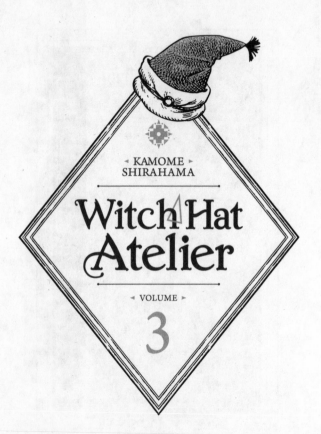

KAMOME
SHIRAHAMA

Witch Hat Atelier

VOLUME

3

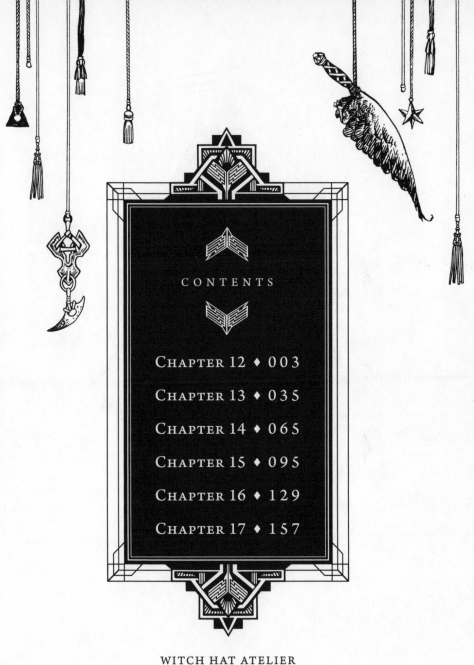

CONTENTS

WITCH HAT ATELIER

◆

KAMOME
SHIRAHAMA

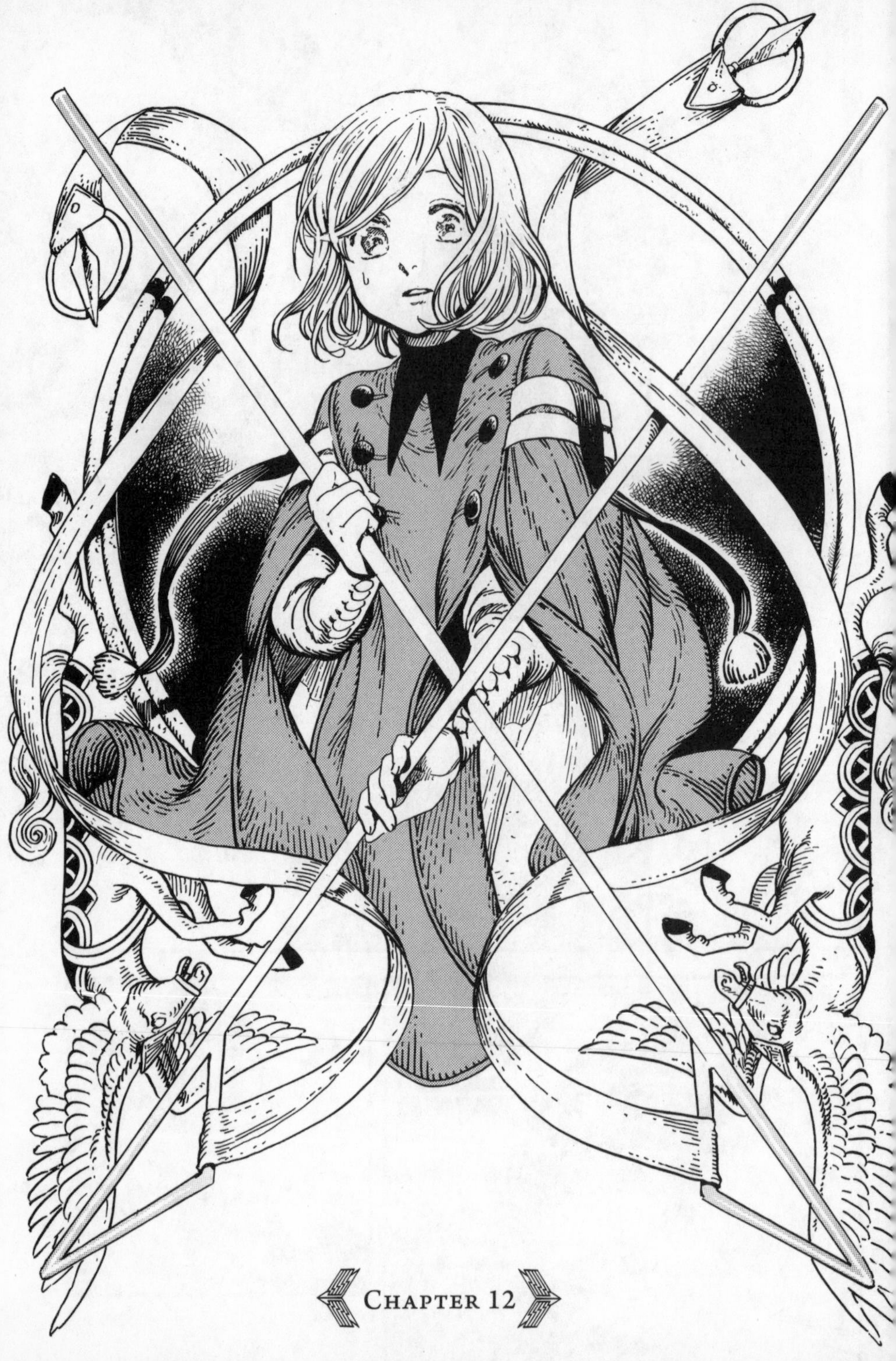

CHAPTER 12

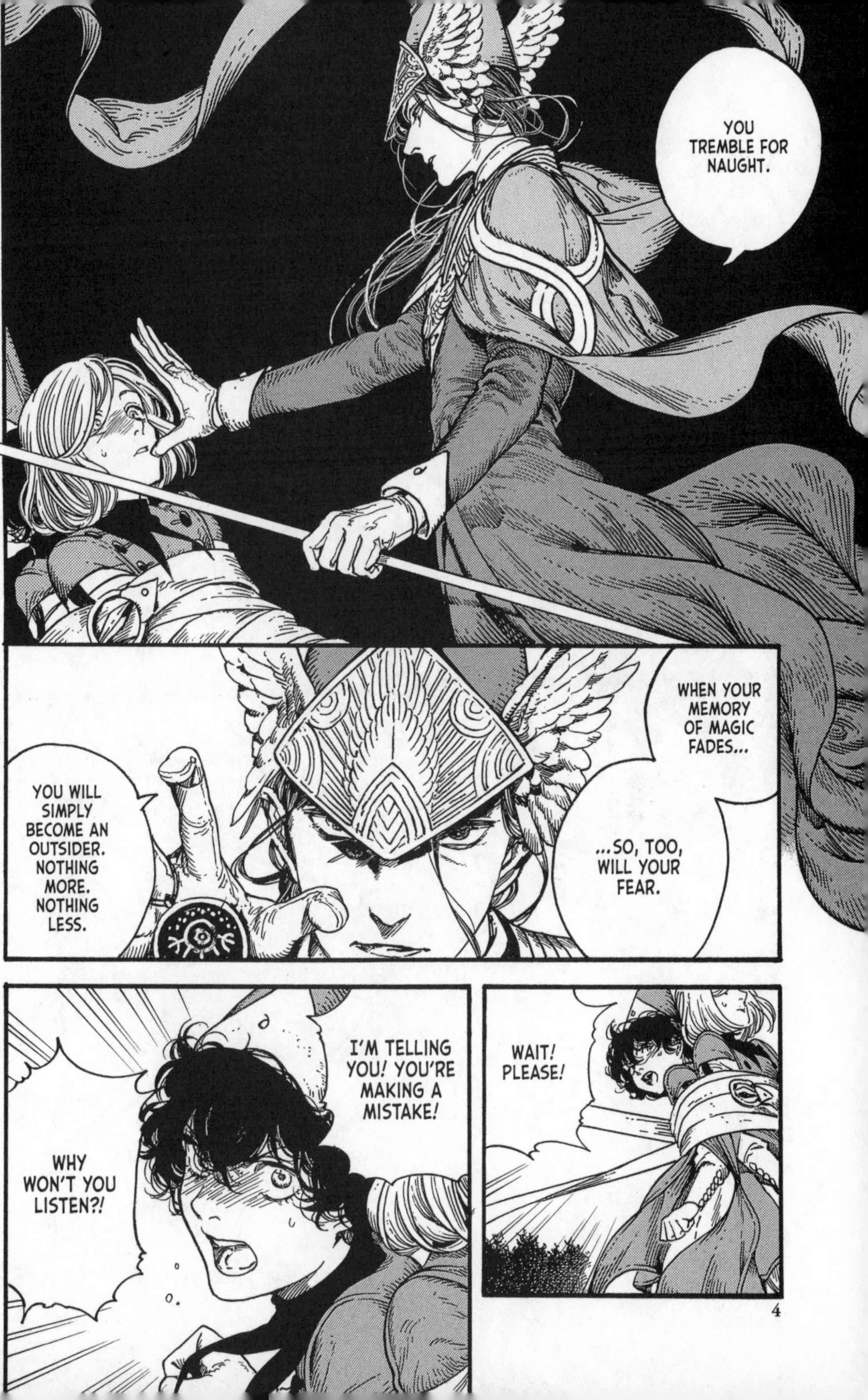
YOU TREMBLE FOR NAUGHT.
WHEN YOUR MEMORY OF MAGIC FADES...
...SO, TOO, WILL YOUR FEAR.
YOU WILL SIMPLY BECOME AN OUTSIDER. NOTHING MORE. NOTHING LESS.
WAIT! PLEASE!
I'M TELLING YOU! YOU'RE MAKING A MISTAKE!
WHY WON'T YOU LISTEN?!

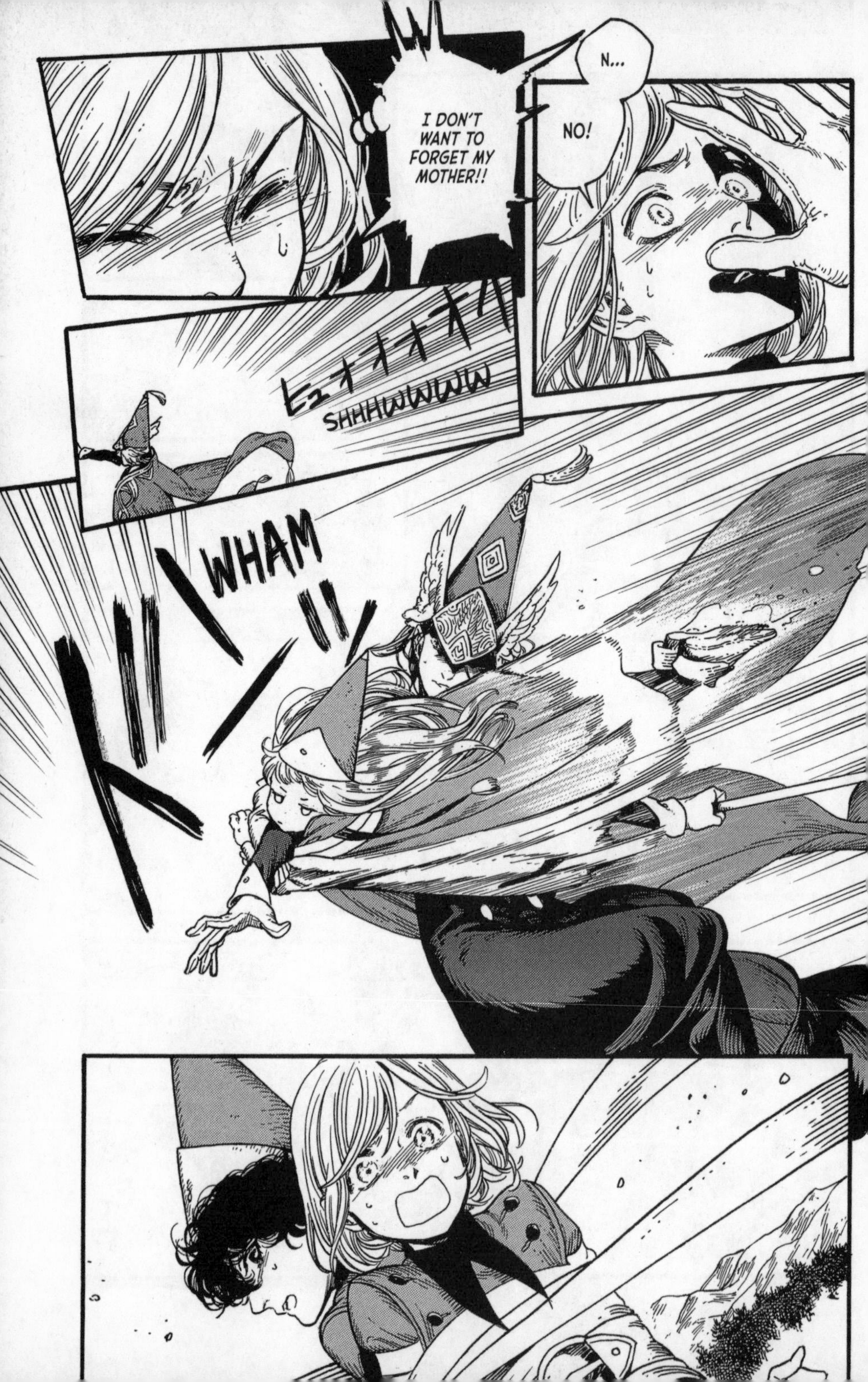
N...
NO!
I DON'T WANT TO FORGET MY MOTHER!!
ヒュオオオオ!!
SHHHWWWWW
WHAM

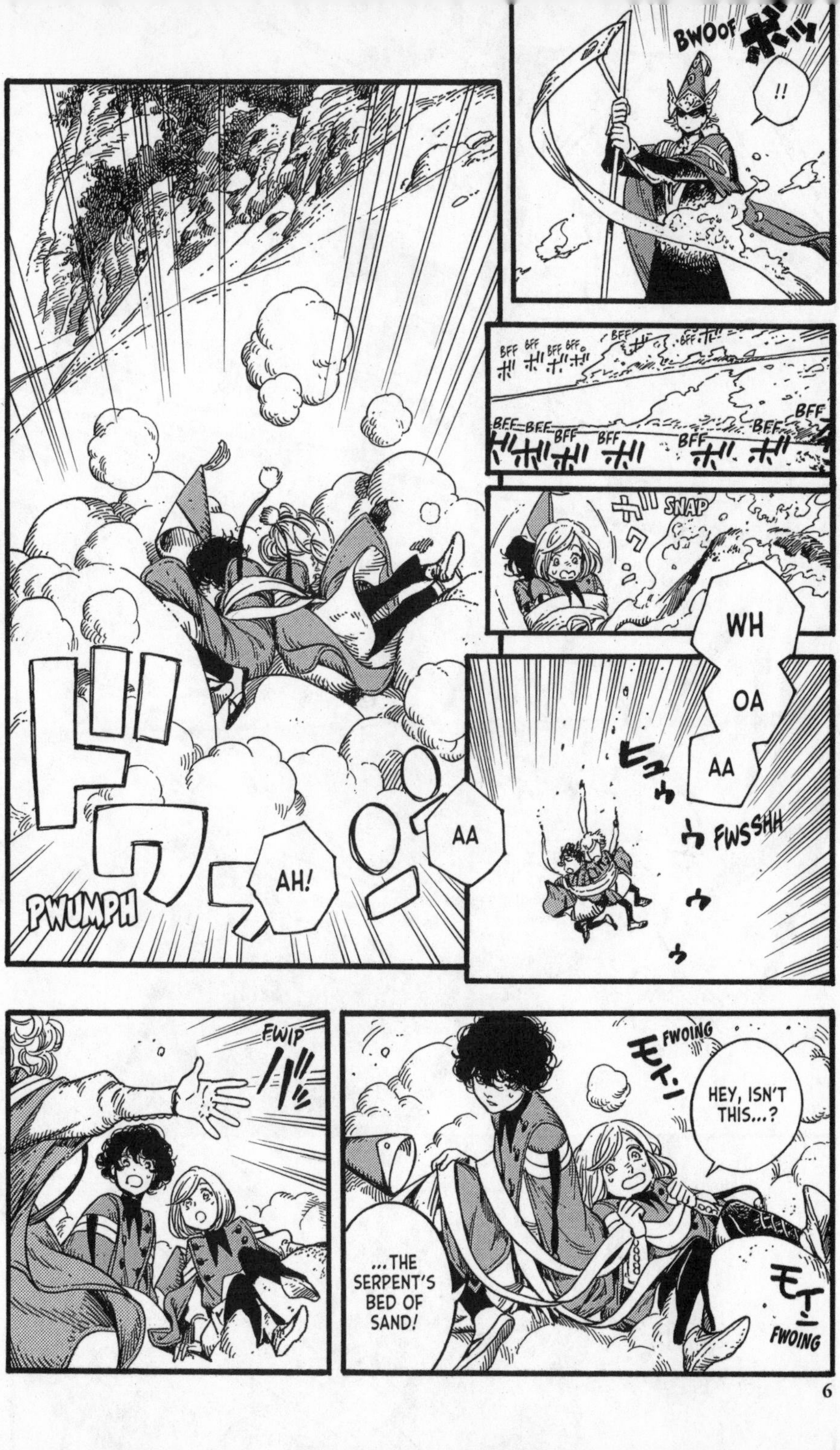
BWOOF
!!
BFF BFF BFF BFF BFF BFF BFF
BFF BFF BFF BFF BFF BFF BFF
SNAP
WH OA AA
FWSSHH
PWUMPH
AH!
AA
FWOING
HEY, ISN'T THIS...?
...THE SERPENT'S BED OF SAND!
FWOING
FWIP

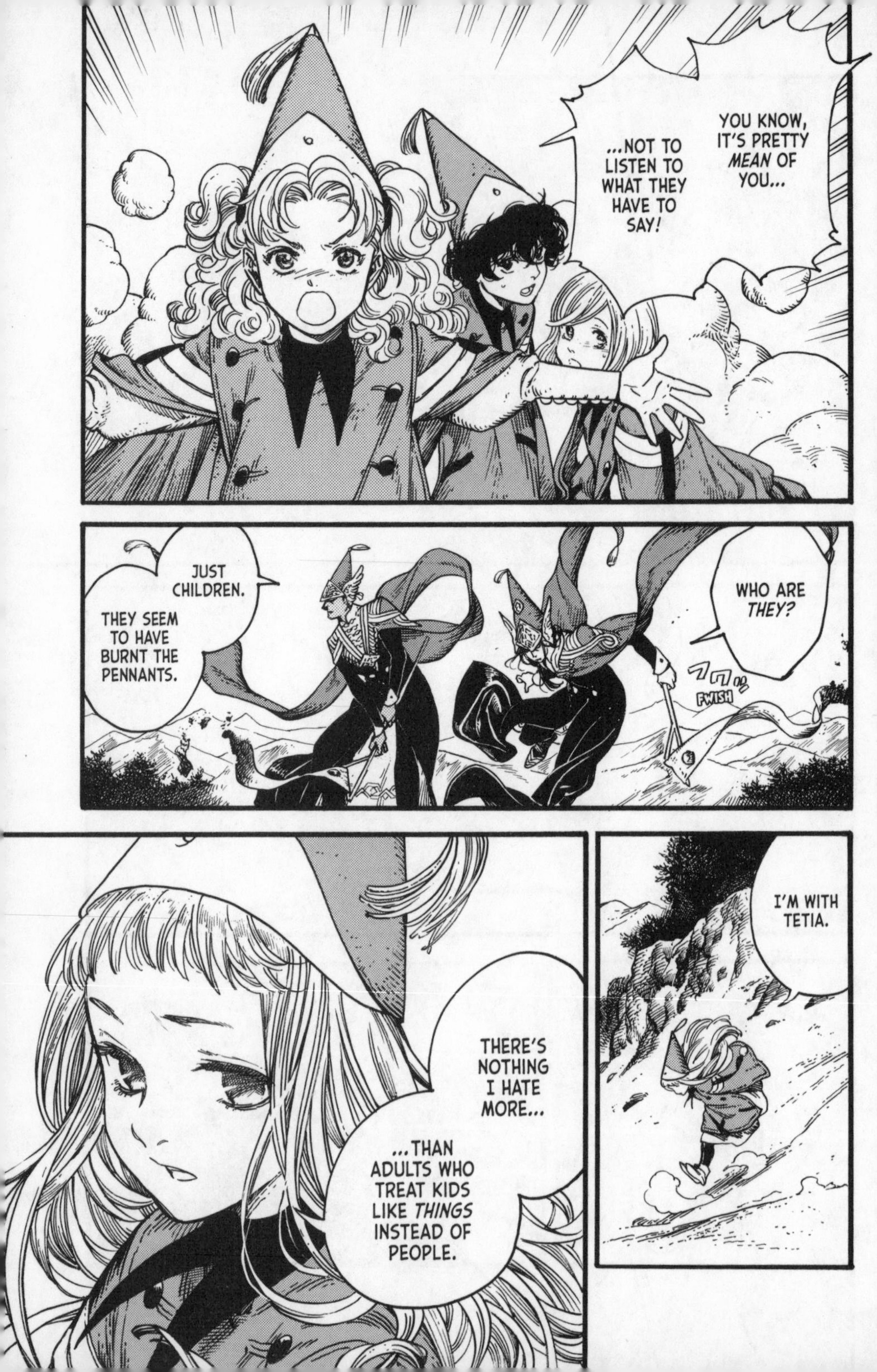
YOU KNOW, IT'S PRETTY *MEAN* OF YOU...
...NOT TO LISTEN TO WHAT THEY HAVE TO SAY!
WHO ARE *THEY?*
FWISH
JUST CHILDREN.
THEY SEEM TO HAVE BURNT THE PENNANTS.
I'M WITH TETIA.
THERE'S NOTHING I HATE MORE...
...THAN ADULTS WHO TREAT KIDS LIKE *THINGS* INSTEAD OF PEOPLE.

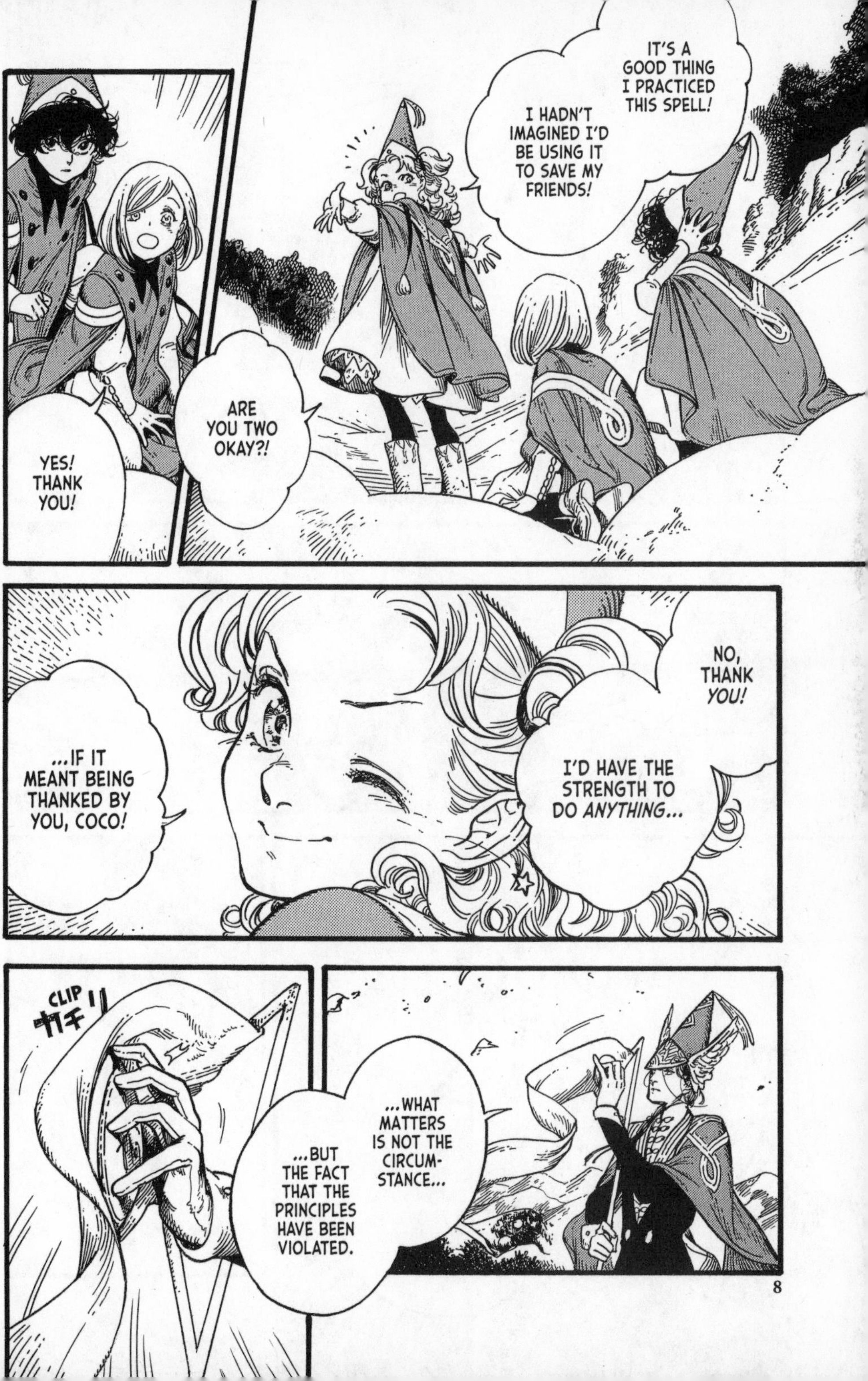
IT'S A GOOD THING I PRACTICED THIS SPELL!
I HADN'T IMAGINED I'D BE USING IT TO SAVE MY FRIENDS!
ARE YOU TWO OKAY?!
YES! THANK YOU!
NO, THANK *YOU!*
I'D HAVE THE STRENGTH TO DO *ANYTHING...*
...IF IT MEANT BEING THANKED BY YOU, COCO!
...WHAT MATTERS IS NOT THE CIRCUM-STANCE...
...BUT THE FACT THAT THE PRINCIPLES HAVE BEEN VIOLATED.
CLIP

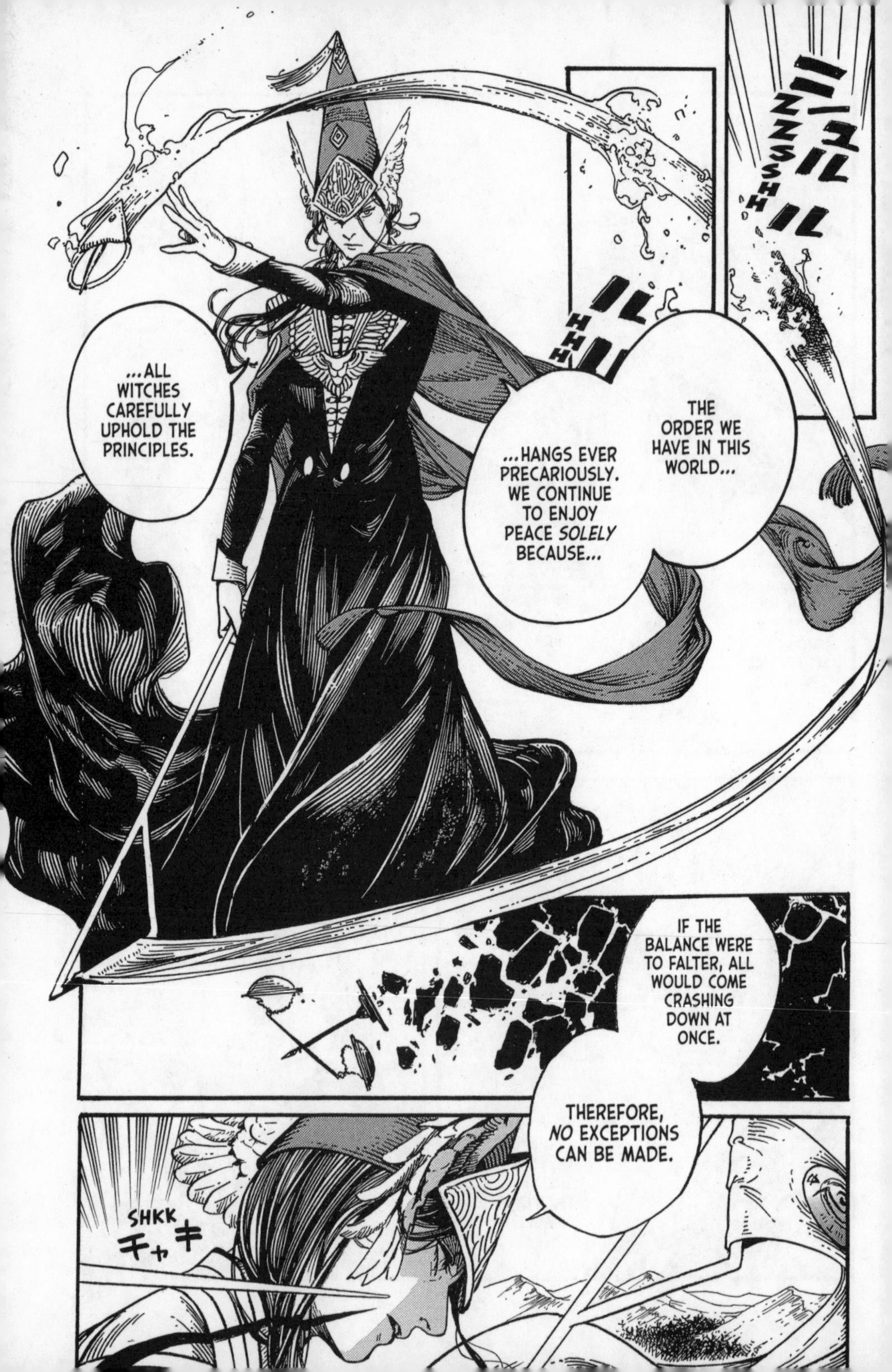
ZZZSSHH
HHHH
THE ORDER WE HAVE IN THIS WORLD...
...HANGS EVER PRECARIOUSLY. WE CONTINUE TO ENJOY PEACE *SOLELY* BECAUSE...
...ALL WITCHES CAREFULLY UPHOLD THE PRINCIPLES.
IF THE BALANCE WERE TO FALTER, ALL WOULD COME CRASHING DOWN AT ONCE.
THEREFORE, *NO* EXCEPTIONS CAN BE MADE.
SHKK
チャキ

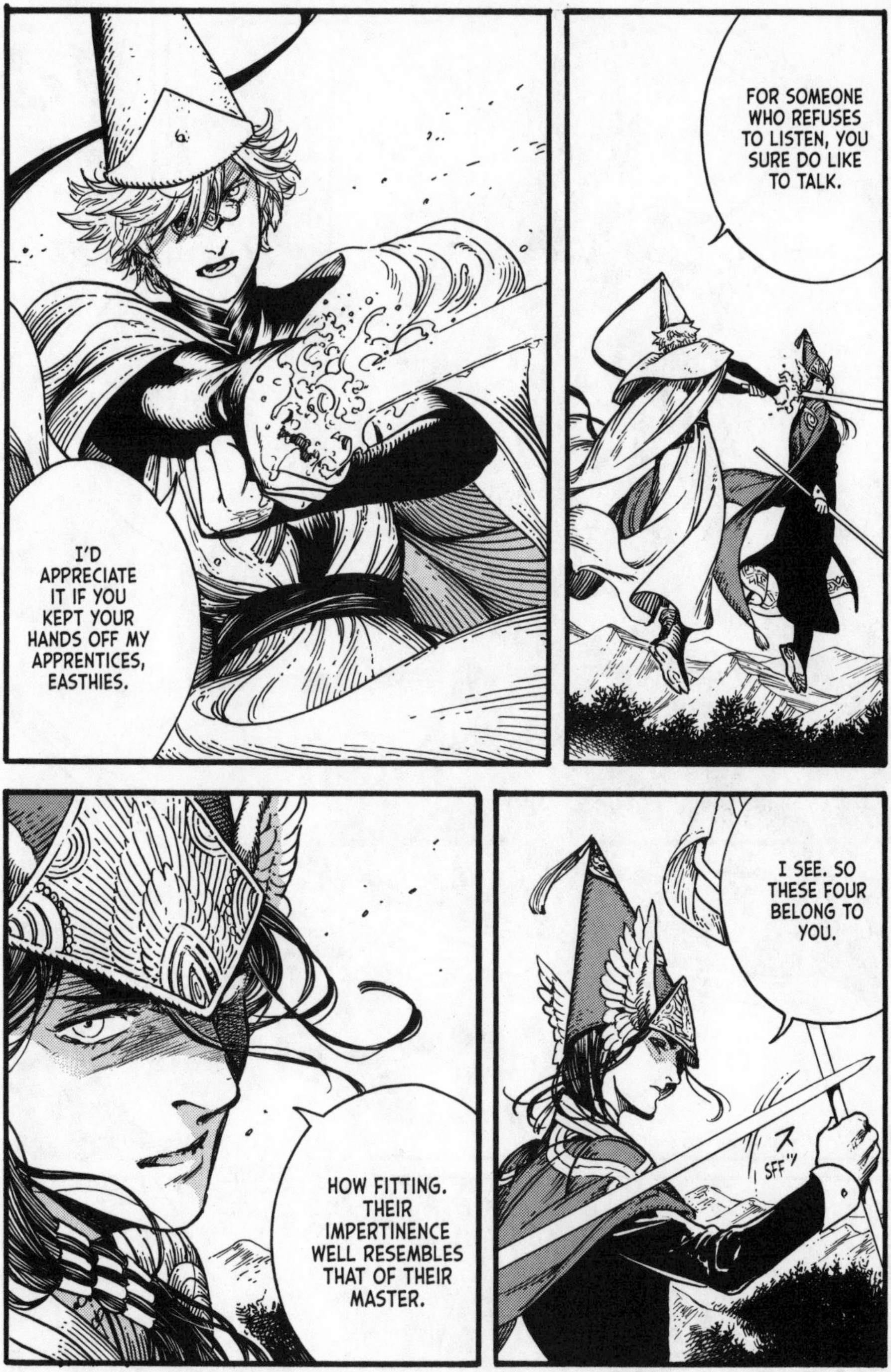
FOR SOMEONE WHO REFUSES TO LISTEN, YOU SURE DO LIKE TO TALK.
I'D APPRECIATE IT IF YOU KEPT YOUR HANDS OFF MY APPRENTICES, EASTHIES.
I SEE. SO THESE FOUR BELONG TO YOU.
スッ
SFF
HOW FITTING. THEIR IMPERTINENCE WELL RESEMBLES THAT OF THEIR MASTER.

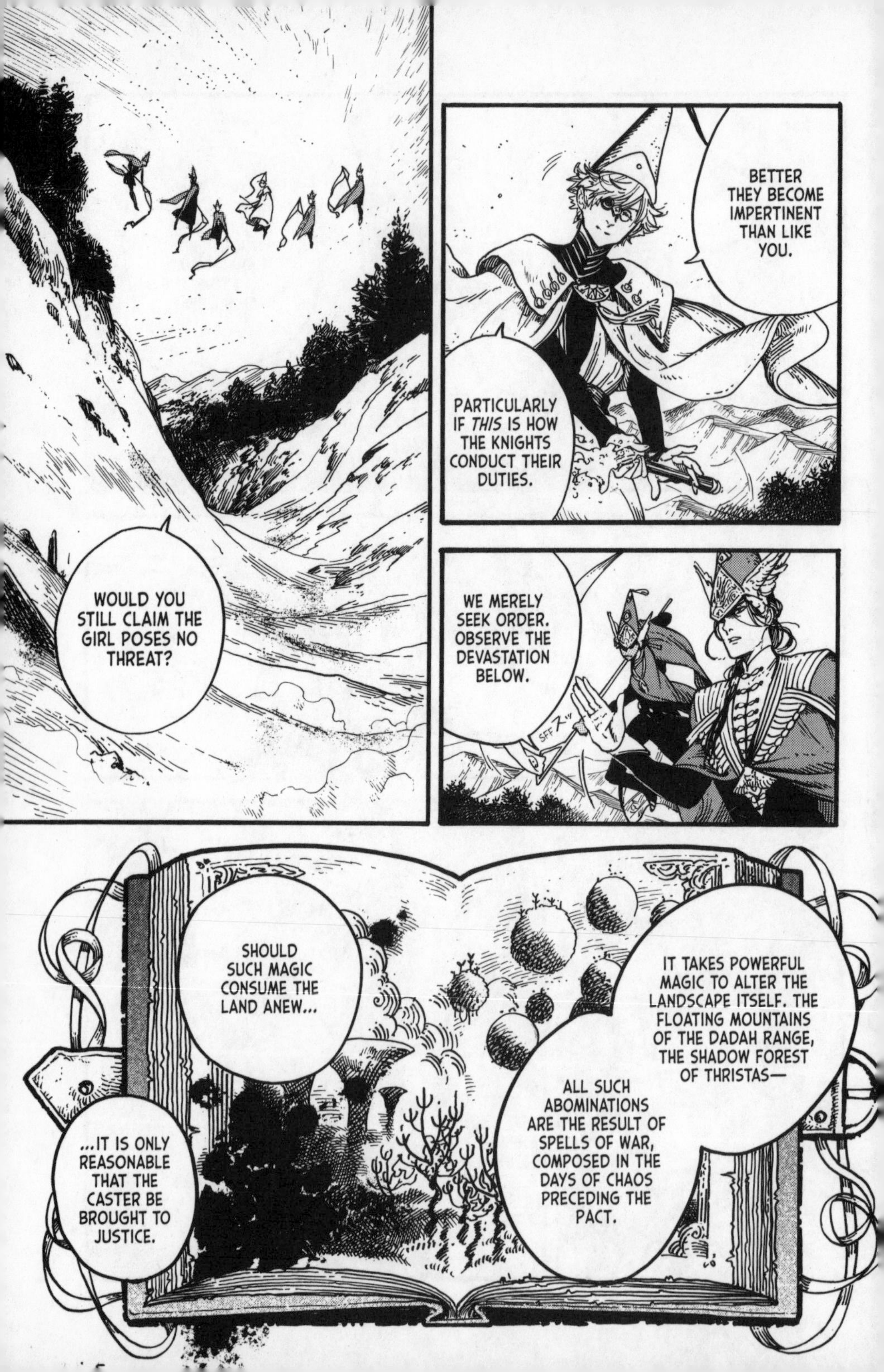
BETTER THEY BECOME IMPERTINENT THAN LIKE YOU.
PARTICULARLY IF *THIS* IS HOW THE KNIGHTS CONDUCT THEIR DUTIES.
WE MERELY SEEK ORDER. OBSERVE THE DEVASTATION BELOW.
SFF スッ
WOULD YOU STILL CLAIM THE GIRL POSES NO THREAT?
IT TAKES POWERFUL MAGIC TO ALTER THE LANDSCAPE ITSELF. THE FLOATING MOUNTAINS OF THE DADAH RANGE, THE SHADOW FOREST OF THRISTAS—
ALL SUCH ABOMINATIONS ARE THE RESULT OF SPELLS OF WAR, COMPOSED IN THE DAYS OF CHAOS PRECEDING THE PACT.
SHOULD SUCH MAGIC CONSUME THE LAND ANEW...
...IT IS ONLY REASONABLE THAT THE CASTER BE BROUGHT TO JUSTICE.

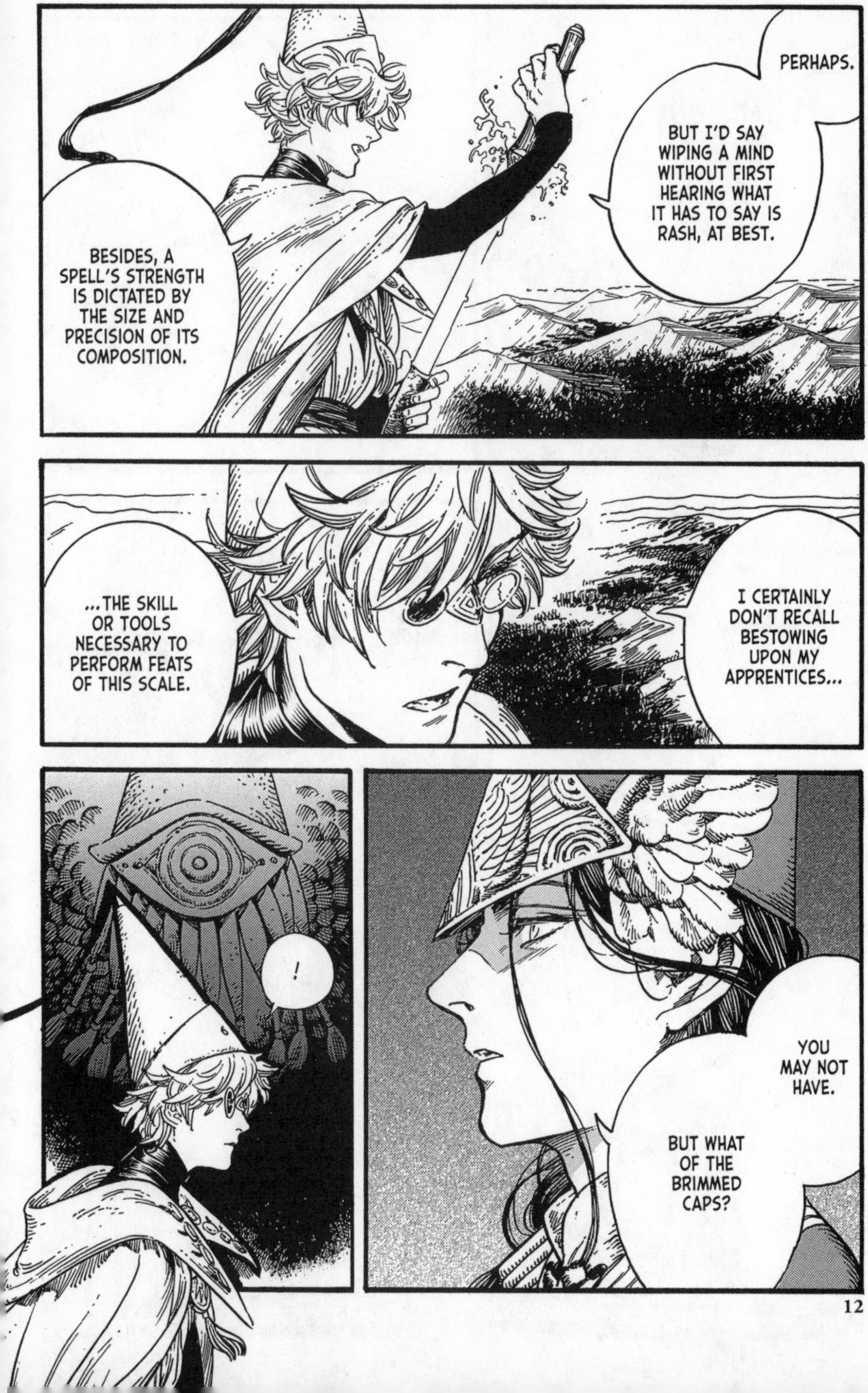
PERHAPS.
BUT I'D SAY WIPING A MIND WITHOUT FIRST HEARING WHAT IT HAS TO SAY IS RASH, AT BEST.
BESIDES, A SPELL'S STRENGTH IS DICTATED BY THE SIZE AND PRECISION OF ITS COMPOSITION.
I CERTAINLY DON'T RECALL BESTOWING UPON MY APPRENTICES...
...THE SKILL OR TOOLS NECESSARY TO PERFORM FEATS OF THIS SCALE.
YOU MAY NOT HAVE.
BUT WHAT OF THE BRIMMED CAPS?
!

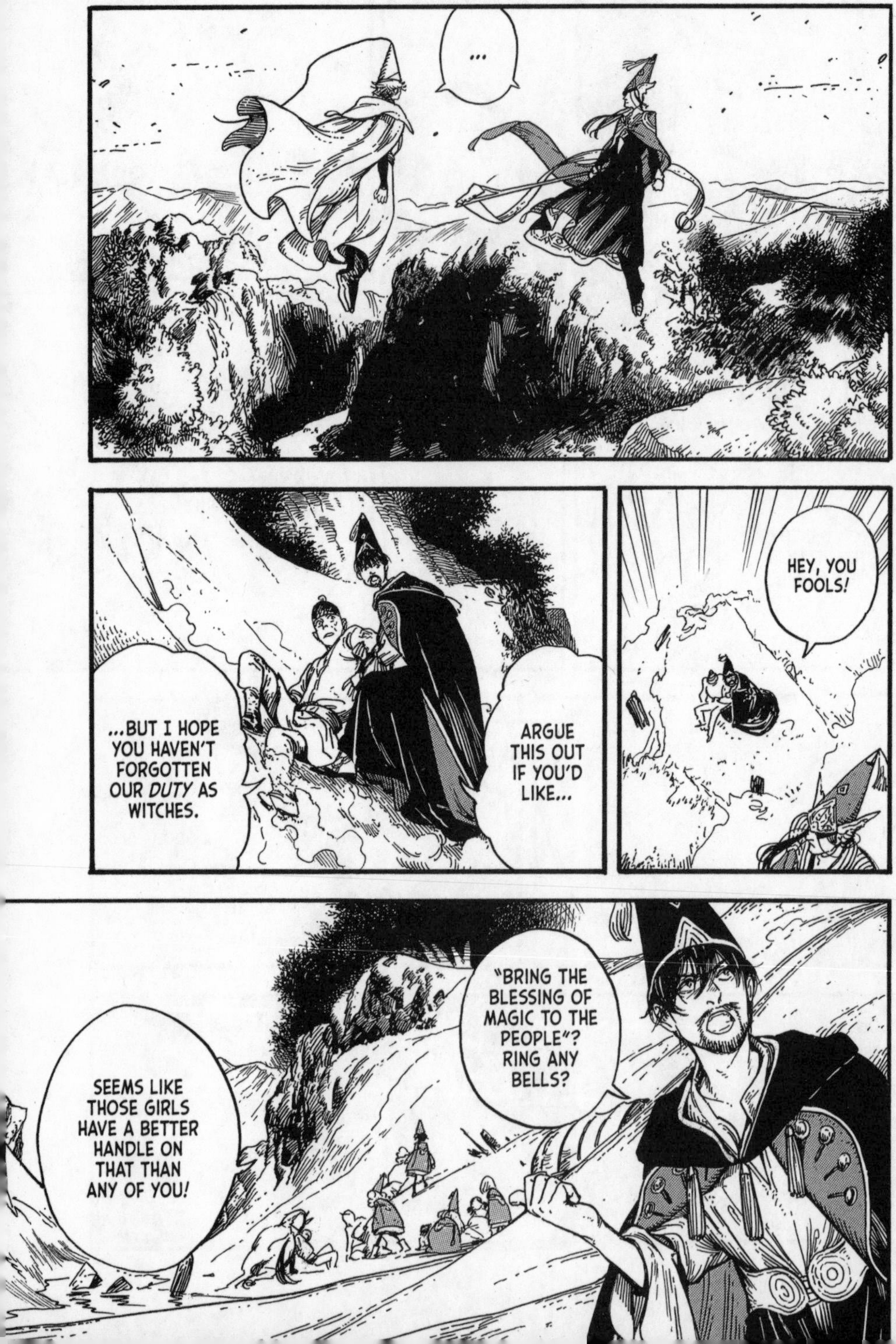
...
HEY, YOU FOOLS!
ARGUE THIS OUT IF YOU'D LIKE...
...BUT I HOPE YOU HAVEN'T FORGOTTEN OUR *DUTY* AS WITCHES.
"BRING THE BLESSING OF MAGIC TO THE PEOPLE"? RING ANY BELLS?
SEEMS LIKE THOSE GIRLS HAVE A BETTER HANDLE ON THAT THAN ANY OF YOU!

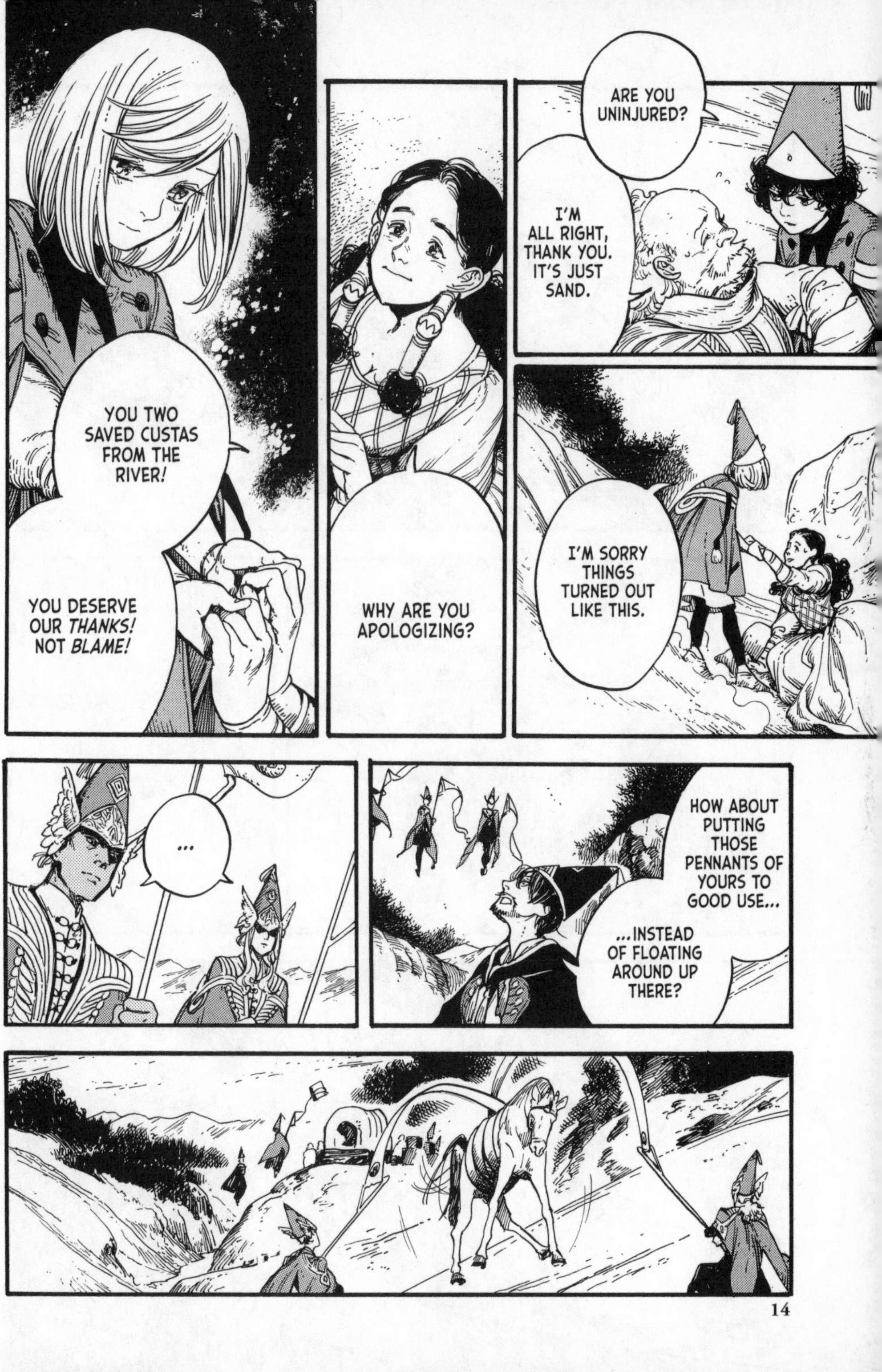
ARE YOU UNINJURED?
I'M ALL RIGHT, THANK YOU. IT'S JUST SAND.
I'M SORRY THINGS TURNED OUT LIKE THIS.
WHY ARE YOU APOLOGIZING?
YOU TWO SAVED CUSTAS FROM THE RIVER!
YOU DESERVE OUR *THANKS!* NOT *BLAME!*
HOW ABOUT PUTTING THOSE PENNANTS OF YOURS TO GOOD USE...
...INSTEAD OF FLOATING AROUND UP THERE?
...

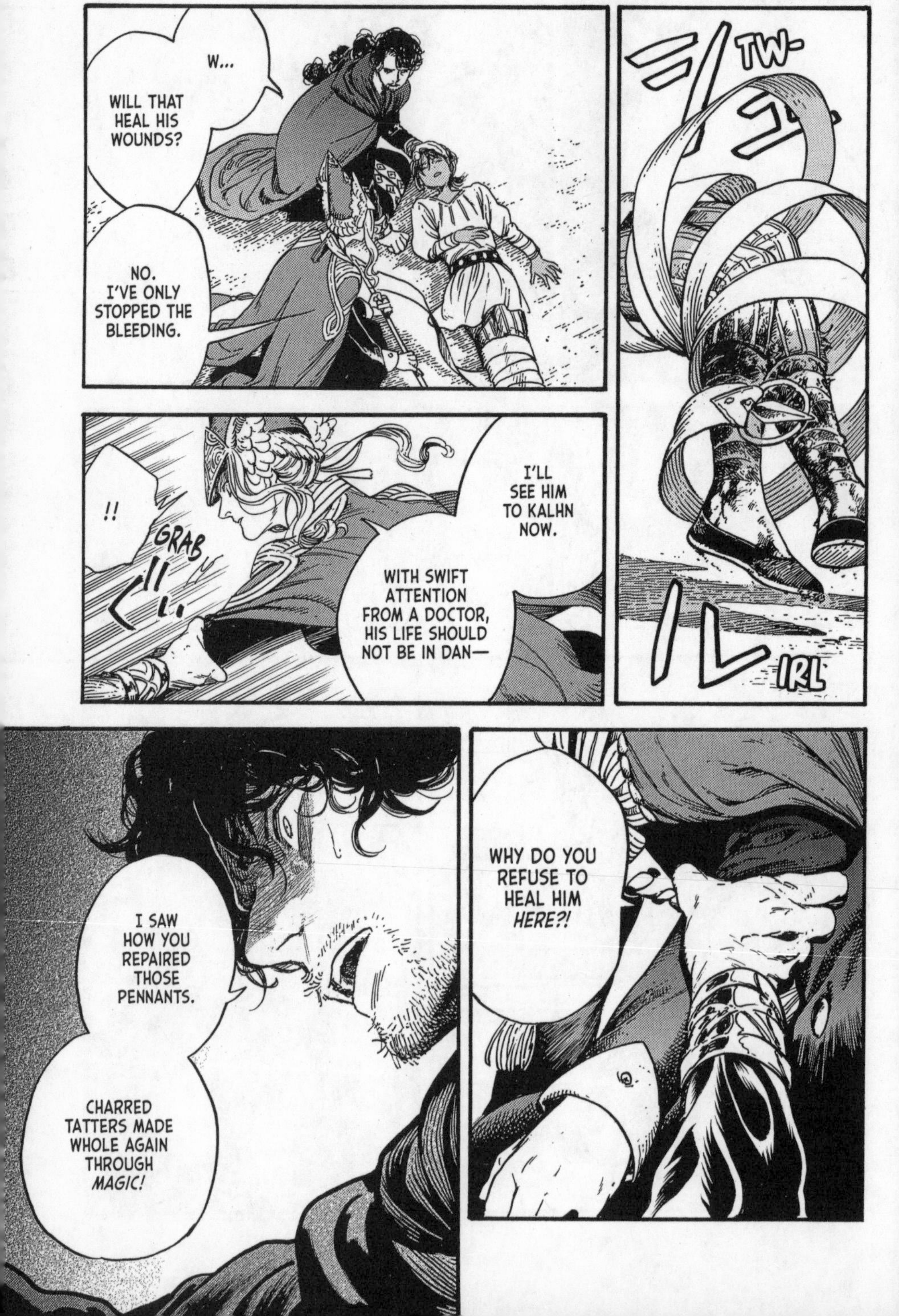
TW-
IRL
W...
WILL THAT HEAL HIS WOUNDS?
NO. I'VE ONLY STOPPED THE BLEEDING.
I'LL SEE HIM TO KALHN NOW.
WITH SWIFT ATTENTION FROM A DOCTOR, HIS LIFE SHOULD NOT BE IN DAN—
!!
GRAB
WHY DO YOU REFUSE TO HEAL HIM *HERE?!*
I SAW HOW YOU REPAIRED THOSE PENNANTS.
CHARRED TATTERS MADE WHOLE AGAIN THROUGH *MAGIC!*

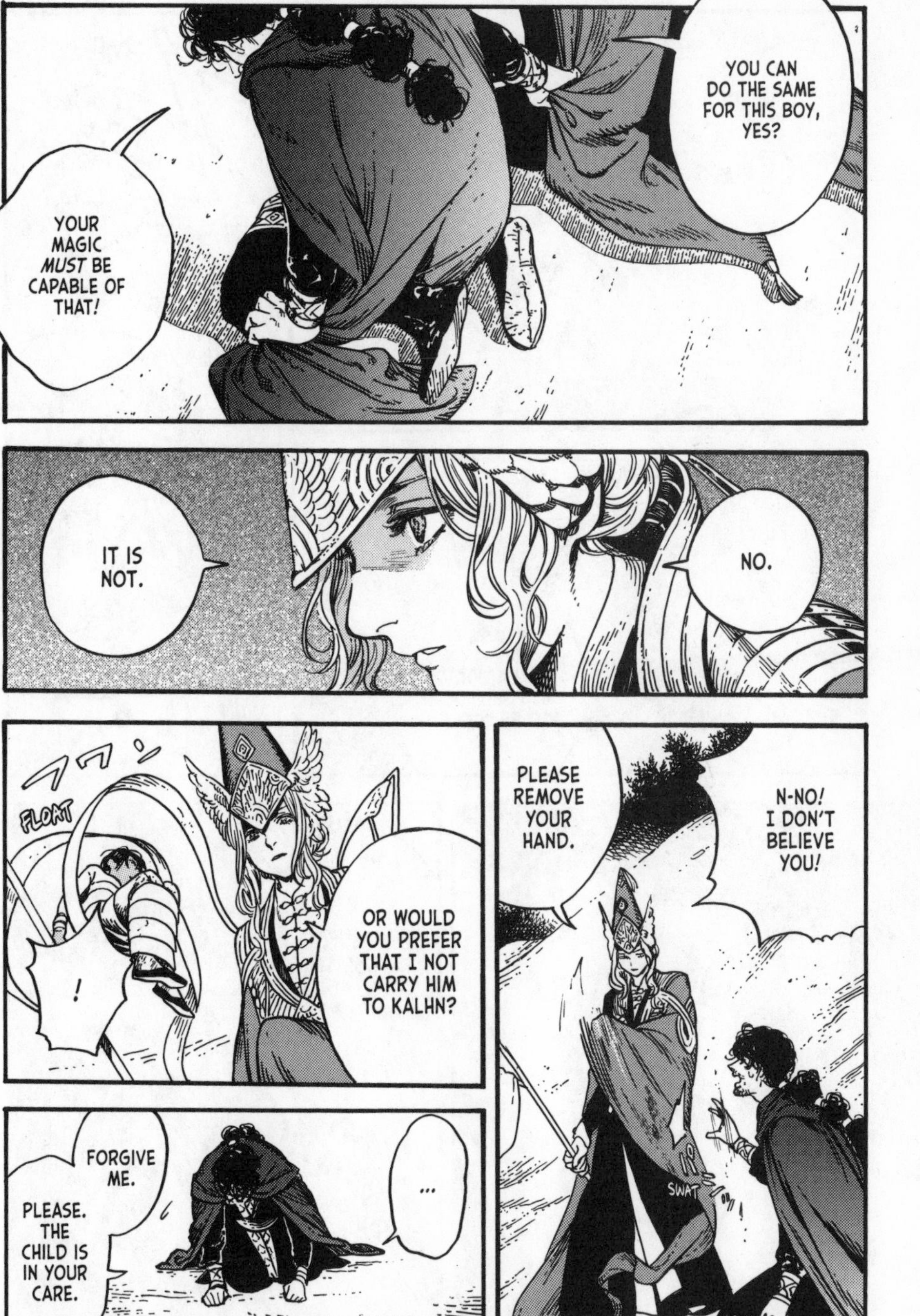
YOU CAN DO THE SAME FOR THIS BOY, YES?
YOUR MAGIC MUST BE CAPABLE OF THAT!
NO.
IT IS NOT.
N-NO! I DON'T BELIEVE YOU!
PLEASE REMOVE YOUR HAND.
SWAT
OR WOULD YOU PREFER THAT I NOT CARRY HIM TO KALHN?
フワン
FLOAT
!
...
FORGIVE ME.
PLEASE. THE CHILD IS IN YOUR CARE.

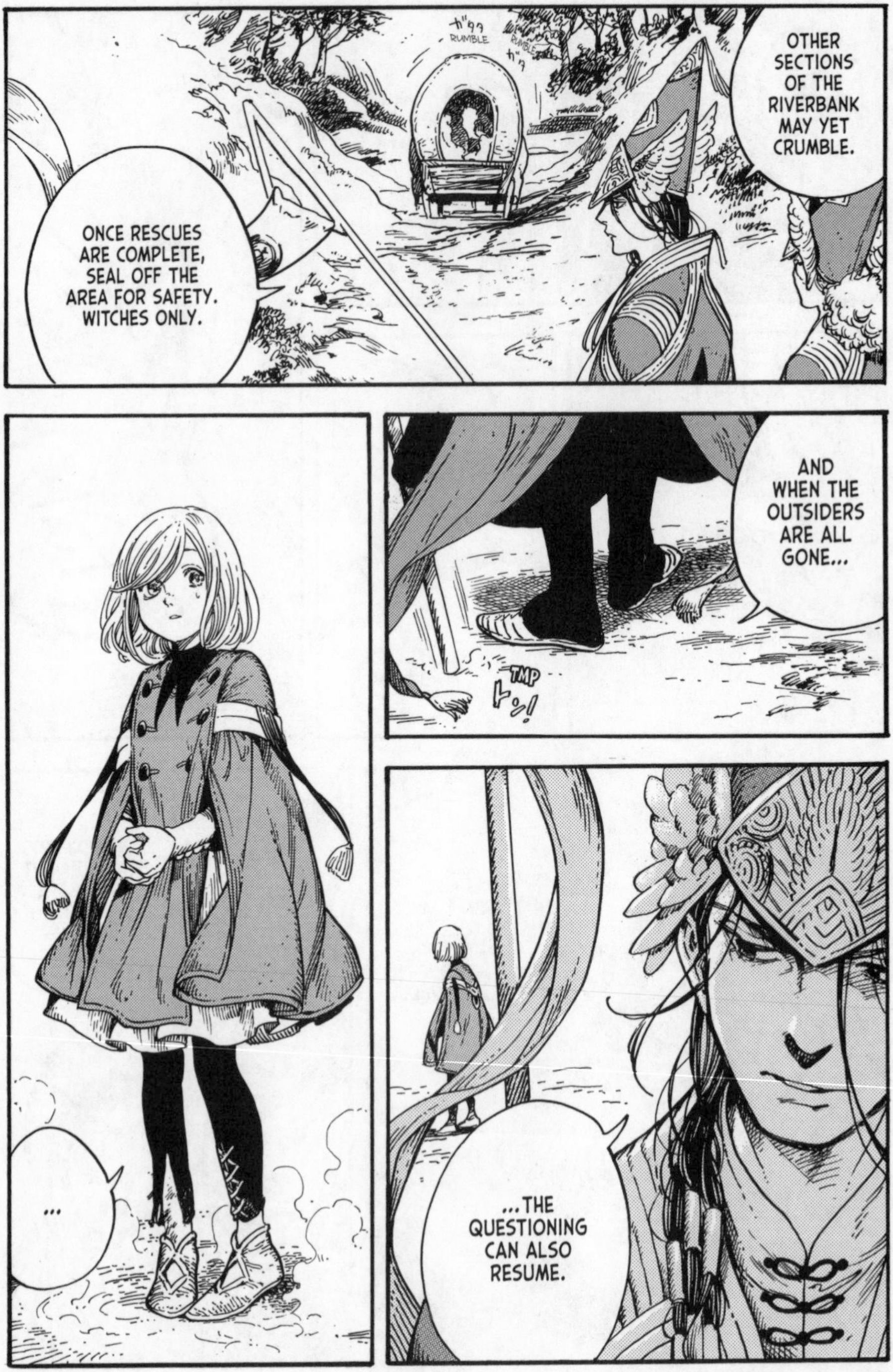
RUMBLE
RUMBLE
OTHER SECTIONS OF THE RIVERBANK MAY YET CRUMBLE.
ONCE RESCUES ARE COMPLETE, SEAL OFF THE AREA FOR SAFETY. WITCHES ONLY.
AND WHEN THE OUTSIDERS ARE ALL GONE...
TMP
トン!
...THE QUESTIONING CAN ALSO RESUME.
...

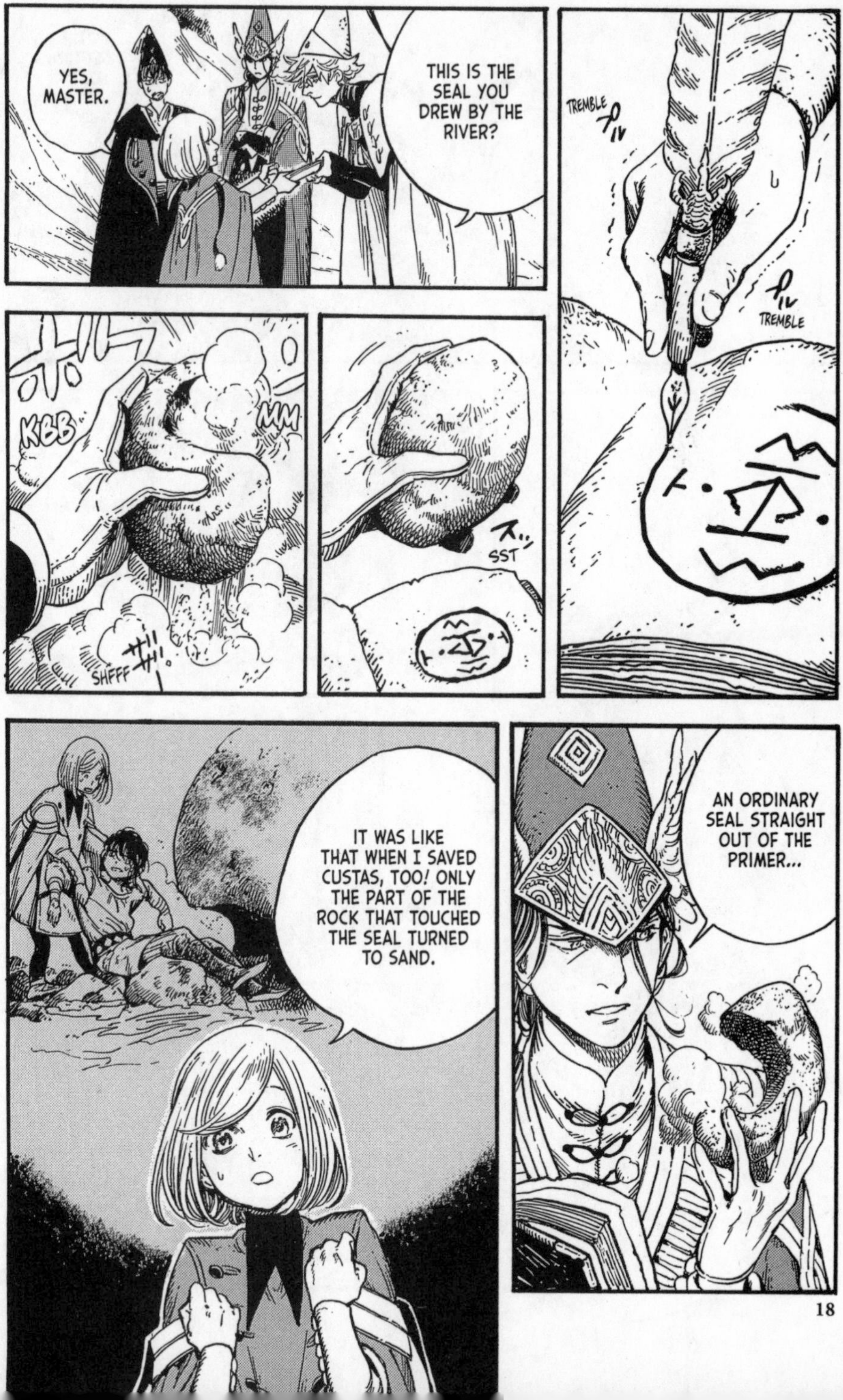

TREMBLE
TREMBLE
THIS IS THE SEAL YOU DREW BY THE RIVER?
YES, MASTER.
SST
MM
KBB
SHFFF
AN ORDINARY SEAL STRAIGHT OUT OF THE PRIMER...
IT WAS LIKE THAT WHEN I SAVED CUSTAS, TOO! ONLY THE PART OF THE ROCK THAT TOUCHED THE SEAL TURNED TO SAND.

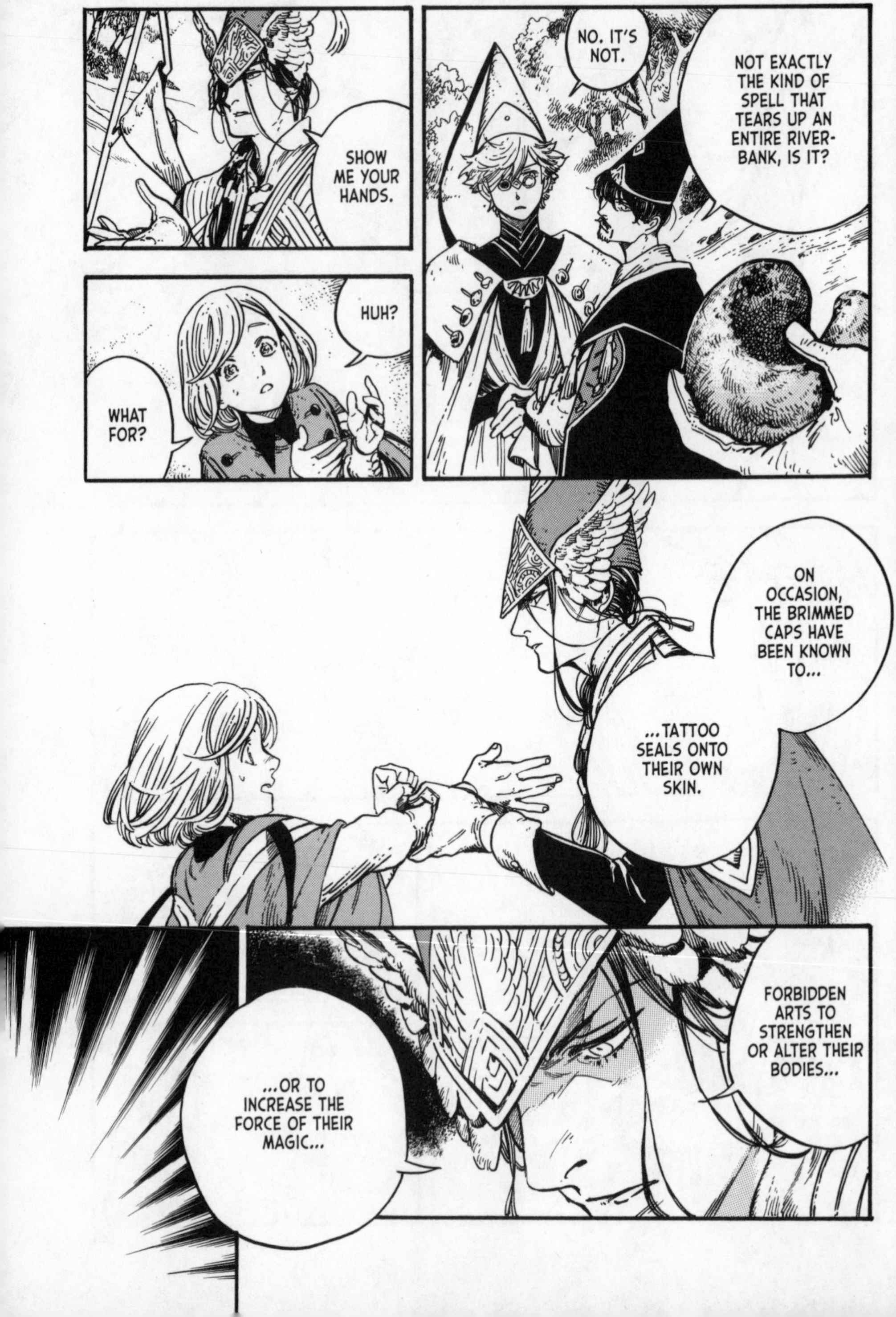
NOT EXACTLY THE KIND OF SPELL THAT TEARS UP AN ENTIRE RIVER-BANK, IS IT?
NO. IT'S NOT.
SHOW ME YOUR HANDS.
HUH?
WHAT FOR?
ON OCCASION, THE BRIMMED CAPS HAVE BEEN KNOWN TO...
...TATTOO SEALS ONTO THEIR OWN SKIN.
FORBIDDEN ARTS TO STRENGTHEN OR ALTER THEIR BODIES...
...OR TO INCREASE THE FORCE OF THEIR MAGIC...

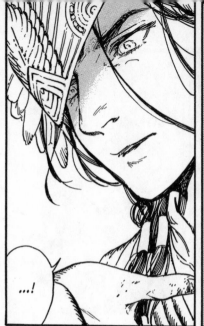

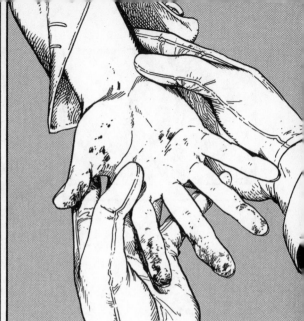

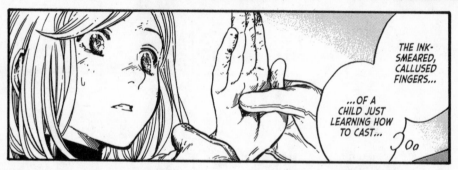

...!
THE INK-SMEARED, CALLUSED FINGERS...
...OF A CHILD JUST LEARNING HOW TO CAST...
HAVE YOU SEEN ENOUGH?
LEAN
...HMPH.
I WILL BE FILING A REPORT OF THIS INCIDENT AT THE GREAT HALL. EXPECT A FORMAL INVESTIGATION.
IF EVIDENCE IS FOUND OF THE GIRL'S INVOLVEMENT...

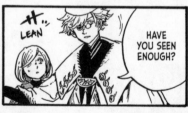

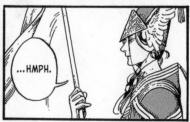

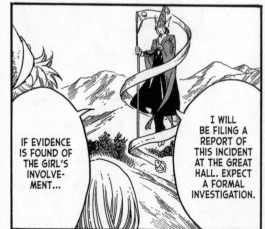

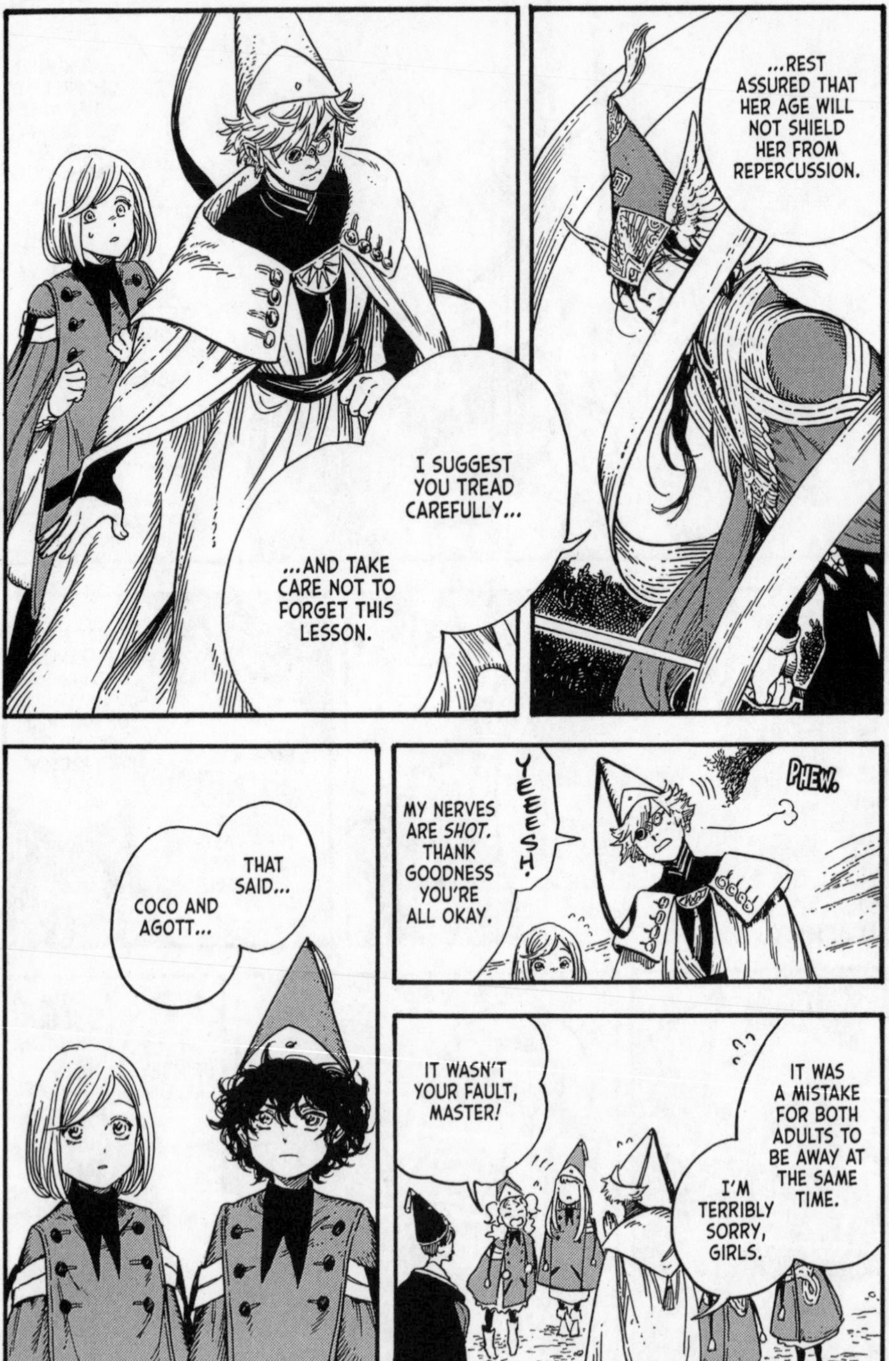
...REST ASSURED THAT HER AGE WILL NOT SHIELD HER FROM REPERCUSSION.
I SUGGEST YOU TREAD CAREFULLY...
...AND TAKE CARE NOT TO FORGET THIS LESSON.
PHEW.
YEEESH.
MY NERVES ARE *SHOT.* THANK GOODNESS YOU'RE ALL OKAY.
IT WAS A MISTAKE FOR BOTH ADULTS TO BE AWAY AT THE SAME TIME.
I'M TERRIBLY SORRY, GIRLS.
IT WASN'T YOUR FAULT, MASTER!
THAT SAID...
COCO AND AGOTT...

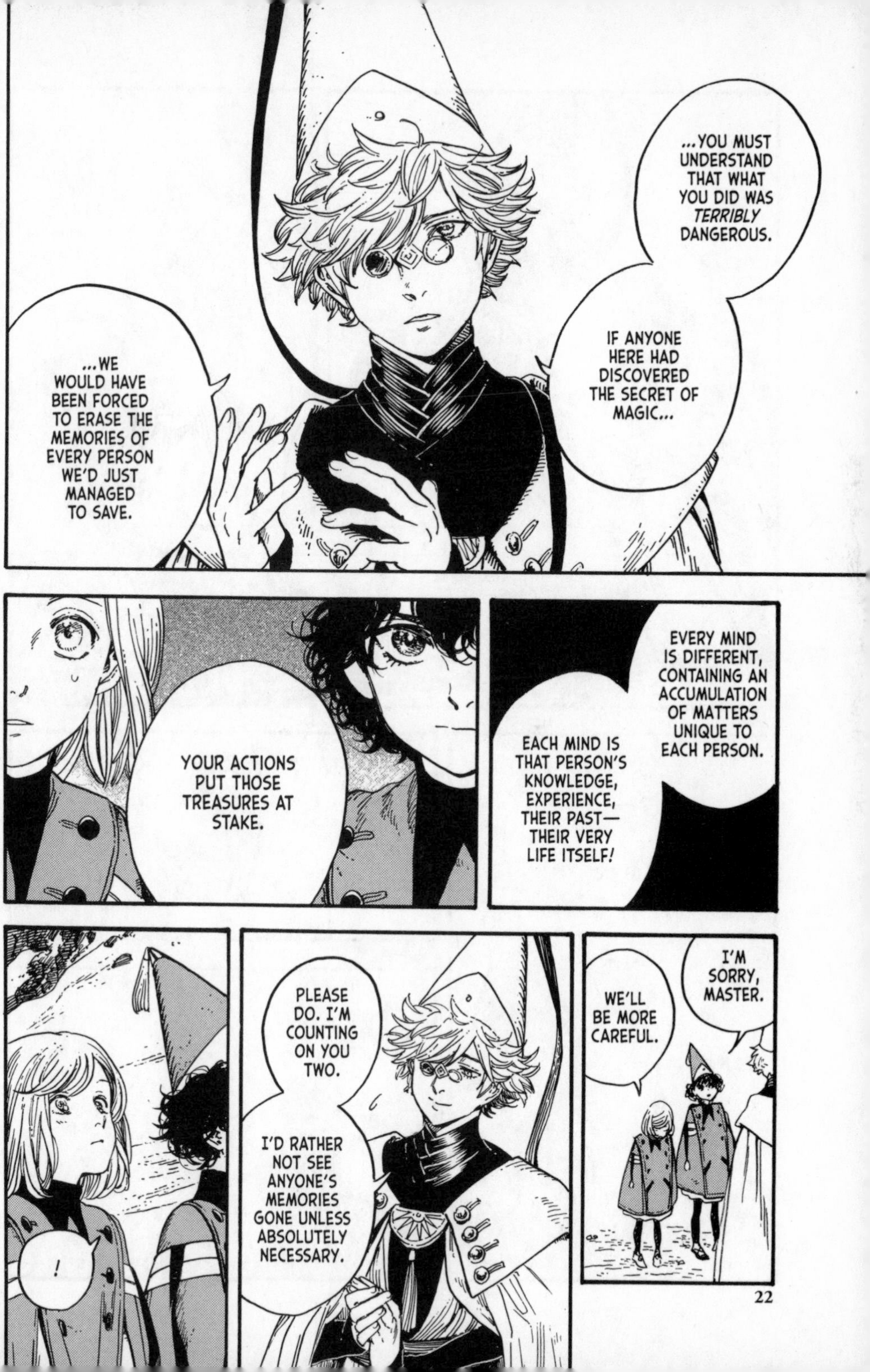
...YOU MUST UNDERSTAND THAT WHAT YOU DID WAS *TERRIBLY* DANGEROUS.
IF ANYONE HERE HAD DISCOVERED THE SECRET OF MAGIC...
...WE WOULD HAVE BEEN FORCED TO ERASE THE MEMORIES OF EVERY PERSON WE'D JUST MANAGED TO SAVE.
EVERY MIND IS DIFFERENT, CONTAINING AN ACCUMULATION OF MATTERS UNIQUE TO EACH PERSON.
EACH MIND IS THAT PERSON'S KNOWLEDGE, EXPERIENCE, THEIR PAST— THEIR VERY LIFE ITSELF!
YOUR ACTIONS PUT THOSE TREASURES AT STAKE.
I'M SORRY, MASTER.
WE'LL BE MORE CAREFUL.
PLEASE DO. I'M COUNTING ON YOU TWO.
I'D RATHER NOT SEE ANYONE'S MEMORIES GONE UNLESS ABSOLUTELY NECESSARY.
!

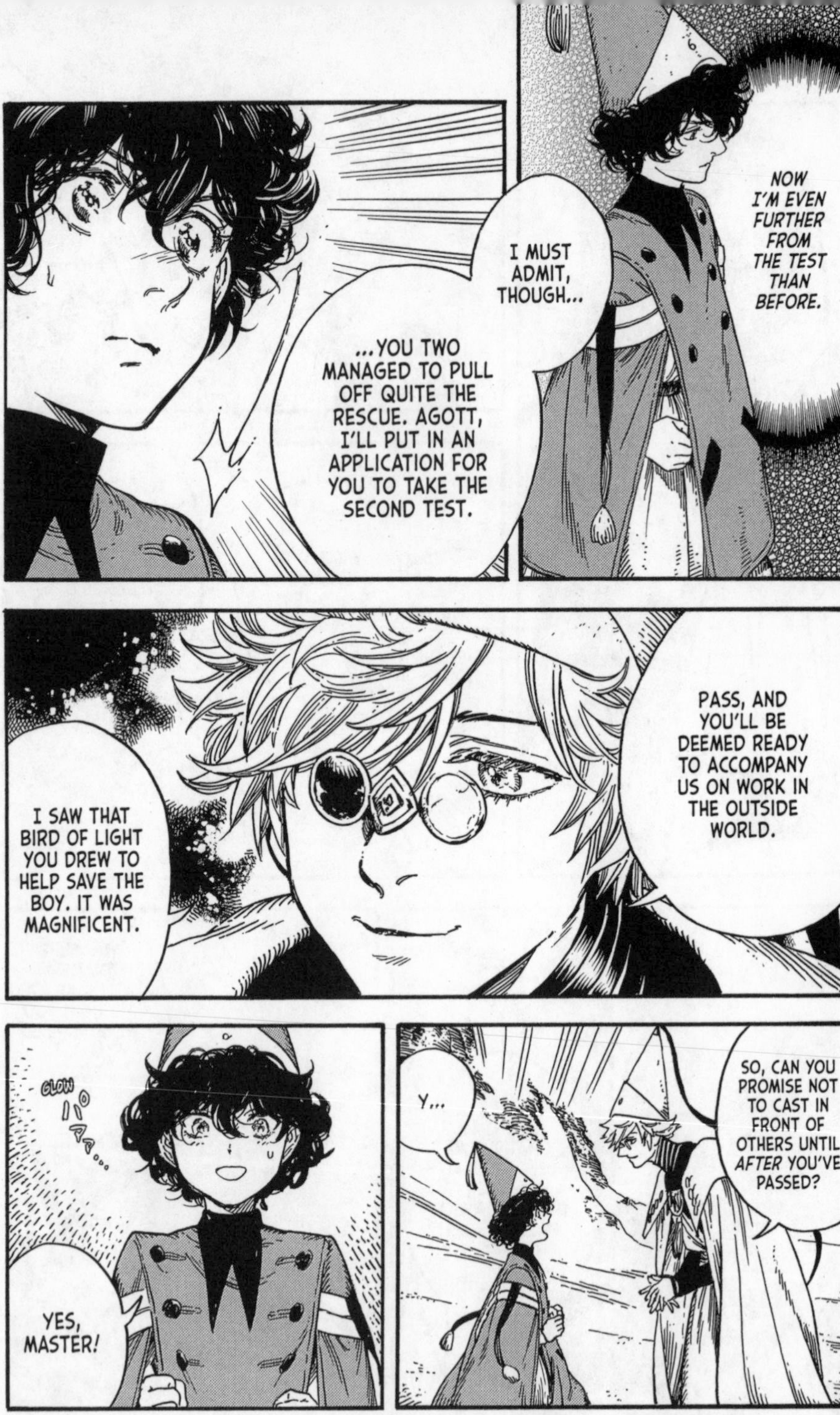
NOW I'M EVEN FURTHER FROM THE TEST THAN BEFORE.
I MUST ADMIT, THOUGH...
...YOU TWO MANAGED TO PULL OFF QUITE THE RESCUE. AGOTT, I'LL PUT IN AN APPLICATION FOR YOU TO TAKE THE SECOND TEST.
PASS, AND YOU'LL BE DEEMED READY TO ACCOMPANY US ON WORK IN THE OUTSIDE WORLD.
I SAW THAT BIRD OF LIGHT YOU DREW TO HELP SAVE THE BOY. IT WAS MAGNIFICENT.
SO, CAN YOU PROMISE NOT TO CAST IN FRONT OF OTHERS UNTIL *AFTER* YOU'VE PASSED?
Y...
GLOW
YES, MASTER!

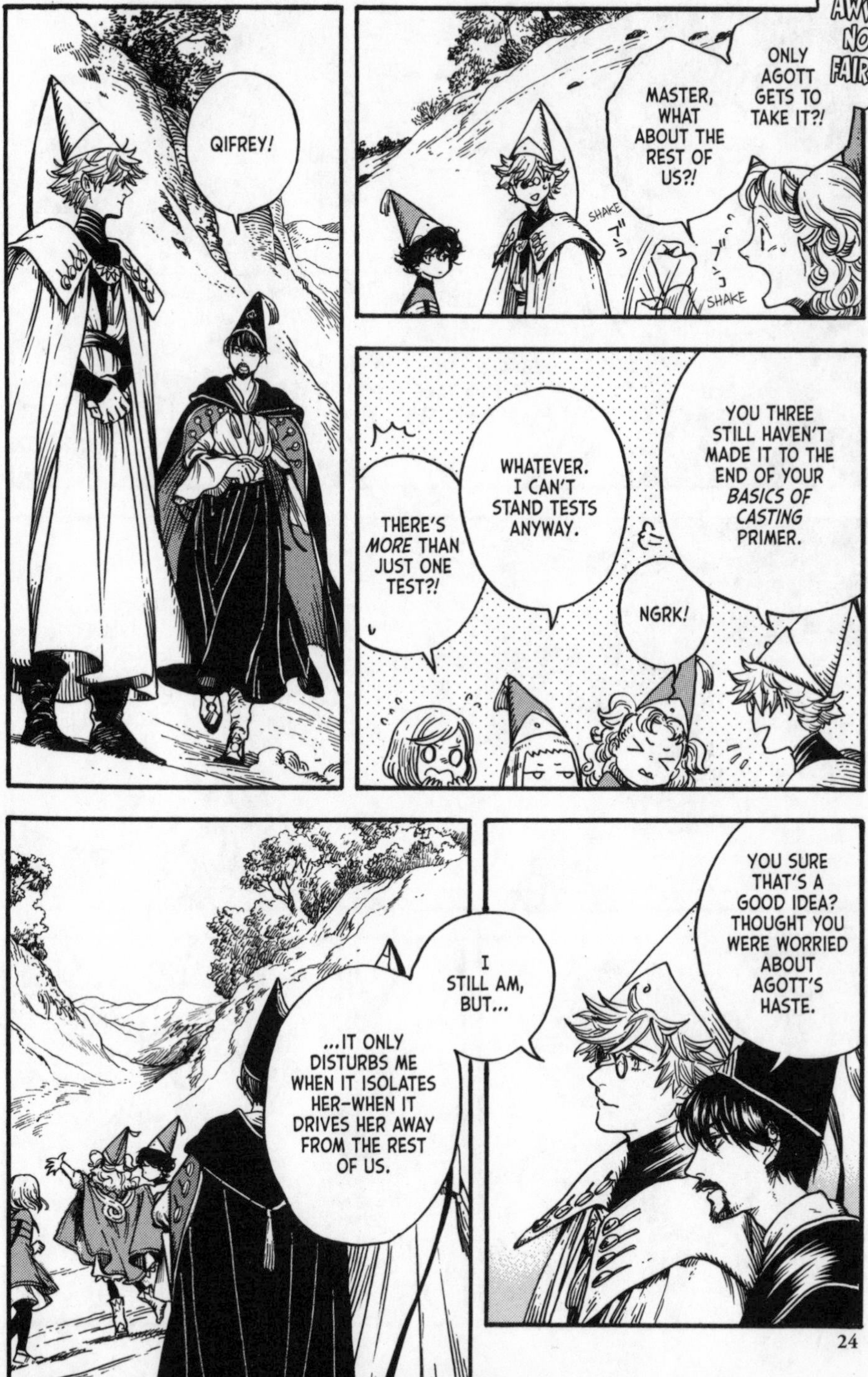
AWW, NO FAIR!
ONLY AGOTT GETS TO TAKE IT?!
MASTER, WHAT ABOUT THE REST OF US?!
SHAKE
SHAKE
YOU THREE STILL HAVEN'T MADE IT TO THE END OF YOUR *BASICS OF CASTING* PRIMER.
NGRK!
WHATEVER. I CAN'T STAND TESTS ANYWAY.
THERE'S *MORE* THAN JUST ONE TEST?!
QIFREY!
YOU SURE THAT'S A GOOD IDEA? THOUGHT YOU WERE WORRIED ABOUT AGOTT'S HASTE.
I STILL AM, BUT...
...IT ONLY DISTURBS ME WHEN IT ISOLATES HER—WHEN IT DRIVES HER AWAY FROM THE REST OF US.

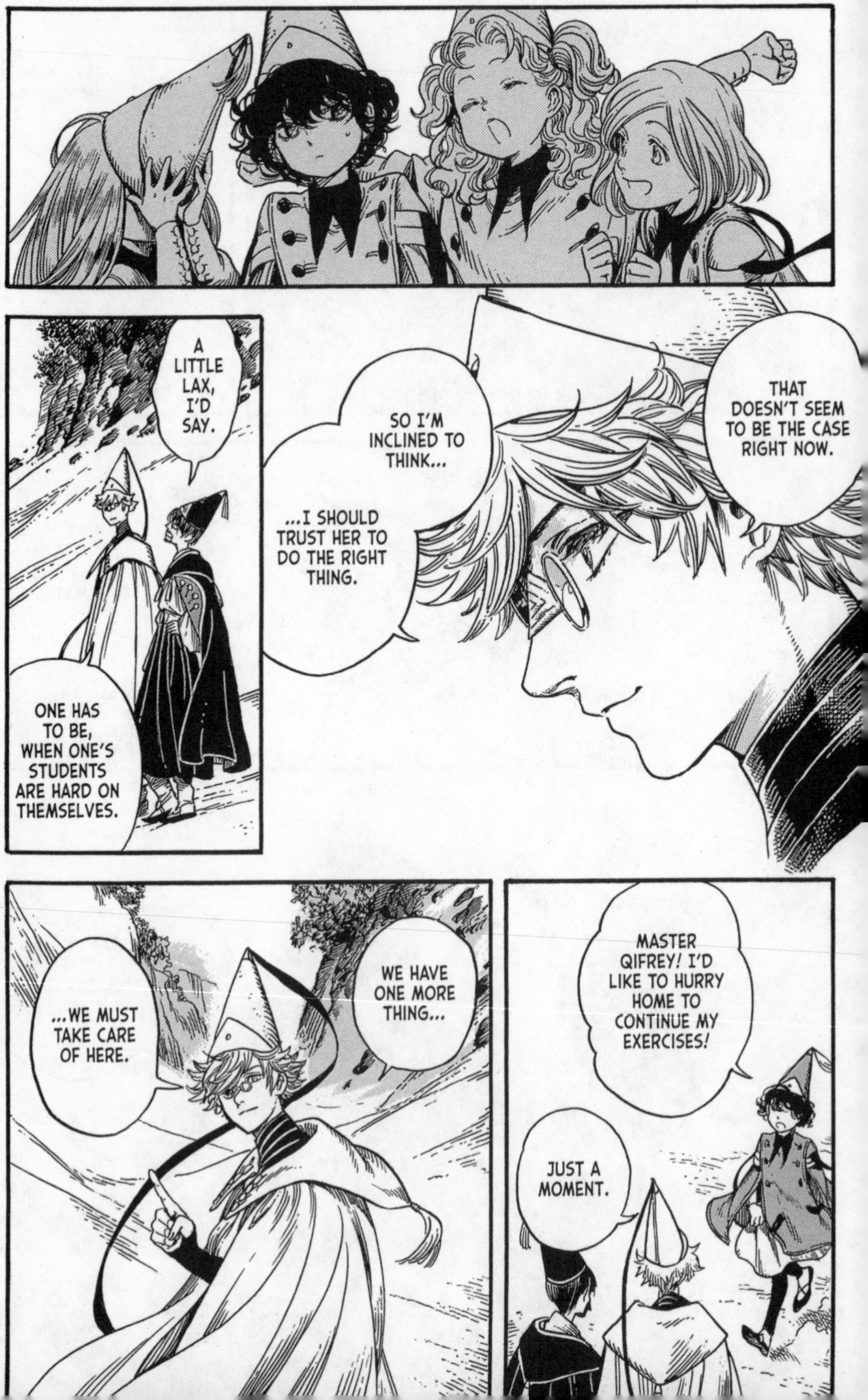
THAT DOESN'T SEEM TO BE THE CASE RIGHT NOW.
SO I'M INCLINED TO THINK...
...I SHOULD TRUST HER TO DO THE RIGHT THING.
A LITTLE LAX, I'D SAY.
ONE HAS TO BE, WHEN ONE'S STUDENTS ARE HARD ON THEMSELVES.
MASTER QIFREY! I'D LIKE TO HURRY HOME TO CONTINUE MY EXERCISES!
JUST A MOMENT.
WE HAVE ONE MORE THING...
...WE MUST TAKE CARE OF HERE.

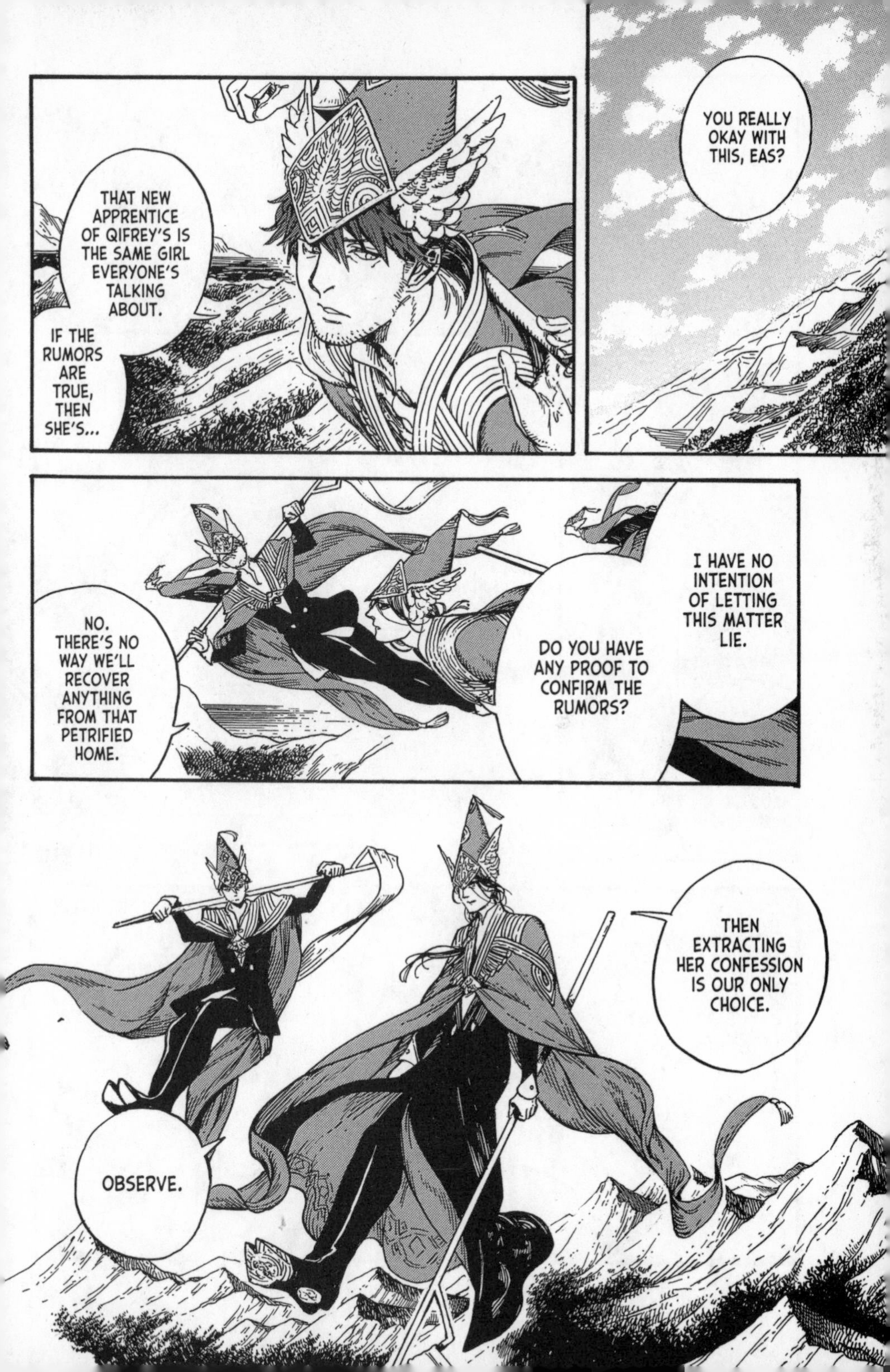
YOU REALLY OKAY WITH THIS, EAS?
THAT NEW APPRENTICE OF QIFREY'S IS THE SAME GIRL EVERYONE'S TALKING ABOUT.
IF THE RUMORS ARE TRUE, THEN SHE'S...
I HAVE NO INTENTION OF LETTING THIS MATTER LIE.
DO YOU HAVE ANY PROOF TO CONFIRM THE RUMORS?
NO. THERE'S NO WAY WE'LL RECOVER ANYTHING FROM THAT PETRIFIED HOME.
THEN EXTRACTING HER CONFESSION IS OUR ONLY CHOICE.
OBSERVE.

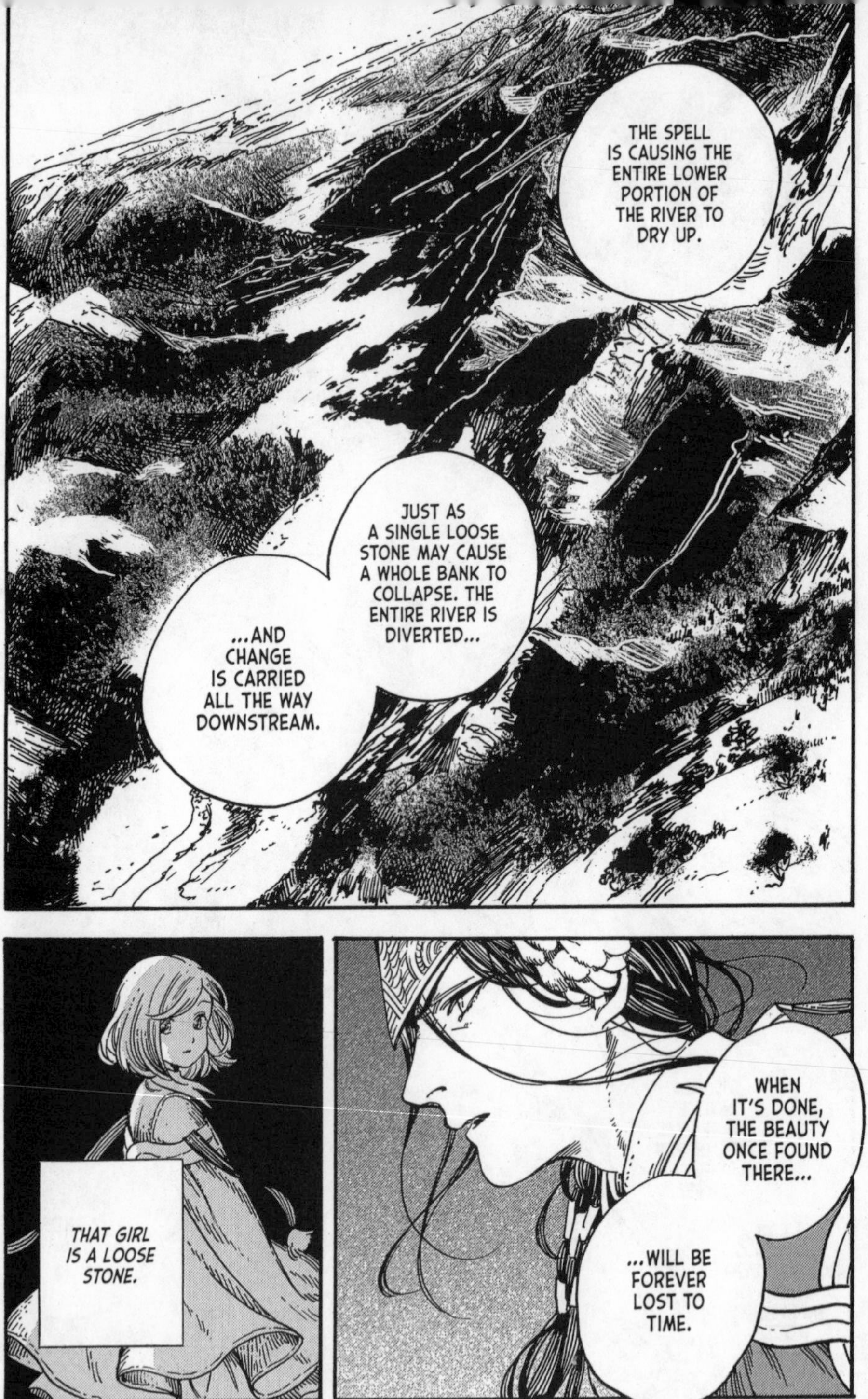
THE SPELL IS CAUSING THE ENTIRE LOWER PORTION OF THE RIVER TO DRY UP.
JUST AS A SINGLE LOOSE STONE MAY CAUSE A WHOLE BANK TO COLLAPSE. THE ENTIRE RIVER IS DIVERTED...
...AND CHANGE IS CARRIED ALL THE WAY DOWNSTREAM.
WHEN IT'S DONE, THE BEAUTY ONCE FOUND THERE...
...WILL BE FOREVER LOST TO TIME.
THAT GIRL IS A LOOSE STONE.

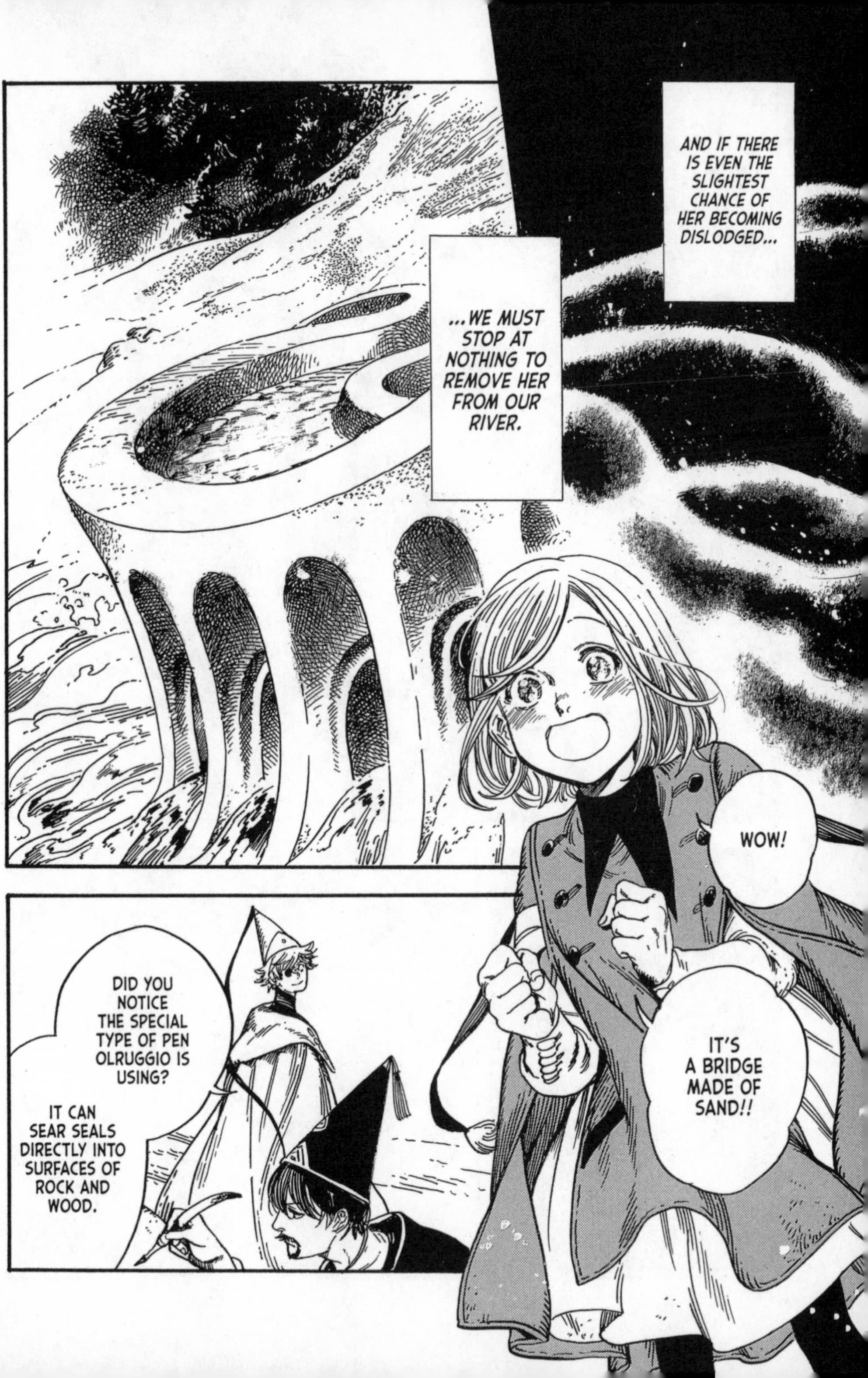
AND IF THERE IS EVEN THE SLIGHTEST CHANCE OF HER BECOMING DISLODGED...
...WE MUST STOP AT NOTHING TO REMOVE HER FROM OUR RIVER.
WOW!
IT'S A BRIDGE MADE OF SAND!!
DID YOU NOTICE THE SPECIAL TYPE OF PEN OLRUGGIO IS USING?
IT CAN SEAR SEALS DIRECTLY INTO SURFACES OF ROCK AND WOOD.

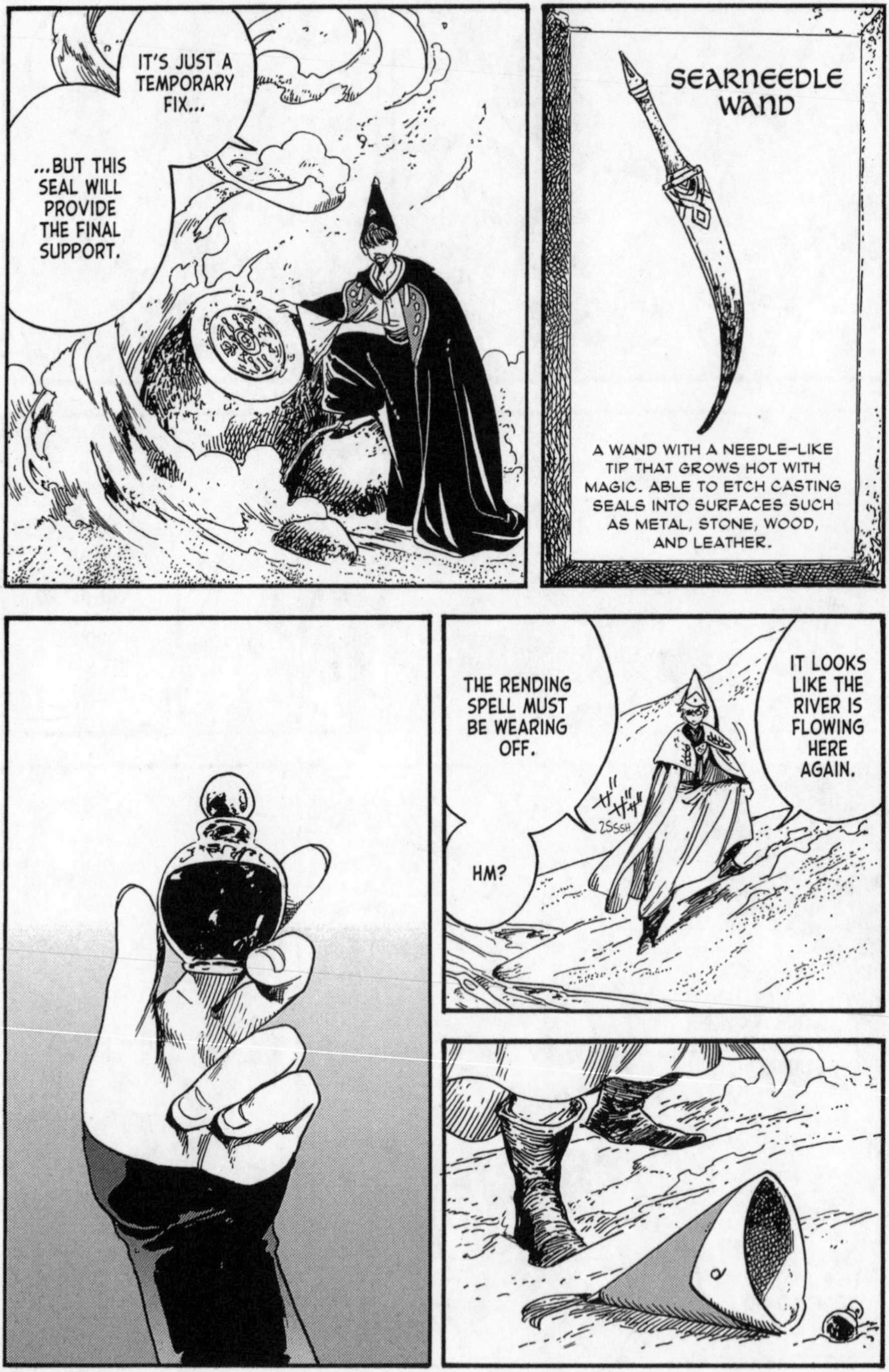
SEARNEEDLE WAND
A WAND WITH A NEEDLE-LIKE TIP THAT GROWS HOT WITH MAGIC. ABLE TO ETCH CASTING SEALS INTO SURFACES SUCH AS METAL, STONE, WOOD, AND LEATHER.
IT'S JUST A TEMPORARY FIX...
...BUT THIS SEAL WILL PROVIDE THE FINAL SUPPORT.
IT LOOKS LIKE THE RIVER IS FLOWING HERE AGAIN.
THE RENDING SPELL MUST BE WEARING OFF.
ZSSSH
HM?

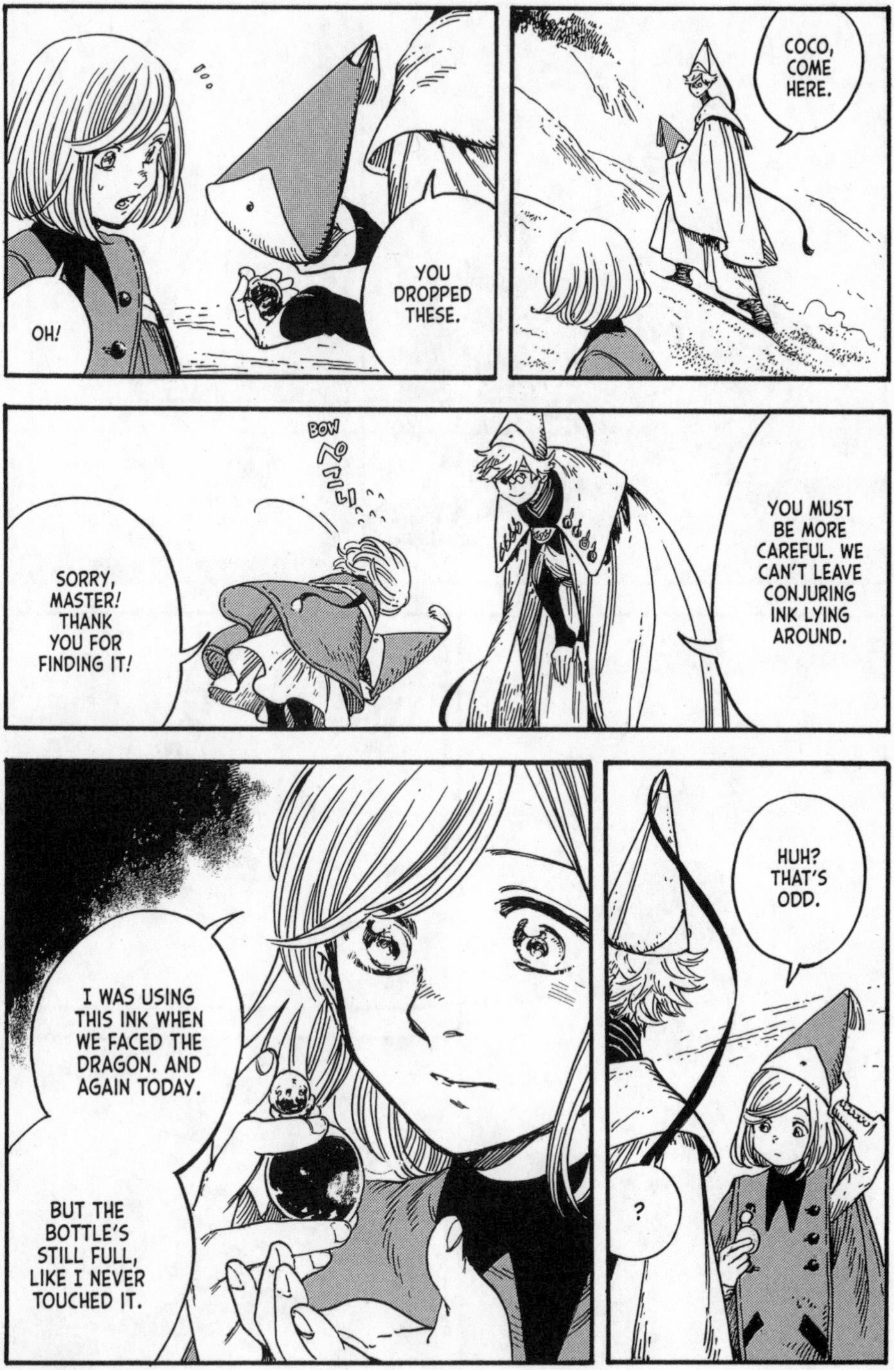
COCO, COME HERE.
YOU DROPPED THESE.
OH!
YOU MUST BE MORE CAREFUL. WE CAN'T LEAVE CONJURING INK LYING AROUND.
BOW
SORRY, MASTER! THANK YOU FOR FINDING IT!
HUH? THAT'S ODD.
?
I WAS USING THIS INK WHEN WE FACED THE DRAGON. AND AGAIN TODAY.
BUT THE BOTTLE'S STILL FULL, LIKE I NEVER TOUCHED IT.

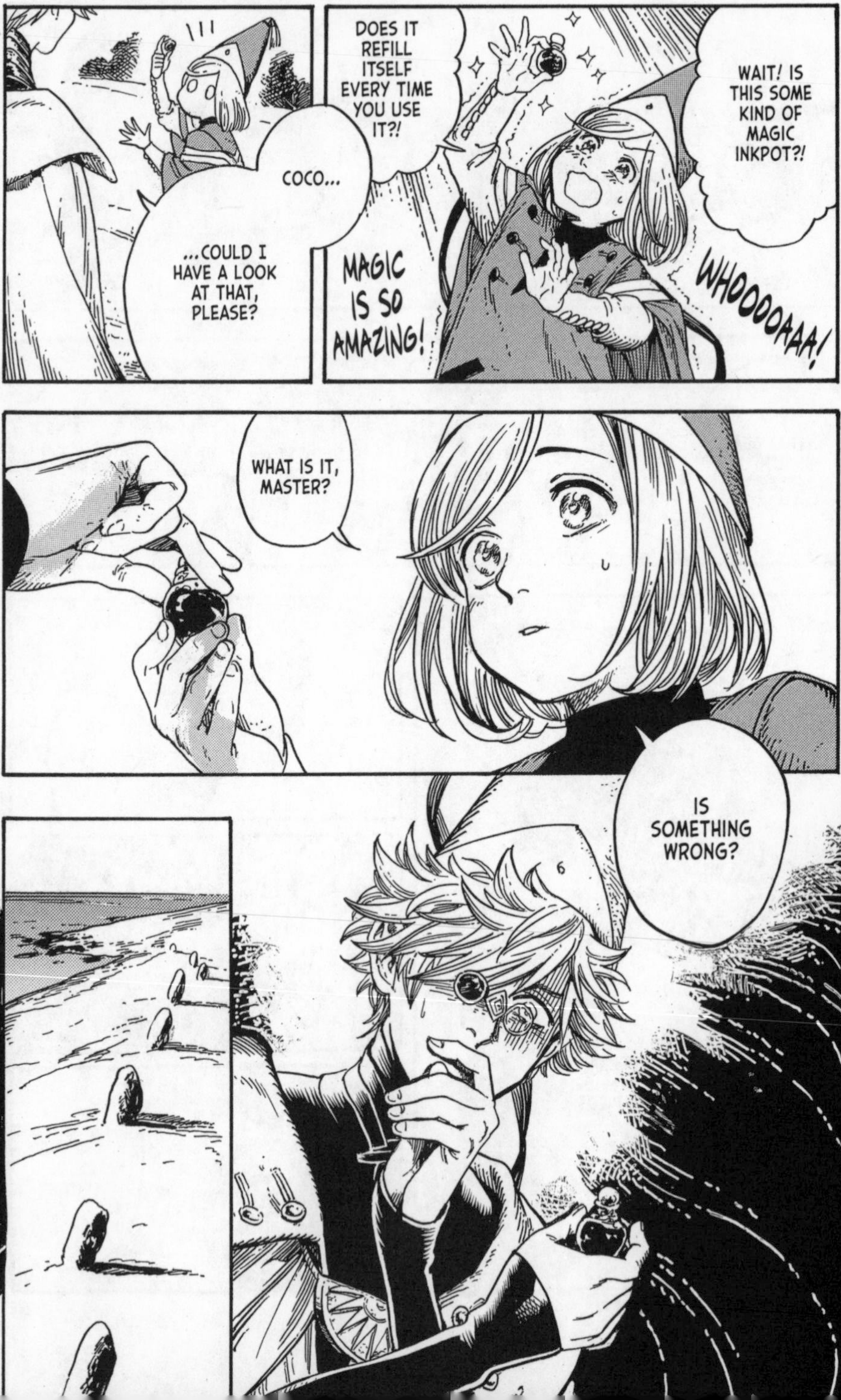
WAIT! IS THIS SOME KIND OF MAGIC INKPOT?!
DOES IT REFILL ITSELF EVERY TIME YOU USE IT?!
WHOOOOAAA!
MAGIC IS SO AMAZING!
COCO...
...COULD I HAVE A LOOK AT THAT, PLEASE?
WHAT IS IT, MASTER?
IS SOMETHING WRONG?

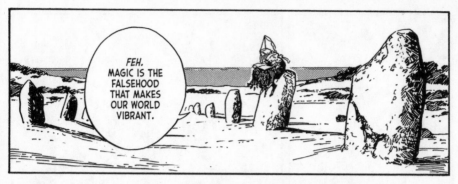

FEH.
MAGIC IS THE FALSEHOOD THAT MAKES OUR WORLD VIBRANT.
SO STAINED WITH POISON ARE THESE HANDS...
...THAT BEAR BEAUTIFUL SPELLS TO FRUIT.
SQUEEZE
AND YET NO LIE...
DR
IP
...CAN SURVIVE CLOSE SCRUTINY.
HOW LONG, I WONDER, CAN THIS RUSE BE MAINTAINED?

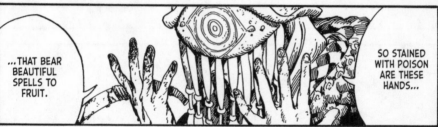

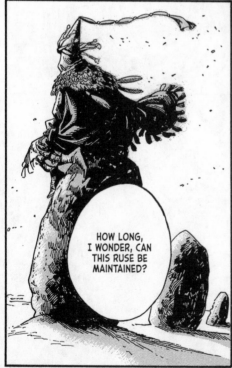

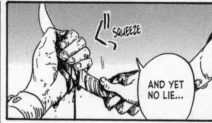

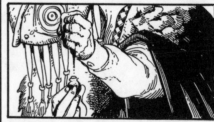

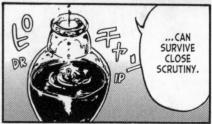

Witch Hat
Atelier

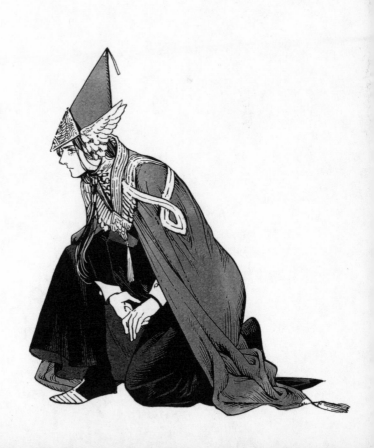

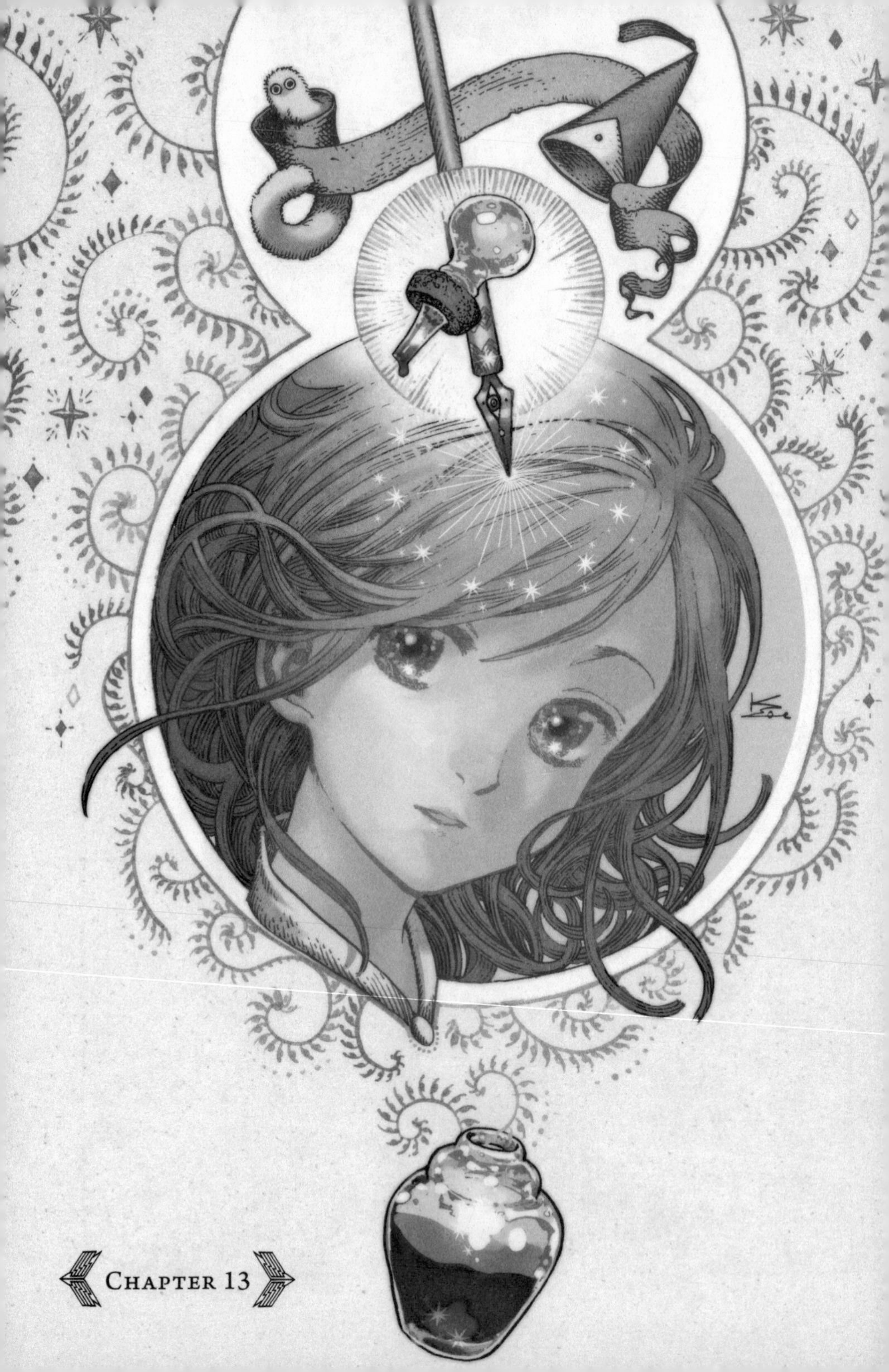

Chapter 13

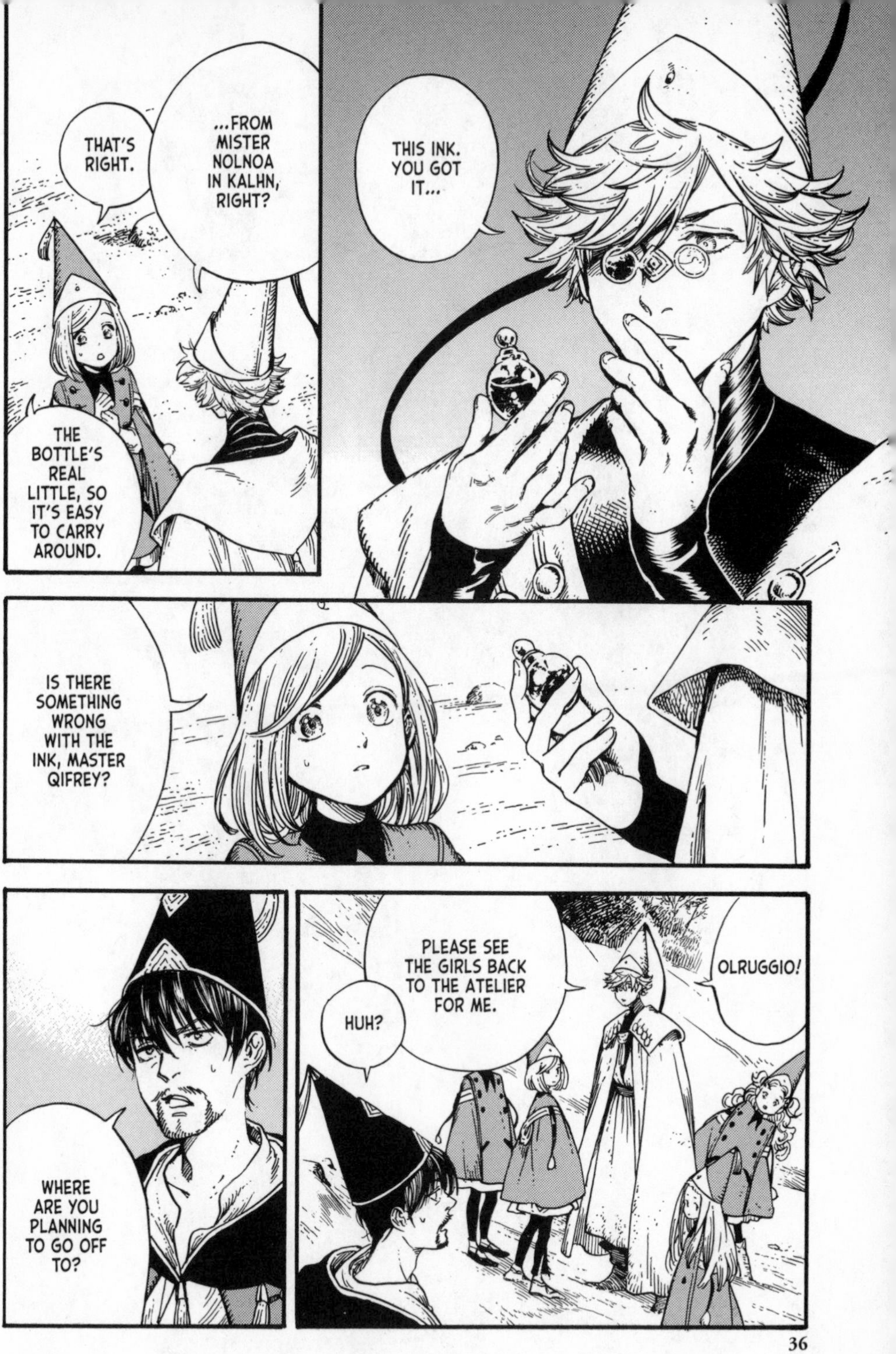
THIS INK. YOU GOT IT...
...FROM MISTER NOLNOA IN KALHN, RIGHT?
THAT'S RIGHT.
THE BOTTLE'S REAL LITTLE, SO IT'S EASY TO CARRY AROUND.
IS THERE SOMETHING WRONG WITH THE INK, MASTER QIFREY?
OLRUGGIO!
PLEASE SEE THE GIRLS BACK TO THE ATELIER FOR ME.
HUH?
WHERE ARE YOU PLANNING TO GO OFF TO?

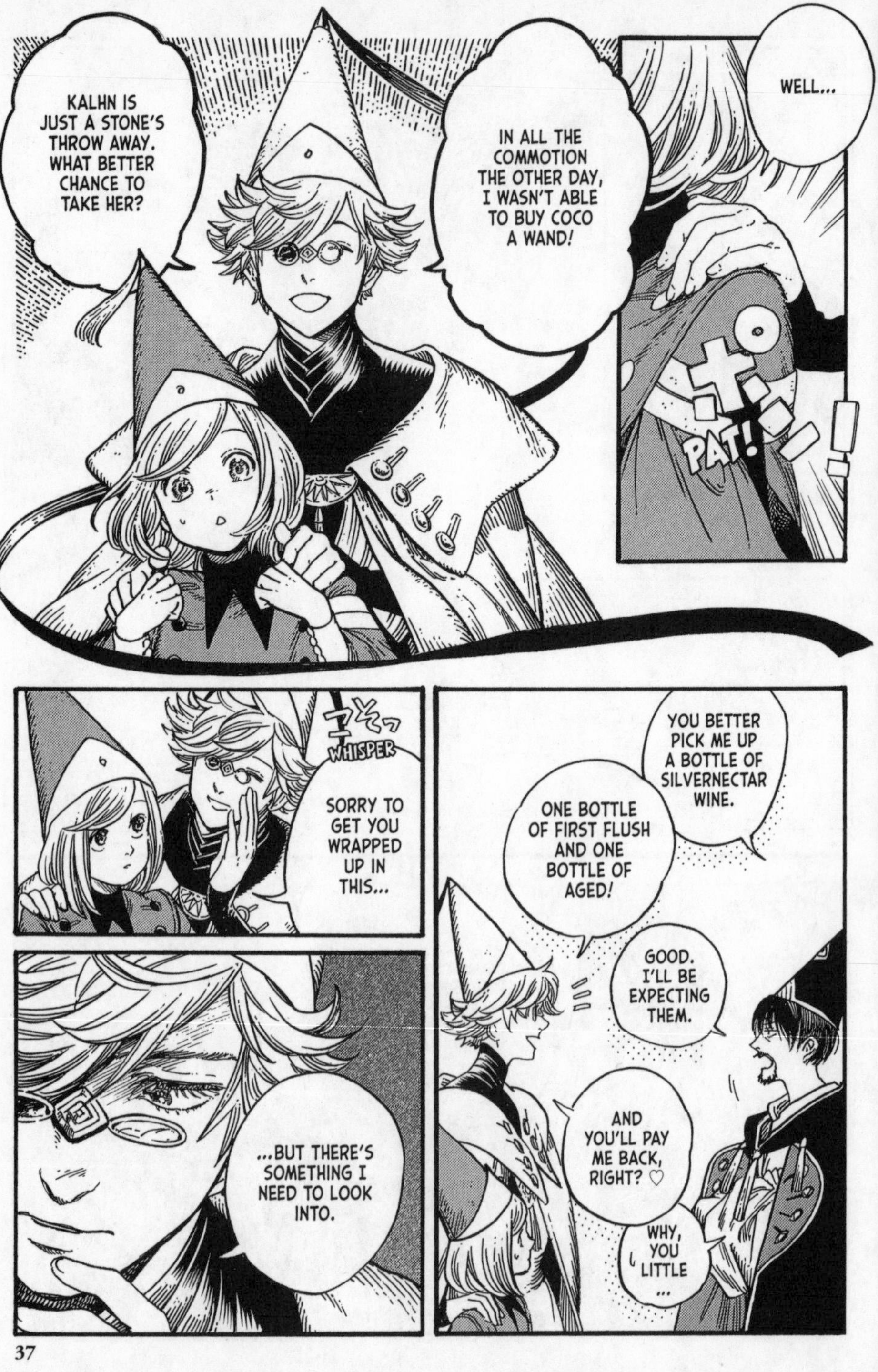
WELL...
PAT!
!
IN ALL THE COMMOTION THE OTHER DAY, I WASN'T ABLE TO BUY COCO A WAND!
KALHN IS JUST A STONE'S THROW AWAY. WHAT BETTER CHANCE TO TAKE HER?
YOU BETTER PICK ME UP A BOTTLE OF SILVERNECTAR WINE.
ONE BOTTLE OF FIRST FLUSH AND ONE BOTTLE OF AGED!
GOOD. I'LL BE EXPECTING THEM.
AND YOU'LL PAY ME BACK, RIGHT? ♡
WHY, YOU LITTLE ...
WHISPER
SORRY TO GET YOU WRAPPED UP IN THIS...
...BUT THERE'S SOMETHING I NEED TO LOOK INTO.

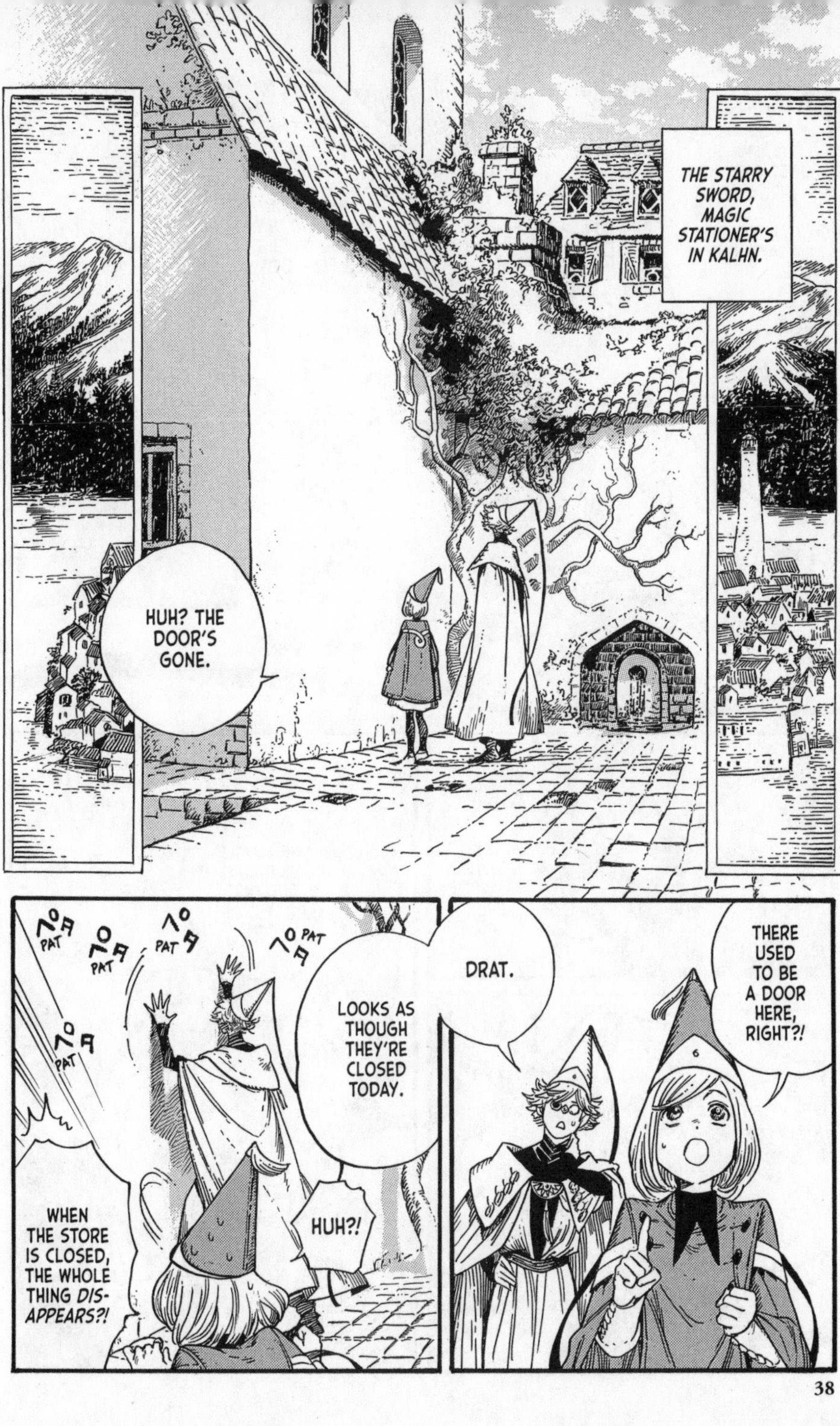
THE STARRY SWORD, MAGIC STATIONER'S IN KALHN.
HUH? THE DOOR'S GONE.
THERE USED TO BE A DOOR HERE, RIGHT?!
DRAT.
PAT
PAT
PAT
PAT
PAT
LOOKS AS THOUGH THEY'RE CLOSED TODAY.
HUH?!
WHEN THE STORE IS CLOSED, THE WHOLE THING *DIS-APPEARS*?!

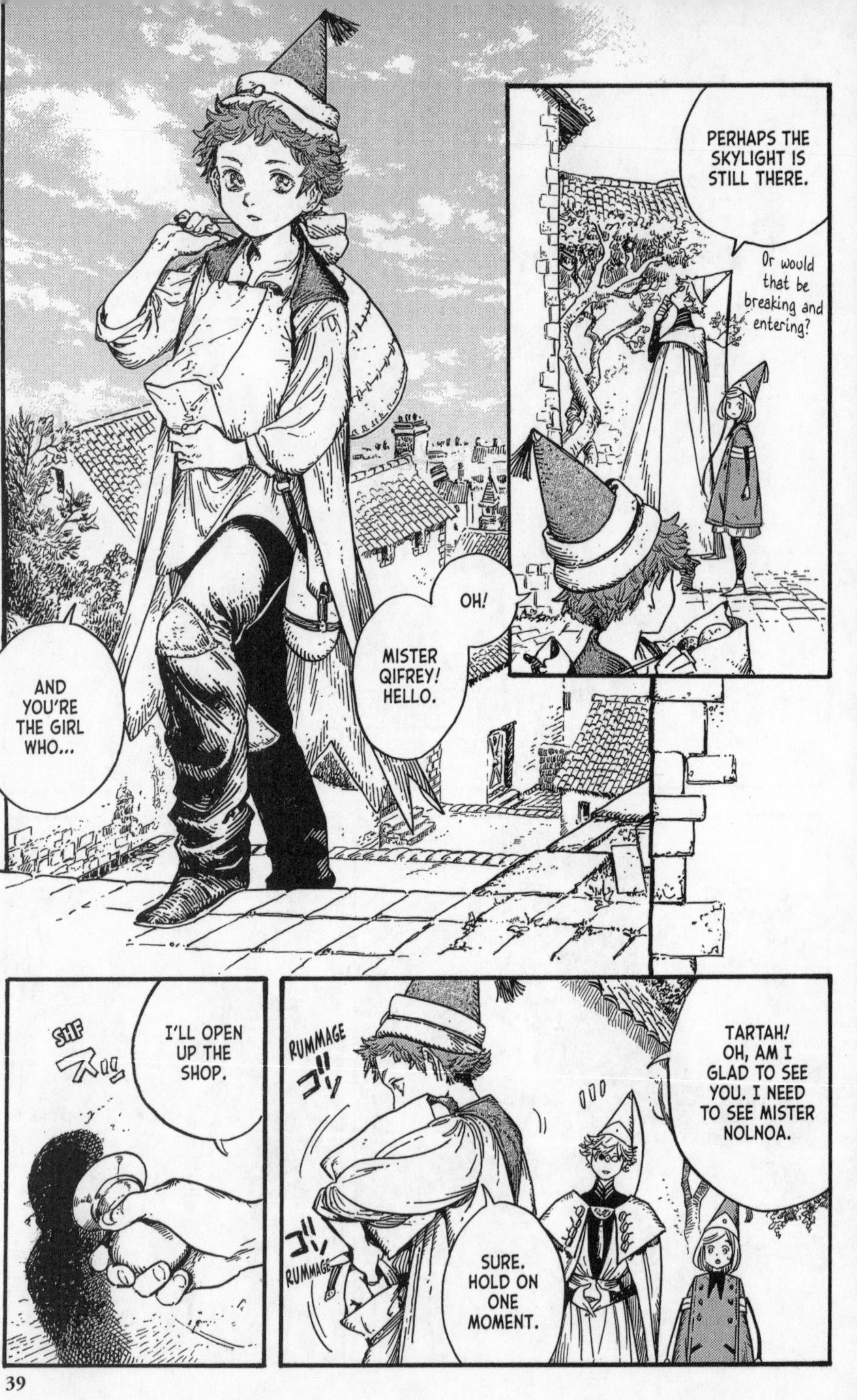
PERHAPS THE SKYLIGHT IS STILL THERE.
Or would that be breaking and entering?
OH!
MISTER QIFREY! HELLO.
AND YOU'RE THE GIRL WHO...
TARTAH! OH, AM I GLAD TO SEE YOU. I NEED TO SEE MISTER NOLNOA.
RUMMAGE
RUMMAGE
SURE. HOLD ON ONE MOMENT.
I'LL OPEN UP THE SHOP.
SHF

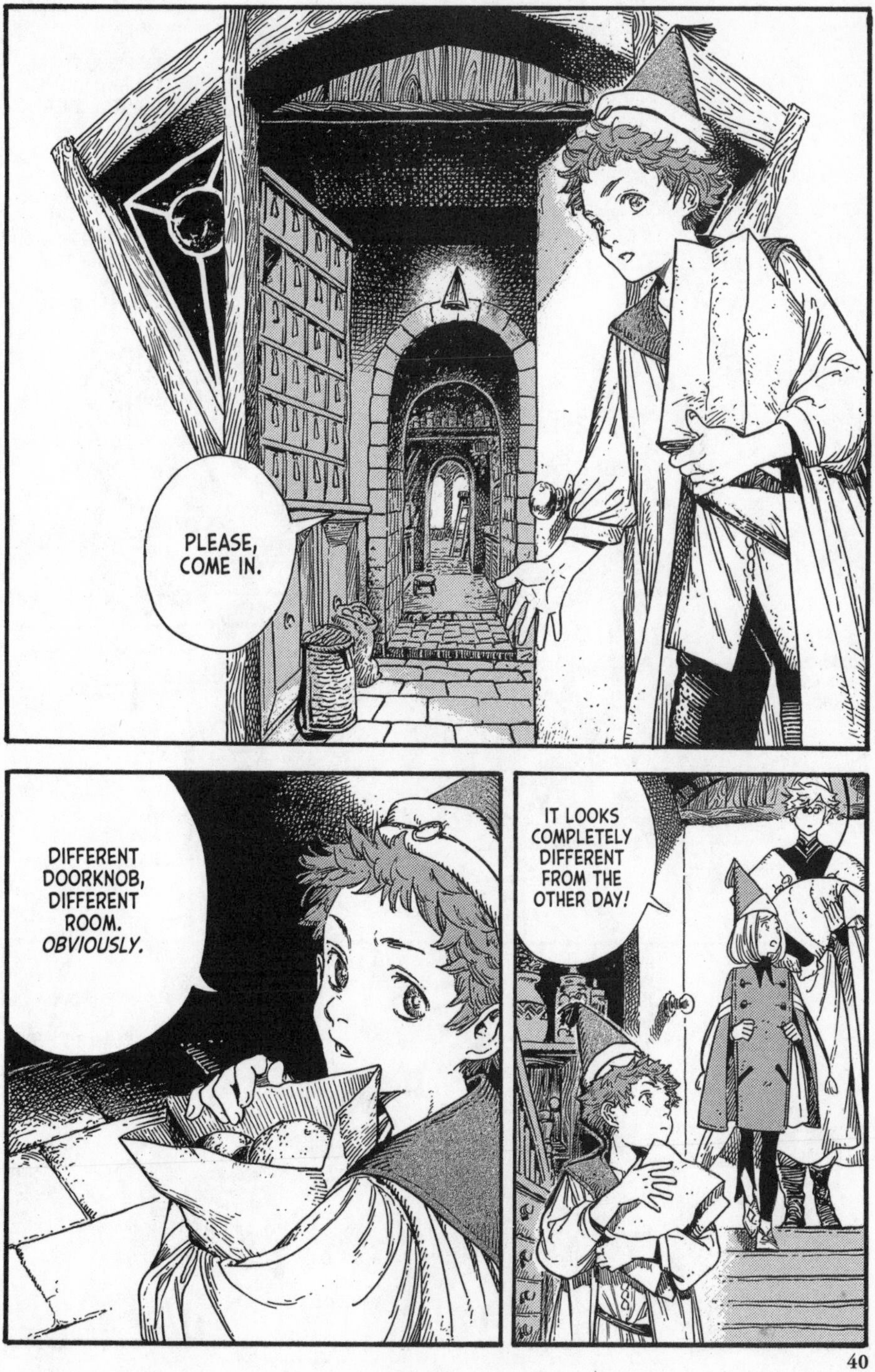
PLEASE, COME IN.
IT LOOKS COMPLETELY DIFFERENT FROM THE OTHER DAY!
DIFFERENT DOORKNOB, DIFFERENT ROOM. *OBVIOUSLY.*

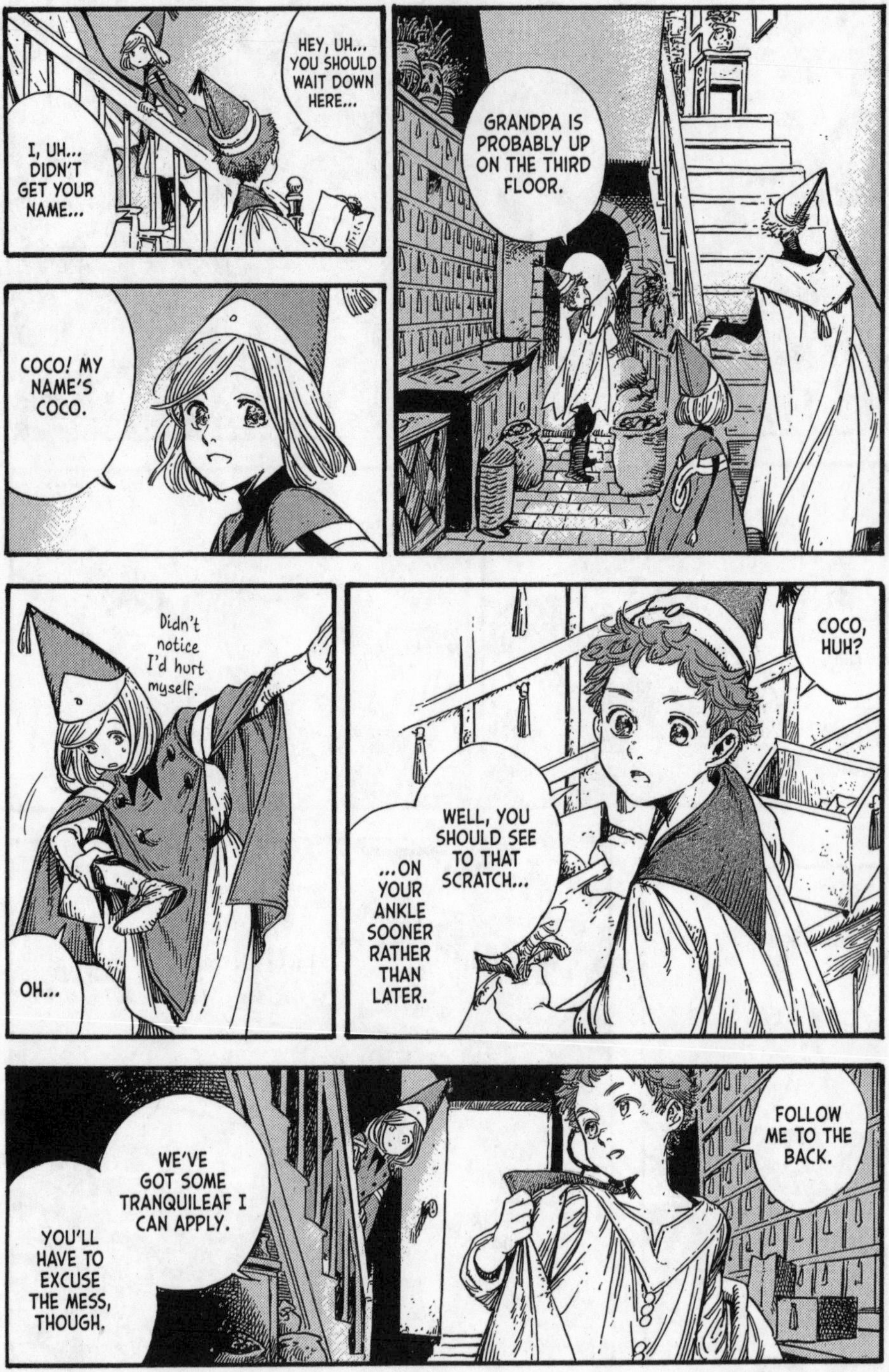
GRANDPA IS PROBABLY UP ON THE THIRD FLOOR.
HEY, UH... YOU SHOULD WAIT DOWN HERE...
I, UH... DIDN'T GET YOUR NAME...
COCO! MY NAME'S COCO.
COCO, HUH?
WELL, YOU SHOULD SEE TO THAT SCRATCH...
...ON YOUR ANKLE SOONER RATHER THAN LATER.
Didn't notice I'd hurt myself.
OH...
FOLLOW ME TO THE BACK.
WE'VE GOT SOME TRANQUILEAF I CAN APPLY.
YOU'LL HAVE TO EXCUSE THE MESS, THOUGH.

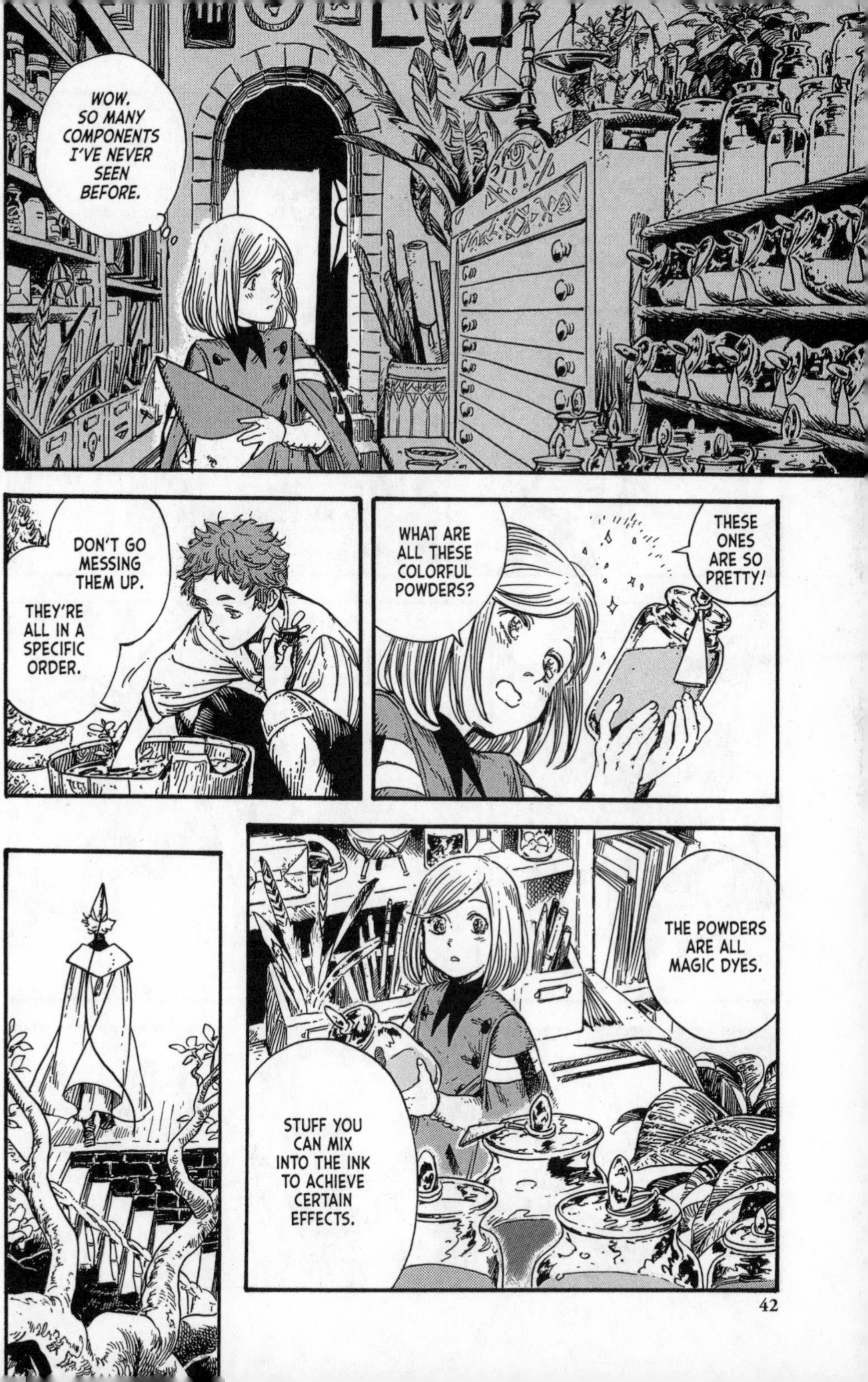
WOW. SO MANY COMPONENTS I'VE NEVER SEEN BEFORE.
THESE ONES ARE SO PRETTY!
WHAT ARE ALL THESE COLORFUL POWDERS?
DON'T GO MESSING THEM UP.
THEY'RE ALL IN A SPECIFIC ORDER.
THE POWDERS ARE ALL MAGIC DYES.
STUFF YOU CAN MIX INTO THE INK TO ACHIEVE CERTAIN EFFECTS.

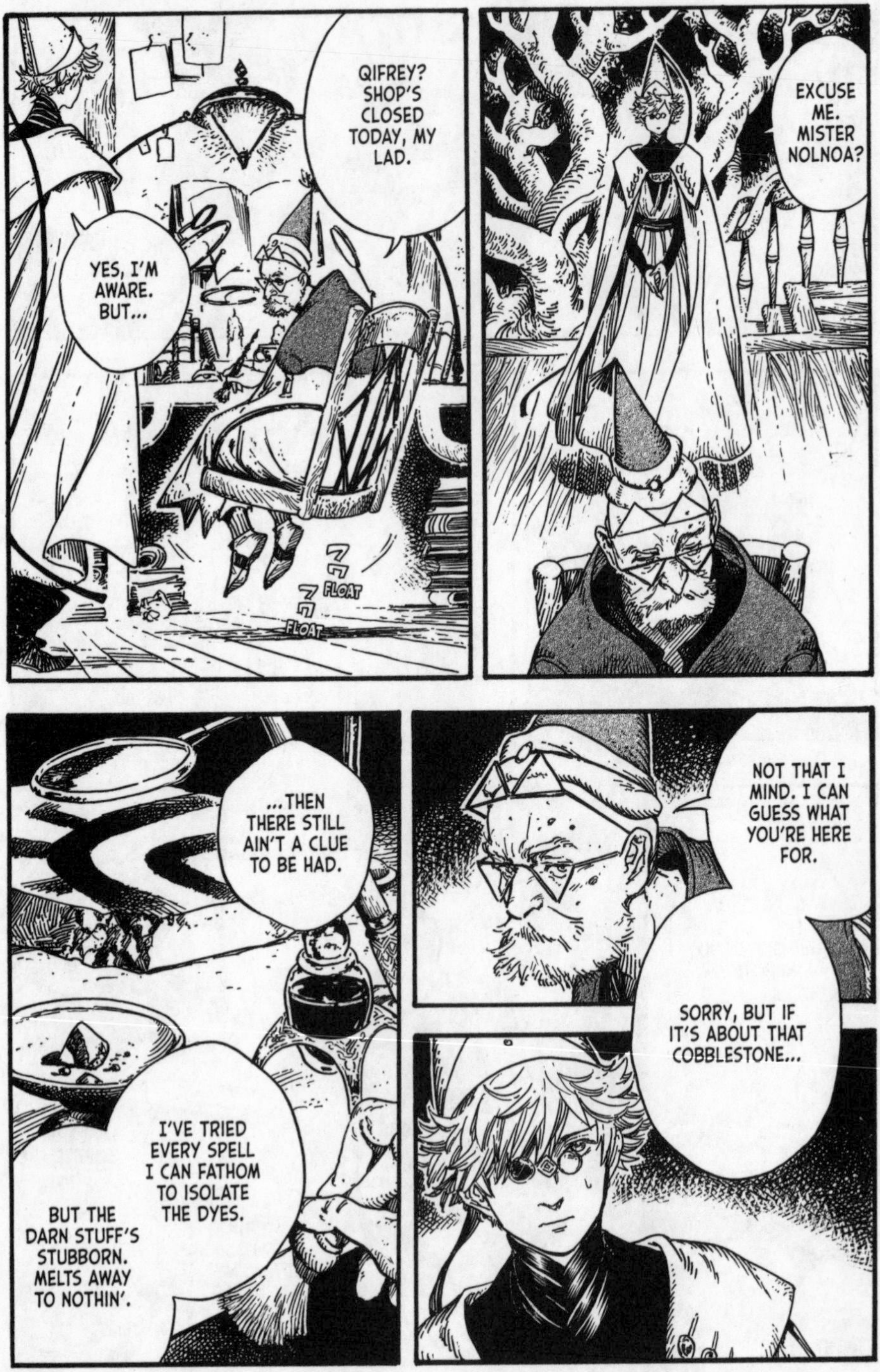
EXCUSE ME. MISTER NOLNOA?
QIFREY? SHOP'S CLOSED TODAY, MY LAD.
YES, I'M AWARE. BUT...
FLOAT
FLOAT
NOT THAT I MIND. I CAN GUESS WHAT YOU'RE HERE FOR.
SORRY, BUT IF IT'S ABOUT THAT COBBLESTONE...
...THEN THERE STILL AIN'T A CLUE TO BE HAD.
I'VE TRIED EVERY SPELL I CAN FATHOM TO ISOLATE THE DYES.
BUT THE DARN STUFF'S STUBBORN. MELTS AWAY TO NOTHIN'.

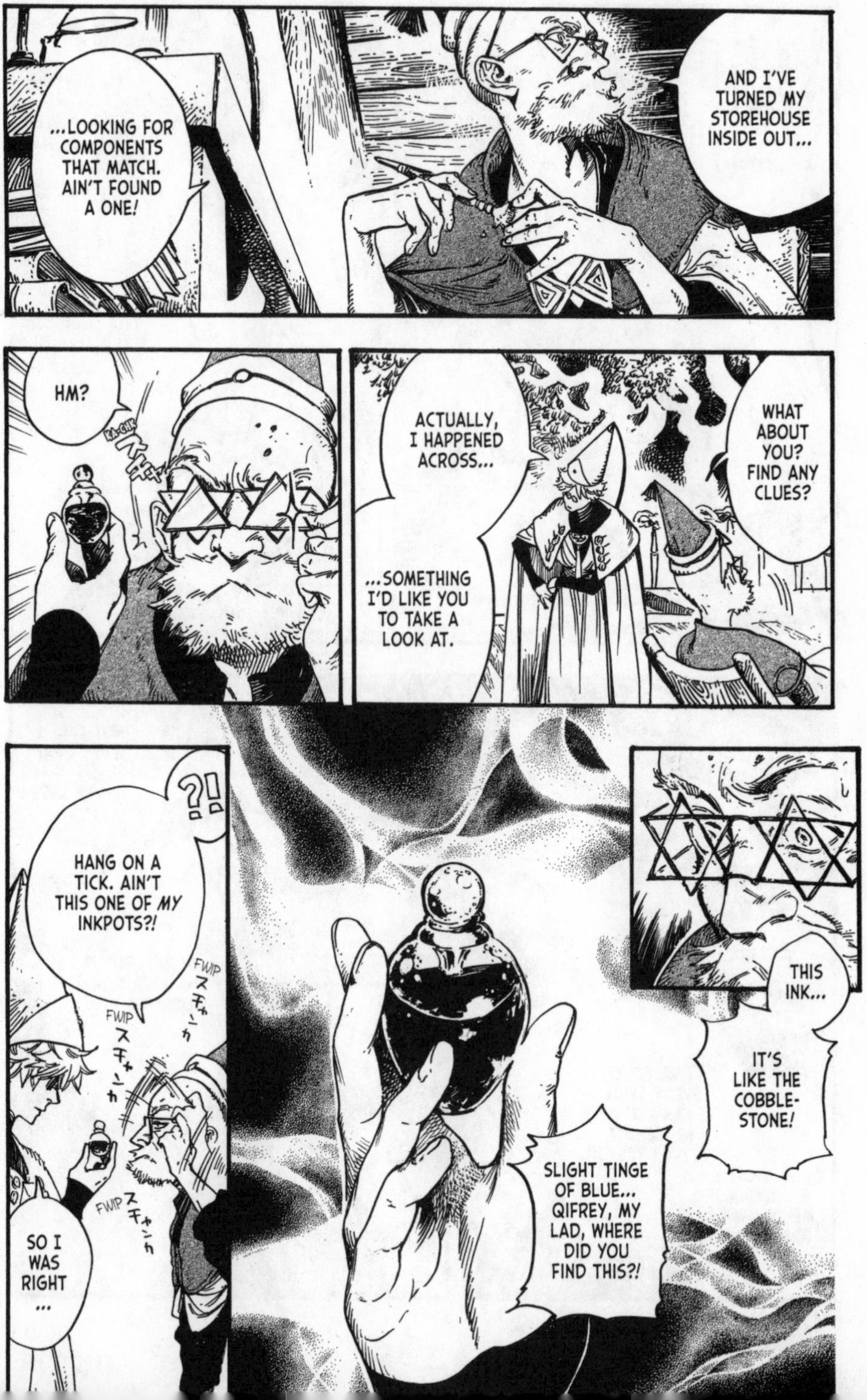
AND I'VE TURNED MY STOREHOUSE INSIDE OUT...
...LOOKING FOR COMPONENTS THAT MATCH. AIN'T FOUND A ONE!
WHAT ABOUT YOU? FIND ANY CLUES?
ACTUALLY, I HAPPENED ACROSS...
...SOMETHING I'D LIKE YOU TO TAKE A LOOK AT.
HM?
KA-CHK
スチャ
THIS INK...
IT'S LIKE THE COBBLESTONE!
SLIGHT TINGE OF BLUE... QIFREY, MY LAD, WHERE DID YOU FIND THIS?!
?!
HANG ON A TICK. AIN'T THIS ONE OF MY INKPOTS?!
FWIP
スチャンカ
FWIP
スチャンカ
FWIP
スチャンカ
SO I WAS RIGHT ...

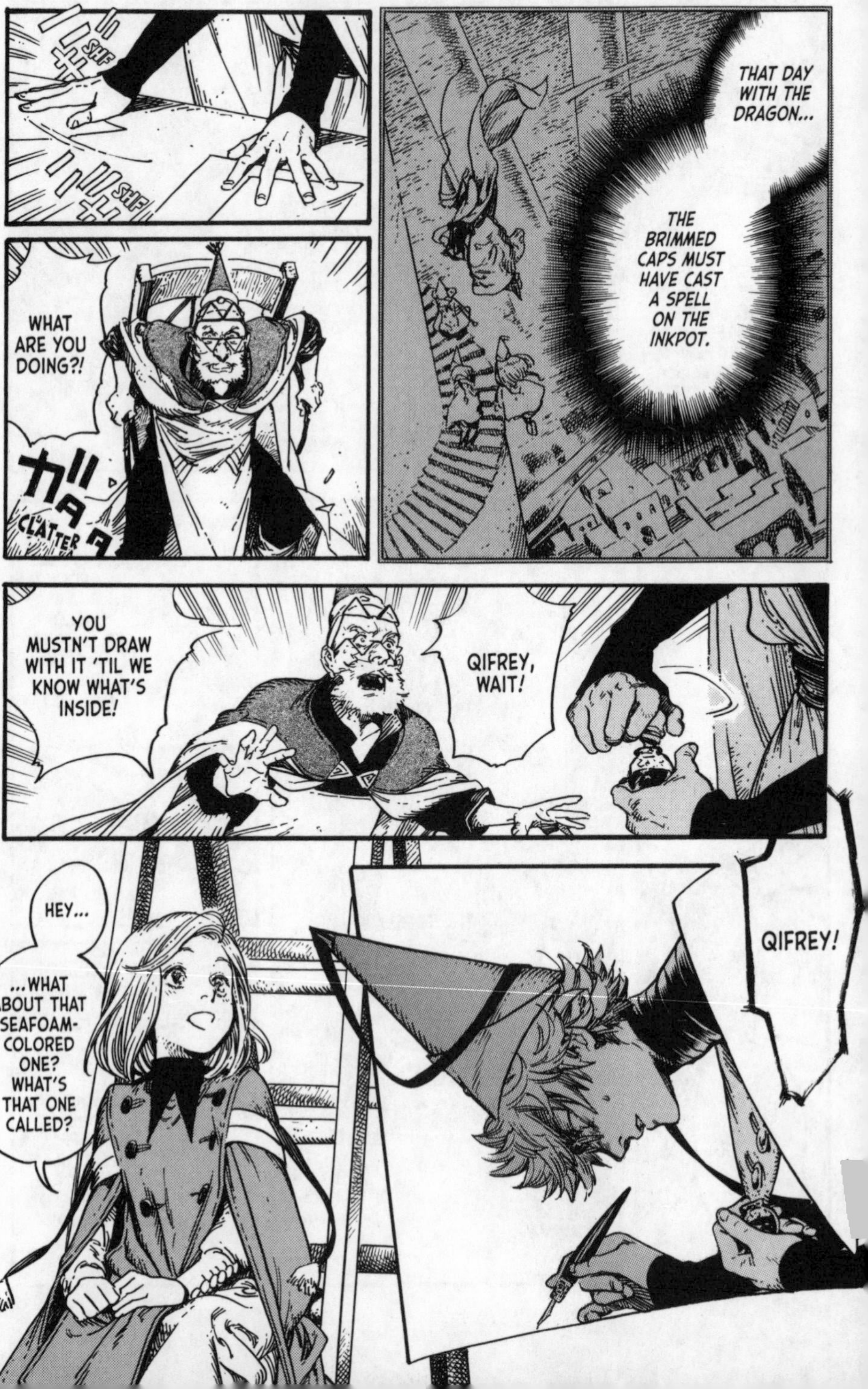
THAT DAY WITH THE DRAGON...
THE BRIMMED CAPS MUST HAVE CAST A SPELL ON THE INKPOT.
SHF
SHF
WHAT ARE YOU DOING?!
CLATTER
QIFREY, WAIT!
YOU MUSTN'T DRAW WITH IT 'TIL WE KNOW WHAT'S INSIDE!
QIFREY!
HEY...
...WHAT ABOUT THAT SEAFOAM-COLORED ONE? WHAT'S THAT ONE CALLED?

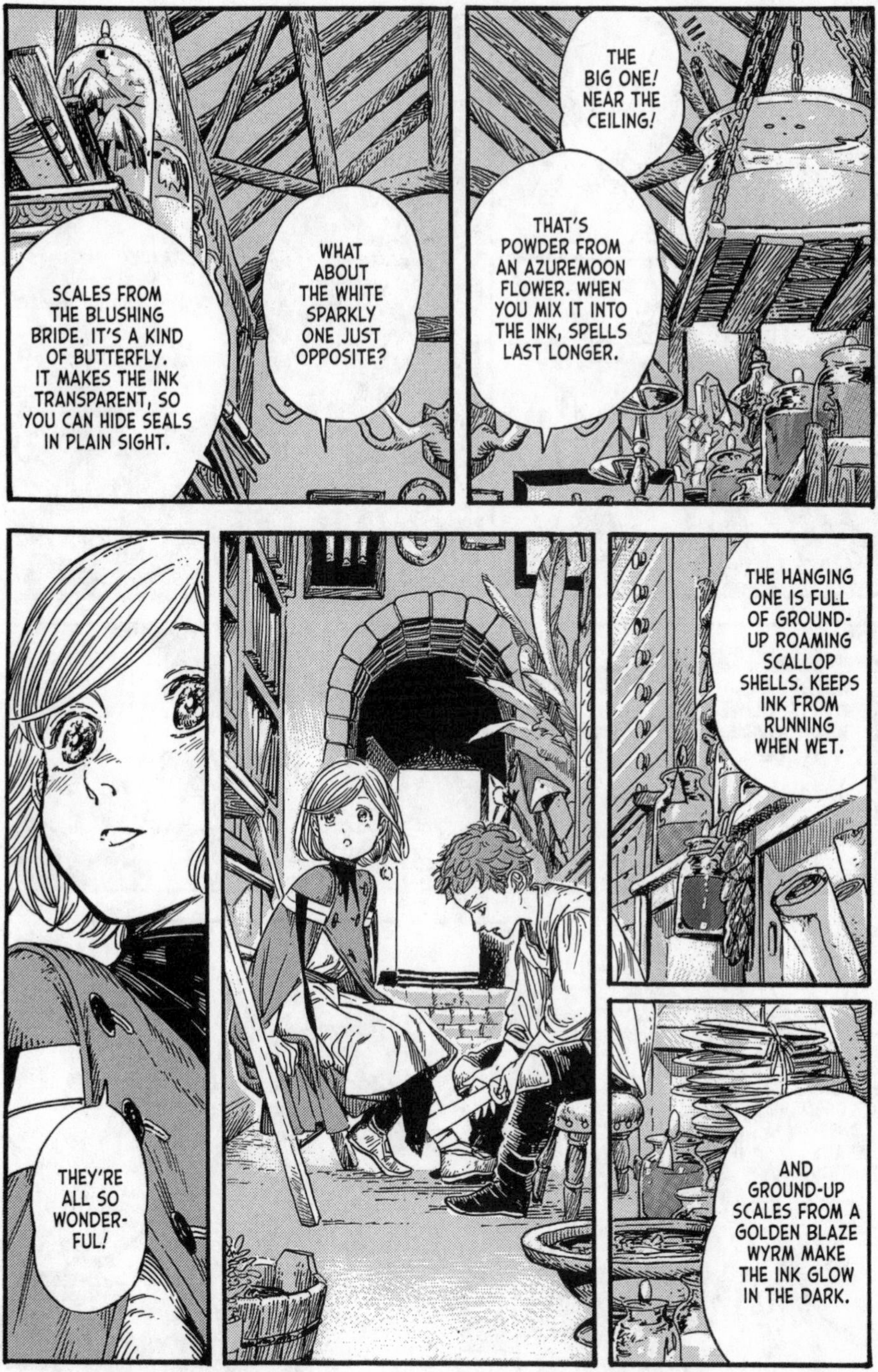
THE BIG ONE! NEAR THE CEILING!
THAT'S POWDER FROM AN AZUREMOON FLOWER. WHEN YOU MIX IT INTO THE INK, SPELLS LAST LONGER.
WHAT ABOUT THE WHITE SPARKLY ONE JUST OPPOSITE?
SCALES FROM THE BLUSHING BRIDE. IT'S A KIND OF BUTTERFLY. IT MAKES THE INK TRANSPARENT, SO YOU CAN HIDE SEALS IN PLAIN SIGHT.
THE HANGING ONE IS FULL OF GROUND-UP ROAMING SCALLOP SHELLS. KEEPS INK FROM RUNNING WHEN WET.
AND GROUND-UP SCALES FROM A GOLDEN BLAZE WYRM MAKE THE INK GLOW IN THE DARK.
THEY'RE ALL SO WONDER-FUL!

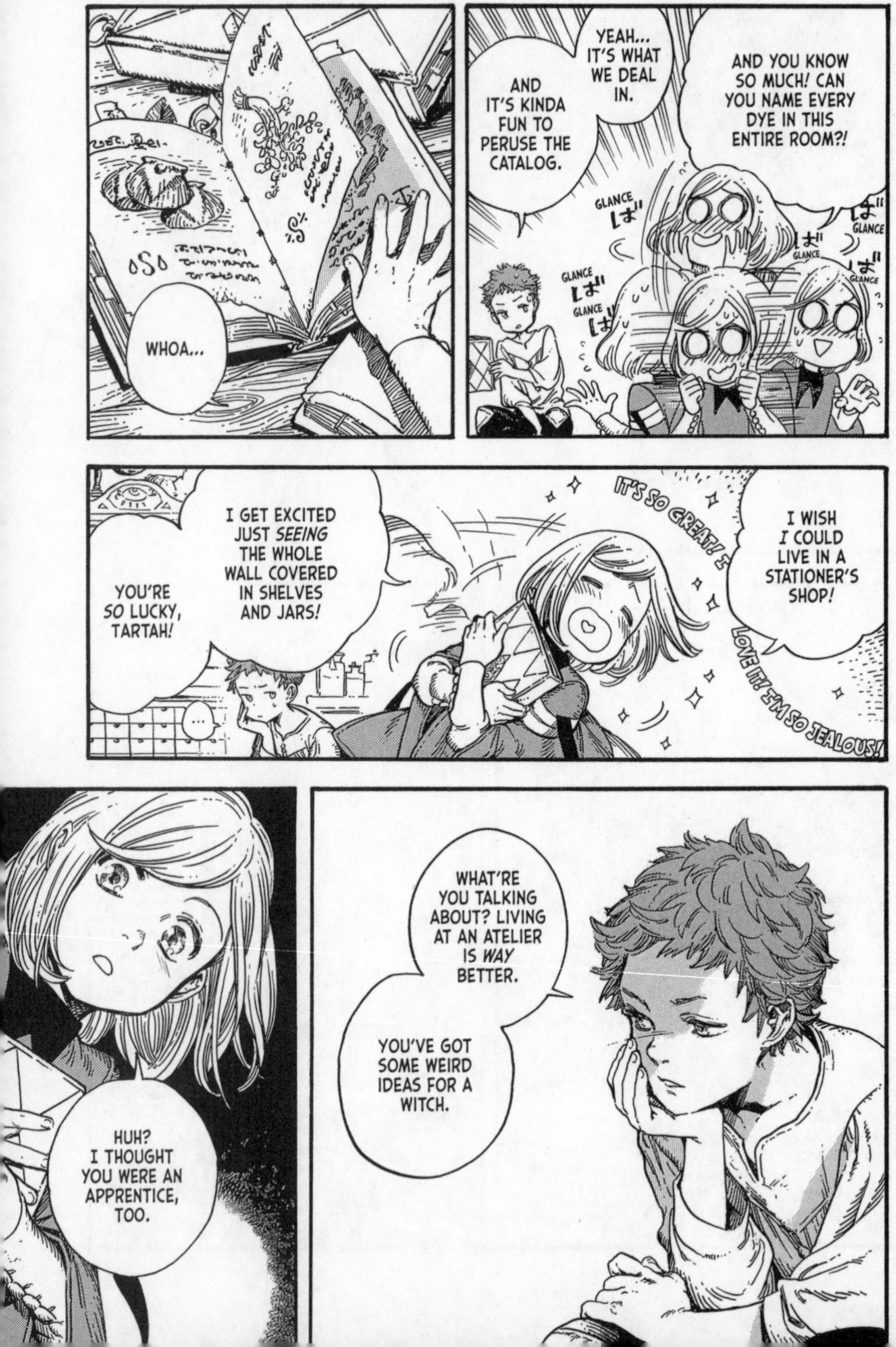
AND YOU KNOW SO MUCH! CAN YOU NAME EVERY DYE IN THIS ENTIRE ROOM?!
GLANCE
GLANCE
GLANCE
GLANCE
GLANCE
YEAH... IT'S WHAT WE DEAL IN.
AND IT'S KINDA FUN TO PERUSE THE CATALOG.
WHOA...
I WISH *I* COULD LIVE IN A STATIONER'S SHOP!
IT'S SO GREAT! I LOVE IT! I'M SO JEALOUS!
I GET EXCITED JUST *SEEING* THE WHOLE WALL COVERED IN SHELVES AND JARS!
YOU'RE *SO* LUCKY, TARTAH!
...
WHAT'RE YOU TALKING ABOUT? LIVING AT AN ATELIER IS *WAY* BETTER.
YOU'VE GOT SOME WEIRD IDEAS FOR A WITCH.
HUH? I THOUGHT YOU WERE AN APPRENTICE, TOO.

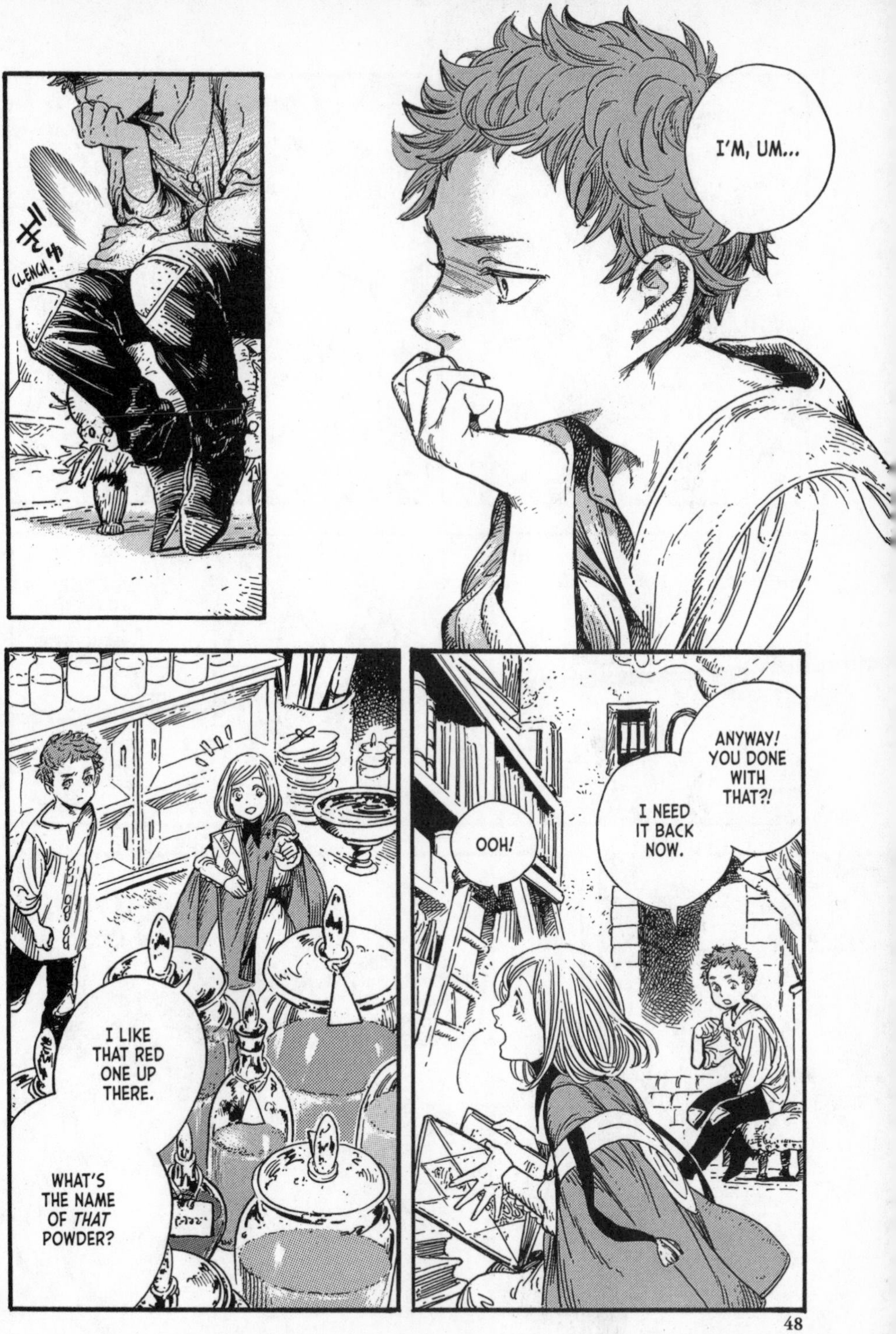
I'M, UM...
CLENCH
ANYWAY! YOU DONE WITH THAT?!
I NEED IT BACK NOW.
OOH!
I LIKE THAT RED ONE UP THERE.
WHAT'S THE NAME OF *THAT* POWDER?

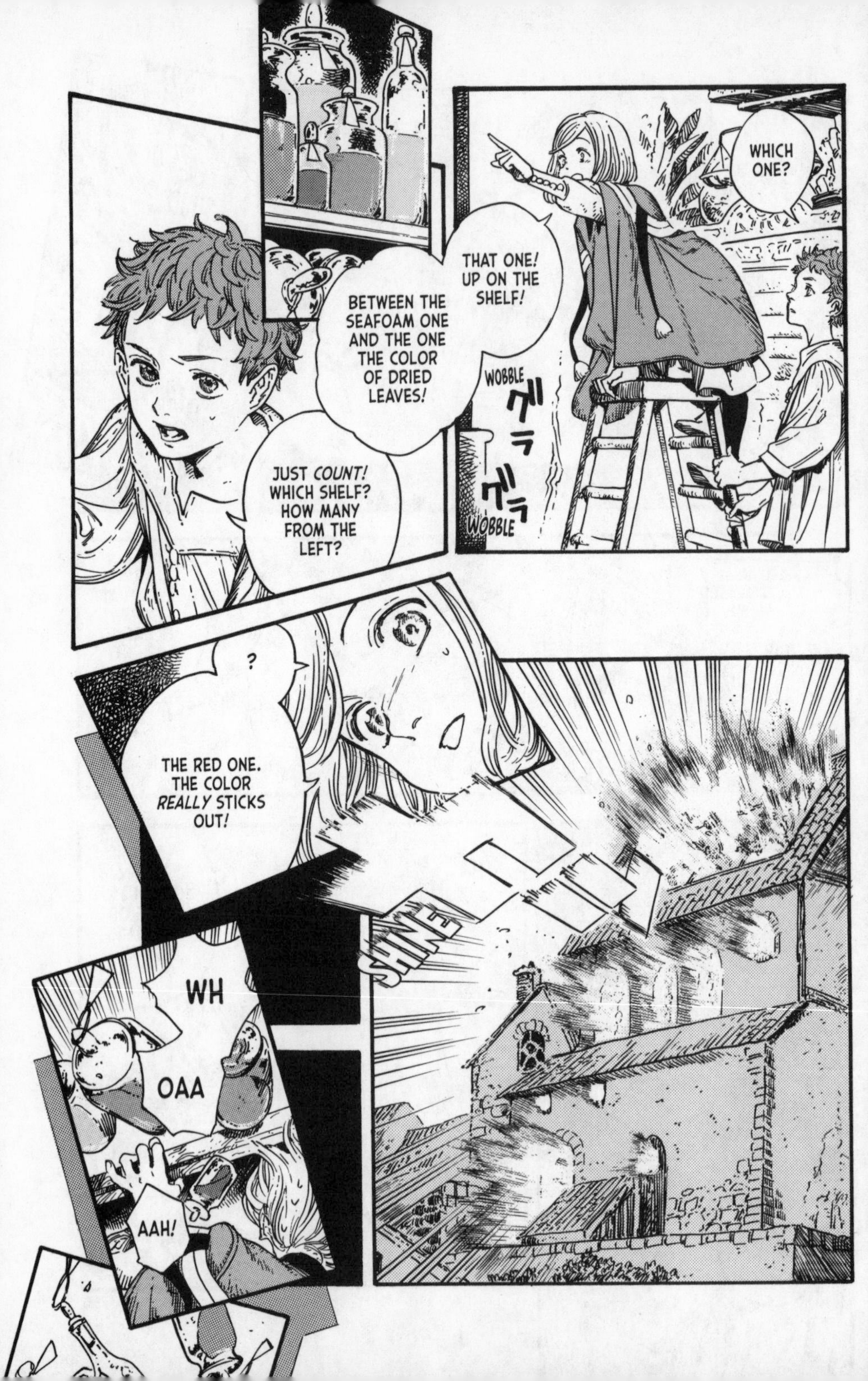
WHICH ONE?
THAT ONE! UP ON THE SHELF!
WOBBLE
グラ
グラ
WOBBLE
BETWEEN THE SEAFOAM ONE AND THE ONE THE COLOR OF DRIED LEAVES!
JUST *COUNT!* WHICH SHELF? HOW MANY FROM THE LEFT?
?
THE RED ONE. THE COLOR *REALLY* STICKS OUT!
SHINE
WH
OAA
AAH!

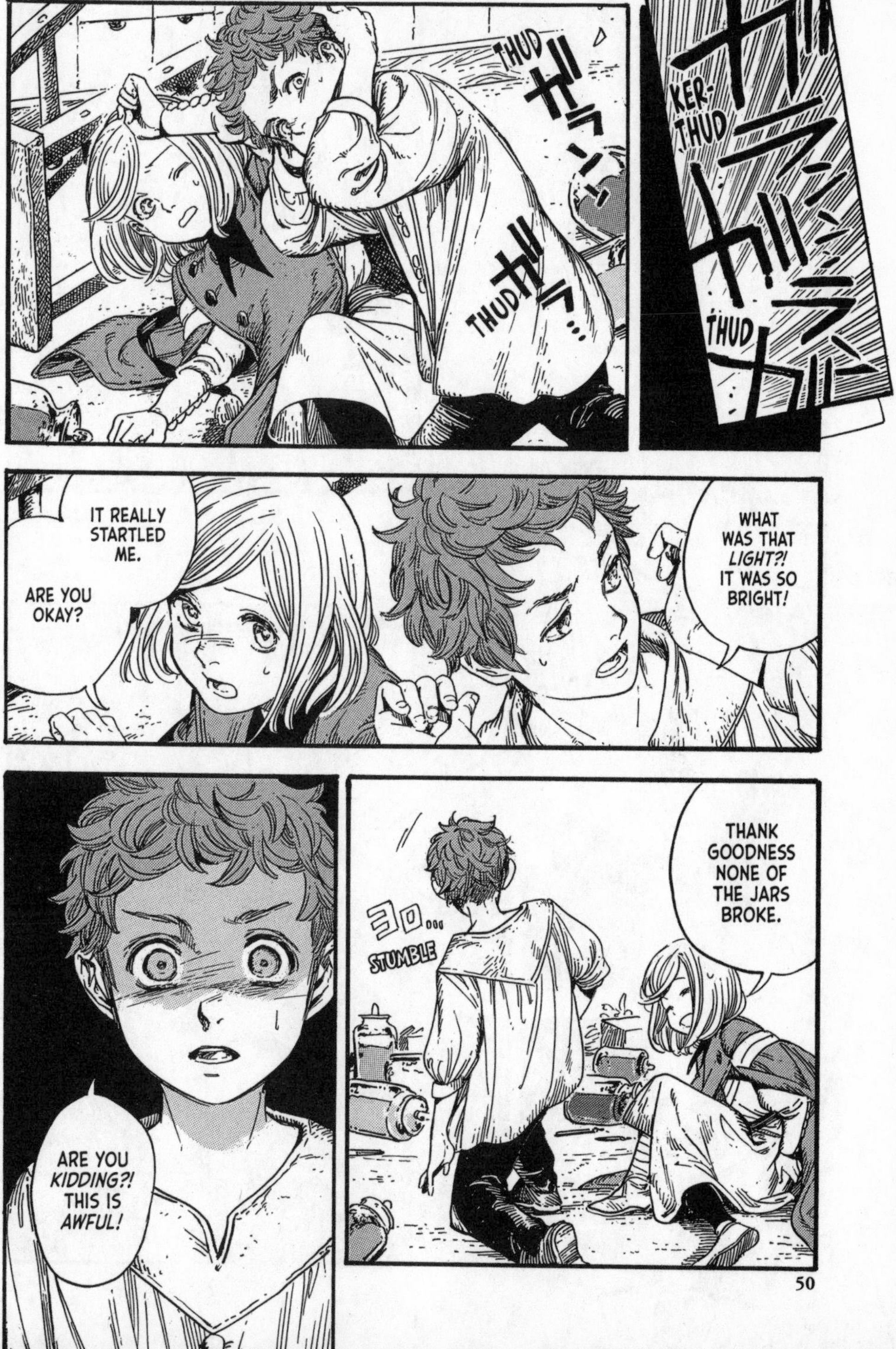
KER-THUD
THUD
THUD
THUD
WHAT WAS THAT *LIGHT?!* IT WAS SO BRIGHT!
IT REALLY STARTLED ME.
ARE YOU OKAY?
THANK GOODNESS NONE OF THE JARS BROKE.
STUMBLE
ARE YOU *KIDDING?!* THIS IS *AWFUL!*

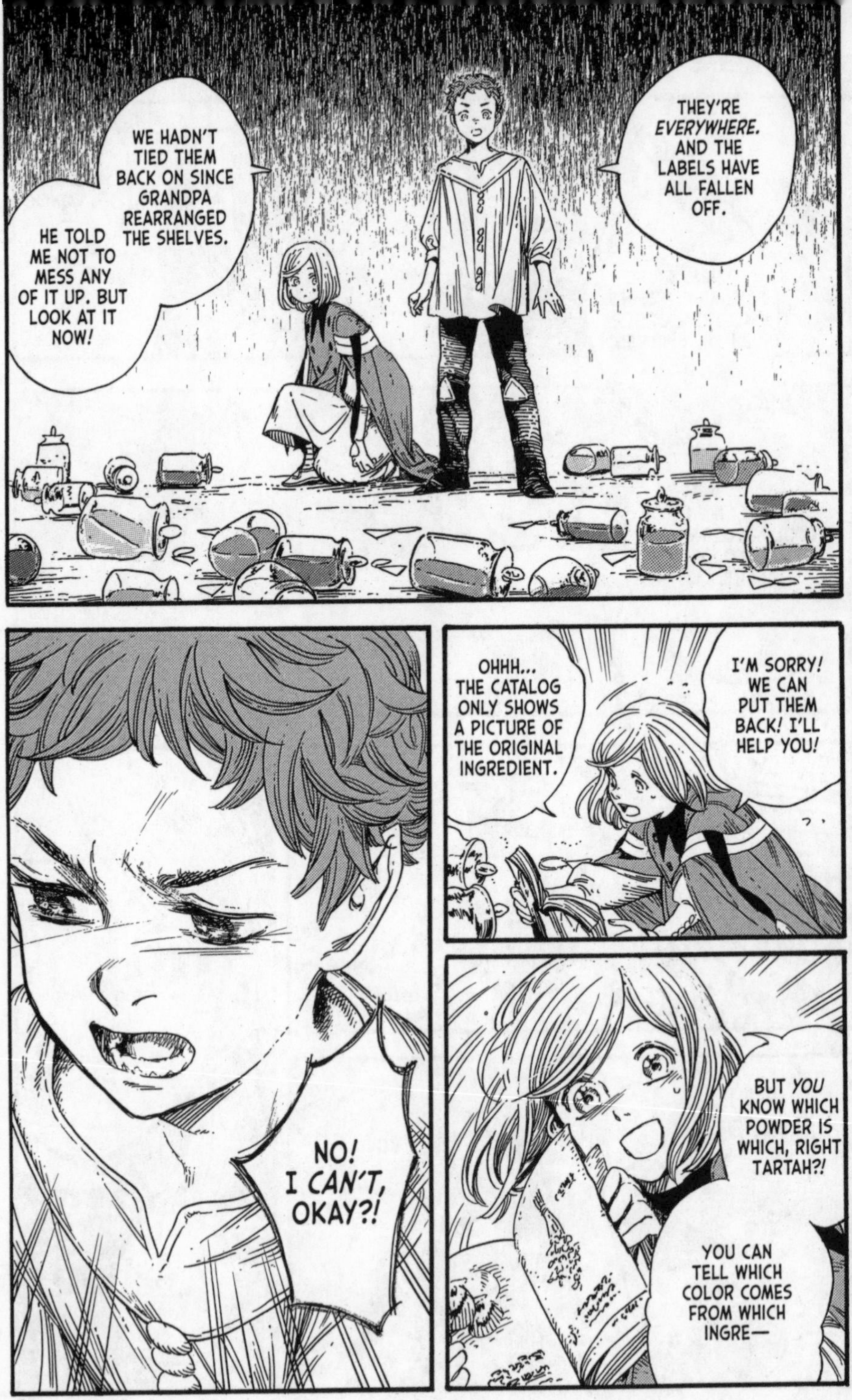
THEY'RE *EVERYWHERE.* AND THE LABELS HAVE ALL FALLEN OFF.
WE HADN'T TIED THEM BACK ON SINCE GRANDPA REARRANGED THE SHELVES.
HE TOLD ME NOT TO MESS ANY OF IT UP. BUT LOOK AT IT NOW!
I'M SORRY! WE CAN PUT THEM BACK! I'LL HELP YOU!
OHHH... THE CATALOG ONLY SHOWS A PICTURE OF THE ORIGINAL INGREDIENT.
BUT *YOU* KNOW WHICH POWDER IS WHICH, RIGHT TARTAH?!
YOU CAN TELL WHICH COLOR COMES FROM WHICH INGRE—
NO! I *CAN'T,* OKAY?!

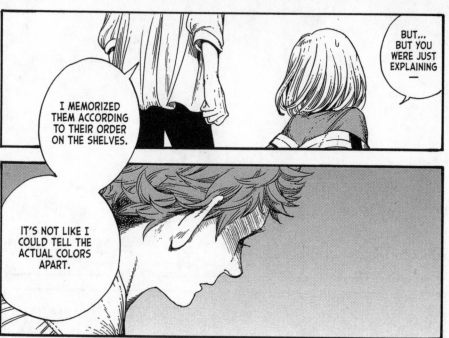

BUT... BUT YOU WERE JUST EXPLAINING —

I MEMORIZED THEM ACCORDING TO THEIR ORDER ON THE SHELVES.

IT'S NOT LIKE I COULD TELL THE ACTUAL COLORS APART.

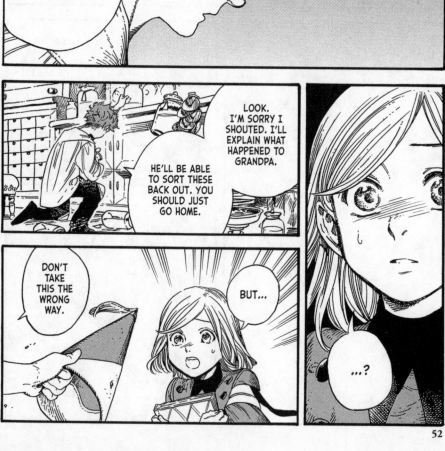

LOOK. I'M SORRY I SHOUTED. I'LL EXPLAIN WHAT HAPPENED TO GRANDPA.

HE'LL BE ABLE TO SORT THESE BACK OUT. YOU SHOULD JUST GO HOME.

DON'T TAKE THIS THE WRONG WAY.

BUT...

...?

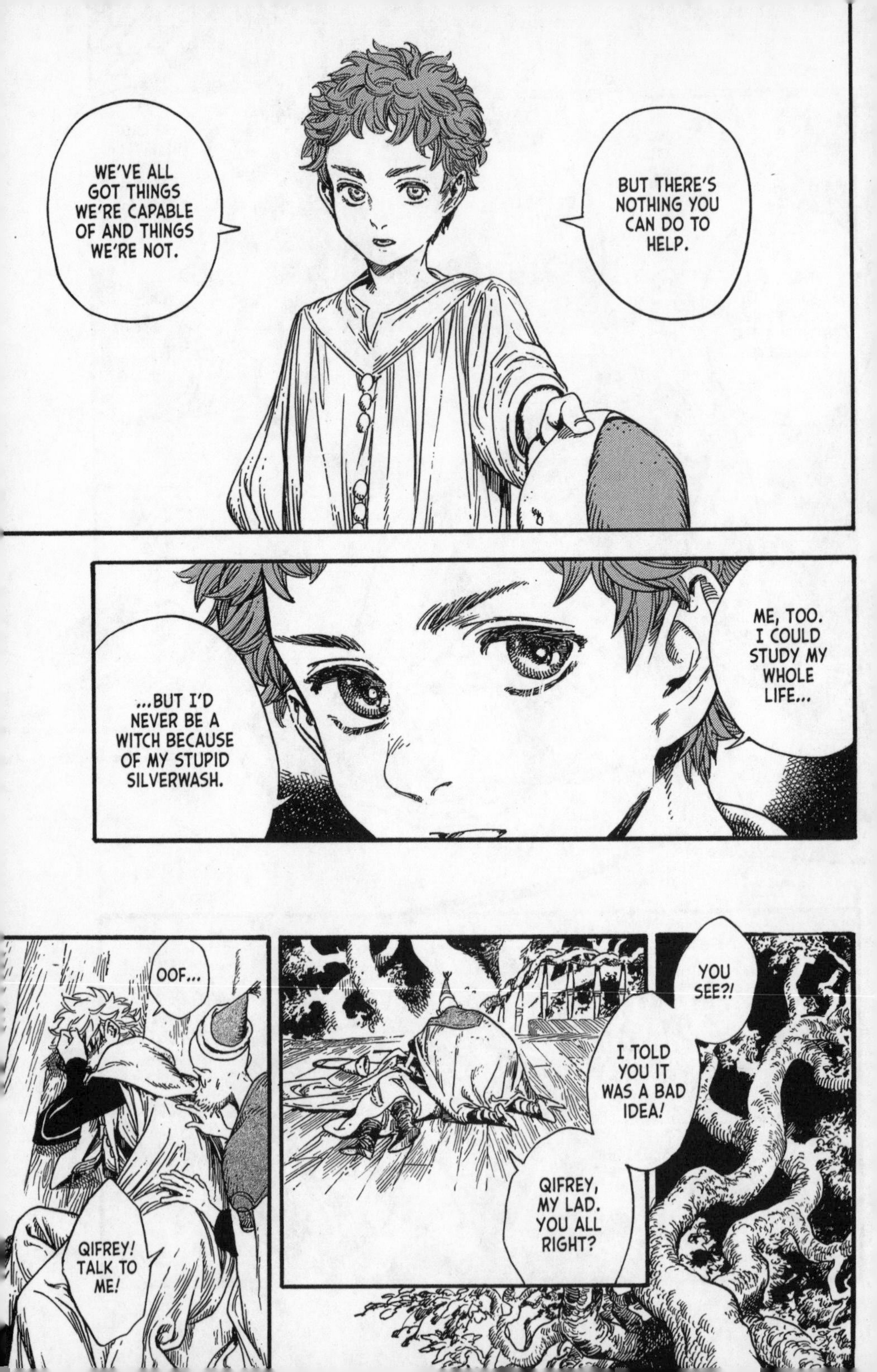

BUT THERE'S NOTHING YOU CAN DO TO HELP.
WE'VE ALL GOT THINGS WE'RE CAPABLE OF AND THINGS WE'RE NOT.
ME, TOO. I COULD STUDY MY WHOLE LIFE...
...BUT I'D NEVER BE A WITCH BECAUSE OF MY STUPID SILVERWASH.
YOU SEE?!
I TOLD YOU IT WAS A BAD IDEA!
QIFREY, MY LAD. YOU ALL RIGHT?
OOF...
QIFREY! TALK TO ME!

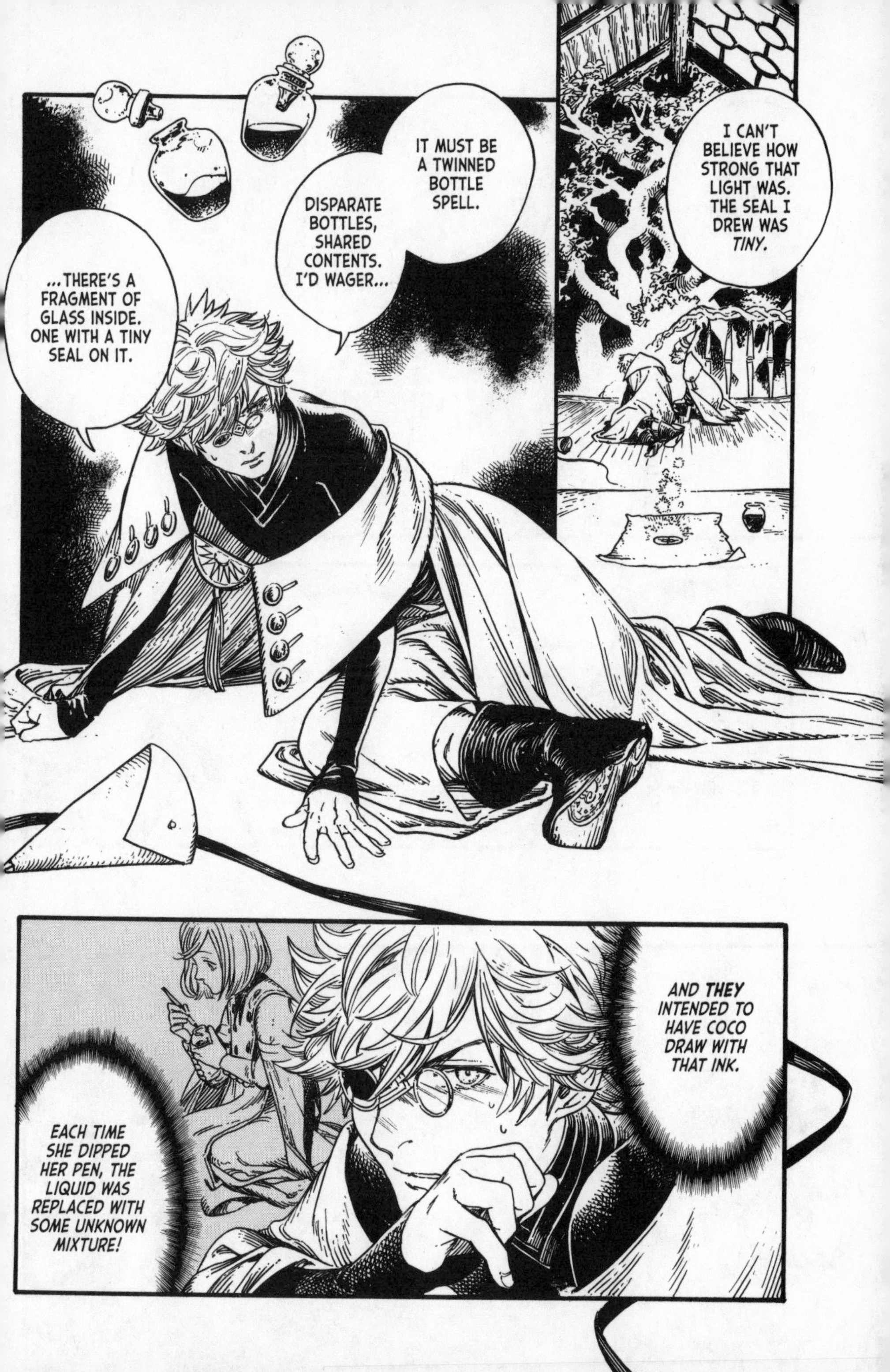
I CAN'T BELIEVE HOW STRONG THAT LIGHT WAS. THE SEAL I DREW WAS *TINY.*
IT MUST BE A TWINNED BOTTLE SPELL.
DISPARATE BOTTLES, SHARED CONTENTS. I'D WAGER...
...THERE'S A FRAGMENT OF GLASS INSIDE. ONE WITH A TINY SEAL ON IT.
AND ***THEY*** *INTENDED TO HAVE COCO DRAW WITH THAT INK.*
EACH TIME SHE DIPPED HER PEN, THE LIQUID WAS REPLACED WITH SOME UNKNOWN MIXTURE!

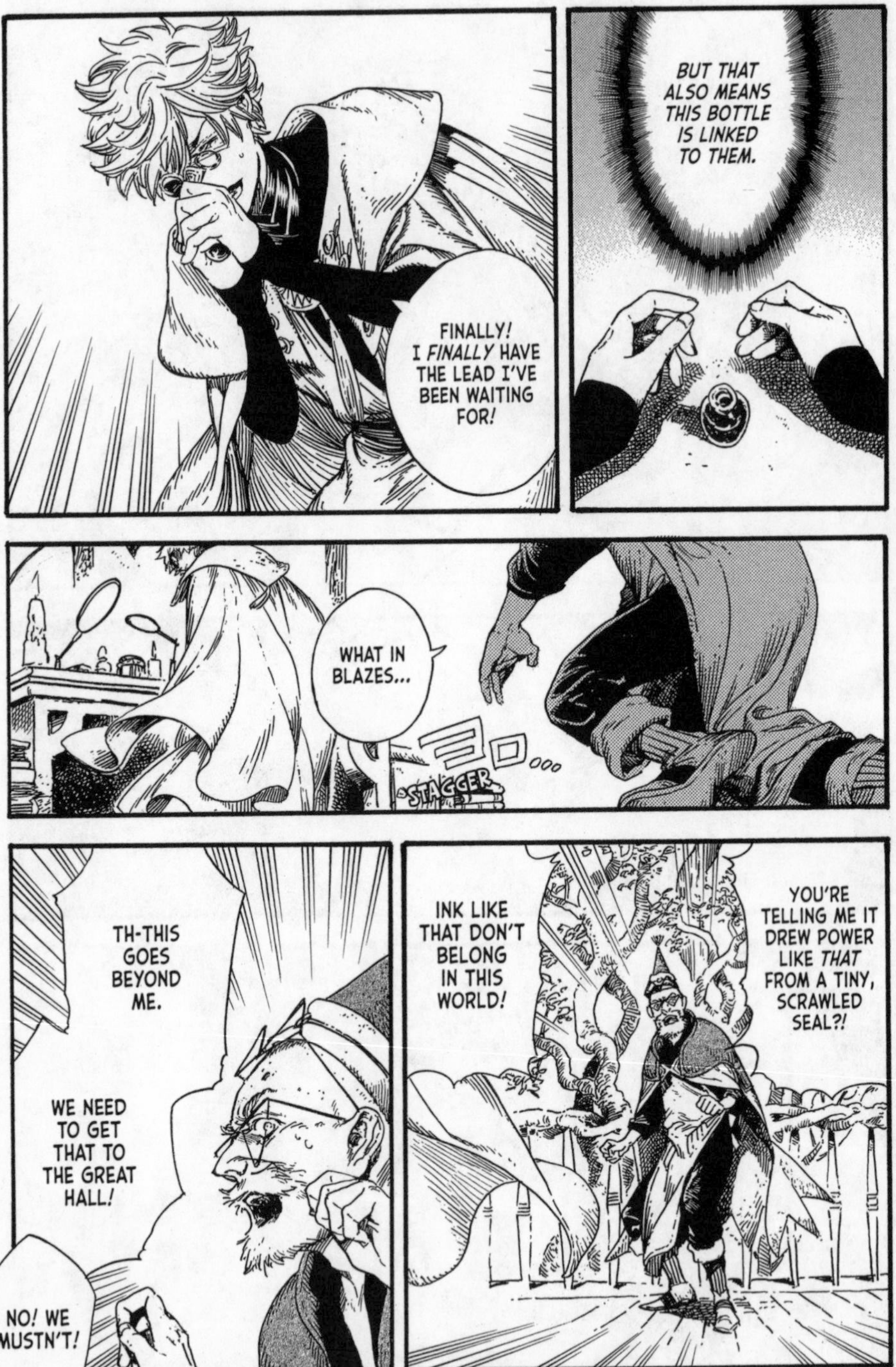
BUT THAT ALSO MEANS THIS BOTTLE IS LINKED TO THEM.
FINALLY! I *FINALLY* HAVE THE LEAD I'VE BEEN WAITING FOR!
WHAT IN BLAZES...
ヨロ
STAGGER
YOU'RE TELLING ME IT DREW POWER LIKE *THAT* FROM A TINY, SCRAWLED SEAL?!
INK LIKE THAT DON'T BELONG IN THIS WORLD!
TH-THIS GOES BEYOND ME.
WE NEED TO GET THAT TO THE GREAT HALL!
NO! WE MUSTN'T!

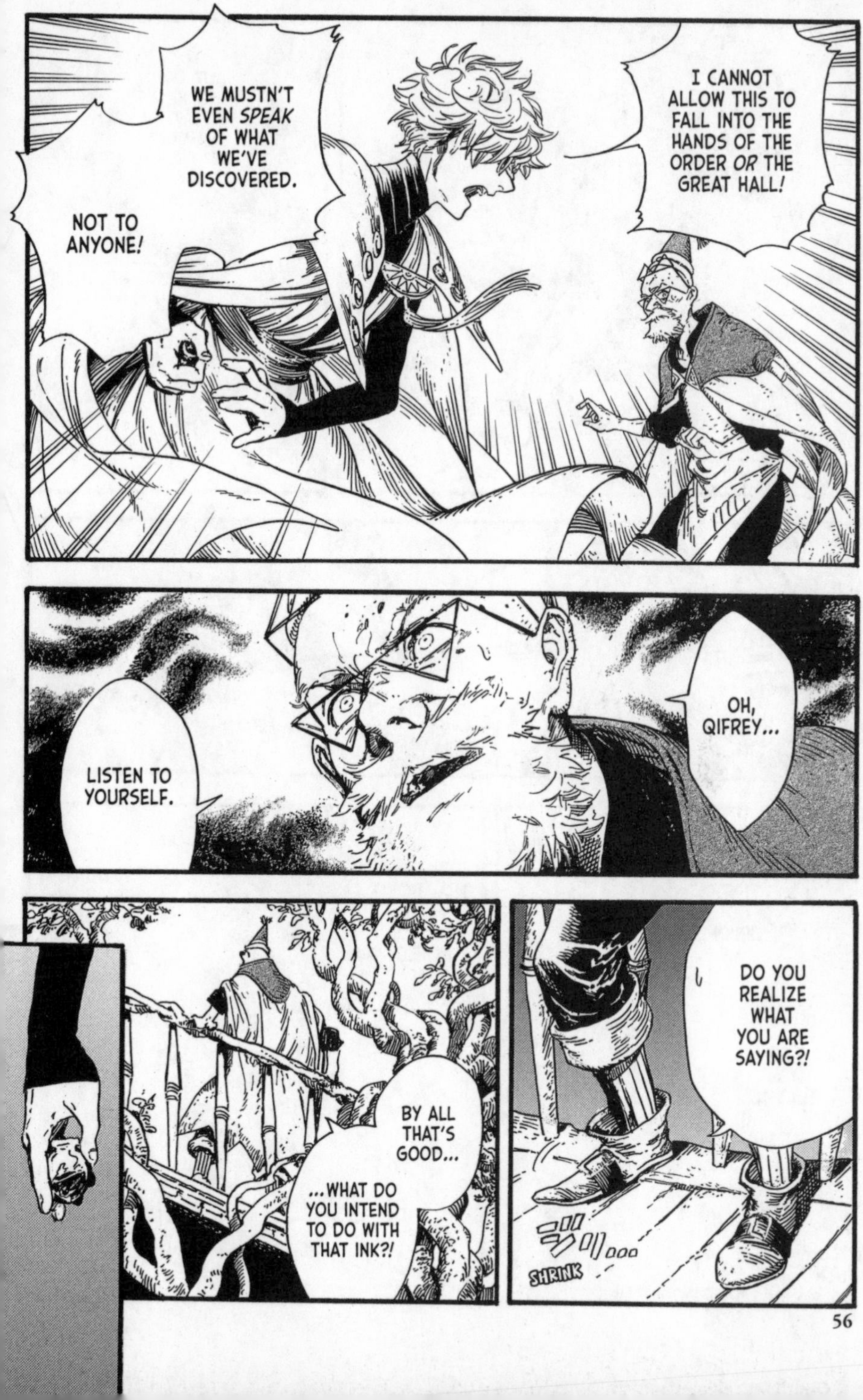
I CANNOT ALLOW THIS TO FALL INTO THE HANDS OF THE ORDER *OR* THE GREAT HALL!
WE MUSTN'T EVEN *SPEAK* OF WHAT WE'VE DISCOVERED.
NOT TO ANYONE!
OH, QIFREY...
LISTEN TO YOURSELF.
DO YOU REALIZE WHAT YOU ARE SAYING?!
SHRINK
BY ALL THAT'S GOOD...
...WHAT DO YOU INTEND TO DO WITH THAT INK?!

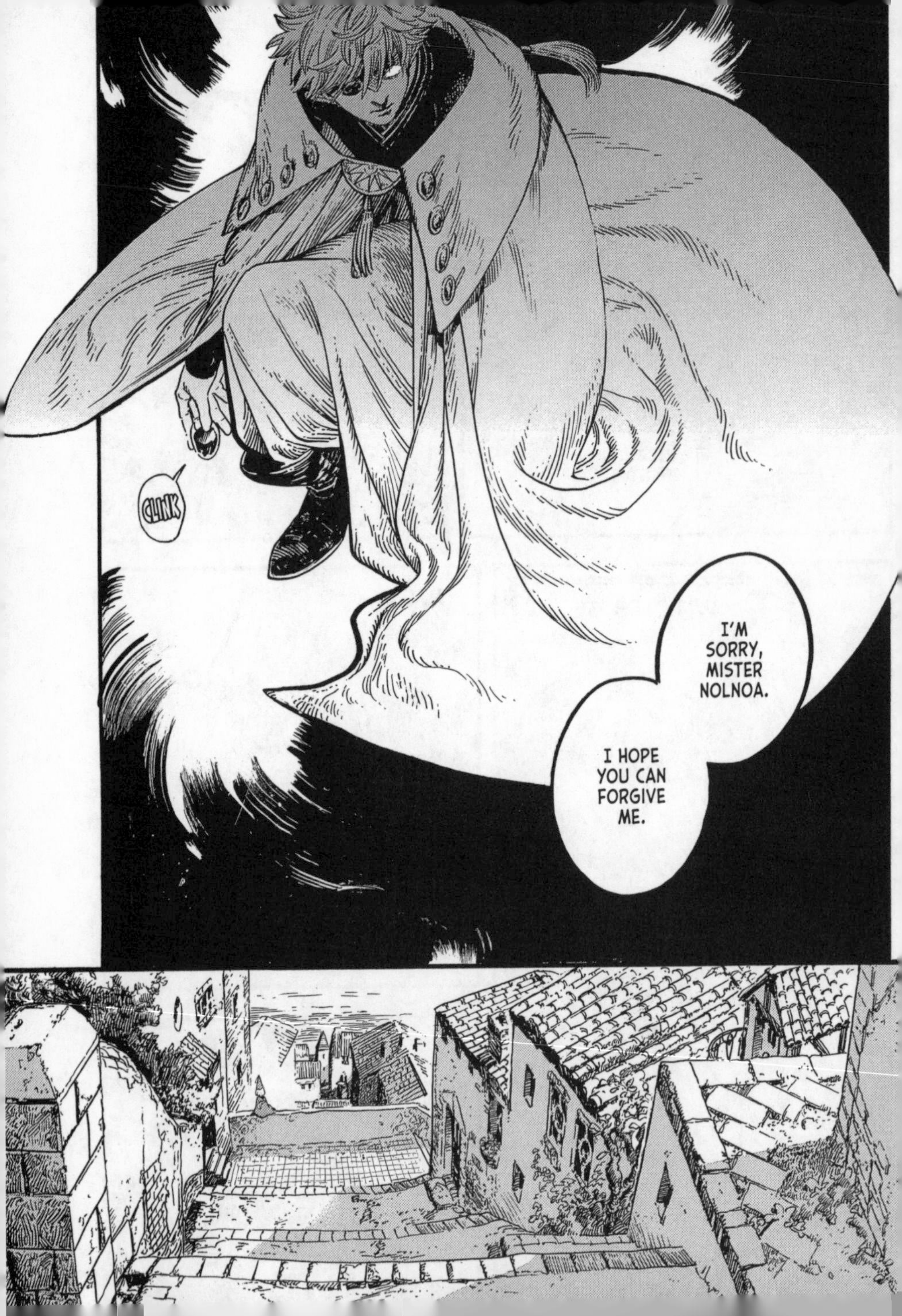
CLINK
I'M SORRY, MISTER NOLNOA.
I HOPE YOU CAN FORGIVE ME.

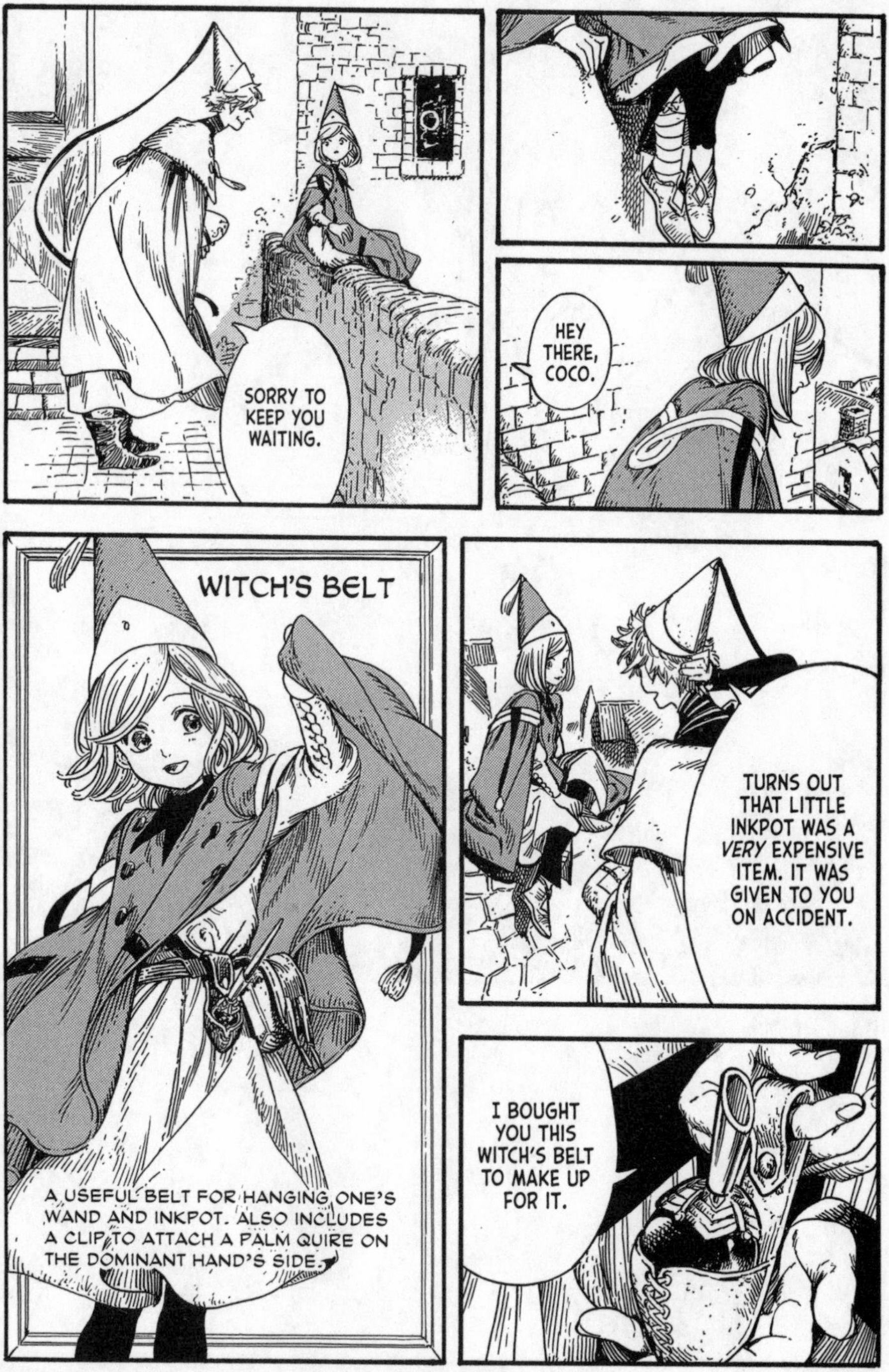
HEY THERE, COCO.
SORRY TO KEEP YOU WAITING.
TURNS OUT THAT LITTLE INKPOT WAS A *VERY* EXPENSIVE ITEM. IT WAS GIVEN TO YOU ON ACCIDENT.
I BOUGHT YOU THIS WITCH'S BELT TO MAKE UP FOR IT.
WITCH'S BELT
A USEFUL BELT FOR HANGING ONE'S WAND AND INKPOT. ALSO INCLUDES A CLIP TO ATTACH A PALM QUIRE ON THE DOMINANT HAND'S SIDE.

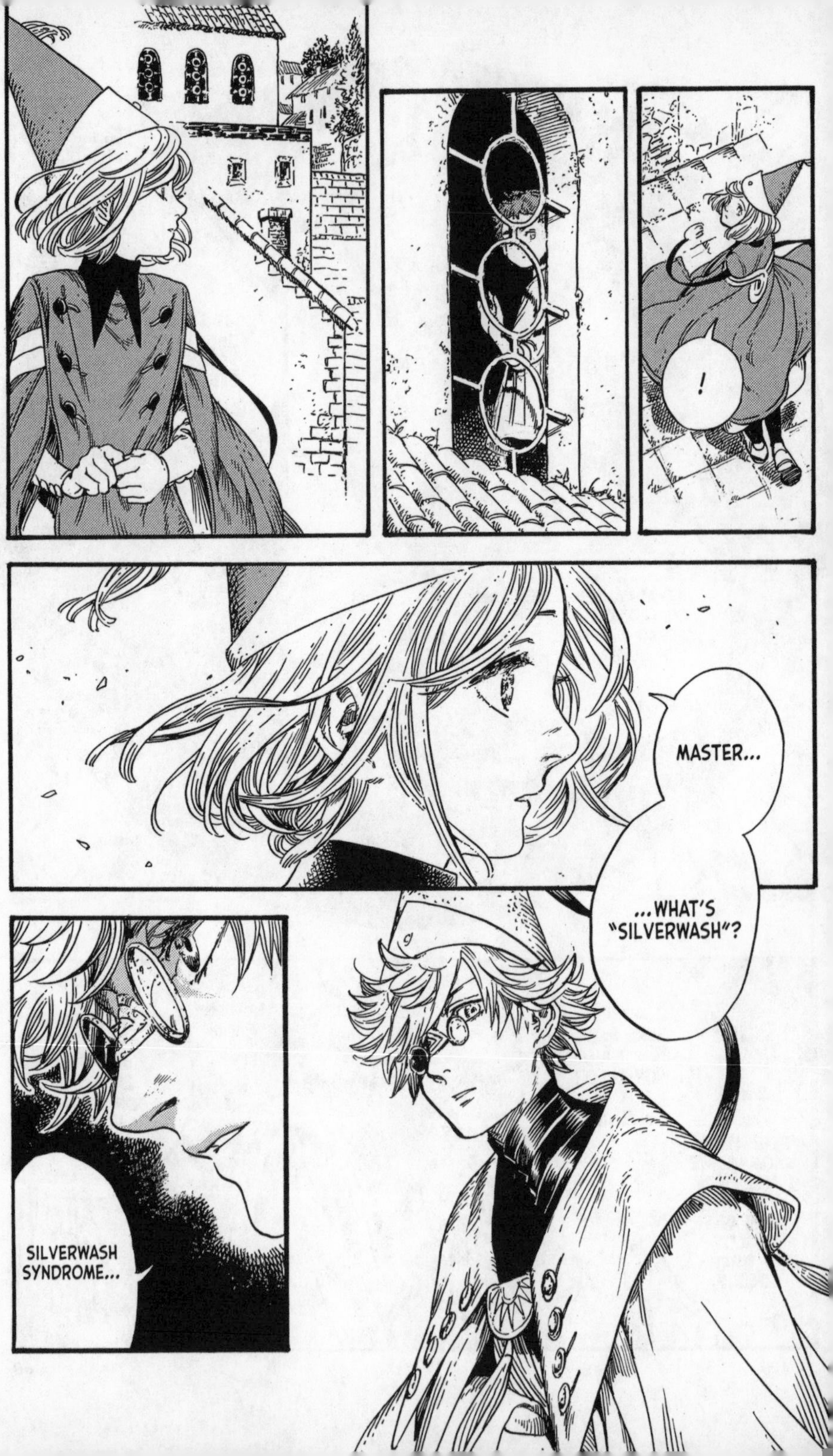
!
MASTER...
...WHAT'S "SILVERWASH"?
SILVERWASH SYNDROME...

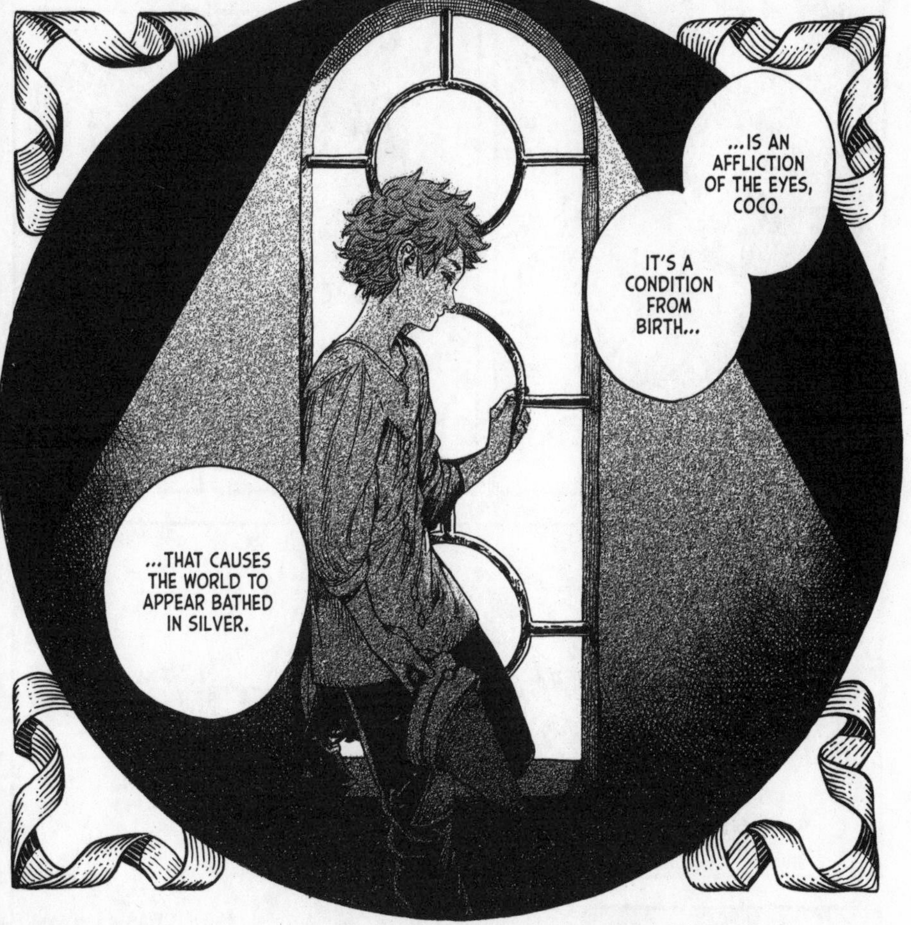
...IS AN AFFLICTION OF THE EYES, COCO.
IT'S A CONDITION FROM BIRTH...
...THAT CAUSES THE WORLD TO APPEAR BATHED IN SILVER.

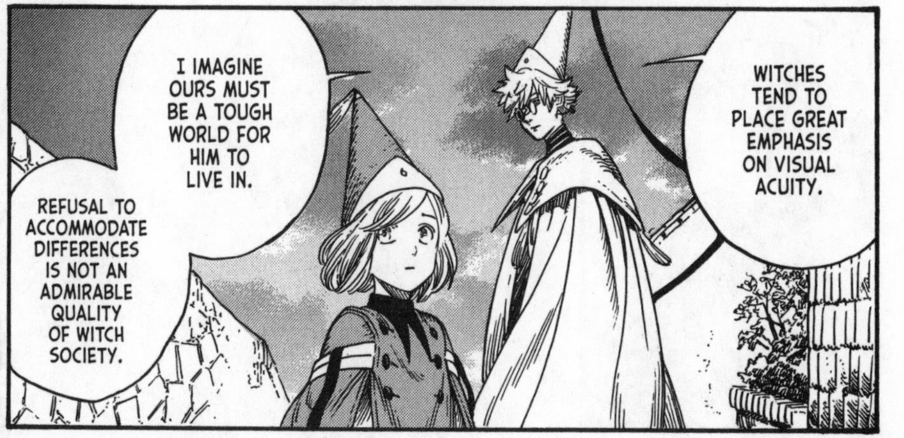
WITCHES TEND TO PLACE GREAT EMPHASIS ON VISUAL ACUITY.
I IMAGINE OURS MUST BE A TOUGH WORLD FOR HIM TO LIVE IN.
REFUSAL TO ACCOMMODATE DIFFERENCES IS NOT AN ADMIRABLE QUALITY OF WITCH SOCIETY.

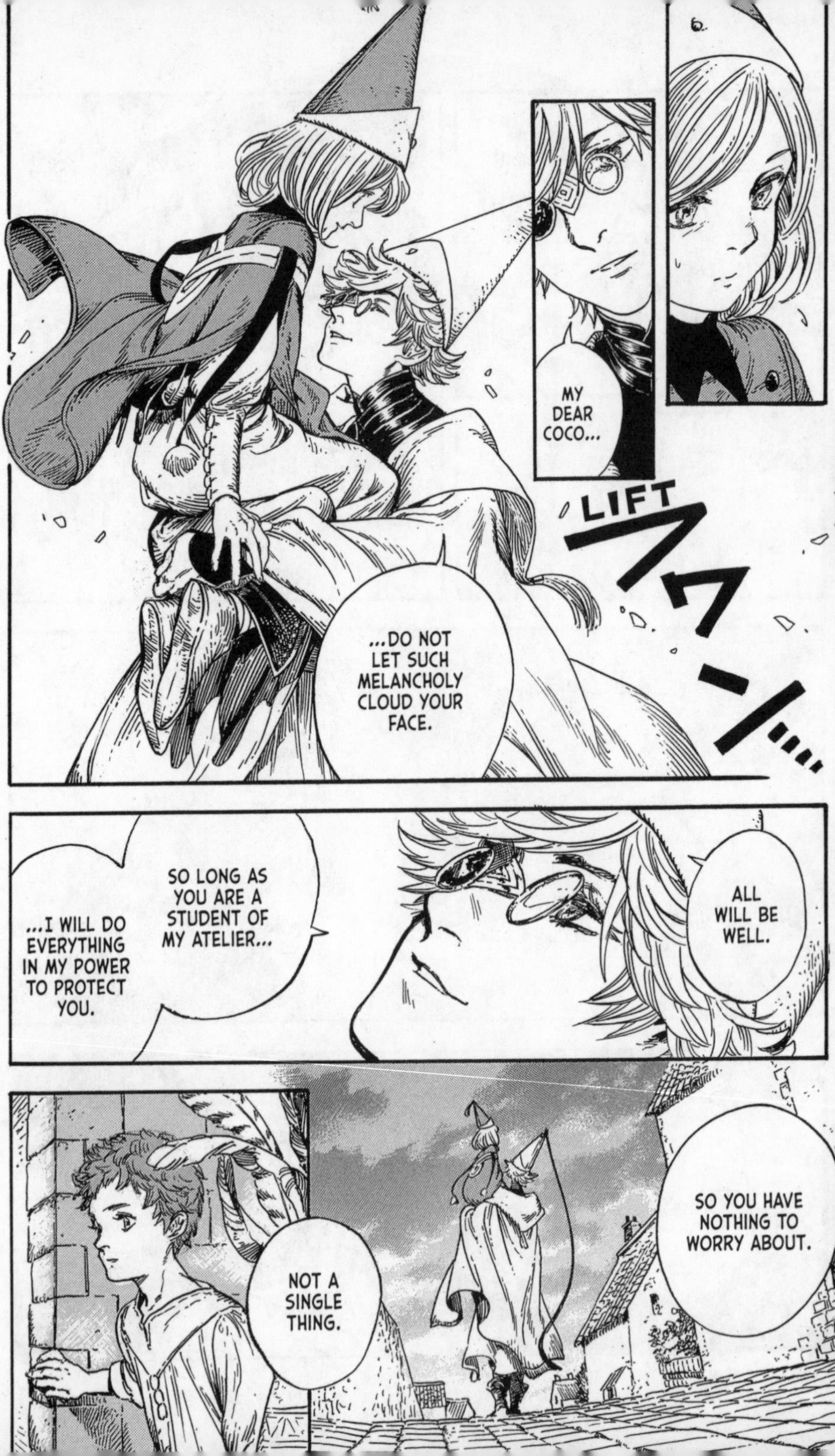
MY DEAR COCO...
LIFT
...DO NOT LET SUCH MELANCHOLY CLOUD YOUR FACE.
ALL WILL BE WELL.
SO LONG AS YOU ARE A STUDENT OF MY ATELIER...
...I WILL DO EVERYTHING IN MY POWER TO PROTECT YOU.
SO YOU HAVE NOTHING TO WORRY ABOUT.
NOT A SINGLE THING.

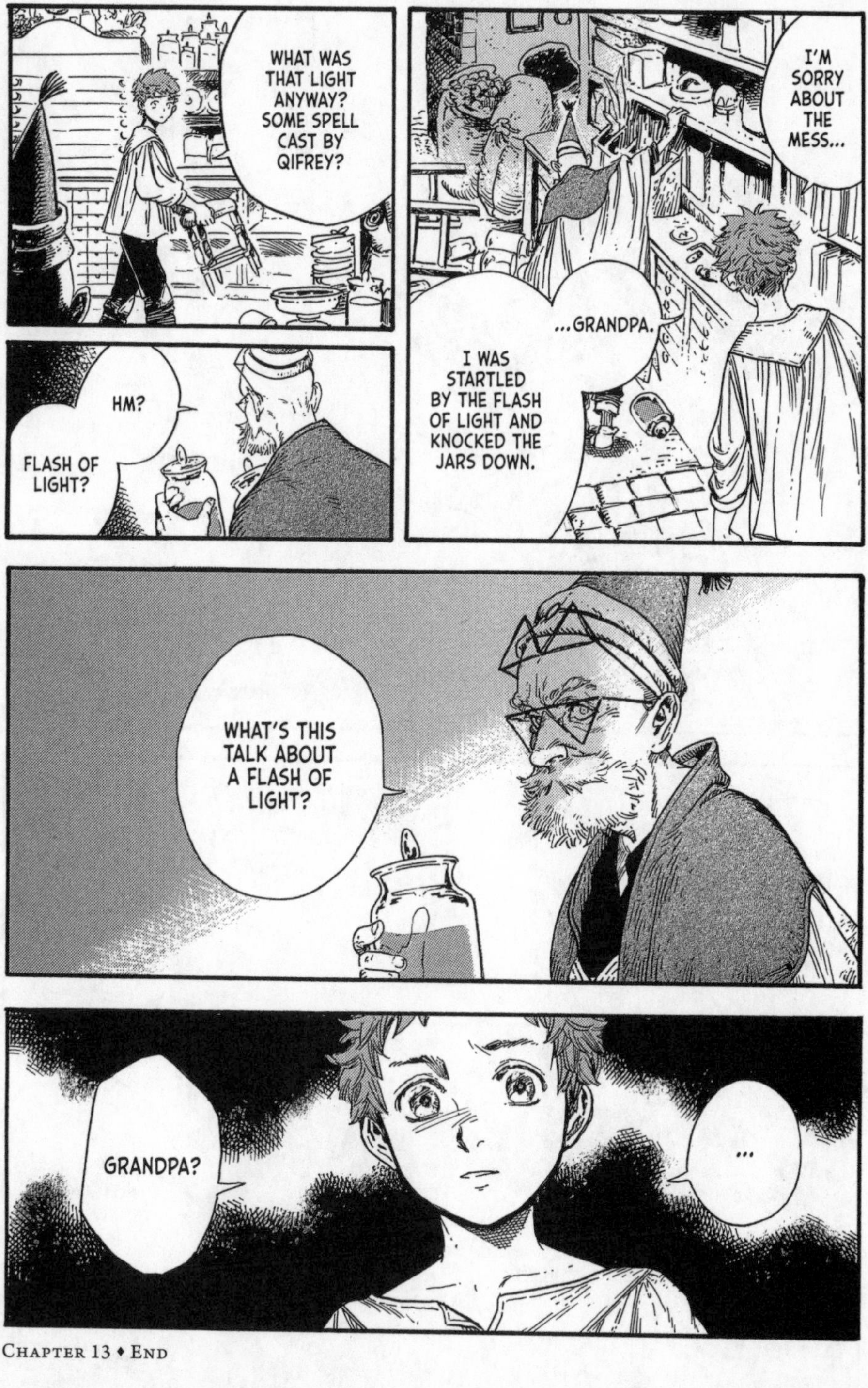
I'M SORRY ABOUT THE MESS...
...GRANDPA.
I WAS STARTLED BY THE FLASH OF LIGHT AND KNOCKED THE JARS DOWN.
WHAT WAS THAT LIGHT ANYWAY? SOME SPELL CAST BY QIFREY?
HM?
FLASH OF LIGHT?
WHAT'S THIS TALK ABOUT A FLASH OF LIGHT?
...
GRANDPA?

CHAPTER 13 ♦ END

Witch Hat Atelier

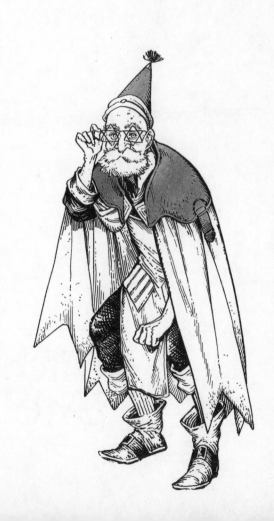

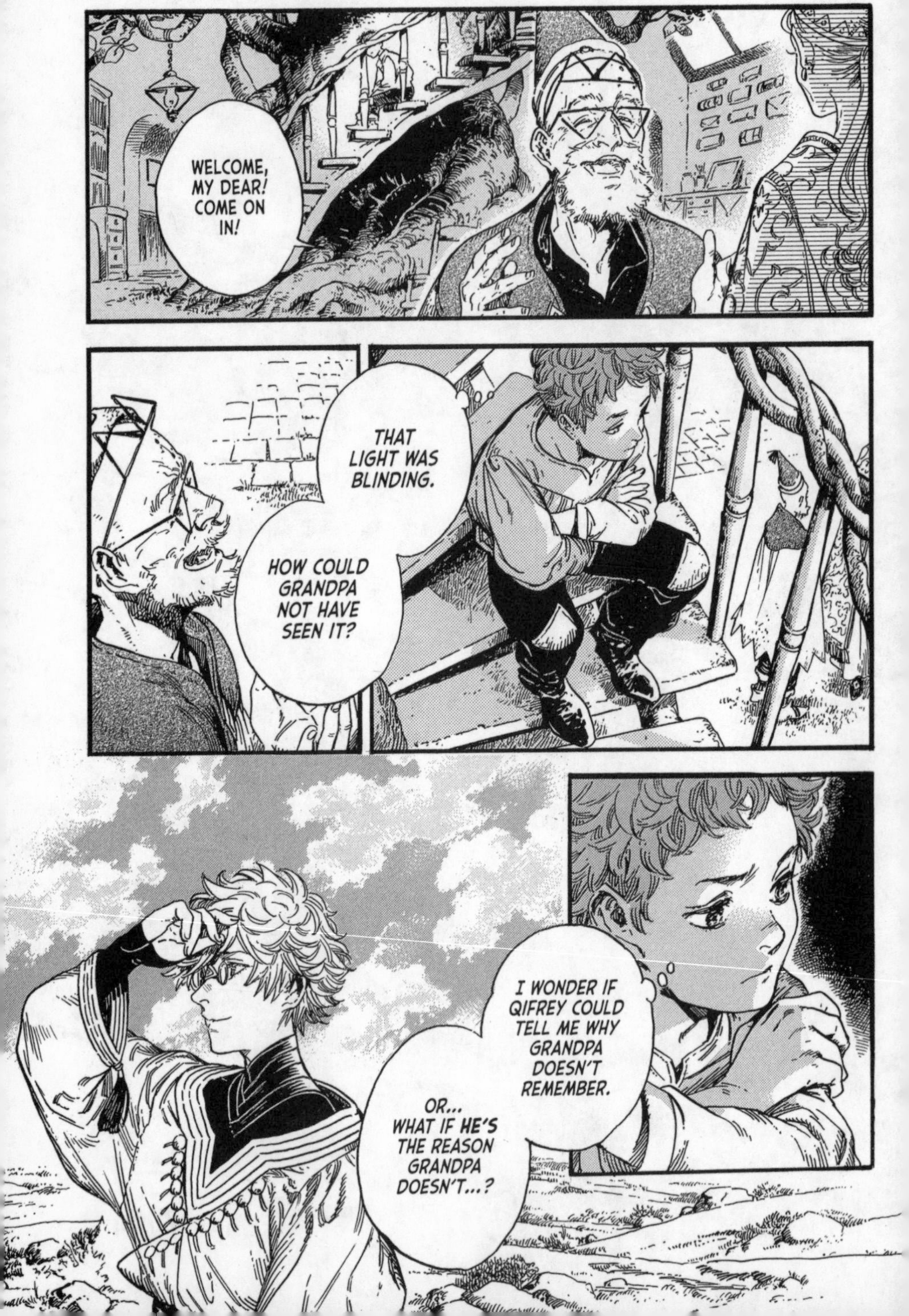
WELCOME, MY DEAR! COME ON IN!
THAT LIGHT WAS BLINDING.
HOW COULD GRANDPA NOT HAVE SEEN IT?
I WONDER IF QIFREY COULD TELL ME WHY GRANDPA DOESN'T REMEMBER.
OR... WHAT IF **HE'S** THE REASON GRANDPA DOESN'T...?

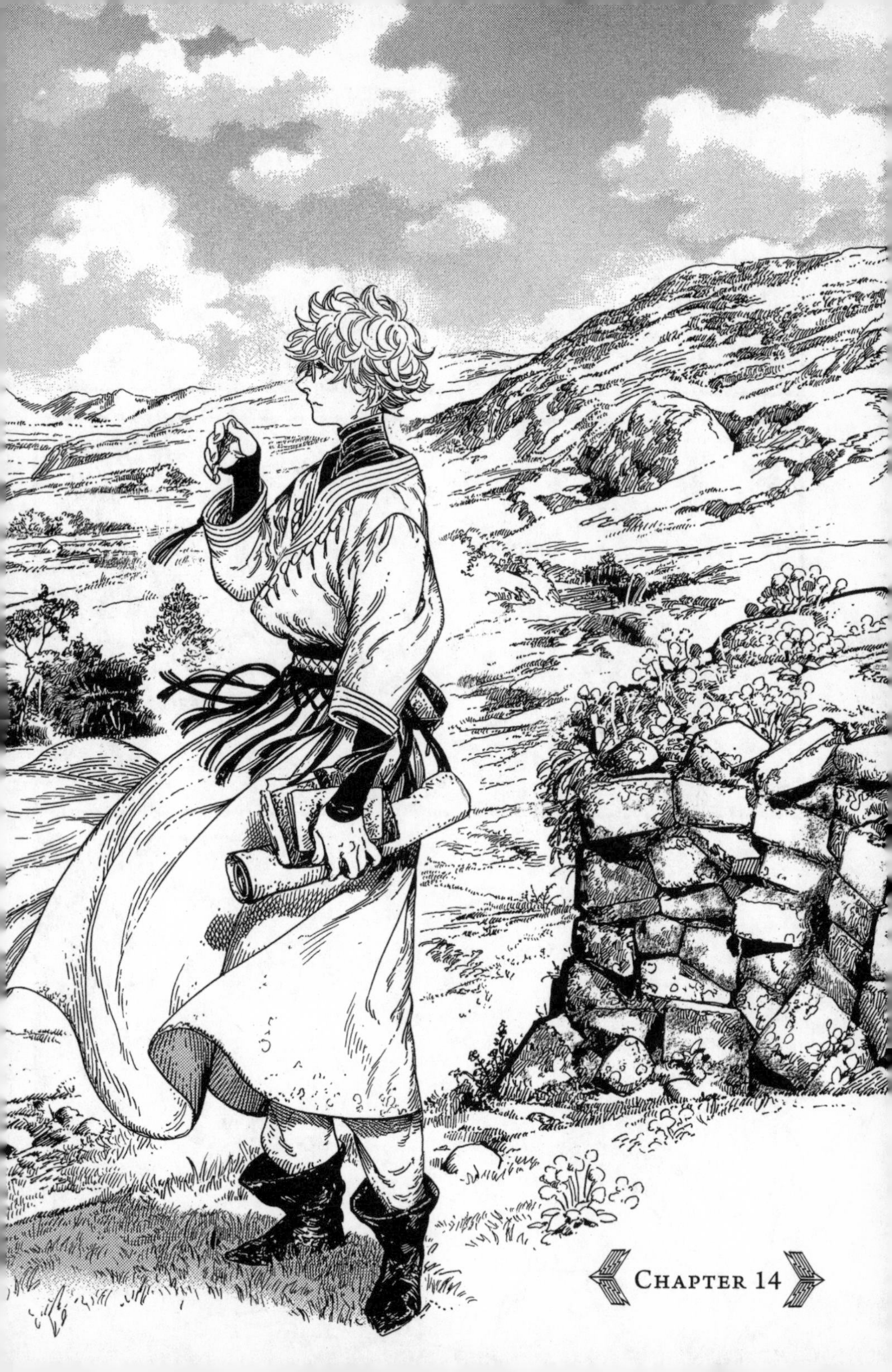

Chapter 14

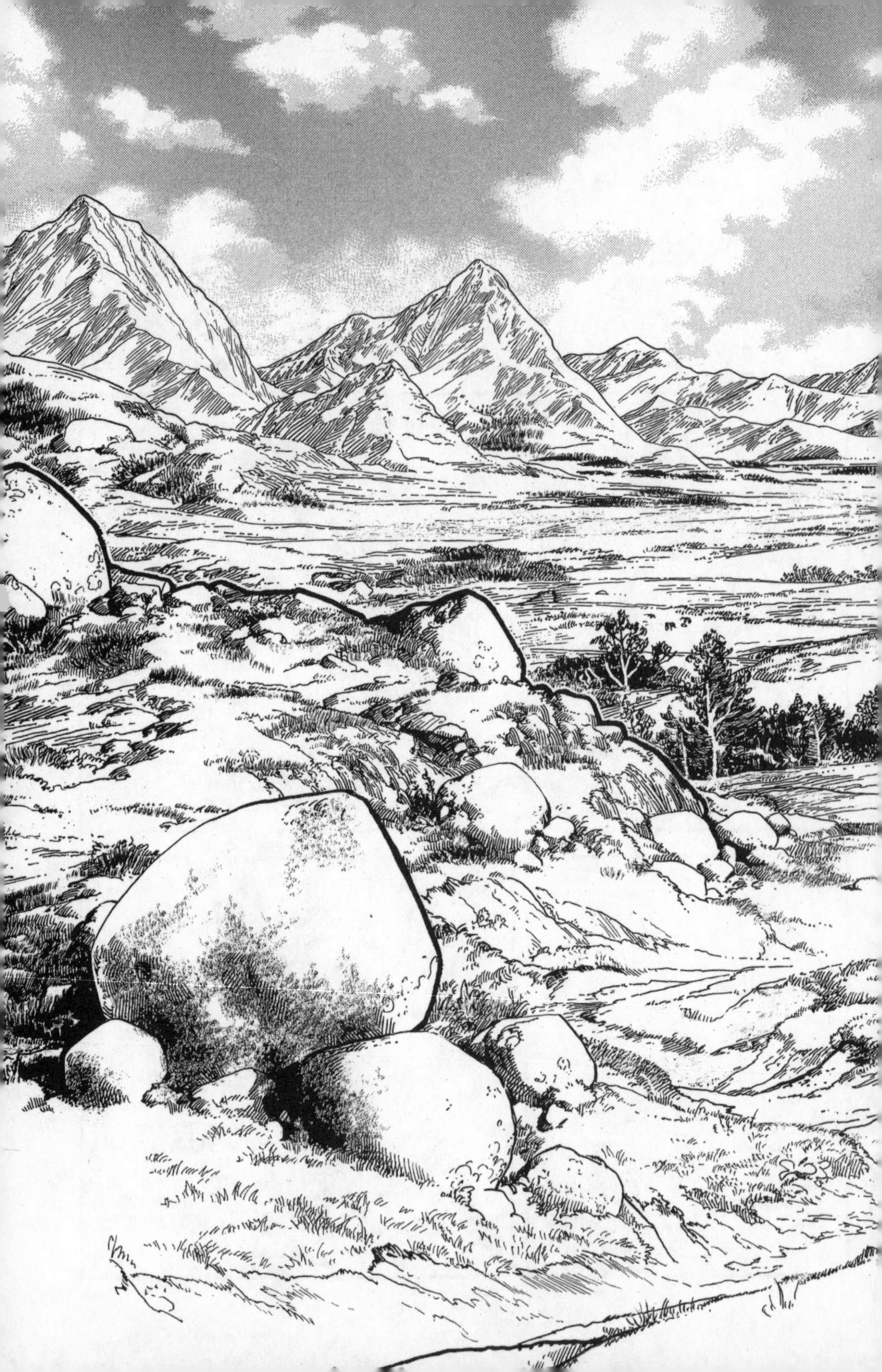

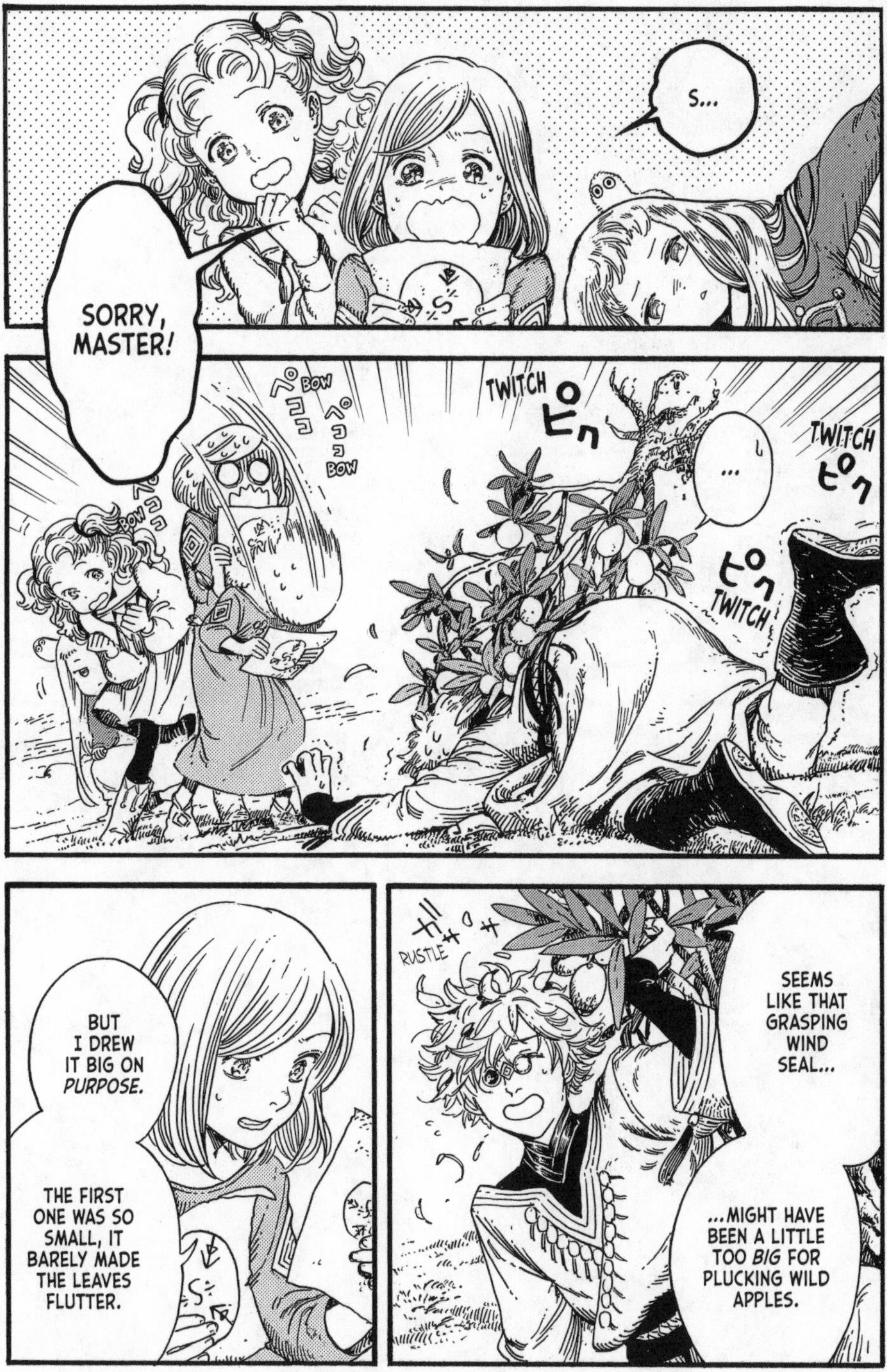
S...
SORRY, MASTER!
TWITCH
TWITCH
...
TWITCH
BOW
BOW
BOW
RUSTLE
SEEMS LIKE THAT GRASPING WIND SEAL...
...MIGHT HAVE BEEN A LITTLE TOO *BIG* FOR PLUCKING WILD APPLES.
BUT I DREW IT BIG ON *PURPOSE.*
THE FIRST ONE WAS SO SMALL, IT BARELY MADE THE LEAVES FLUTTER.

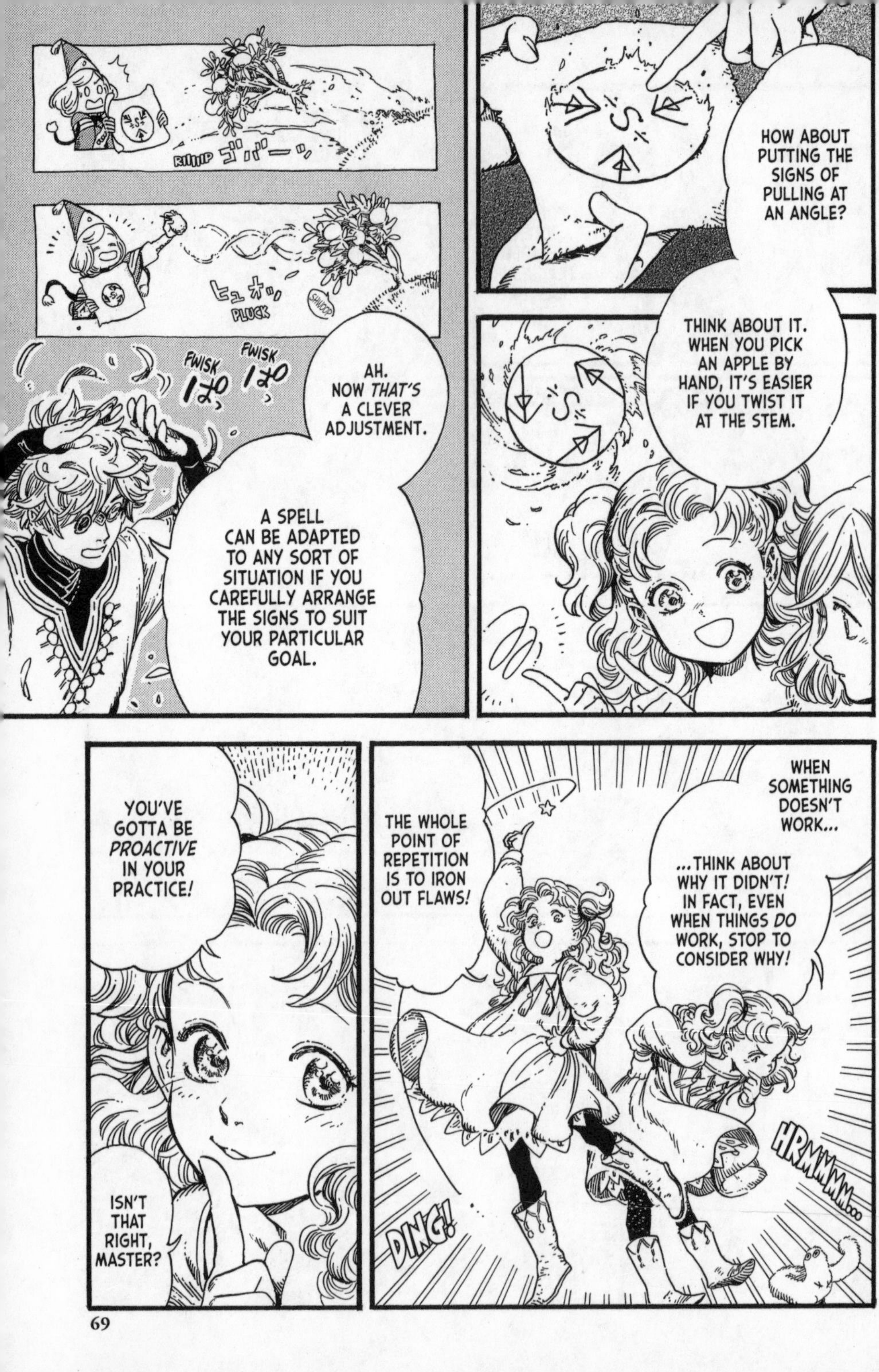

HOW ABOUT PUTTING THE SIGNS OF PULLING AT AN ANGLE?
THINK ABOUT IT. WHEN YOU PICK AN APPLE BY HAND, IT'S EASIER IF YOU TWIST IT AT THE STEM.
RIIIIP
SHWOOP
PLUCK
FWISK
FWISK
AH. NOW *THAT'S* A CLEVER ADJUSTMENT.
A SPELL CAN BE ADAPTED TO ANY SORT OF SITUATION IF YOU CAREFULLY ARRANGE THE SIGNS TO SUIT YOUR PARTICULAR GOAL.
WHEN SOMETHING DOESN'T WORK...
...THINK ABOUT WHY IT DIDN'T! IN FACT, EVEN WHEN THINGS *DO* WORK, STOP TO CONSIDER WHY!
THE WHOLE POINT OF REPETITION IS TO IRON OUT FLAWS!
HRMMMM...
DING!
YOU'VE GOTTA BE *PROACTIVE* IN YOUR PRACTICE!
ISN'T THAT RIGHT, MASTER?

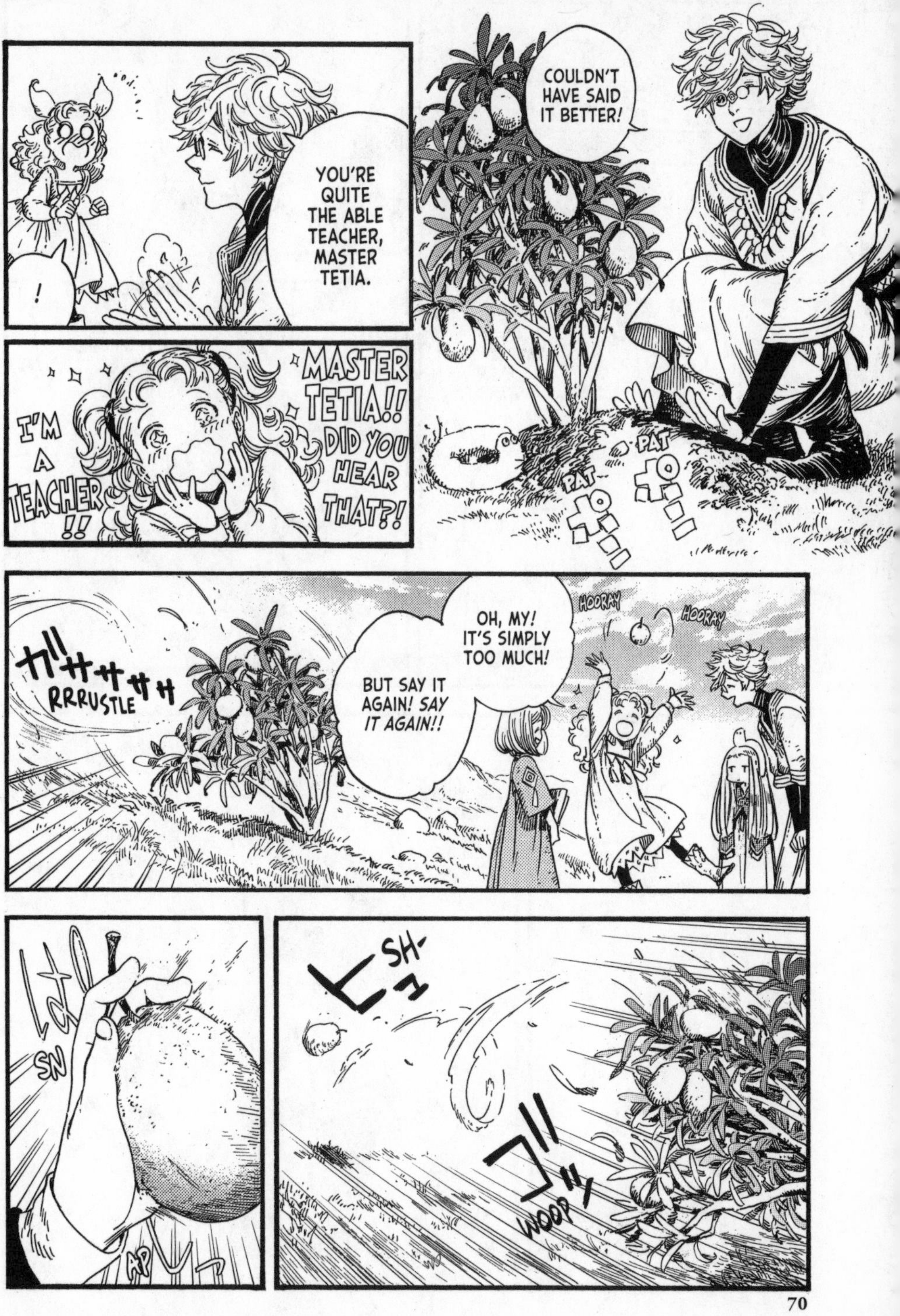
COULDN'T HAVE SAID IT BETTER!
PAT
PAT
YOU'RE QUITE THE ABLE TEACHER, MASTER TETIA.
!
MASTER TETIA!! DID YOU HEAR THAT?!
I'M A TEACHER!!
HOORAY
HOORAY
OH, MY! IT'S SIMPLY TOO MUCH!
BUT SAY IT AGAIN! SAY IT AGAIN!!
RRRUSTLE
SH-
WOOP
SN
AP

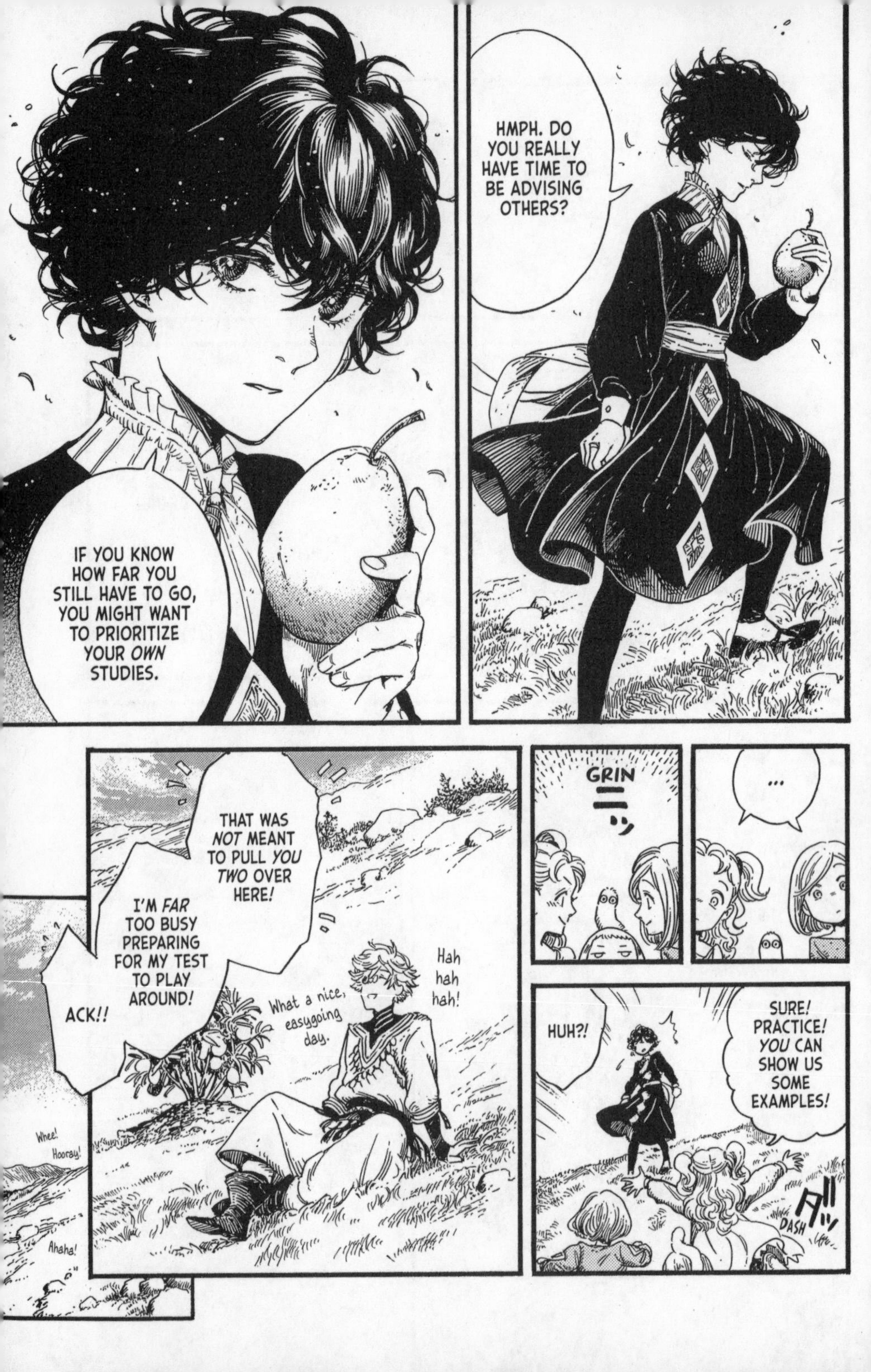

HMPH. DO YOU REALLY HAVE TIME TO BE ADVISING OTHERS?
IF YOU KNOW HOW FAR YOU STILL HAVE TO GO, YOU MIGHT WANT TO PRIORITIZE YOUR *OWN* STUDIES.
...
GRIN
SURE! PRACTICE! *YOU* CAN SHOW US SOME EXAMPLES!
HUH?!
DASH
THAT WAS *NOT* MEANT TO PULL *YOU TWO* OVER HERE!
I'M *FAR* TOO BUSY PREPARING FOR MY TEST TO PLAY AROUND!
Hah hah hah!
What a nice, easygoing day.
ACK!!
Whee!
Hooray!
Ahaha!

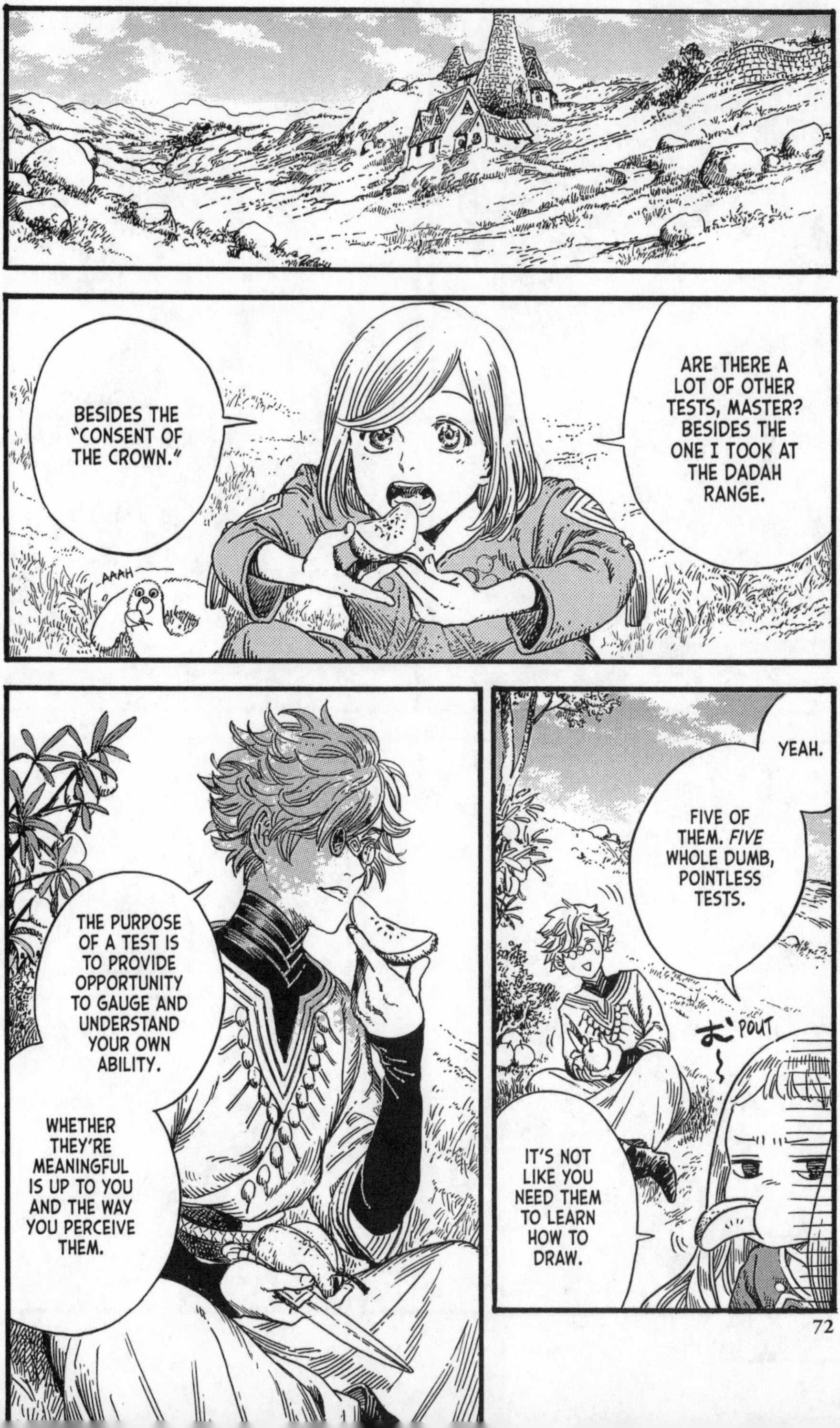
ARE THERE A LOT OF OTHER TESTS, MASTER? BESIDES THE ONE I TOOK AT THE DADAH RANGE.
BESIDES THE "CONSENT OF THE CROWN."
AAAH
YEAH.
FIVE OF THEM. *FIVE* WHOLE DUMB, POINTLESS TESTS.
お~ POUT
IT'S NOT LIKE YOU NEED THEM TO LEARN HOW TO DRAW.
THE PURPOSE OF A TEST IS TO PROVIDE OPPORTUNITY TO GAUGE AND UNDERSTAND YOUR OWN ABILITY.
WHETHER THEY'RE MEANINGFUL IS UP TO YOU AND THE WAY YOU PERCEIVE THEM.

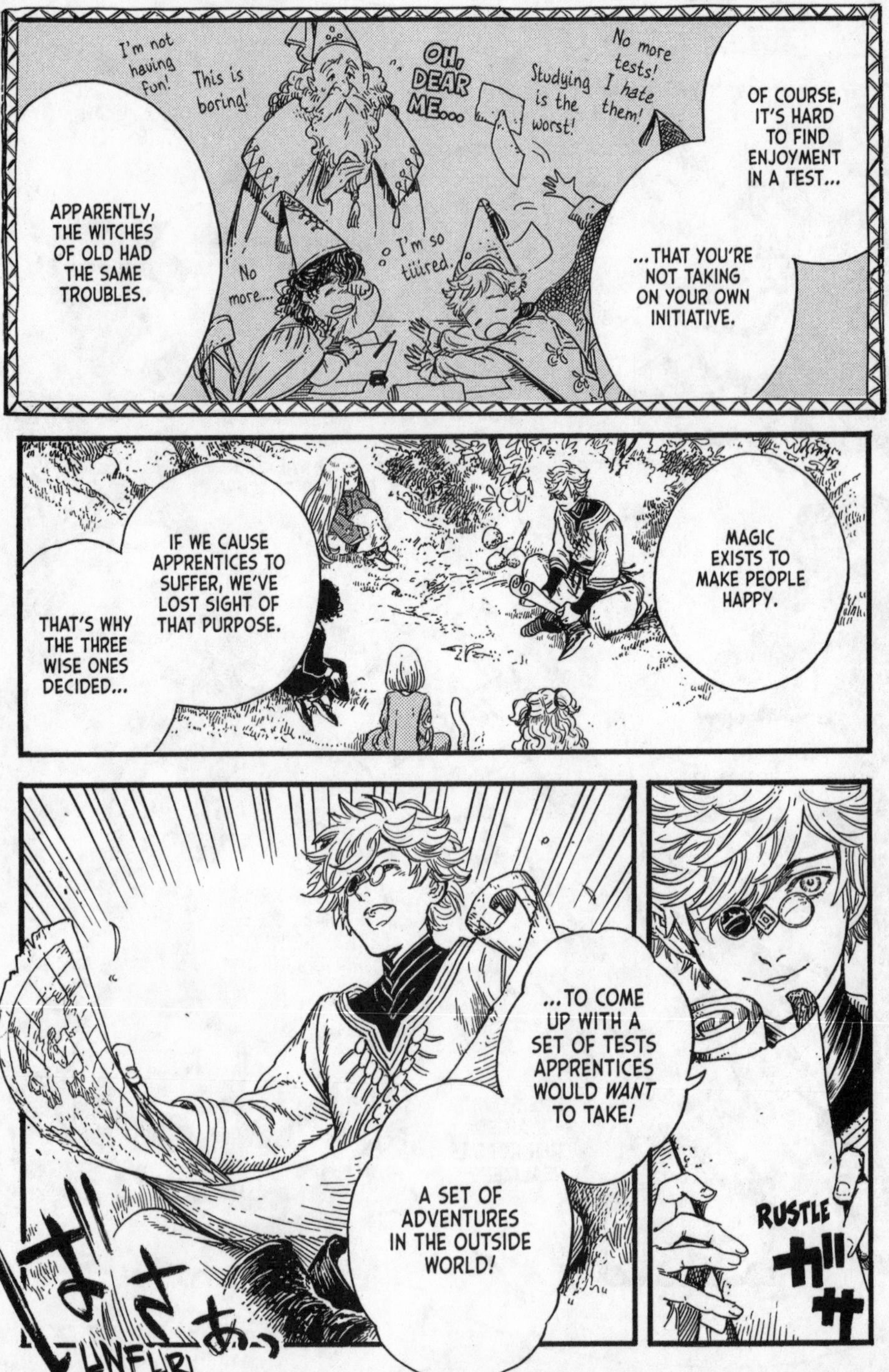
No more tests! I hate them!
OF COURSE, IT'S HARD TO FIND ENJOYMENT IN A TEST...
...THAT YOU'RE NOT TAKING ON YOUR OWN INITIATIVE.
Studying is the worst!
OH, DEAR ME...
This is boring!
I'm not having fun!
I'm so tiiired.
APPARENTLY, THE WITCHES OF OLD HAD THE SAME TROUBLES.
No more...
MAGIC EXISTS TO MAKE PEOPLE HAPPY.
IF WE CAUSE APPRENTICES TO SUFFER, WE'VE LOST SIGHT OF THAT PURPOSE.
THAT'S WHY THE THREE WISE ONES DECIDED...
RUSTLE
ガサ
...TO COME UP WITH A SET OF TESTS APPRENTICES WOULD *WANT* TO TAKE!
A SET OF ADVENTURES IN THE OUTSIDE WORLD!
ばさあっ
UNFURL

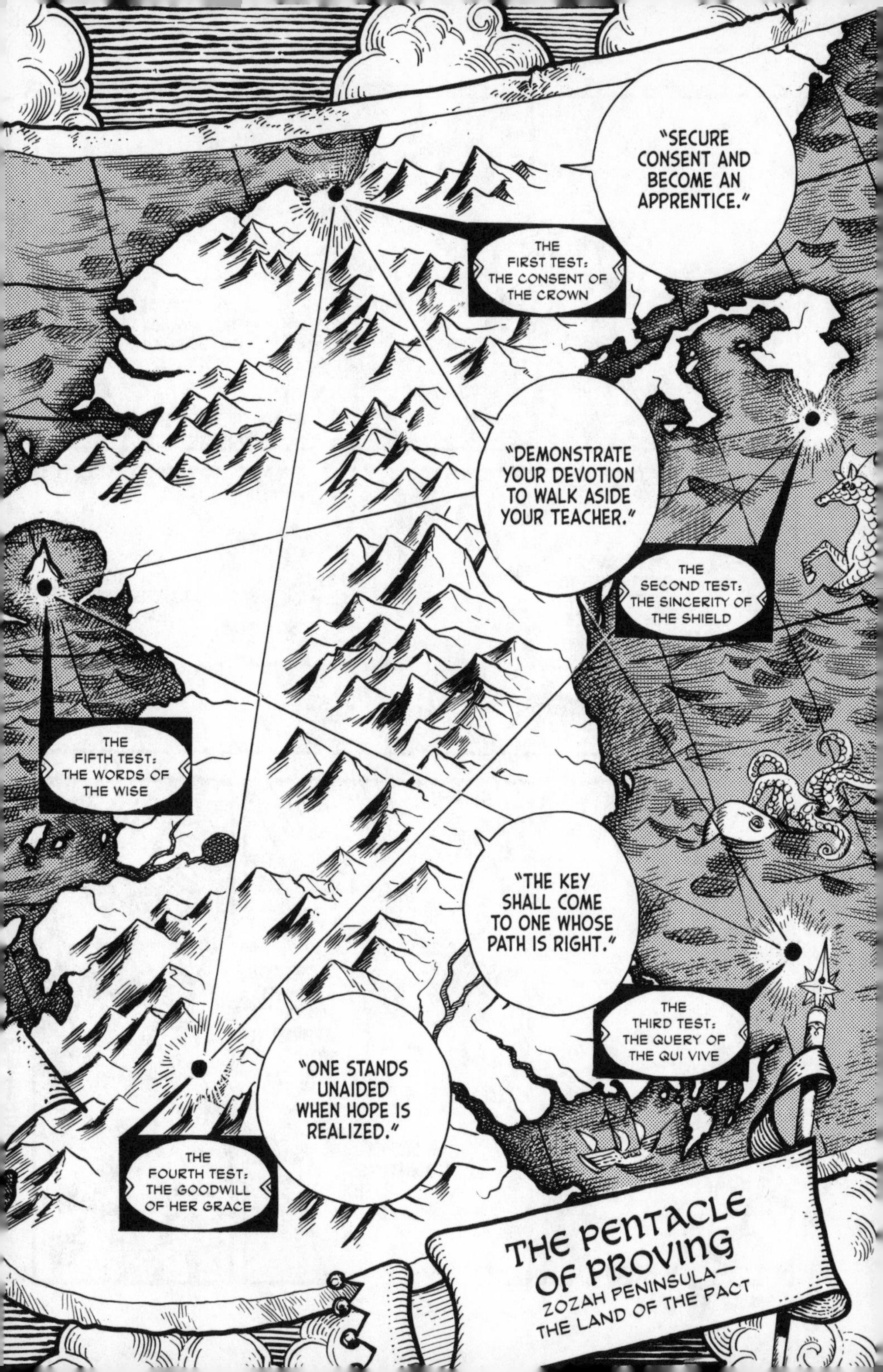
"SECURE CONSENT AND BECOME AN APPRENTICE."
THE FIRST TEST: THE CONSENT OF THE CROWN
"DEMONSTRATE YOUR DEVOTION TO WALK ASIDE YOUR TEACHER."
THE SECOND TEST: THE SINCERITY OF THE SHIELD
"THE KEY SHALL COME TO ONE WHOSE PATH IS RIGHT."
THE THIRD TEST: THE QUERY OF THE QUI VIVE
"ONE STANDS UNAIDED WHEN HOPE IS REALIZED."
THE FOURTH TEST: THE GOODWILL OF HER GRACE
THE FIFTH TEST: THE WORDS OF THE WISE
THE PENTACLE OF PROVING
ZOZAH PENINSULA— THE LAND OF THE PACT

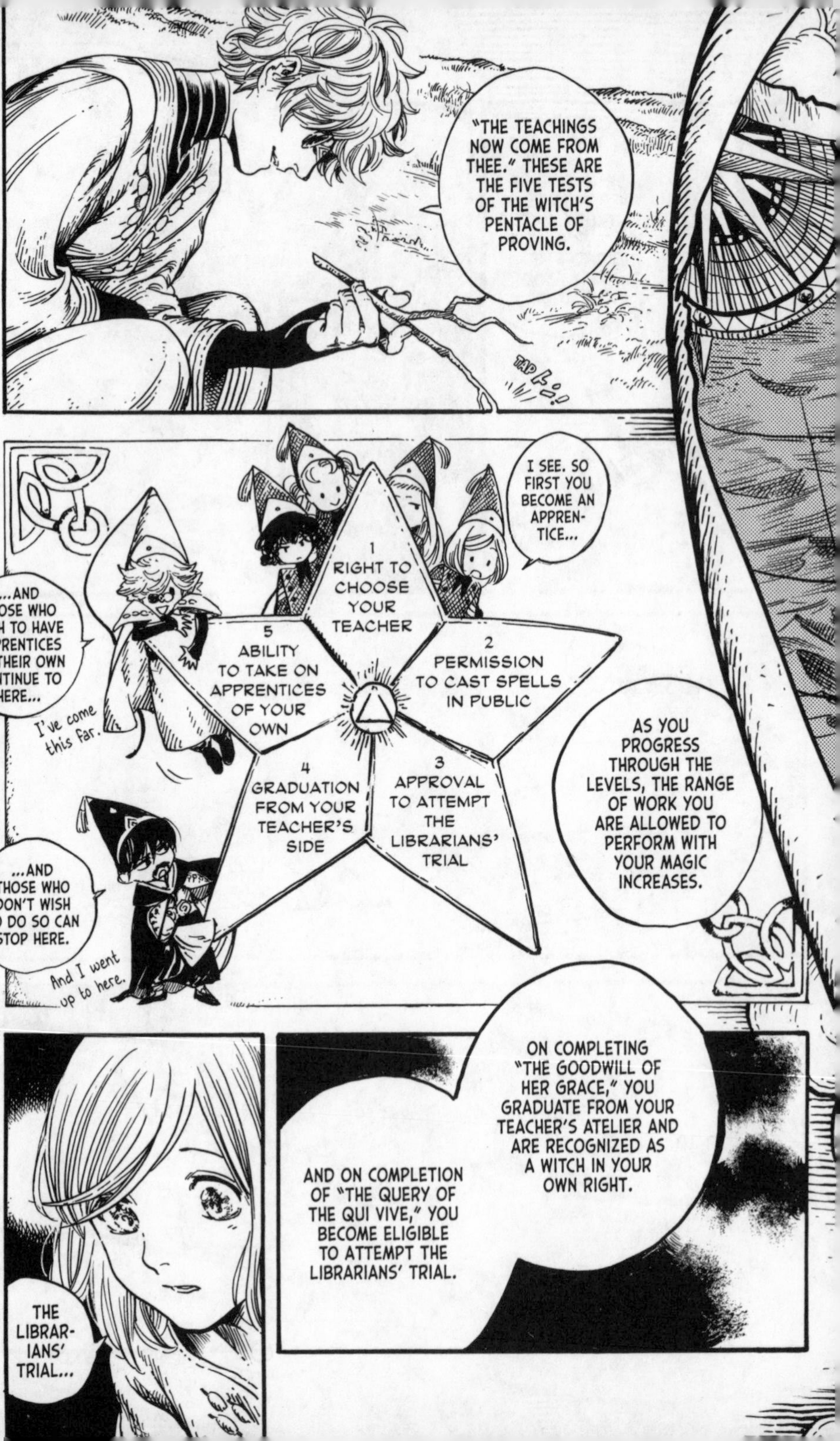
"THE TEACHINGS NOW COME FROM THEE." THESE ARE THE FIVE TESTS OF THE WITCH'S PENTACLE OF PROVING.
TAP
I SEE. SO FIRST YOU BECOME AN APPREN-TICE...
1 RIGHT TO CHOOSE YOUR TEACHER
2 PERMISSION TO CAST SPELLS IN PUBLIC
3 APPROVAL TO ATTEMPT THE LIBRARIANS' TRIAL
4 GRADUATION FROM YOUR TEACHER'S SIDE
5 ABILITY TO TAKE ON APPRENTICES OF YOUR OWN
AS YOU PROGRESS THROUGH THE LEVELS, THE RANGE OF WORK YOU ARE ALLOWED TO PERFORM WITH YOUR MAGIC INCREASES.
...AND THOSE WHO WISH TO HAVE APPRENTICES OF THEIR OWN CONTINUE TO HERE...
I've come this far.
...AND THOSE WHO DON'T WISH TO DO SO CAN STOP HERE.
And I went up to here.
ON COMPLETING "THE GOODWILL OF HER GRACE," YOU GRADUATE FROM YOUR TEACHER'S ATELIER AND ARE RECOGNIZED AS A WITCH IN YOUR OWN RIGHT.
AND ON COMPLETION OF "THE QUERY OF THE QUI VIVE," YOU BECOME ELIGIBLE TO ATTEMPT THE LIBRARIANS' TRIAL.
THE LIBRAR-IANS' TRIAL...

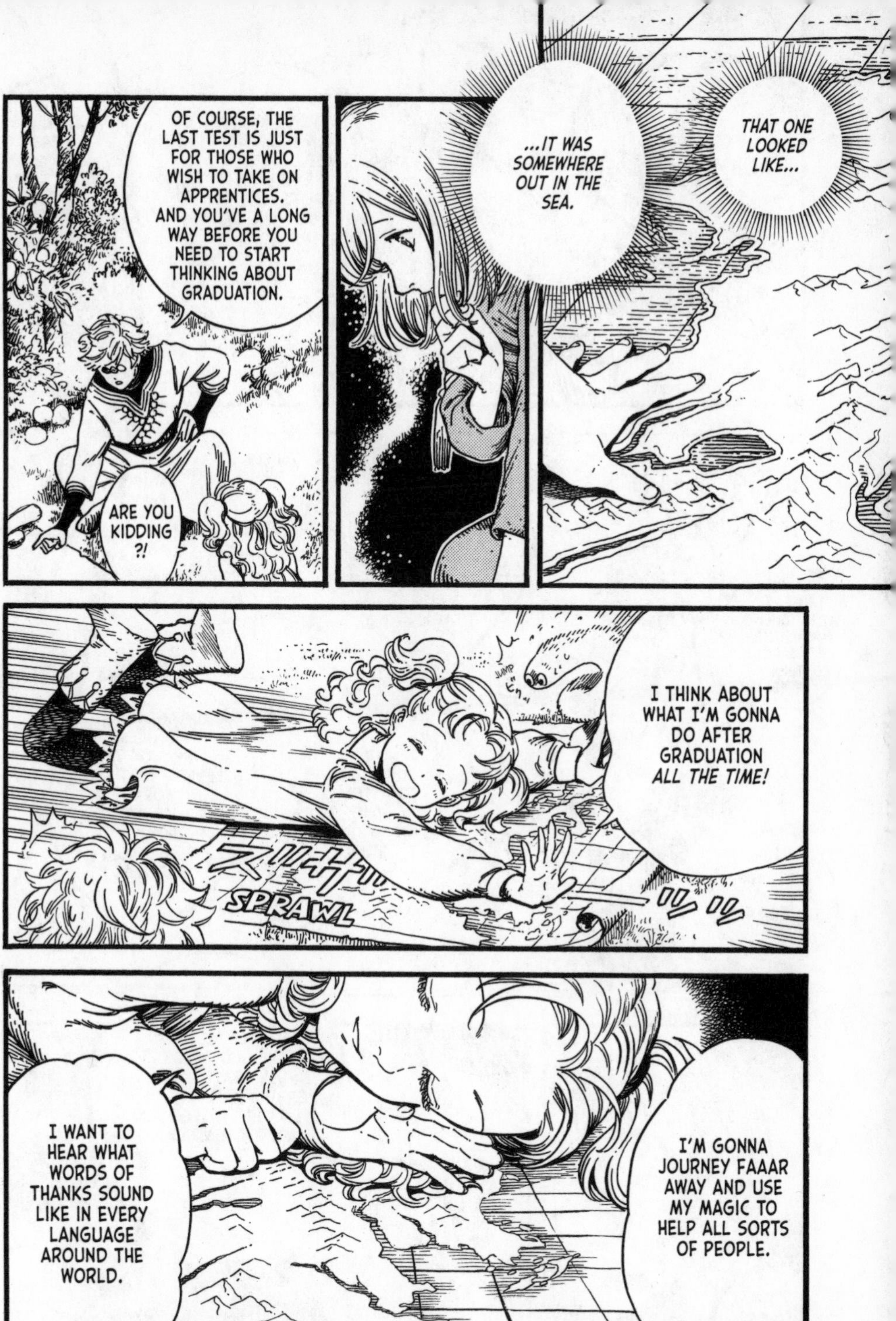
THAT ONE LOOKED LIKE...
...IT WAS SOMEWHERE OUT IN THE SEA.
OF COURSE, THE LAST TEST IS JUST FOR THOSE WHO WISH TO TAKE ON APPRENTICES. AND YOU'VE A LONG WAY BEFORE YOU NEED TO START THINKING ABOUT GRADUATION.
ARE YOU KIDDING ?!
JUMP
I THINK ABOUT WHAT I'M GONNA DO AFTER GRADUATION *ALL THE TIME!*
SPRAWL
I'M GONNA JOURNEY FAAAR AWAY AND USE MY MAGIC TO HELP ALL SORTS OF PEOPLE.
I WANT TO HEAR WHAT WORDS OF THANKS SOUND LIKE IN EVERY LANGUAGE AROUND THE WORLD.

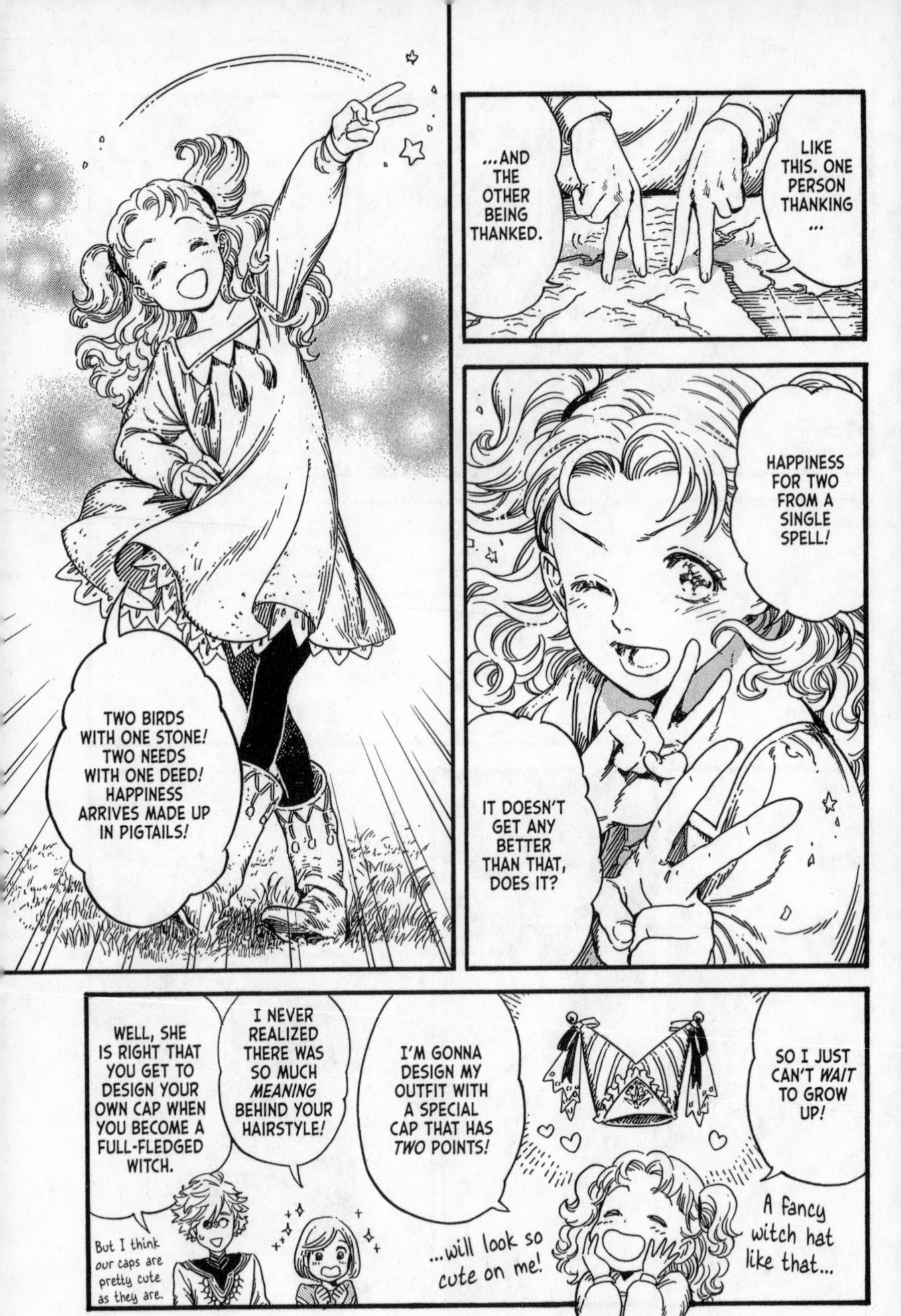
LIKE THIS. ONE PERSON THANKING ...
...AND THE OTHER BEING THANKED.
HAPPINESS FOR TWO FROM A SINGLE SPELL!
IT DOESN'T GET ANY BETTER THAN THAT, DOES IT?
TWO BIRDS WITH ONE STONE! TWO NEEDS WITH ONE DEED! HAPPINESS ARRIVES MADE UP IN PIGTAILS!
SO I JUST CAN'T *WAIT* TO GROW UP!
A fancy witch hat like that...
I'M GONNA DESIGN MY OUTFIT WITH A SPECIAL CAP THAT HAS *TWO* POINTS!
...will look so cute on me!
I NEVER REALIZED THERE WAS SO MUCH *MEANING* BEHIND YOUR HAIRSTYLE!
WELL, SHE IS RIGHT THAT YOU GET TO DESIGN YOUR OWN CAP WHEN YOU BECOME A FULL-FLEDGED WITCH.
But I think our caps are pretty cute as they are.

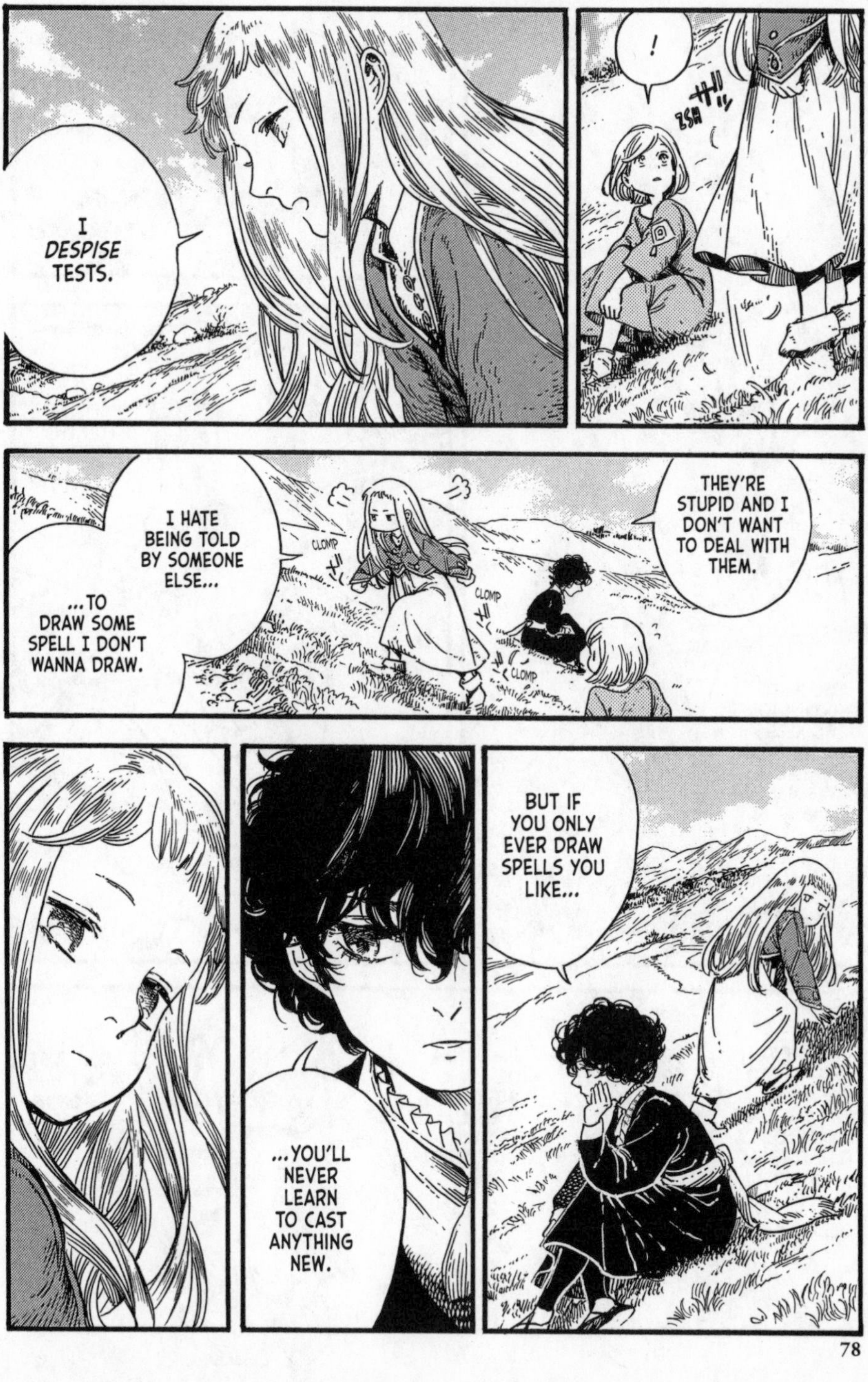
!
ZSH
I DESPISE TESTS.
THEY'RE STUPID AND I DON'T WANT TO DEAL WITH THEM.
CLOMP
CLOMP
CLOMP
I HATE BEING TOLD BY SOMEONE ELSE...
...TO DRAW SOME SPELL I DON'T WANNA DRAW.
BUT IF YOU ONLY EVER DRAW SPELLS YOU LIKE...
...YOU'LL NEVER LEARN TO CAST ANYTHING NEW.

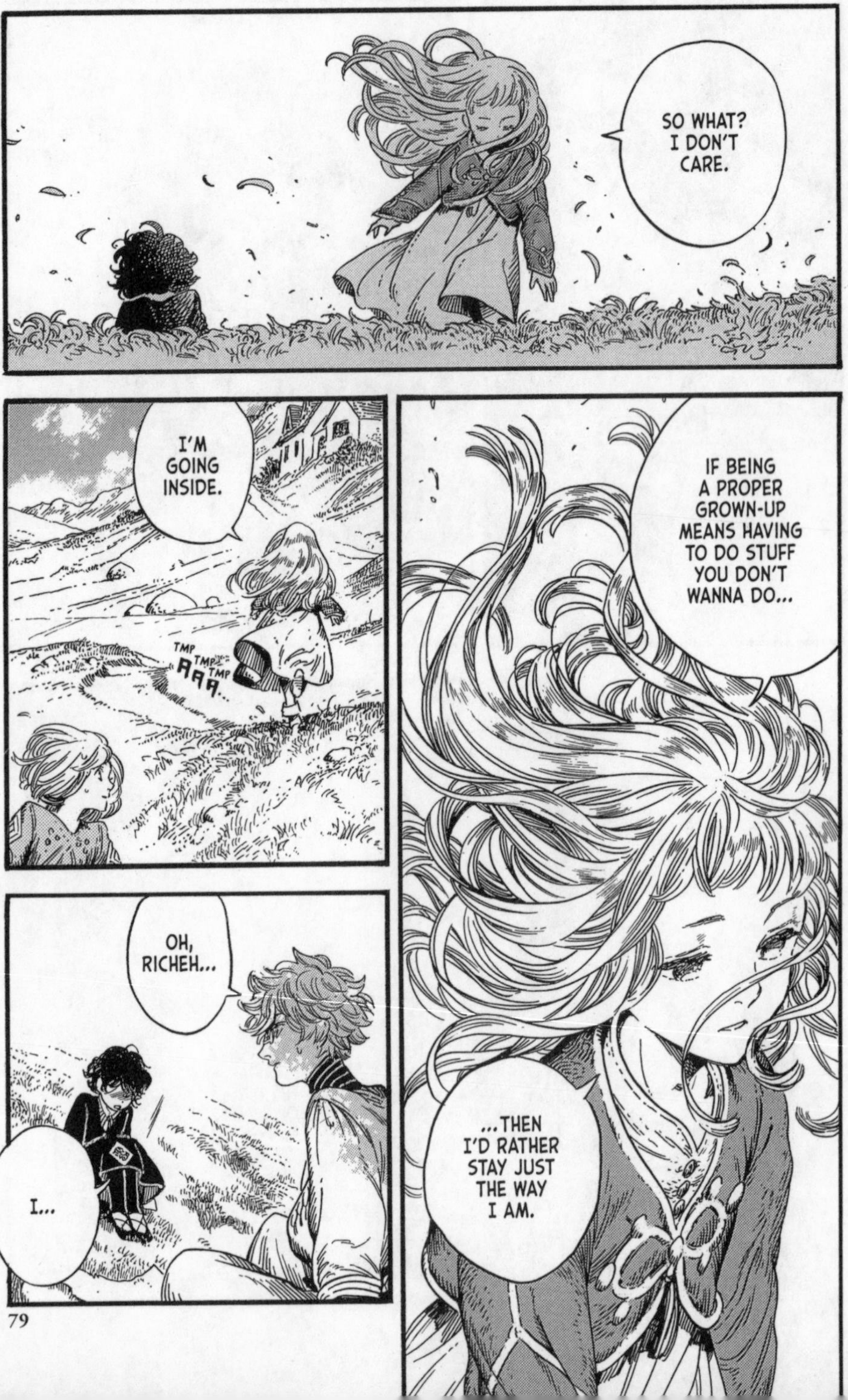
SO WHAT? I DON'T CARE.
IF BEING A PROPER GROWN-UP MEANS HAVING TO DO STUFF YOU DON'T WANNA DO...
...THEN I'D RATHER STAY JUST THE WAY I AM.
I'M GOING INSIDE.
TMP TMP TMP
OH, RICHEH...
I...

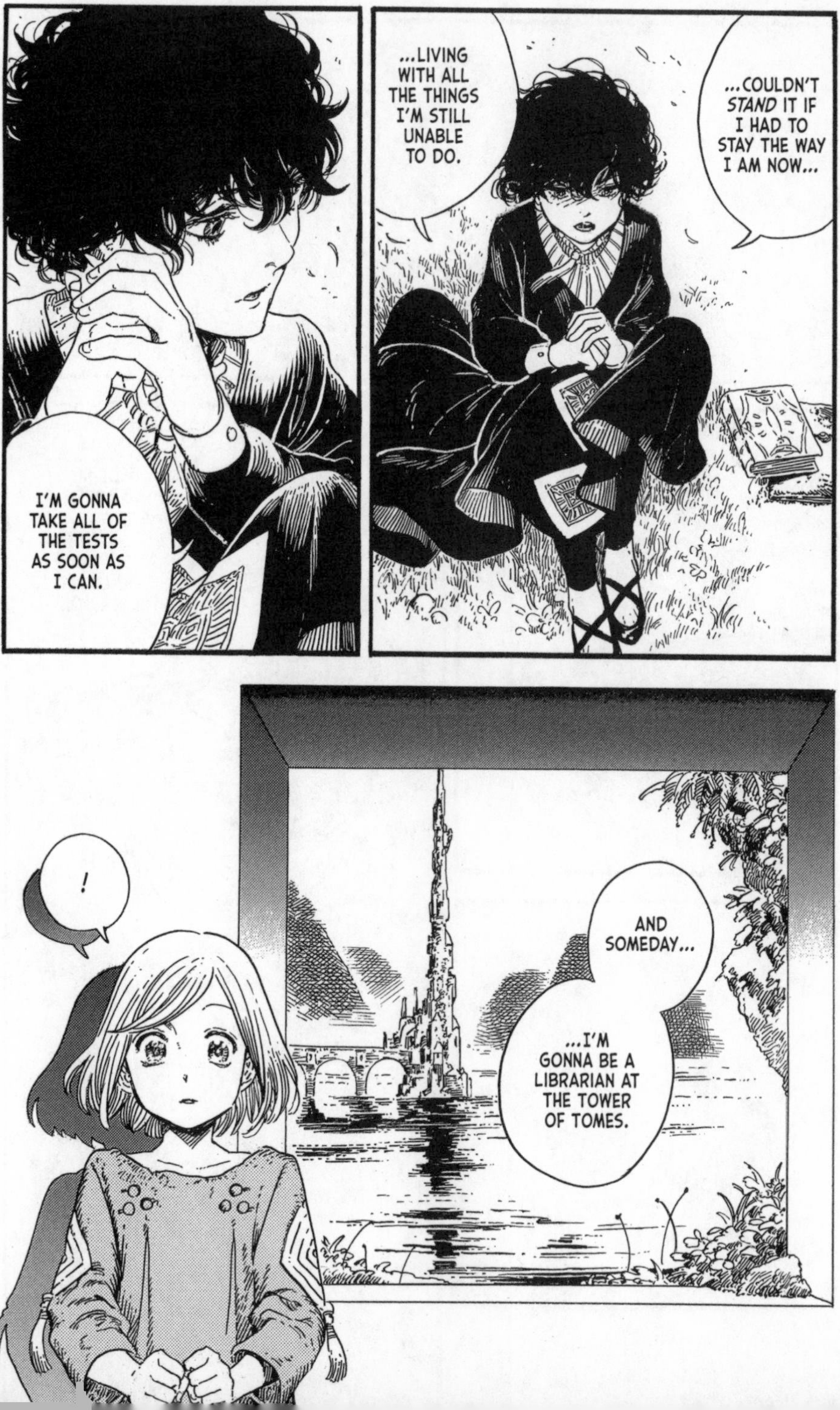
...COULDN'T *STAND* IT IF I HAD TO STAY THE WAY I AM NOW...
...LIVING WITH ALL THE THINGS I'M STILL UNABLE TO DO.
I'M GONNA TAKE ALL OF THE TESTS AS SOON AS I CAN.
AND SOMEDAY...
...I'M GONNA BE A LIBRARIAN AT THE TOWER OF TOMES.
!

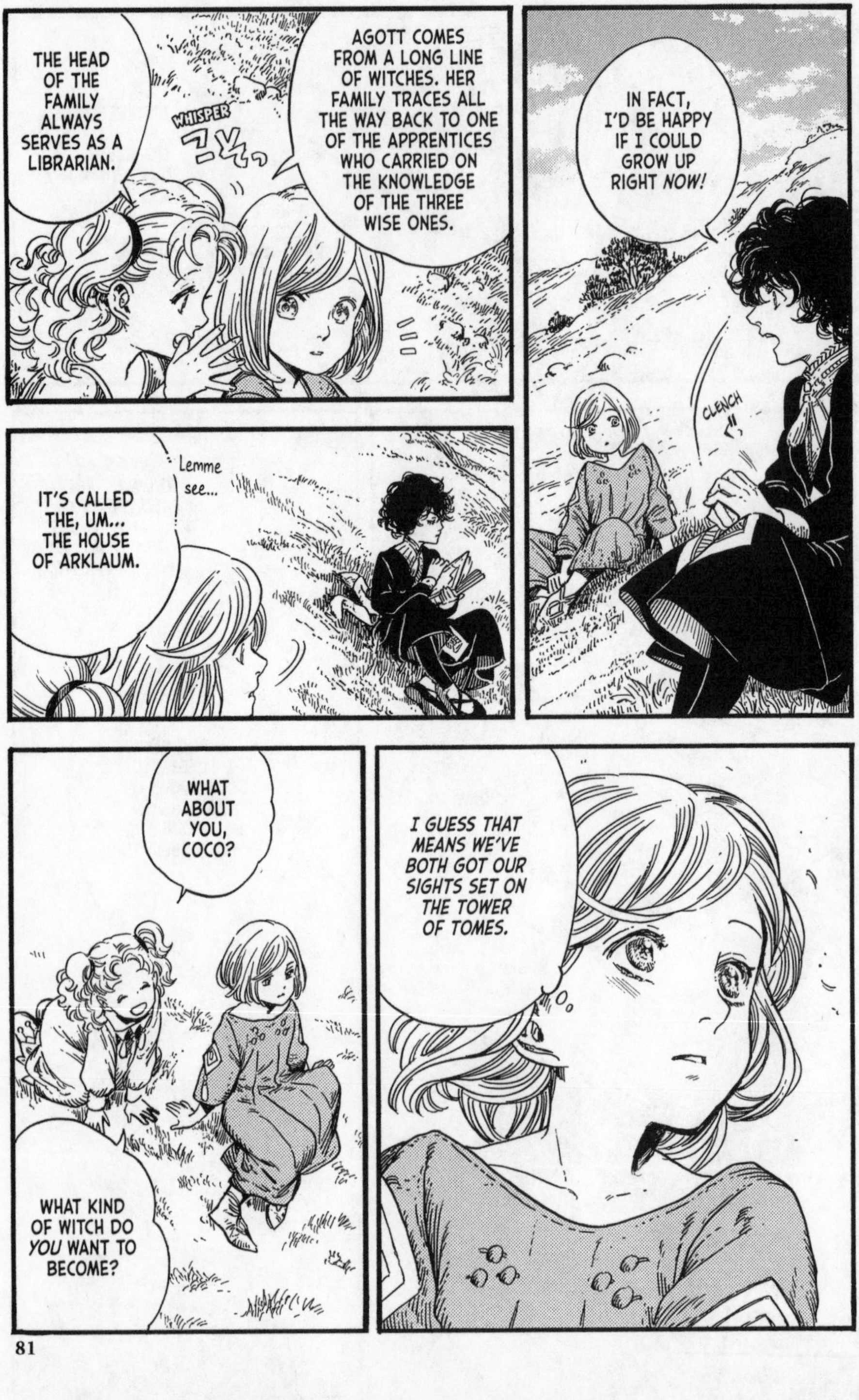
IN FACT, I'D BE HAPPY IF I COULD GROW UP RIGHT *NOW!*
CLENCH
AGOTT COMES FROM A LONG LINE OF WITCHES. HER FAMILY TRACES ALL THE WAY BACK TO ONE OF THE APPRENTICES WHO CARRIED ON THE KNOWLEDGE OF THE THREE WISE ONES.
WHISPER
THE HEAD OF THE FAMILY ALWAYS SERVES AS A LIBRARIAN.
Lemme see...
IT'S CALLED THE, UM... THE HOUSE OF ARKLAUM.
I GUESS THAT MEANS WE'VE BOTH GOT OUR SIGHTS SET ON THE TOWER OF TOMES.
WHAT ABOUT YOU, COCO?
WHAT KIND OF WITCH DO *YOU* WANT TO BECOME?

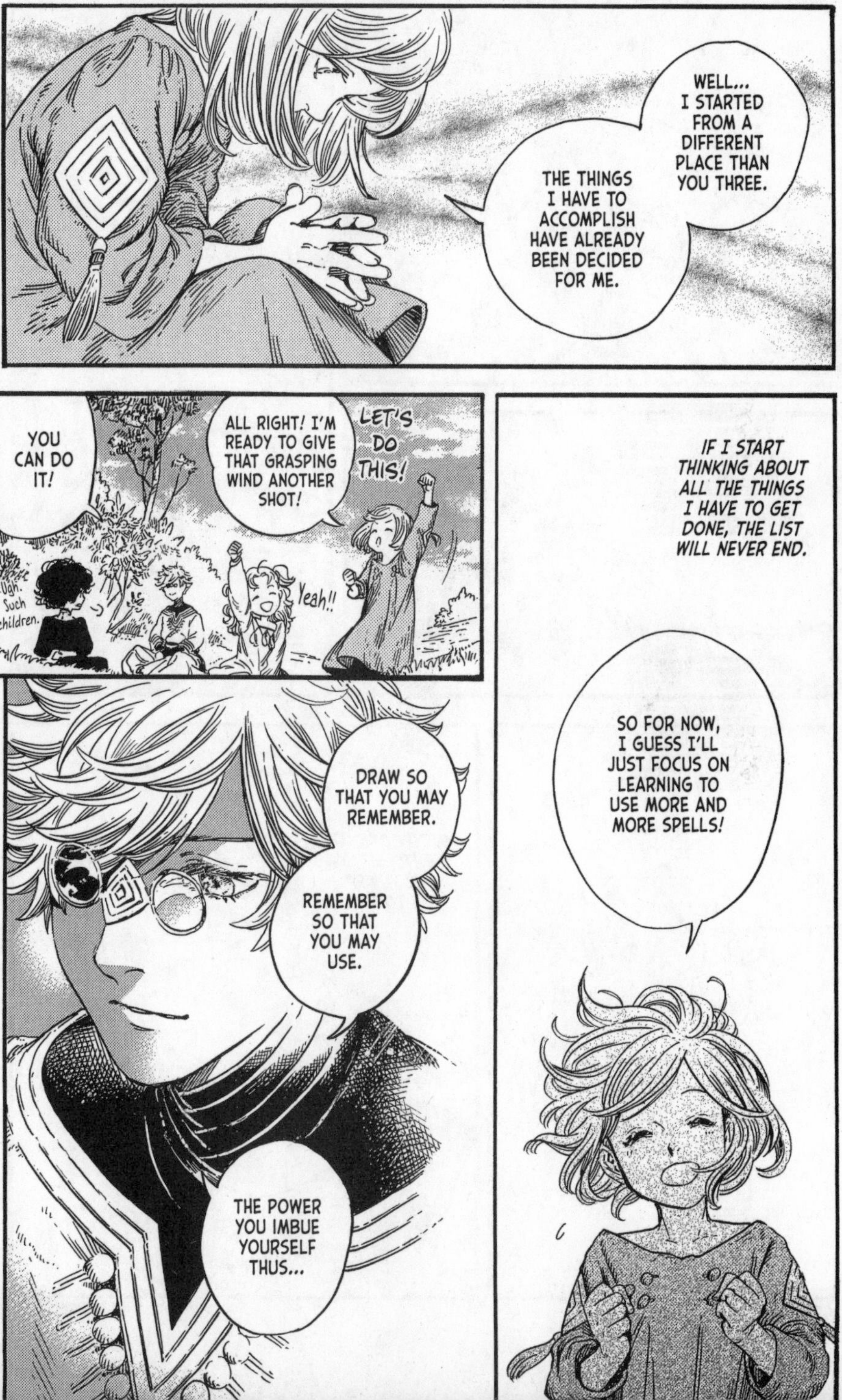
WELL... I STARTED FROM A DIFFERENT PLACE THAN YOU THREE.
THE THINGS I HAVE TO ACCOMPLISH HAVE ALREADY BEEN DECIDED FOR ME.
IF I START THINKING ABOUT ALL THE THINGS I HAVE TO GET DONE, THE LIST WILL NEVER END.
SO FOR NOW, I GUESS I'LL JUST FOCUS ON LEARNING TO USE MORE AND MORE SPELLS!
LET'S DO THIS!
ALL RIGHT! I'M READY TO GIVE THAT GRASPING WIND ANOTHER SHOT!
YOU CAN DO IT!
Yeah!!
Ugh. Such children.
DRAW SO THAT YOU MAY REMEMBER.
REMEMBER SO THAT YOU MAY USE.
THE POWER YOU IMBUE YOURSELF THUS...

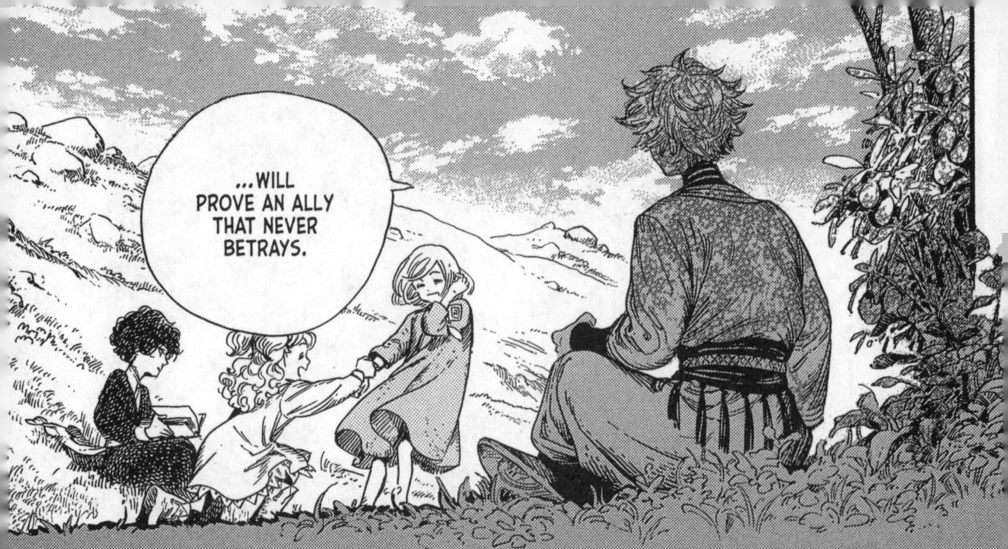
...WILL PROVE AN ALLY THAT NEVER BETRAYS.

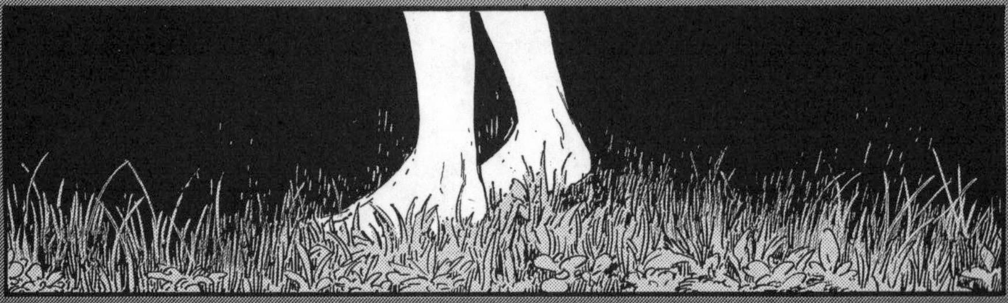

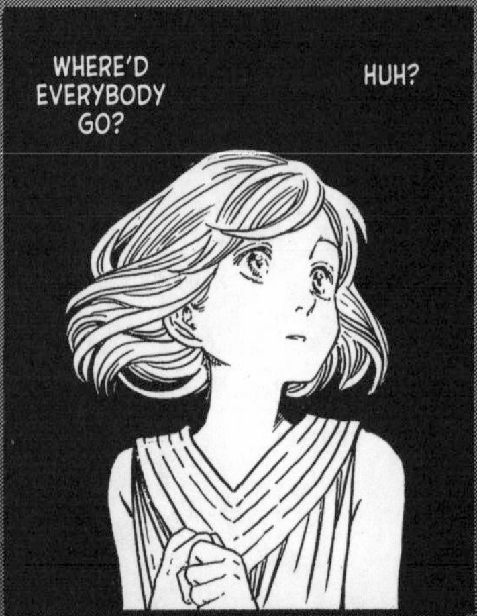
HUH?
WHERE'D EVERYBODY GO?

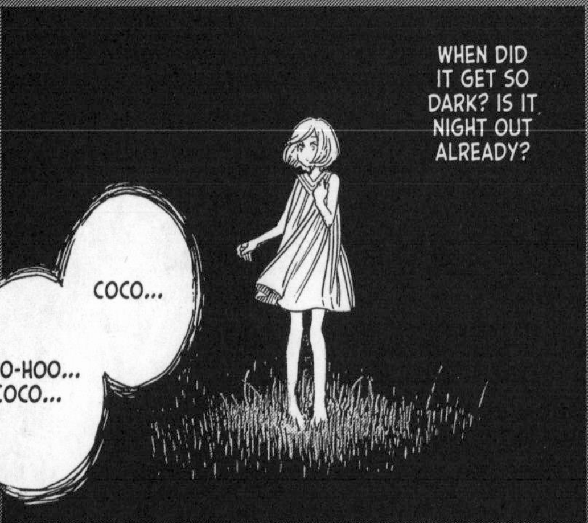
WHEN DID IT GET SO DARK? IS IT NIGHT OUT ALREADY?
COCO...
YOO-HOO... COCO...

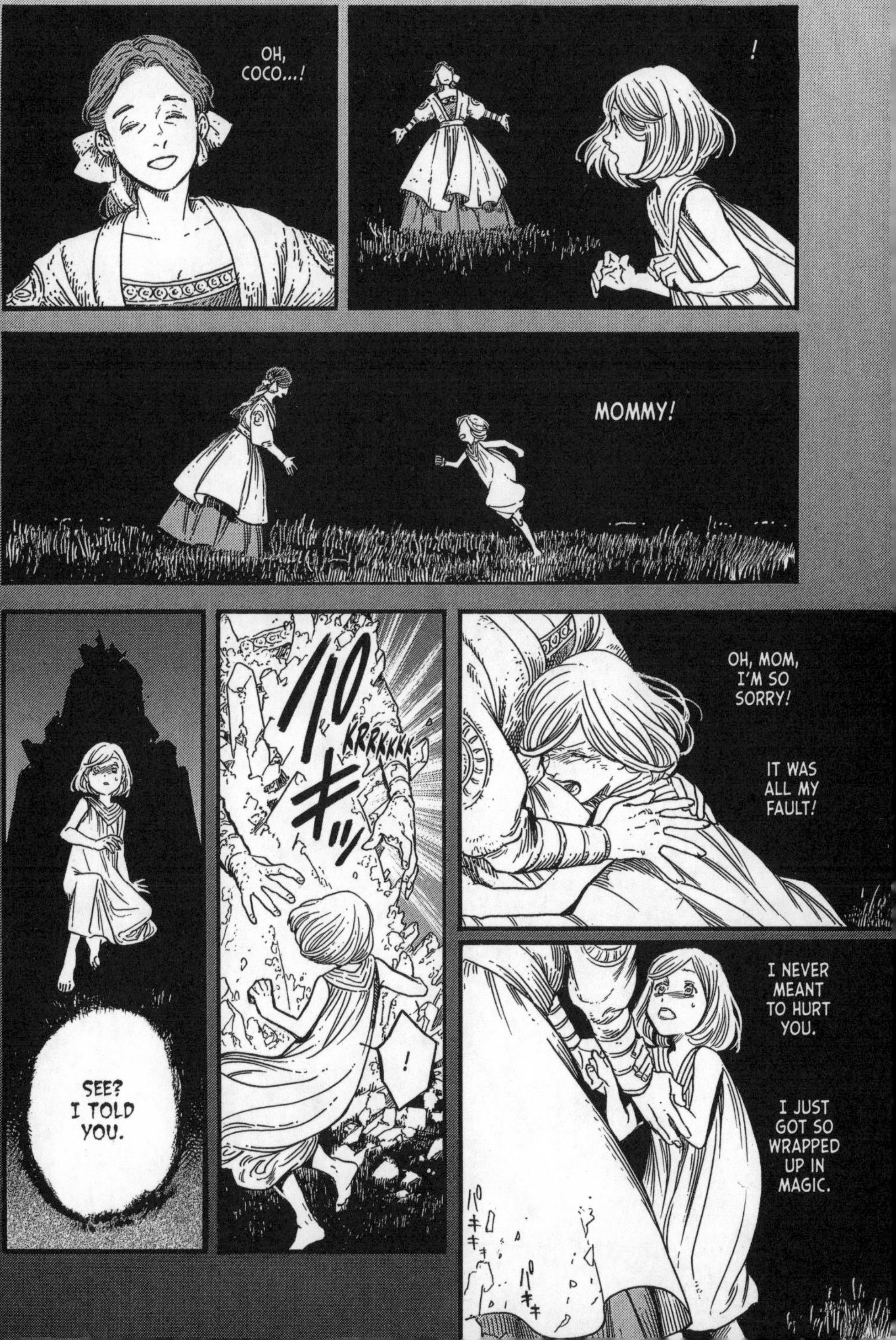
!
OH, COCO...!
MOMMY!
OH, MOM, I'M SO SORRY!
IT WAS ALL MY FAULT!
I NEVER MEANT TO HURT YOU.
I JUST GOT SO WRAPPED UP IN MAGIC.
KRRKKKK
!
SEE? I TOLD YOU.

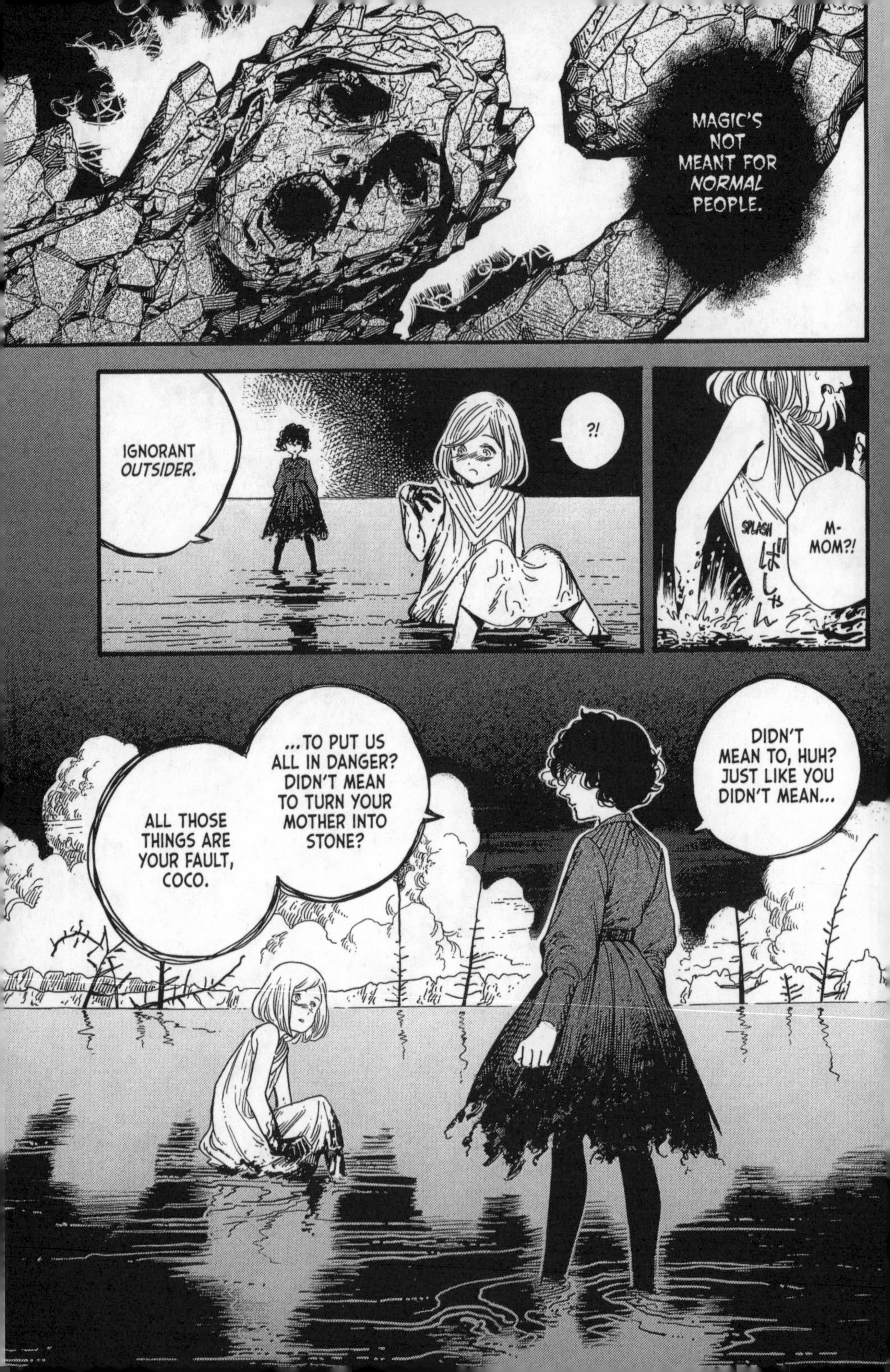
MAGIC'S NOT MEANT FOR *NORMAL* PEOPLE.
M-MOM?!
SPLASH
ばしゃん
?!
IGNORANT *OUTSIDER.*
DIDN'T MEAN TO, HUH? JUST LIKE YOU DIDN'T MEAN...
...TO PUT US ALL IN DANGER? DIDN'T MEAN TO TURN YOUR MOTHER INTO STONE?
ALL THOSE THINGS ARE YOUR FAULT, COCO.

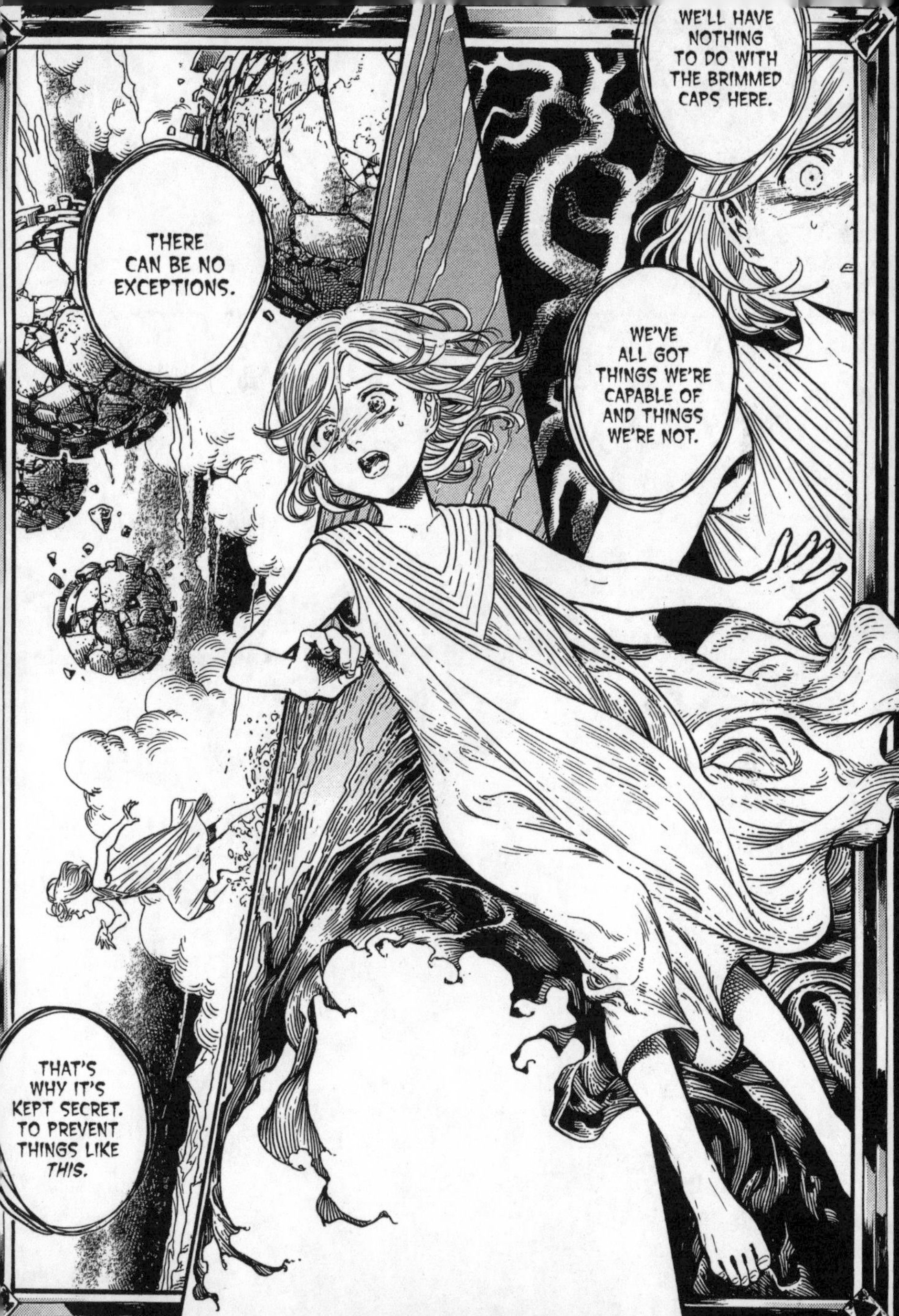
WE'LL HAVE NOTHING TO DO WITH THE BRIMMED CAPS HERE.
WE'VE ALL GOT THINGS WE'RE CAPABLE OF AND THINGS WE'RE NOT.
THERE CAN BE NO EXCEPTIONS.
THAT'S WHY IT'S KEPT SECRET. TO PREVENT THINGS LIKE *THIS.*

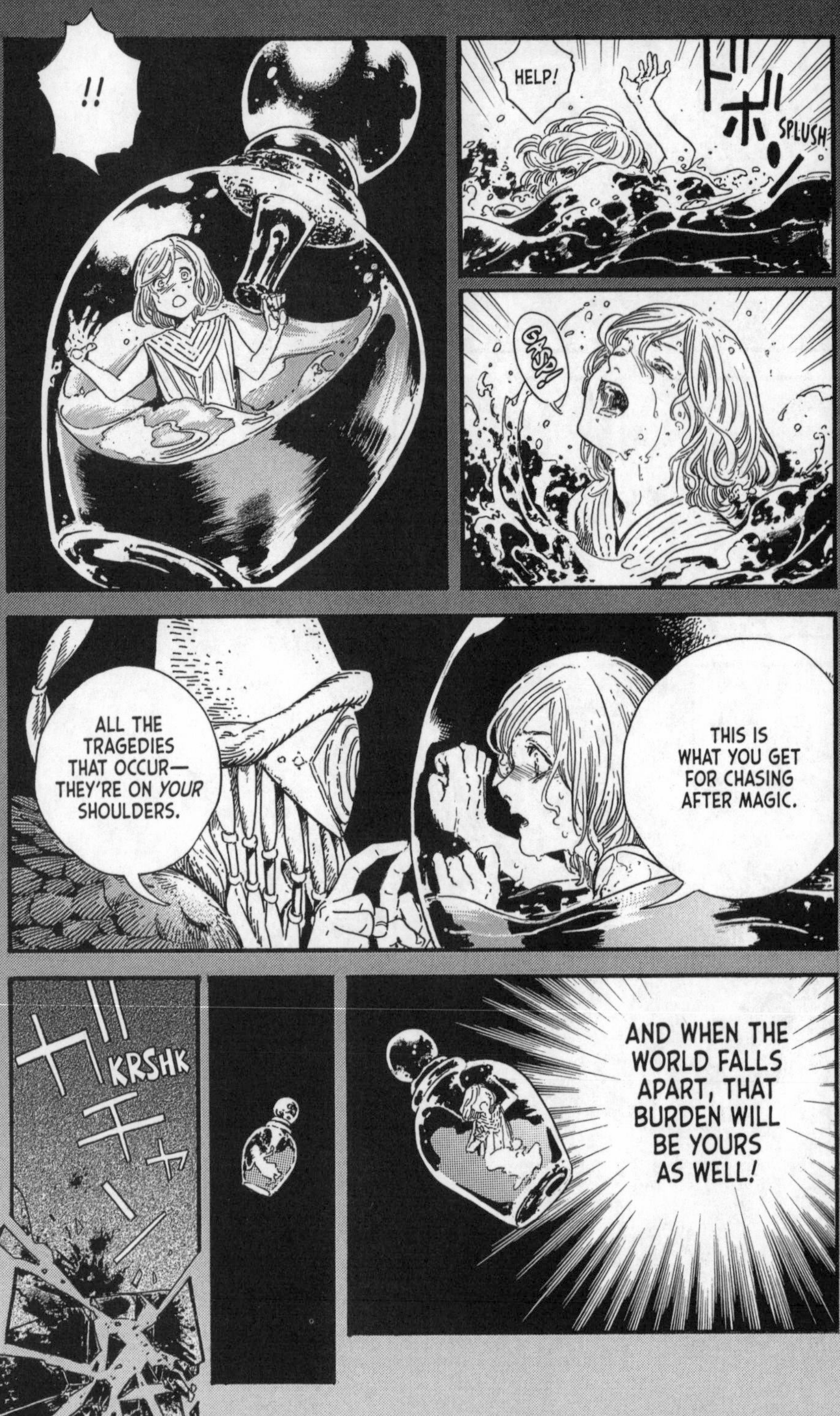
HELP!
SPLUSH
GASP!
!!
THIS IS WHAT YOU GET FOR CHASING AFTER MAGIC.
ALL THE TRAGEDIES THAT OCCUR—THEY'RE ON *YOUR* SHOULDERS.
AND WHEN THE WORLD FALLS APART, THAT BURDEN WILL BE YOURS AS WELL!
KRSHK

Haah.
Haah.
Haah.
Haaah.
Haaah.
Haaah.
TREMBLE
TREMBLE
RUB
CLASP

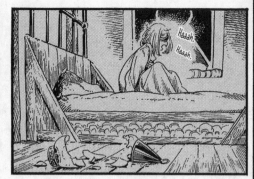

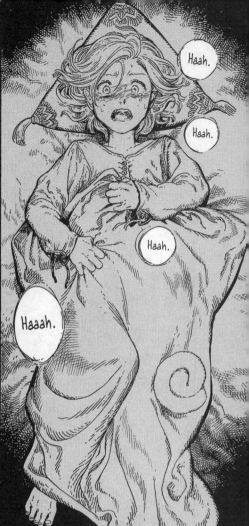

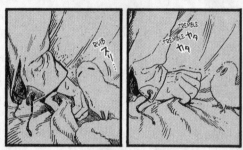

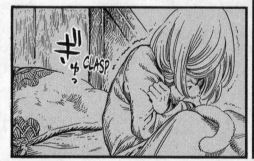

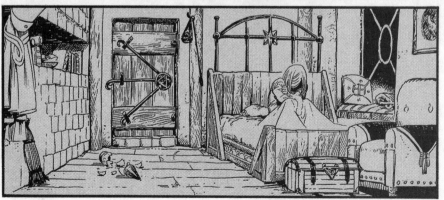

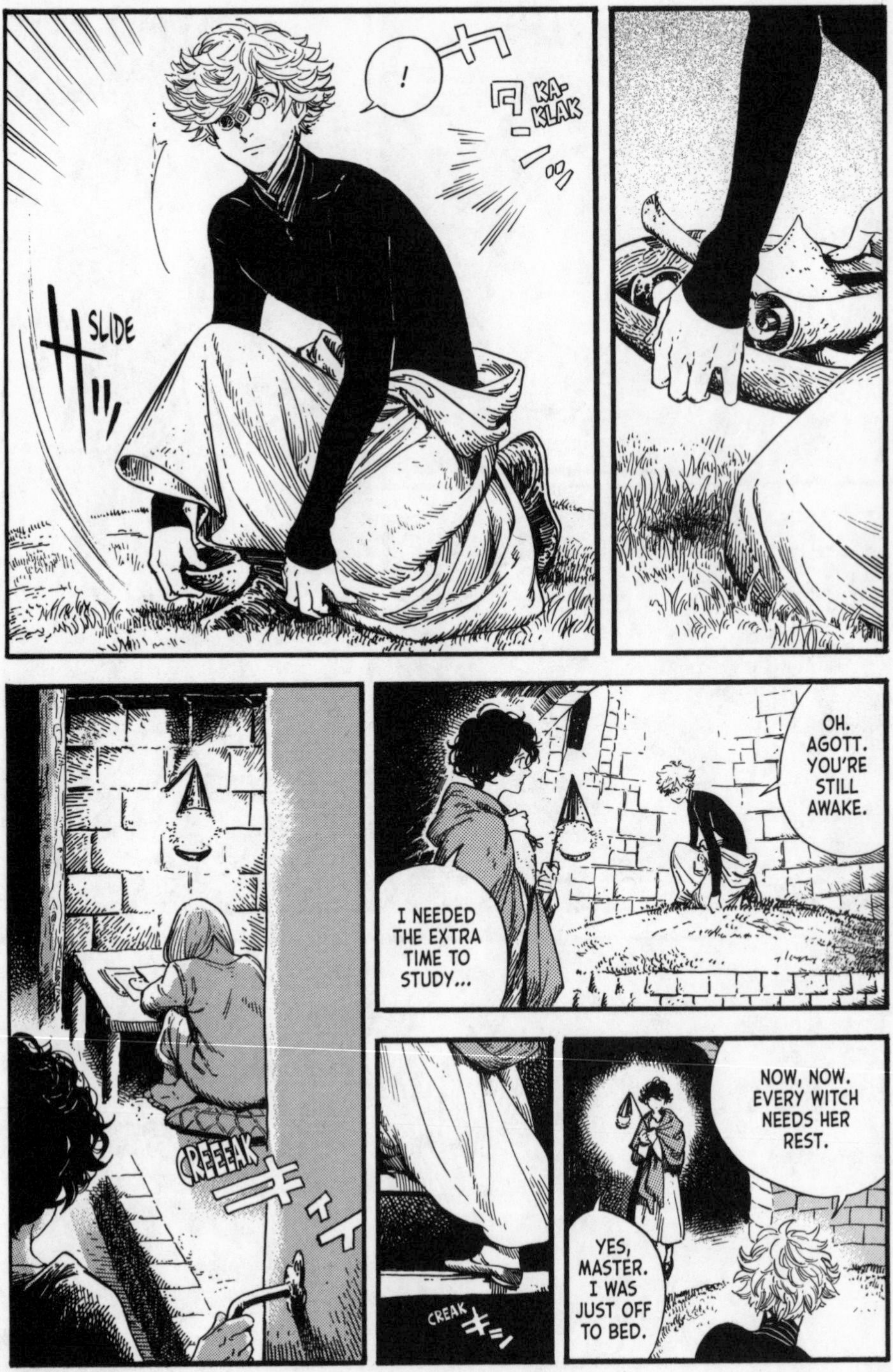
!
KA-KLAK
SLIDE
OH. AGOTT. YOU'RE STILL AWAKE.
I NEEDED THE EXTRA TIME TO STUDY...
NOW, NOW. EVERY WITCH NEEDS HER REST.
YES, MASTER. I WAS JUST OFF TO BED.
CREAK
CREEEAK

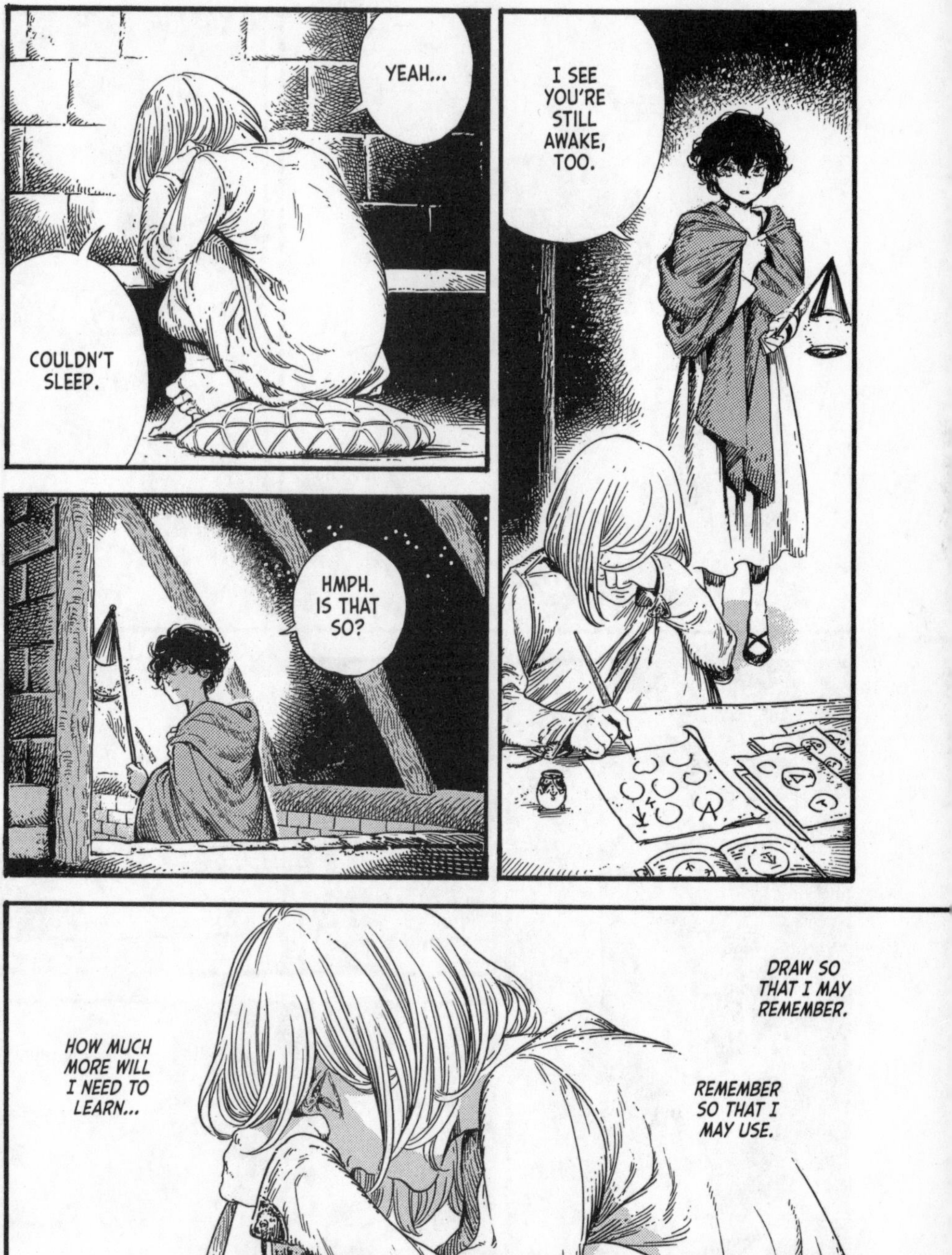
I SEE YOU'RE STILL AWAKE, TOO.
YEAH...
COULDN'T SLEEP.
HMPH. IS THAT SO?
DRAW SO THAT I MAY REMEMBER.
REMEMBER SO THAT I MAY USE.
HOW MUCH MORE WILL I NEED TO LEARN...

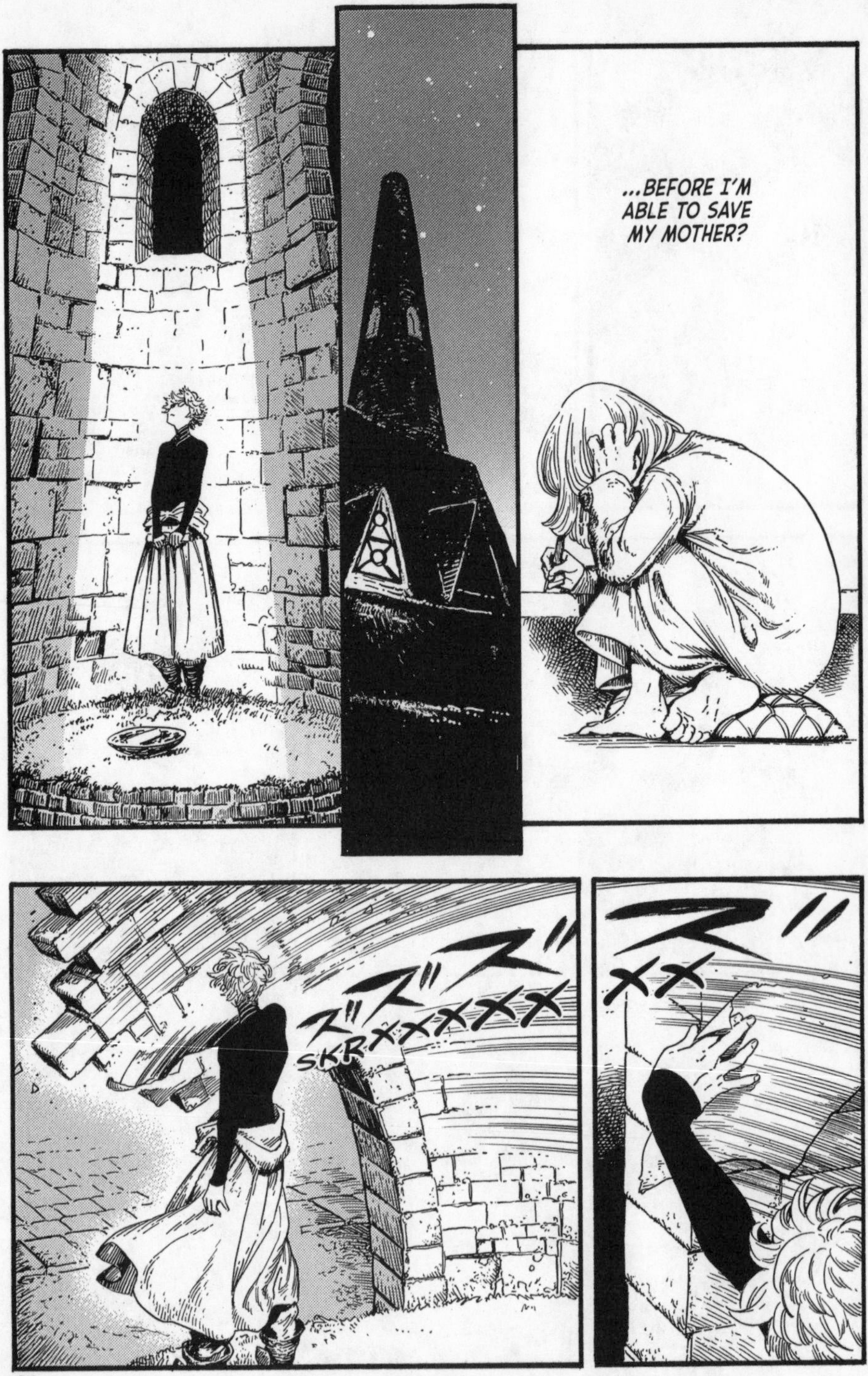
...BEFORE I'M ABLE TO SAVE MY MOTHER?
ズ
SKRXXXXXX

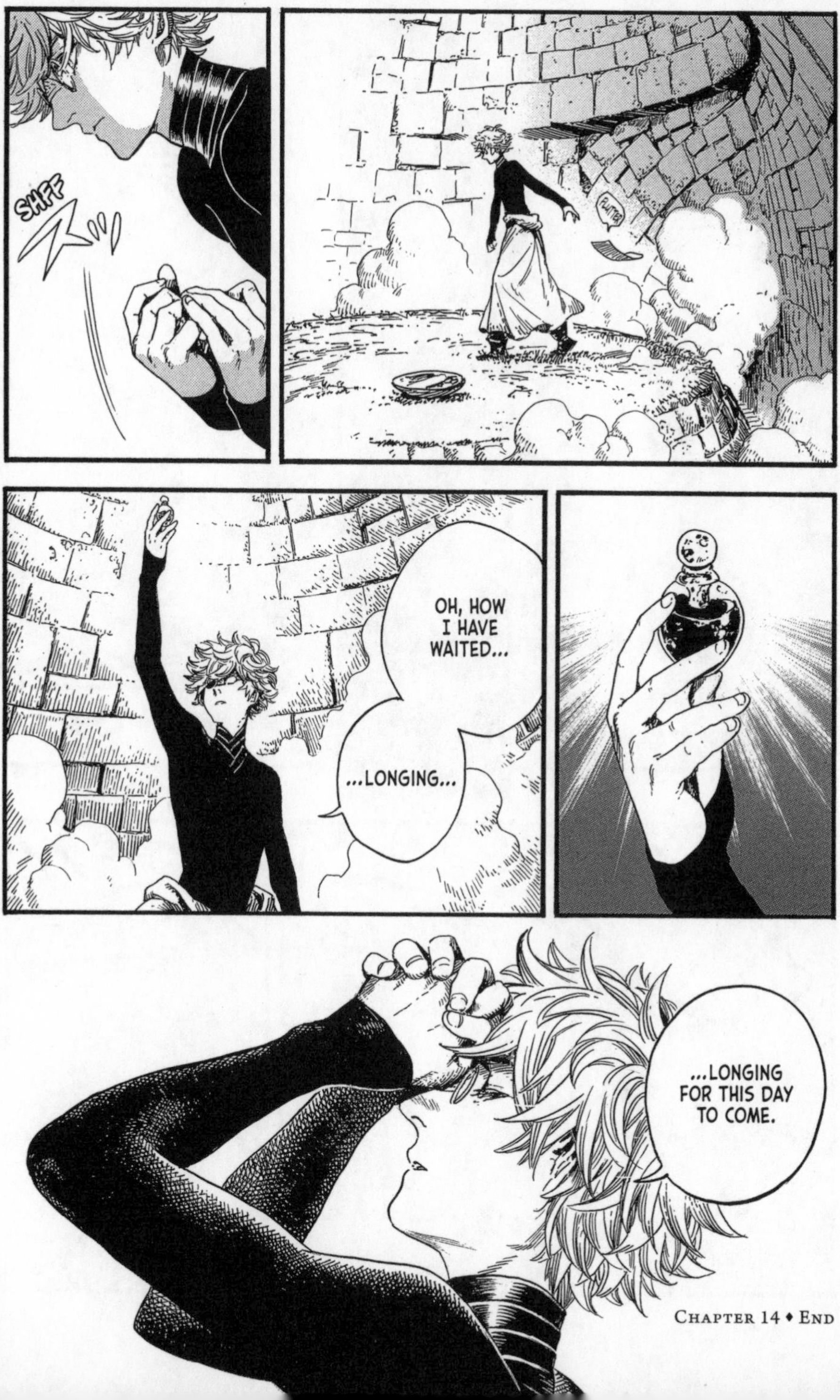
FLUTTER
SHFF
OH, HOW I HAVE WAITED...
...LONGING...
...LONGING FOR THIS DAY TO COME.

Chapter 14 • End

Witch Hat Atelier

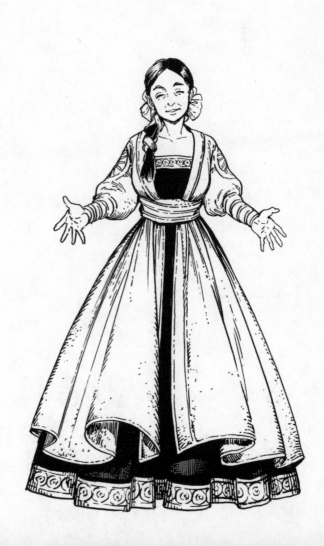

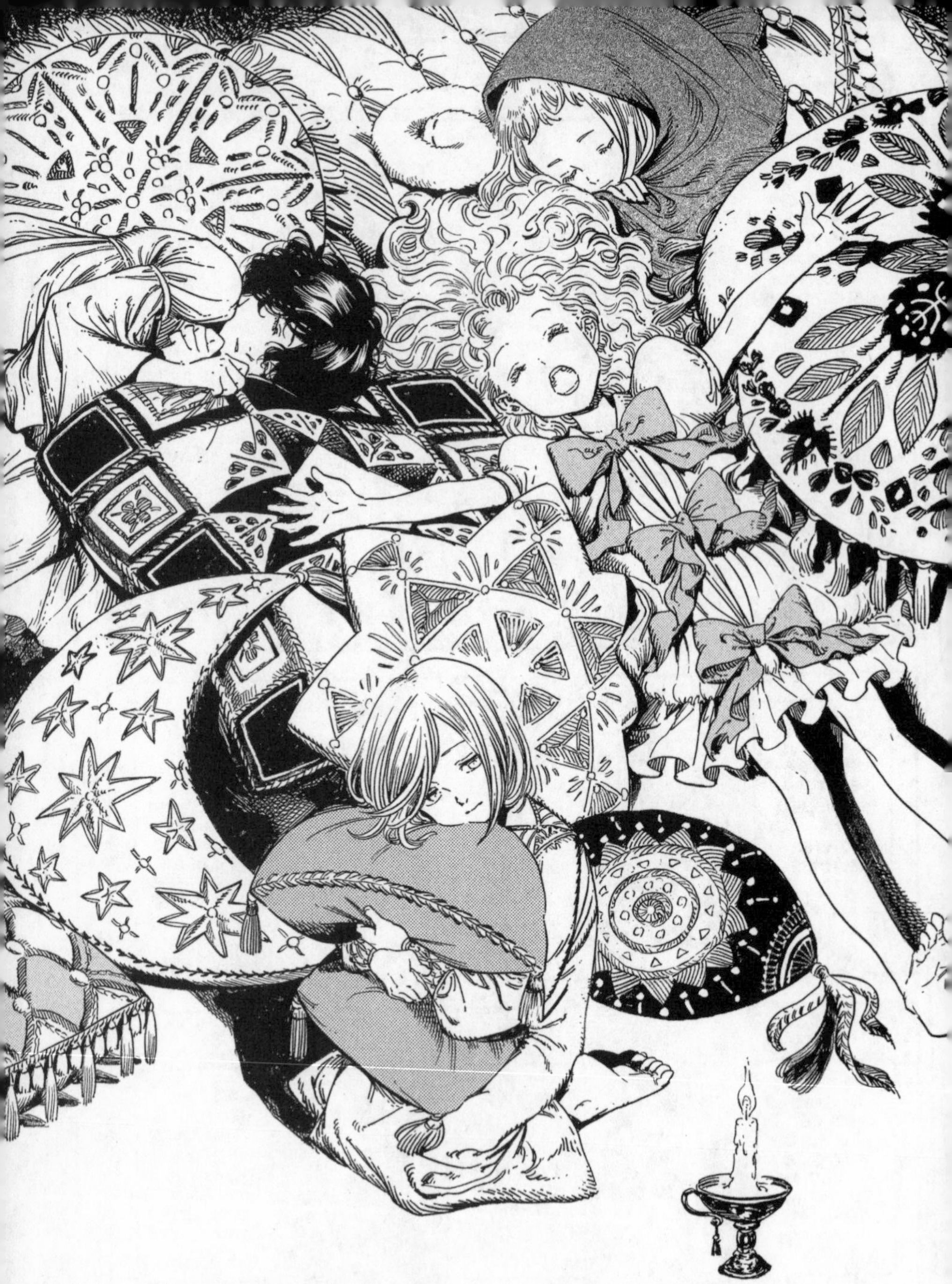

Chapter 15

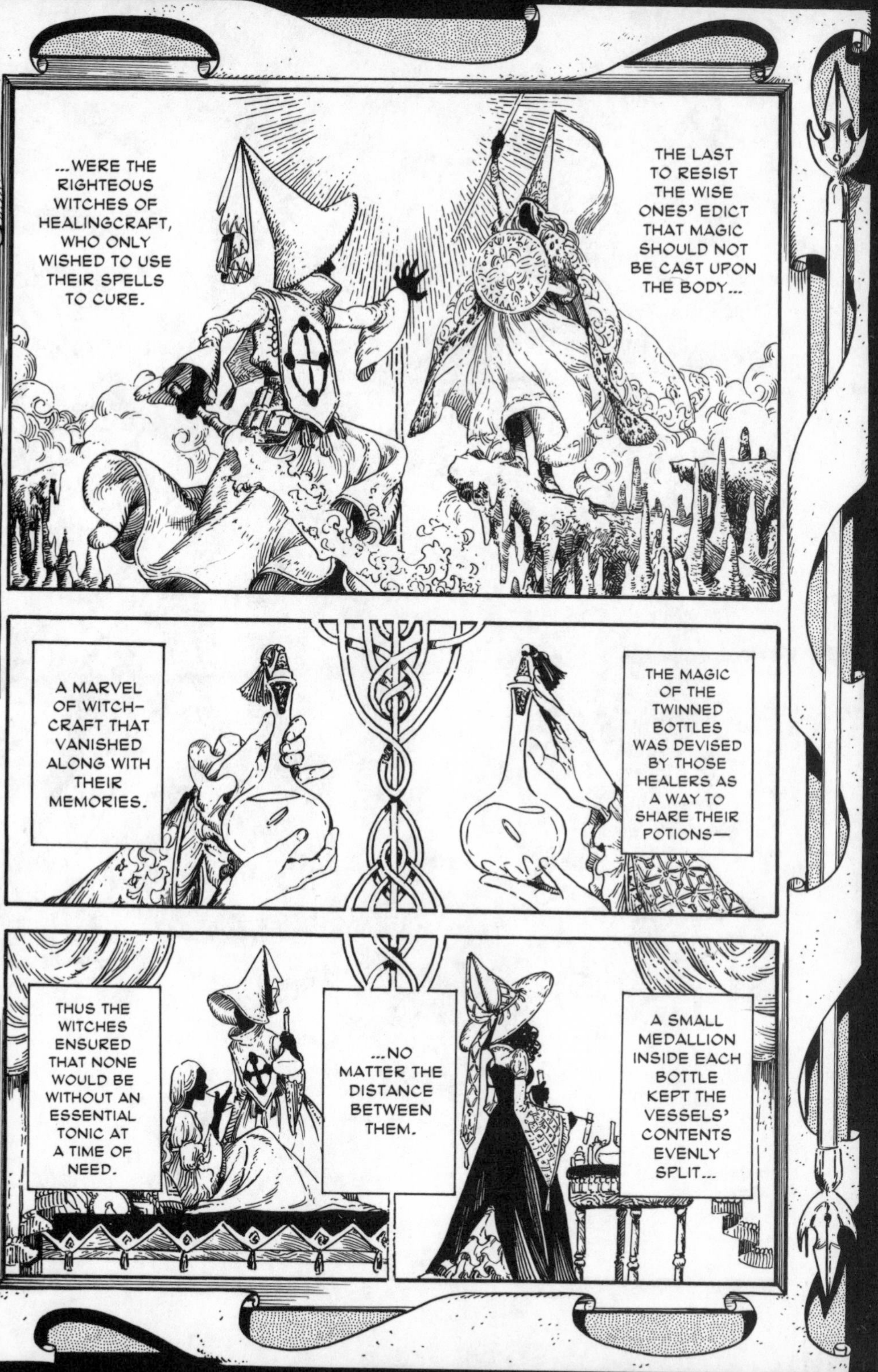
THE LAST TO RESIST THE WISE ONES' EDICT THAT MAGIC SHOULD NOT BE CAST UPON THE BODY...
...WERE THE RIGHTEOUS WITCHES OF HEALINGCRAFT, WHO ONLY WISHED TO USE THEIR SPELLS TO CURE.
THE MAGIC OF THE TWINNED BOTTLES WAS DEVISED BY THOSE HEALERS AS A WAY TO SHARE THEIR POTIONS—
A MARVEL OF WITCH-CRAFT THAT VANISHED ALONG WITH THEIR MEMORIES.
A SMALL MEDALLION INSIDE EACH BOTTLE KEPT THE VESSELS' CONTENTS EVENLY SPLIT...
...NO MATTER THE DISTANCE BETWEEN THEM.
THUS THE WITCHES ENSURED THAT NONE WOULD BE WITHOUT AN ESSENTIAL TONIC AT A TIME OF NEED.

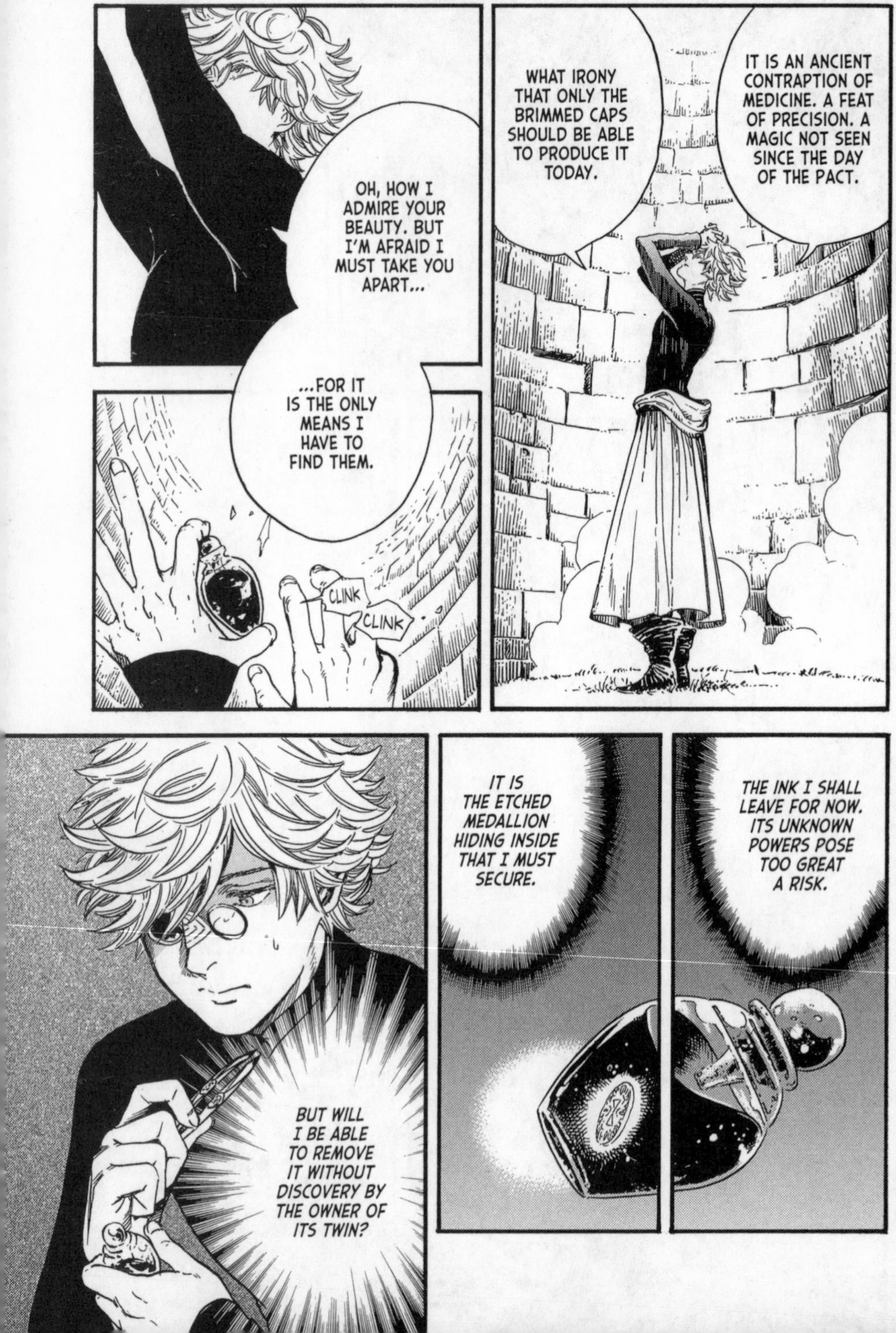
IT IS AN ANCIENT CONTRAPTION OF MEDICINE. A FEAT OF PRECISION. A MAGIC NOT SEEN SINCE THE DAY OF THE PACT.
WHAT IRONY THAT ONLY THE BRIMMED CAPS SHOULD BE ABLE TO PRODUCE IT TODAY.
OH, HOW I ADMIRE YOUR BEAUTY. BUT I'M AFRAID I MUST TAKE YOU APART...
...FOR IT IS THE ONLY MEANS I HAVE TO FIND THEM.
CLINK
CLINK
THE INK I SHALL LEAVE FOR NOW. ITS UNKNOWN POWERS POSE TOO GREAT A RISK.
IT IS THE ETCHED MEDALLION HIDING INSIDE THAT I MUST SECURE.
BUT WILL I BE ABLE TO REMOVE IT WITHOUT DISCOVERY BY THE OWNER OF ITS TWIN?

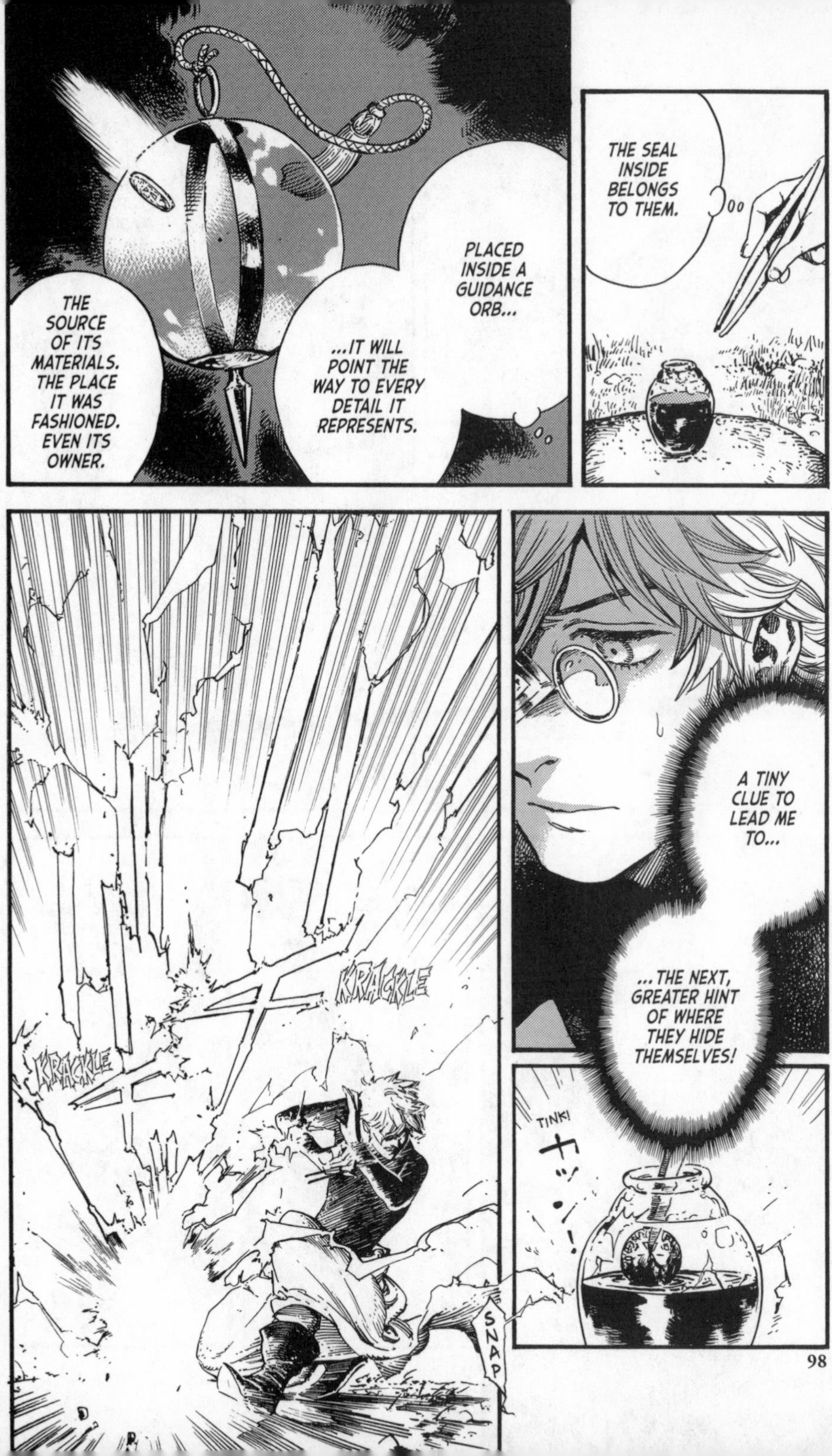
THE SEAL INSIDE BELONGS TO THEM.
PLACED INSIDE A GUIDANCE ORB...
...IT WILL POINT THE WAY TO EVERY DETAIL IT REPRESENTS.
THE SOURCE OF ITS MATERIALS. THE PLACE IT WAS FASHIONED. EVEN ITS OWNER.
A TINY CLUE TO LEAD ME TO...
...THE NEXT, GREATER HINT OF WHERE THEY HIDE THEMSELVES!
TINK!
KRACKLE
KRACKLE
SNAP

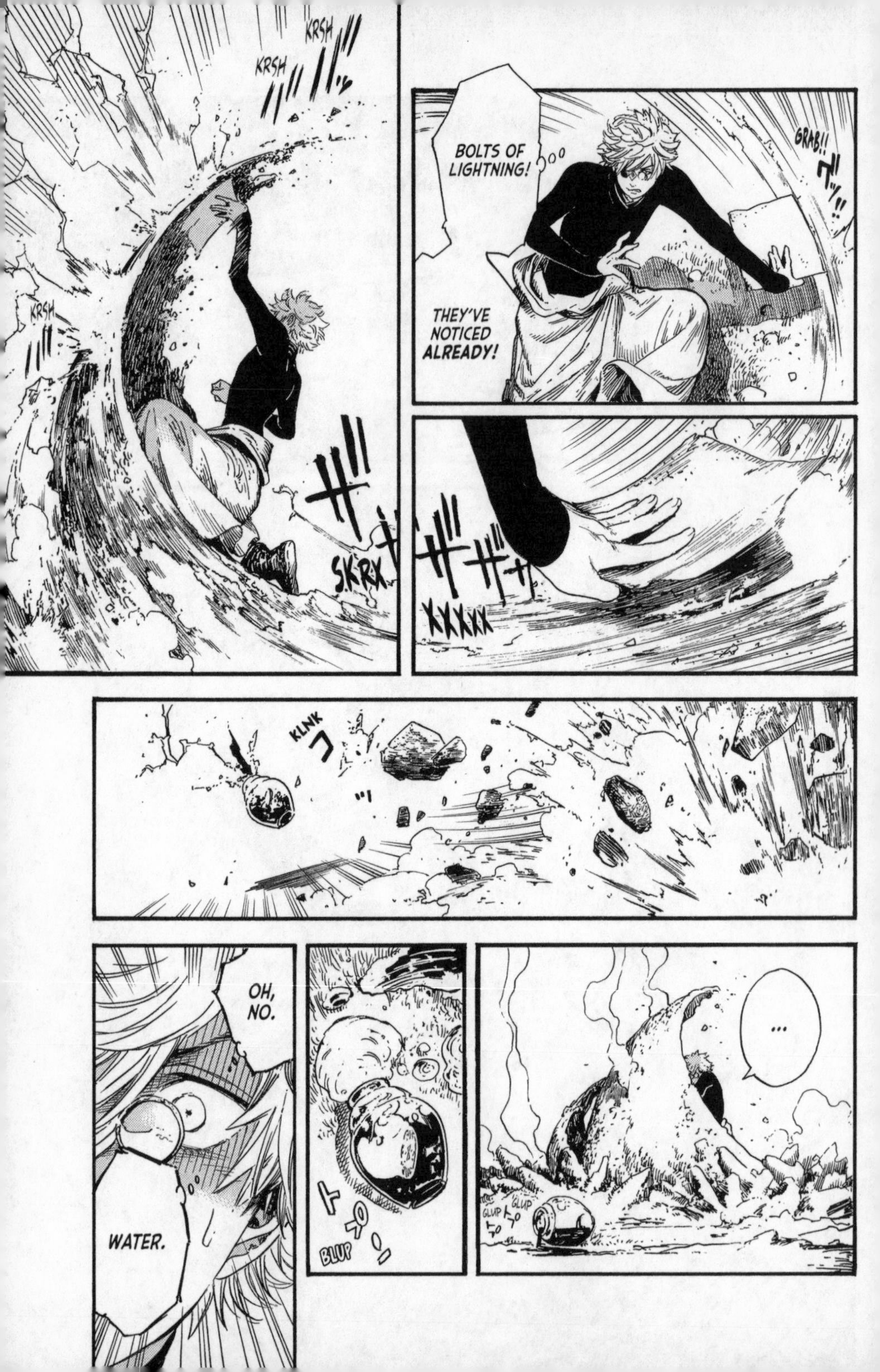
GRAB!!
BOLTS OF LIGHTNING!
THEY'VE NOTICED ALREADY!
SKRX
XXXXX
KRSH
KRSH
KRSH
KLNK
...
GLUP
GLUP
BLUP
OH, NO.
WATER.

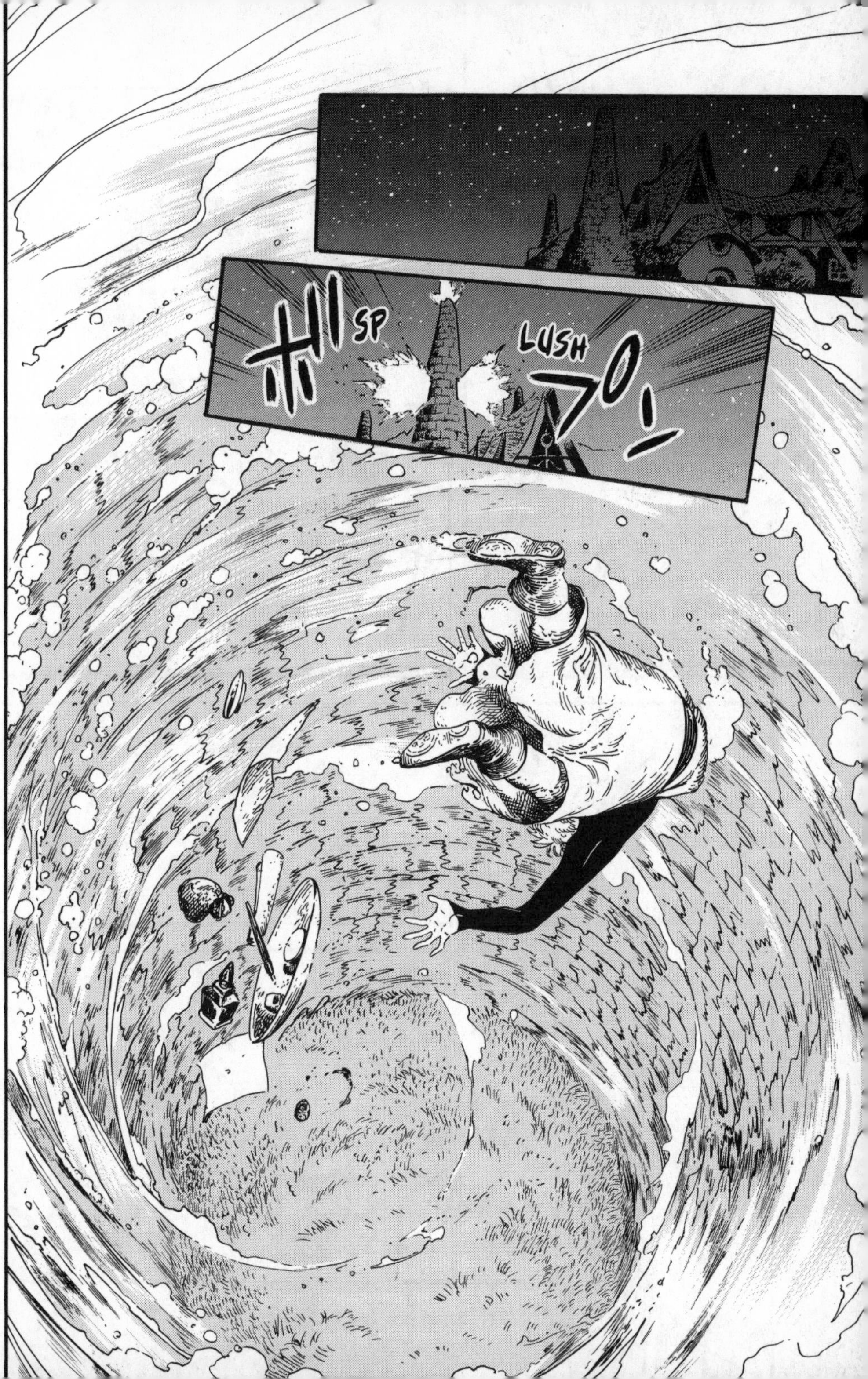
SP LUSH

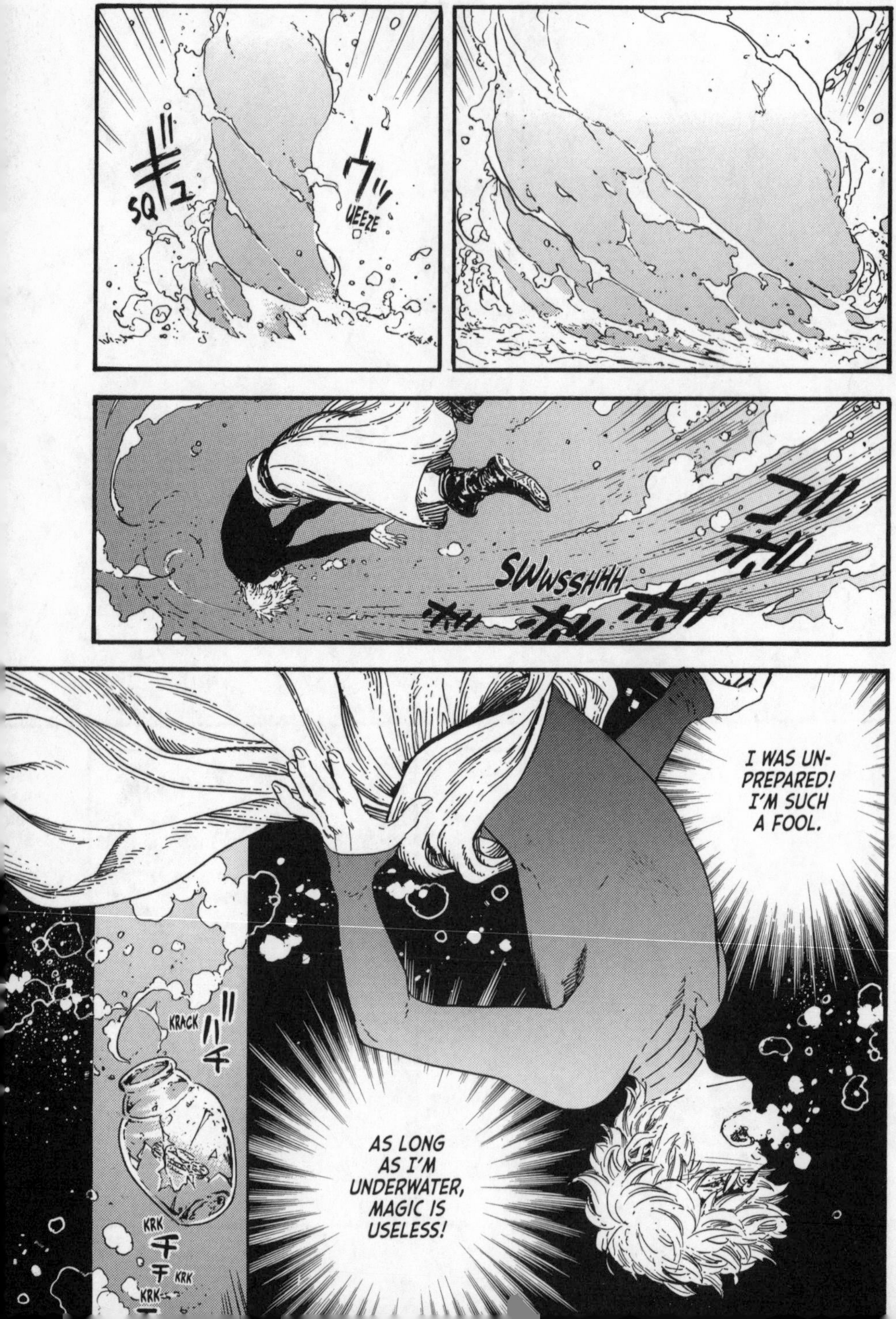

SQUEEZE
SWWSSHHH
I WAS UN-PREPARED! I'M SUCH A FOOL.
AS LONG AS I'M UNDERWATER, MAGIC IS USELESS!
KRACK
KRK
KRK
KRK

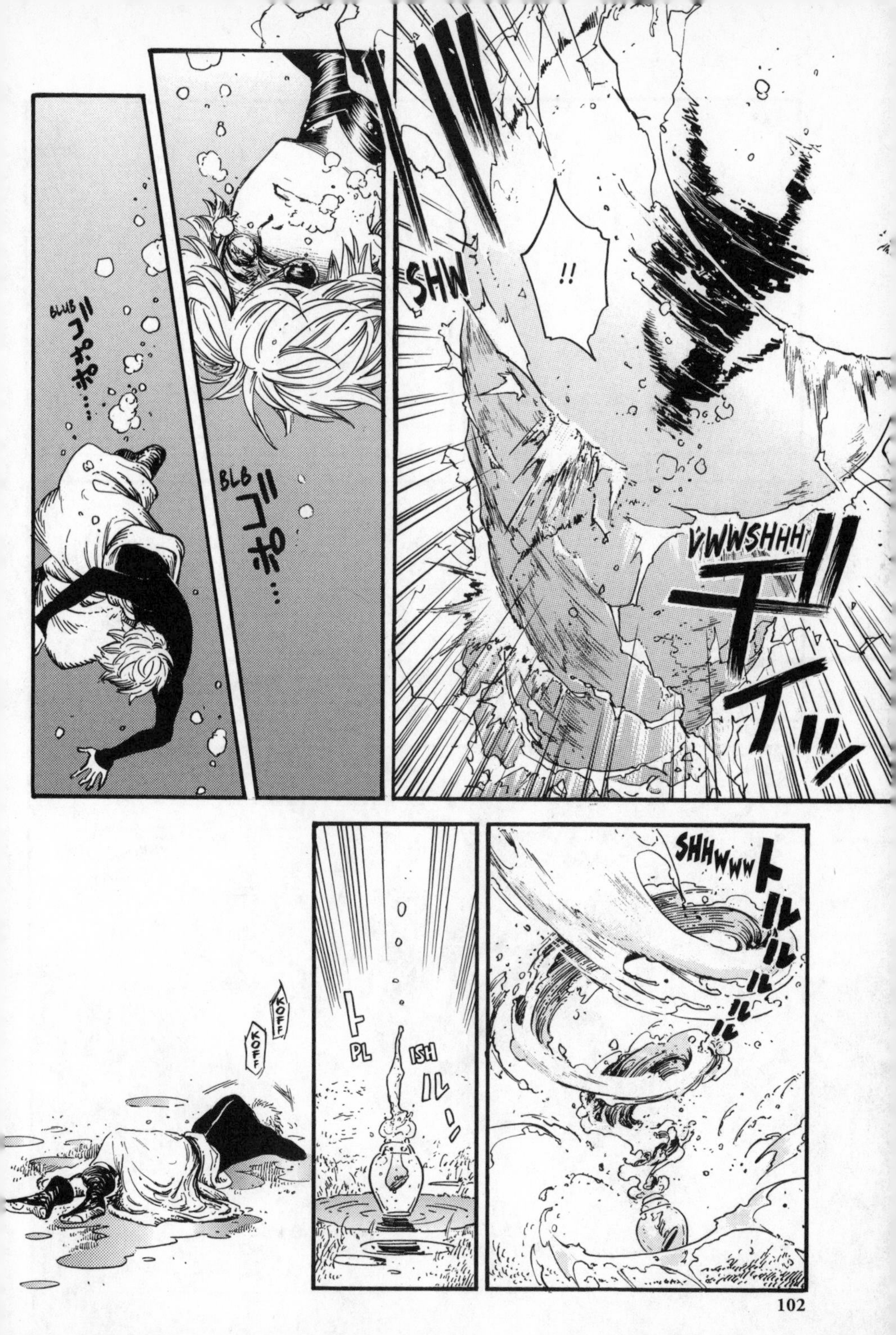
SHW
!!
VWWSHHH
BLB
ゴポ…
BLUB
ゴポポ……
SHHWWW
トルルルル…
PL
ISH
トルッ
KOFF
KOFF

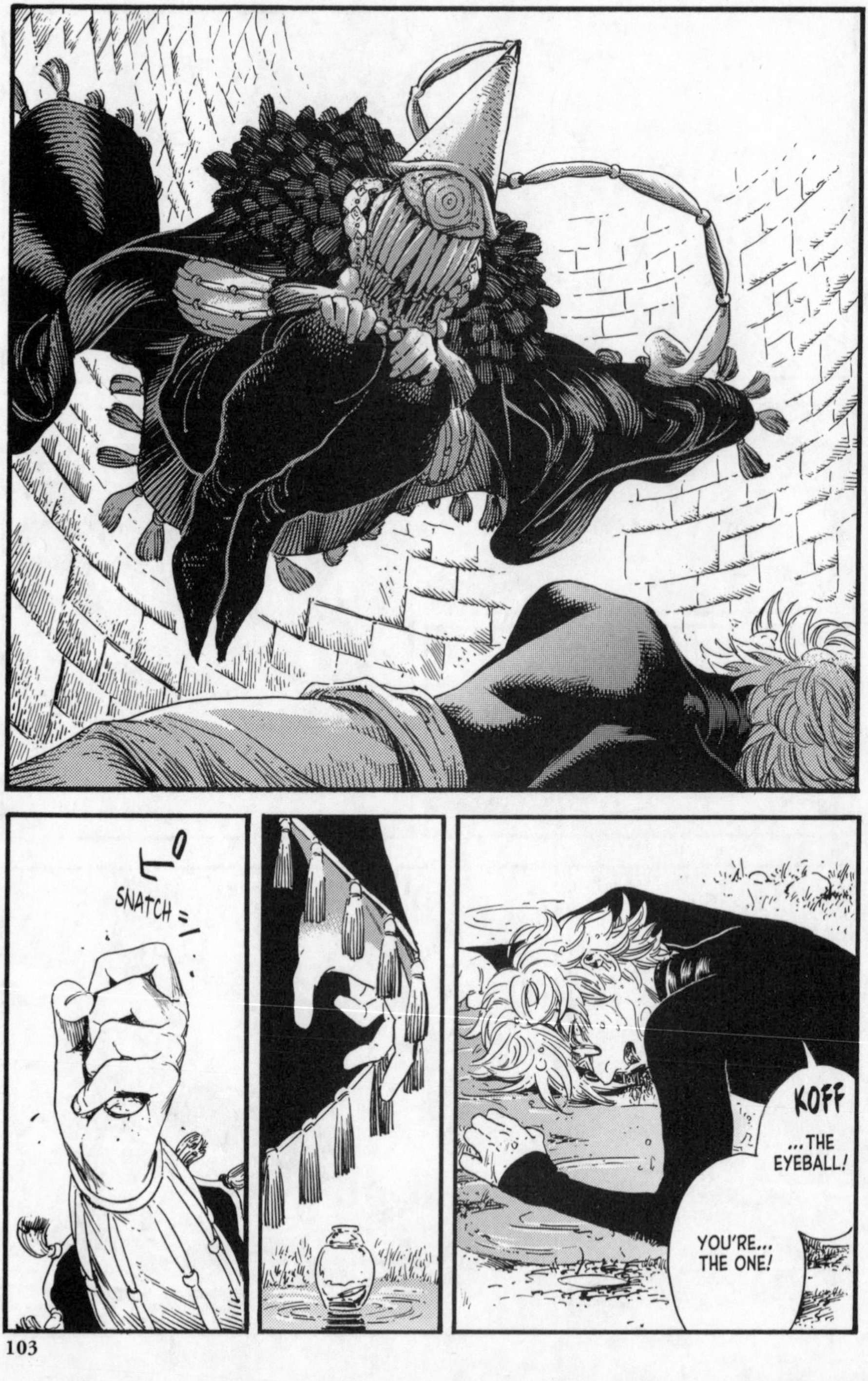
KOFF
...THE EYEBALL!
YOU'RE... THE ONE!
SNATCH

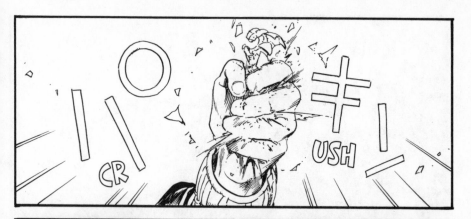

I'M NOT DONE WITH—

W...

WAIT.

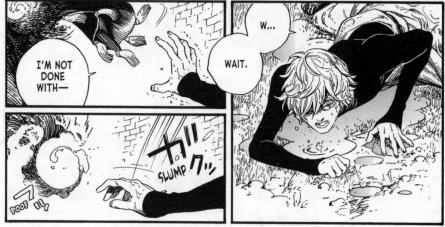

SLUMP

POOF

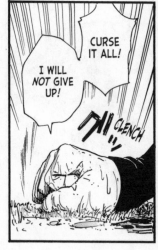

CURSE IT ALL!

I WILL *NOT* GIVE UP!

CLENCH

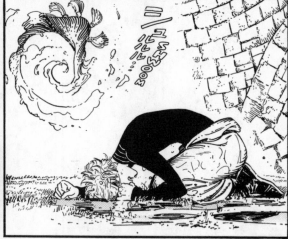

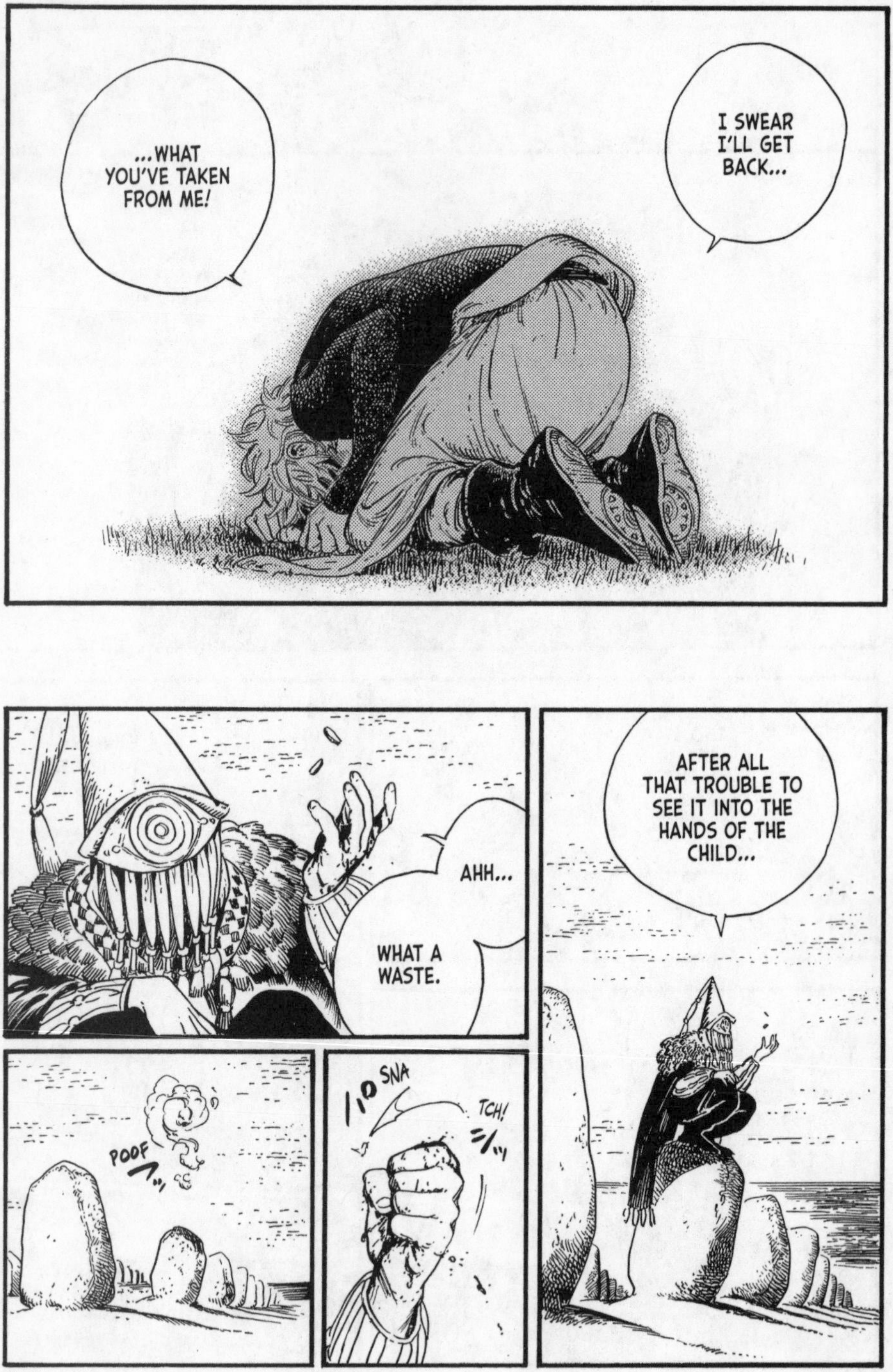
I SWEAR I'LL GET BACK...
...WHAT YOU'VE TAKEN FROM ME!
AFTER ALL THAT TROUBLE TO SEE IT INTO THE HANDS OF THE CHILD...
AHH...
WHAT A WASTE.
SNA
TCH!
POOF

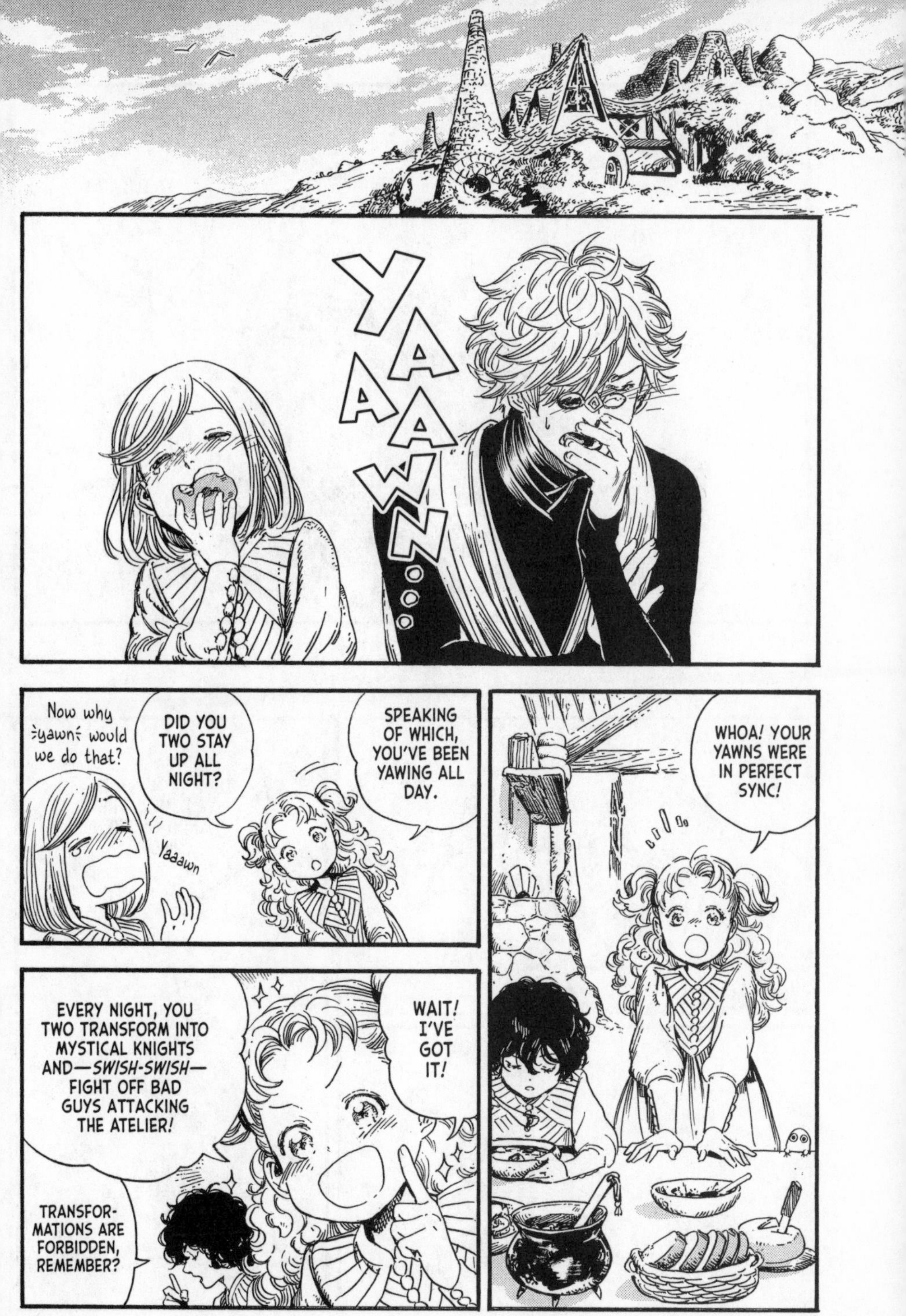

YAAAWN
WHOA! YOUR YAWNS WERE IN PERFECT SYNC!
SPEAKING OF WHICH, YOU'VE BEEN YAWING ALL DAY.
DID YOU TWO STAY UP ALL NIGHT?
Now why ≈yawn≈ would we do that?
Yaaawn
WAIT! I'VE GOT IT!
EVERY NIGHT, YOU TWO TRANSFORM INTO MYSTICAL KNIGHTS AND—*SWISH-SWISH*—FIGHT OFF BAD GUYS ATTACKING THE ATELIER!
TRANSFORMATIONS ARE FORBIDDEN, REMEMBER?

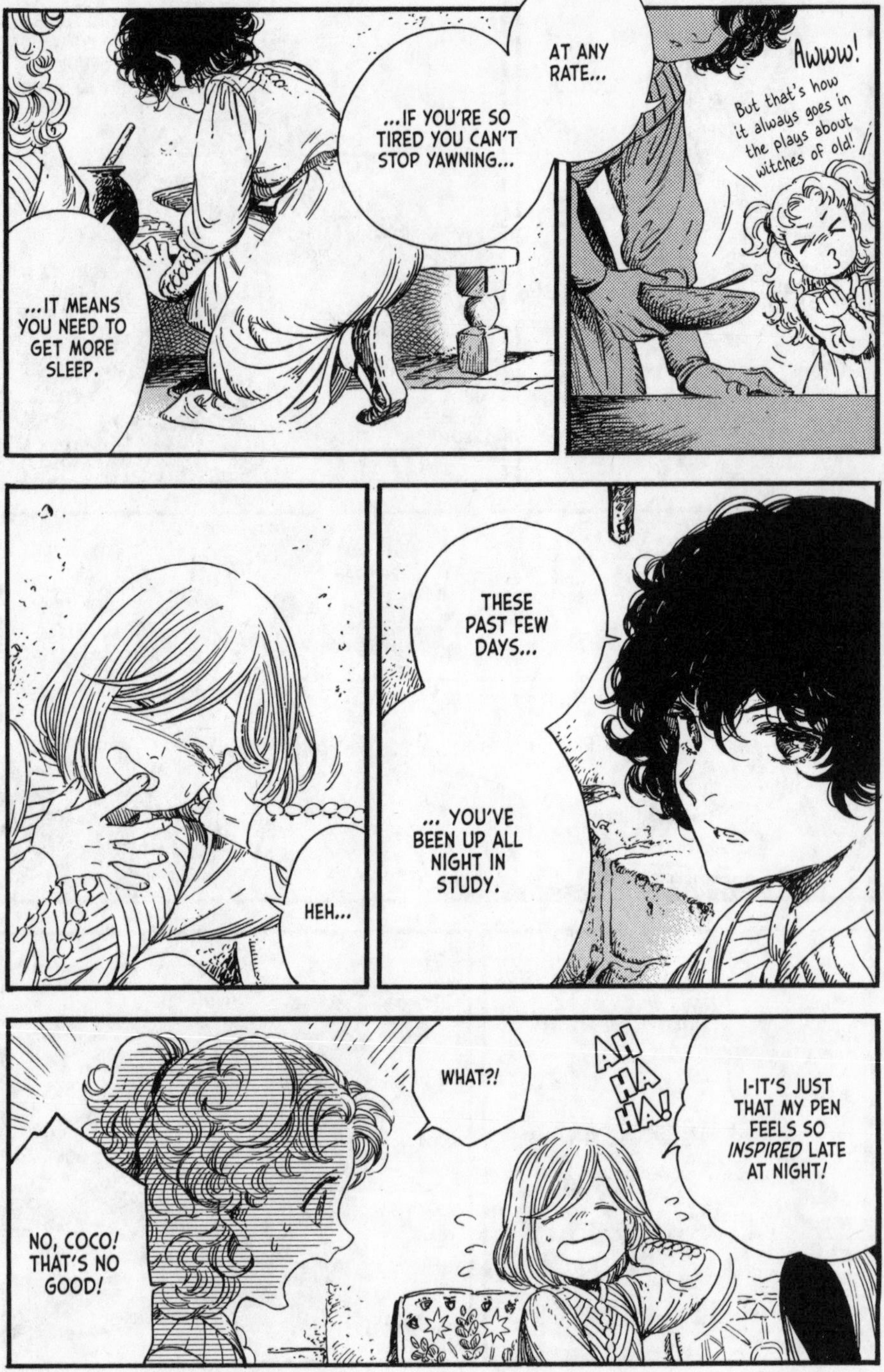
Awww!
But that's how it always goes in the plays about witches of old!
AT ANY RATE...
...IF YOU'RE SO TIRED YOU CAN'T STOP YAWNING...
...IT MEANS YOU NEED TO GET MORE SLEEP.
THESE PAST FEW DAYS...
... YOU'VE BEEN UP ALL NIGHT IN STUDY.
HEH...
I-IT'S JUST THAT MY PEN FEELS SO *INSPIRED* LATE AT NIGHT!
AH HA HA!
WHAT?!
NO, COCO! THAT'S NO GOOD!

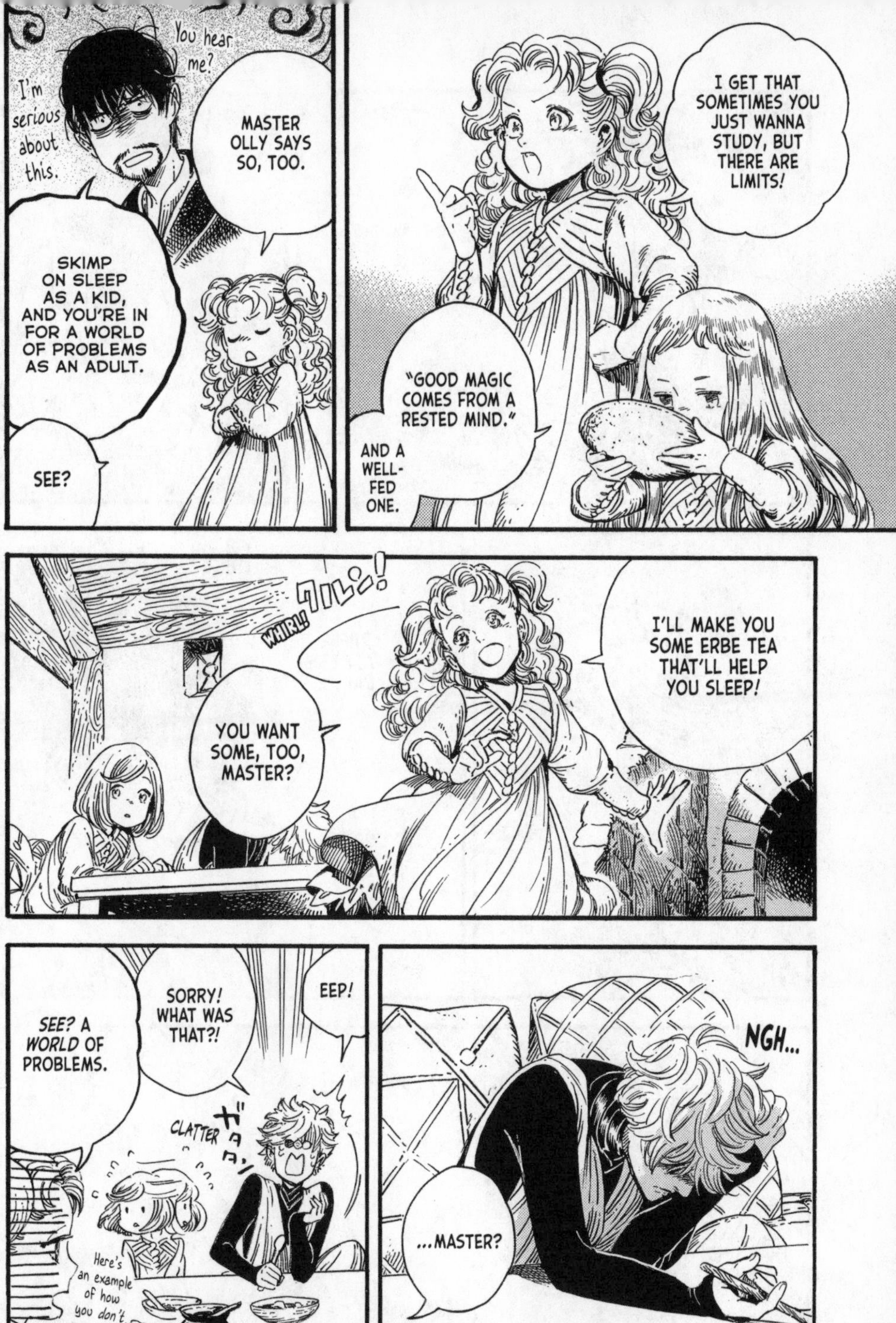
I GET THAT SOMETIMES YOU JUST WANNA STUDY, BUT THERE ARE LIMITS!
"GOOD MAGIC COMES FROM A RESTED MIND."
AND A WELL-FED ONE.
You hear me?
MASTER OLLY SAYS SO, TOO.
I'm serious about this.
SKIMP ON SLEEP AS A KID, AND YOU'RE IN FOR A WORLD OF PROBLEMS AS AN ADULT.
SEE?
I'LL MAKE YOU SOME ERBE TEA THAT'LL HELP YOU SLEEP!
WHIRL!
YOU WANT SOME, TOO, MASTER?
NGH...
...MASTER?
EEP!
SORRY! WHAT WAS THAT?!
CLATTER
SEE? A WORLD OF PROBLEMS.
Here's an example of how you don't wanna be.

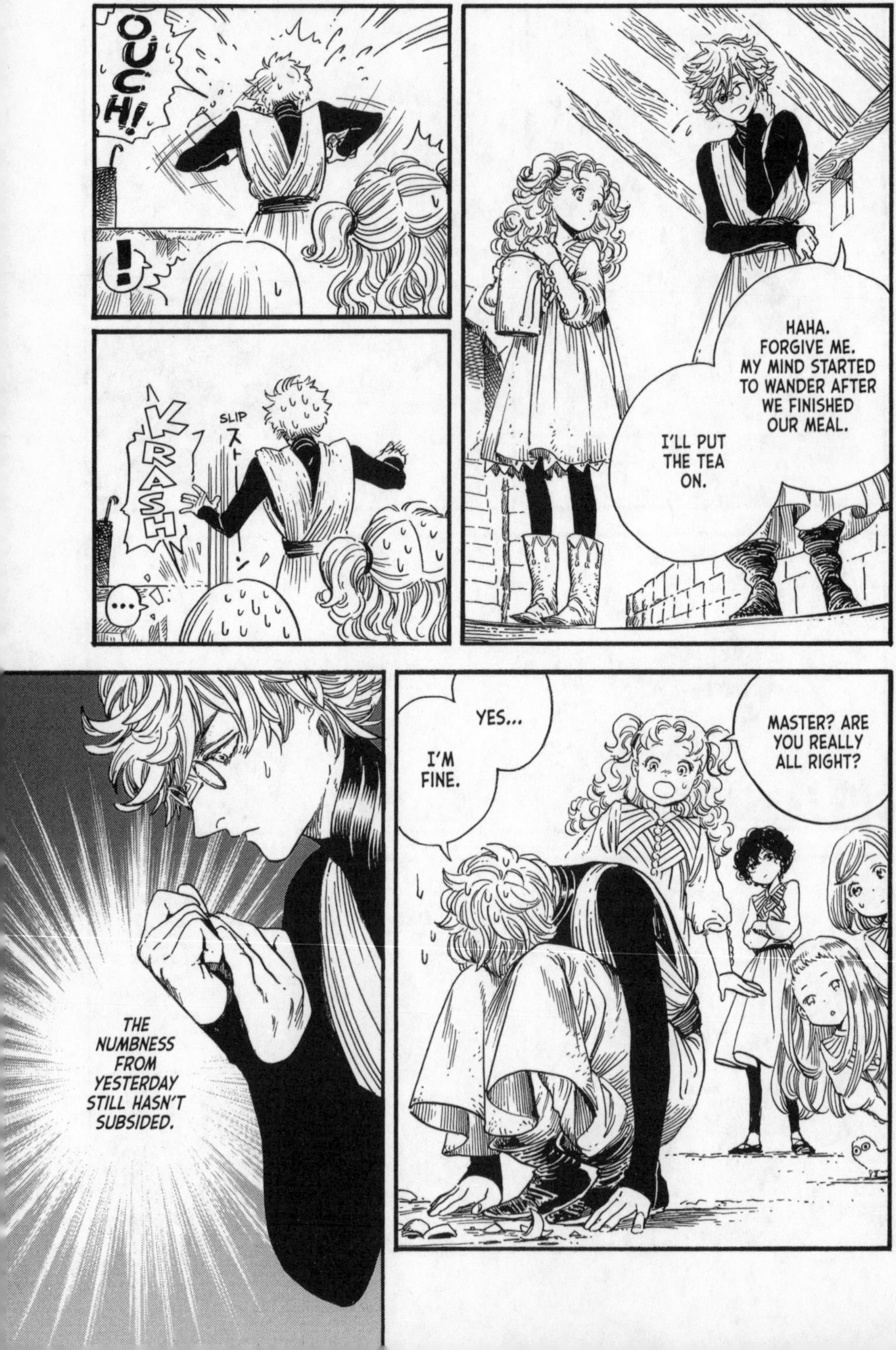
HAHA. FORGIVE ME. MY MIND STARTED TO WANDER AFTER WE FINISHED OUR MEAL.
I'LL PUT THE TEA ON.
OUCH!
!
SLIP
スト
KRASH
...
MASTER? ARE YOU REALLY ALL RIGHT?
YES...
I'M FINE.
THE NUMBNESS FROM YESTERDAY STILL HASN'T SUBSIDED.

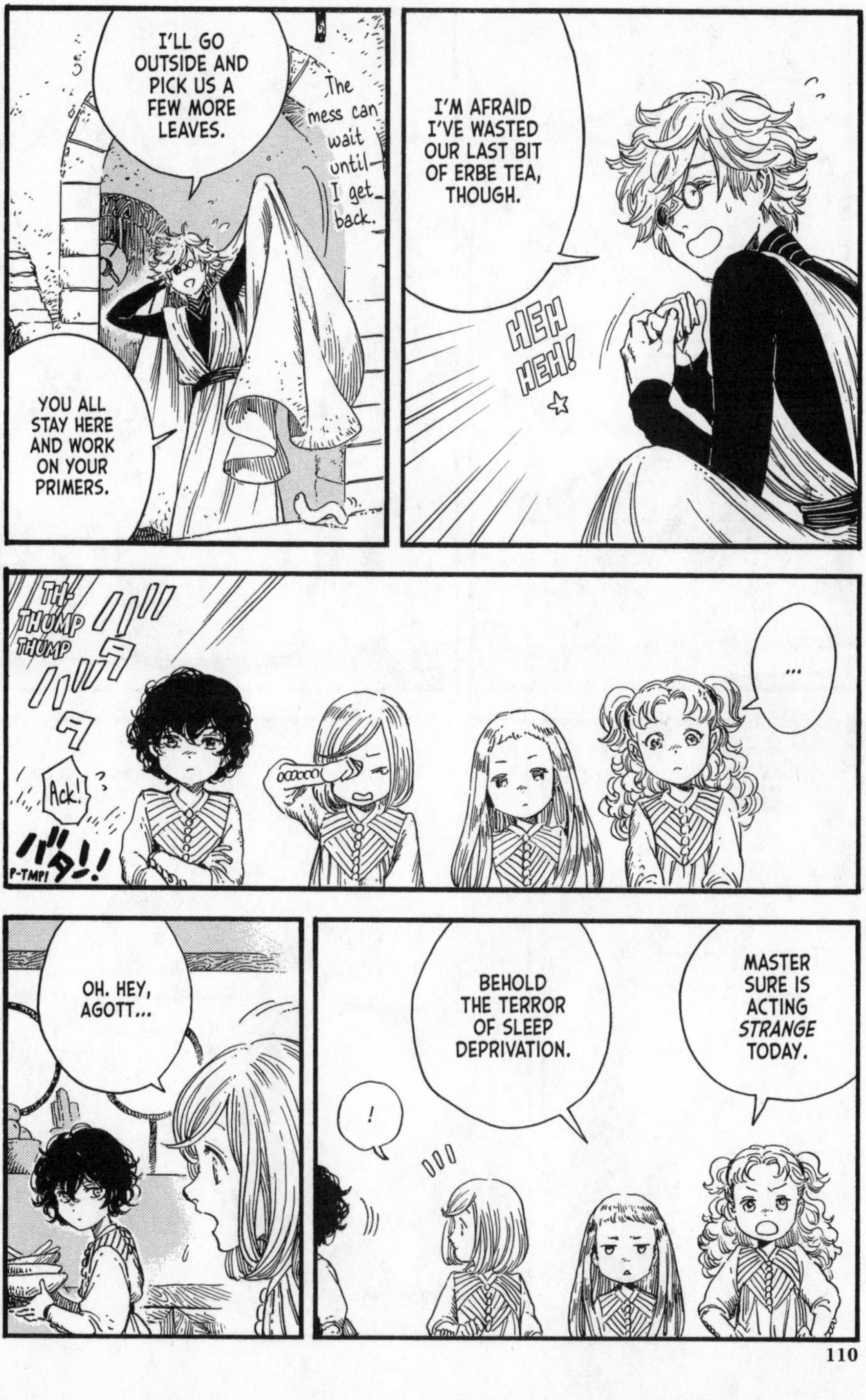
I'M AFRAID I'VE WASTED OUR LAST BIT OF ERBE TEA, THOUGH.
HEH HEH!
I'LL GO OUTSIDE AND PICK US A FEW MORE LEAVES.
The mess can wait until I get back.
YOU ALL STAY HERE AND WORK ON YOUR PRIMERS.
...
TH-THUMP THUMP
Ack!
P-TMP!
MASTER SURE IS ACTING STRANGE TODAY.
BEHOLD THE TERROR OF SLEEP DEPRIVATION.
!
OH. HEY, AGOTT...

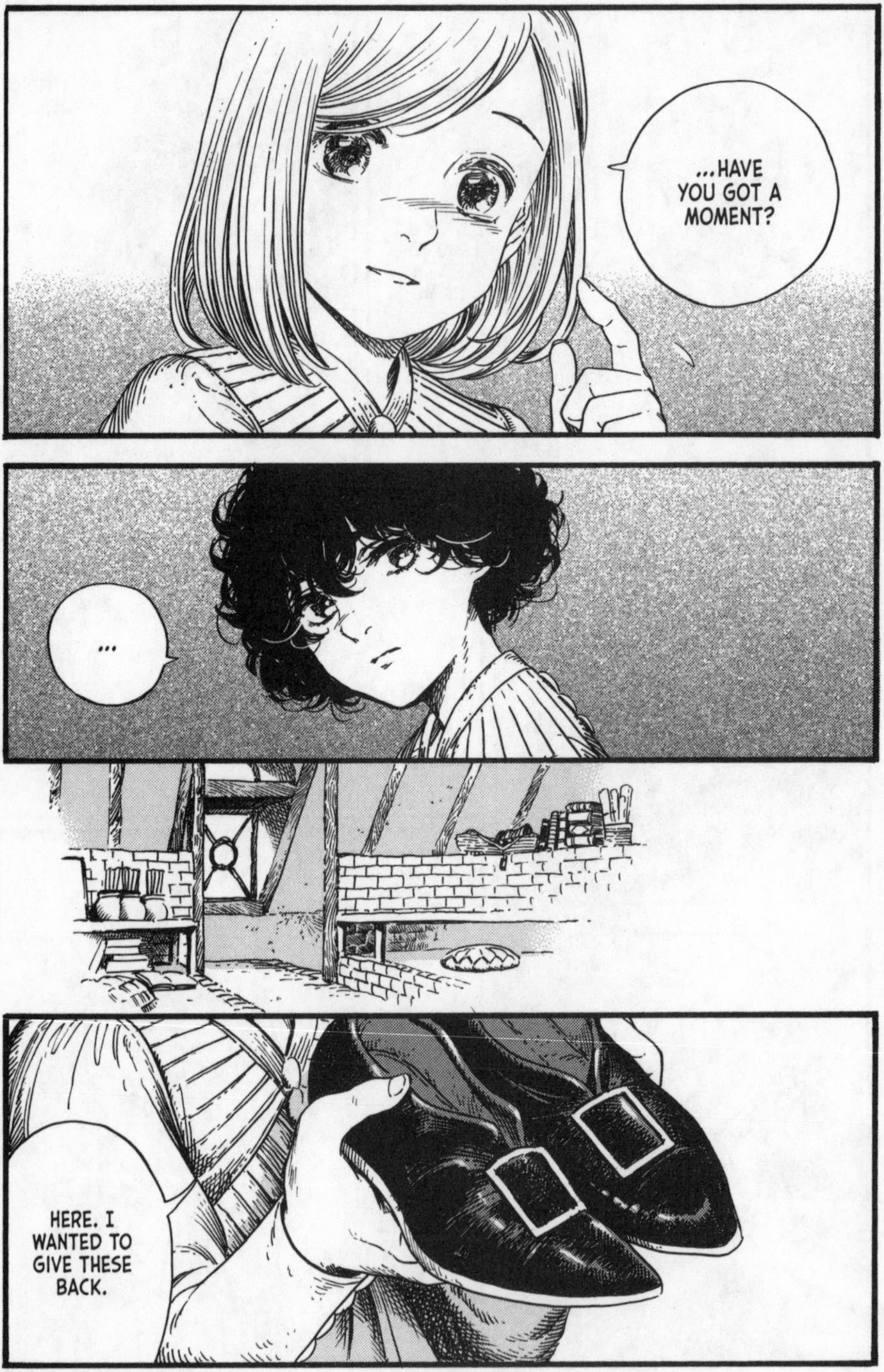
...HAVE YOU GOT A MOMENT?
...
HERE. I WANTED TO GIVE THESE BACK.

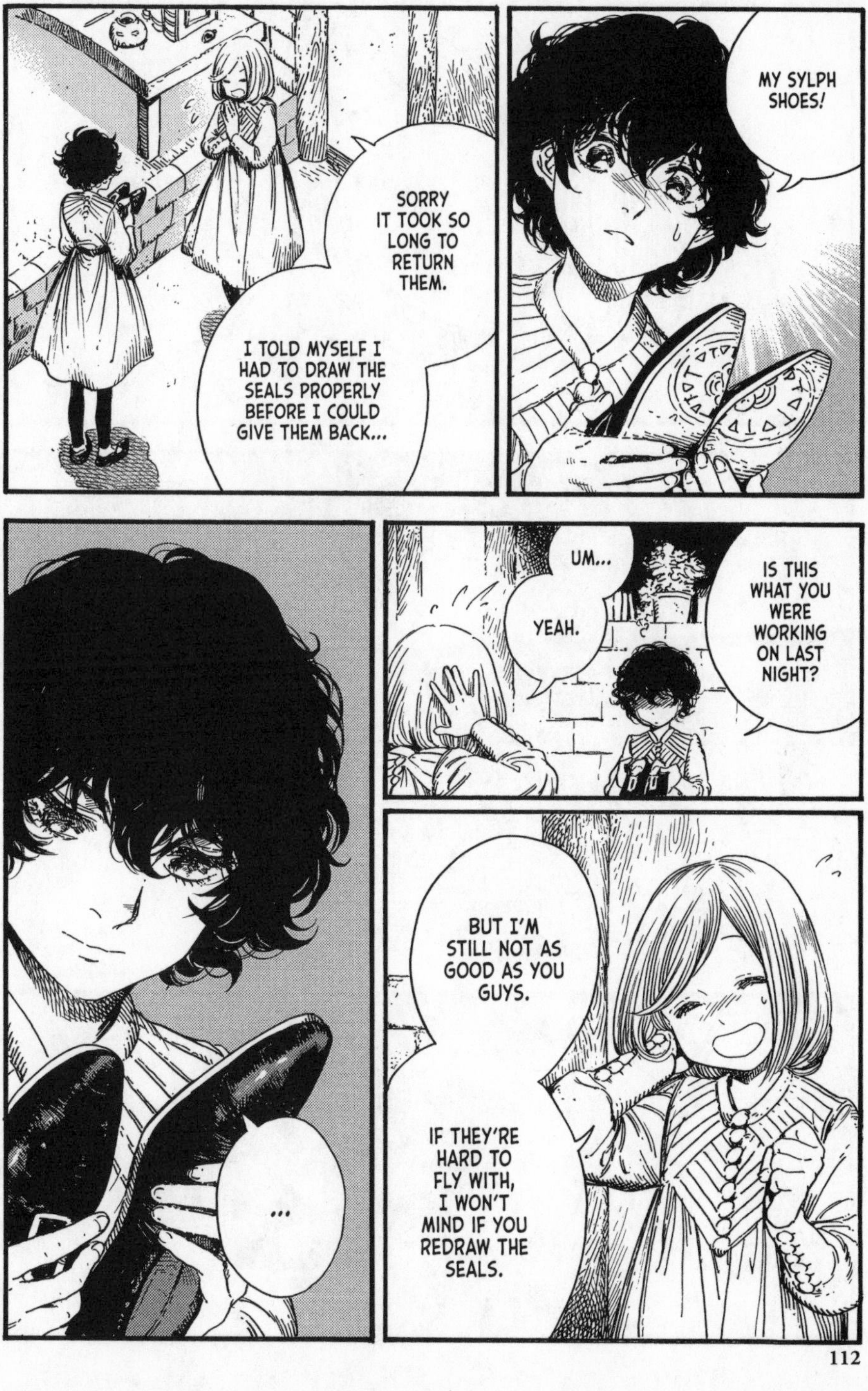
MY SYLPH SHOES!
SORRY IT TOOK SO LONG TO RETURN THEM.
I TOLD MYSELF I HAD TO DRAW THE SEALS PROPERLY BEFORE I COULD GIVE THEM BACK...
IS THIS WHAT YOU WERE WORKING ON LAST NIGHT?
UM...
YEAH.
BUT I'M STILL NOT AS GOOD AS YOU GUYS.
IF THEY'RE HARD TO FLY WITH, I WON'T MIND IF YOU REDRAW THE SEALS.
...

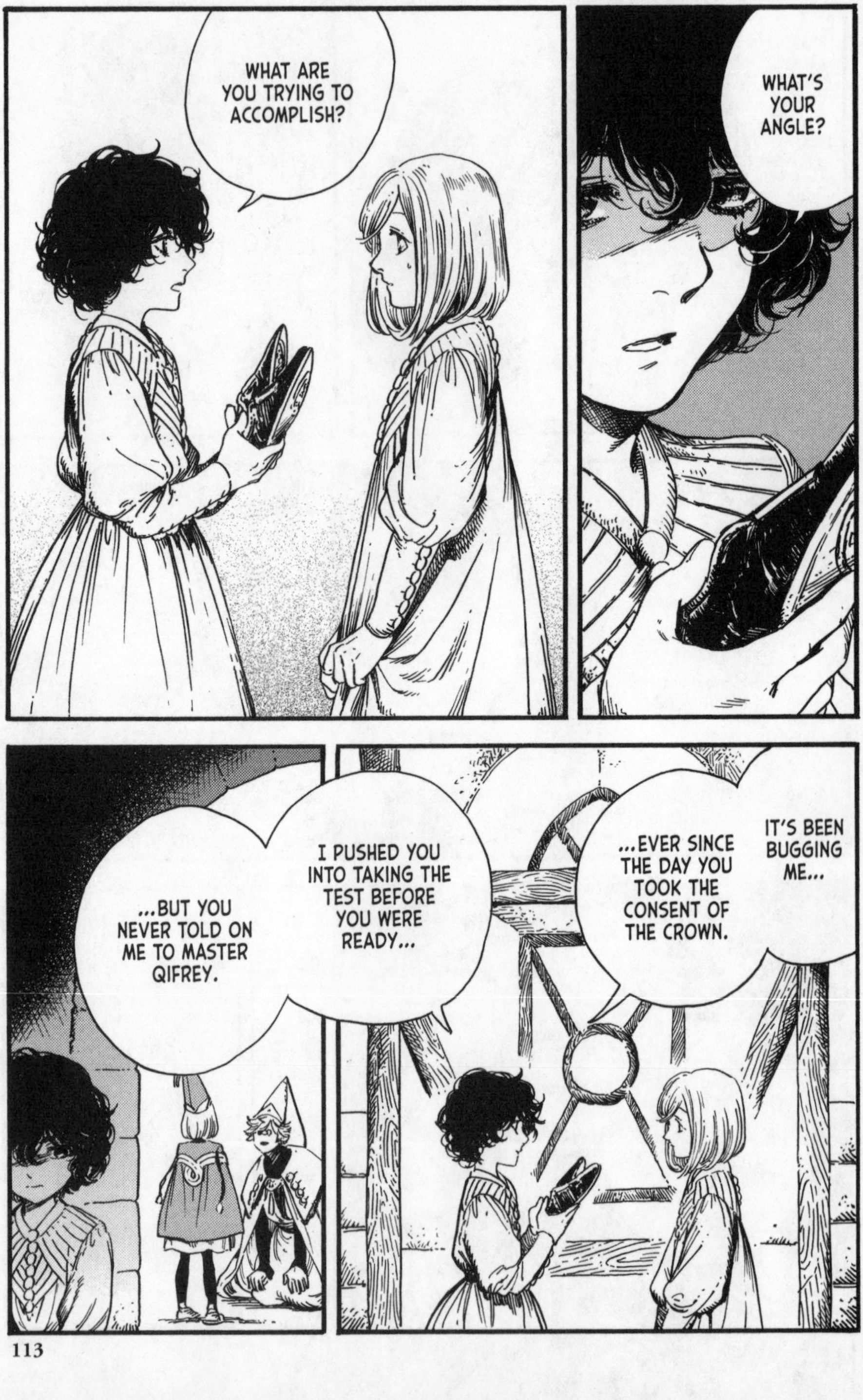
WHAT'S YOUR ANGLE?
WHAT ARE YOU TRYING TO ACCOMPLISH?
IT'S BEEN BUGGING ME...
...EVER SINCE THE DAY YOU TOOK THE CONSENT OF THE CROWN.
I PUSHED YOU INTO TAKING THE TEST BEFORE YOU WERE READY...
...BUT YOU NEVER TOLD ON ME TO MASTER QIFREY.

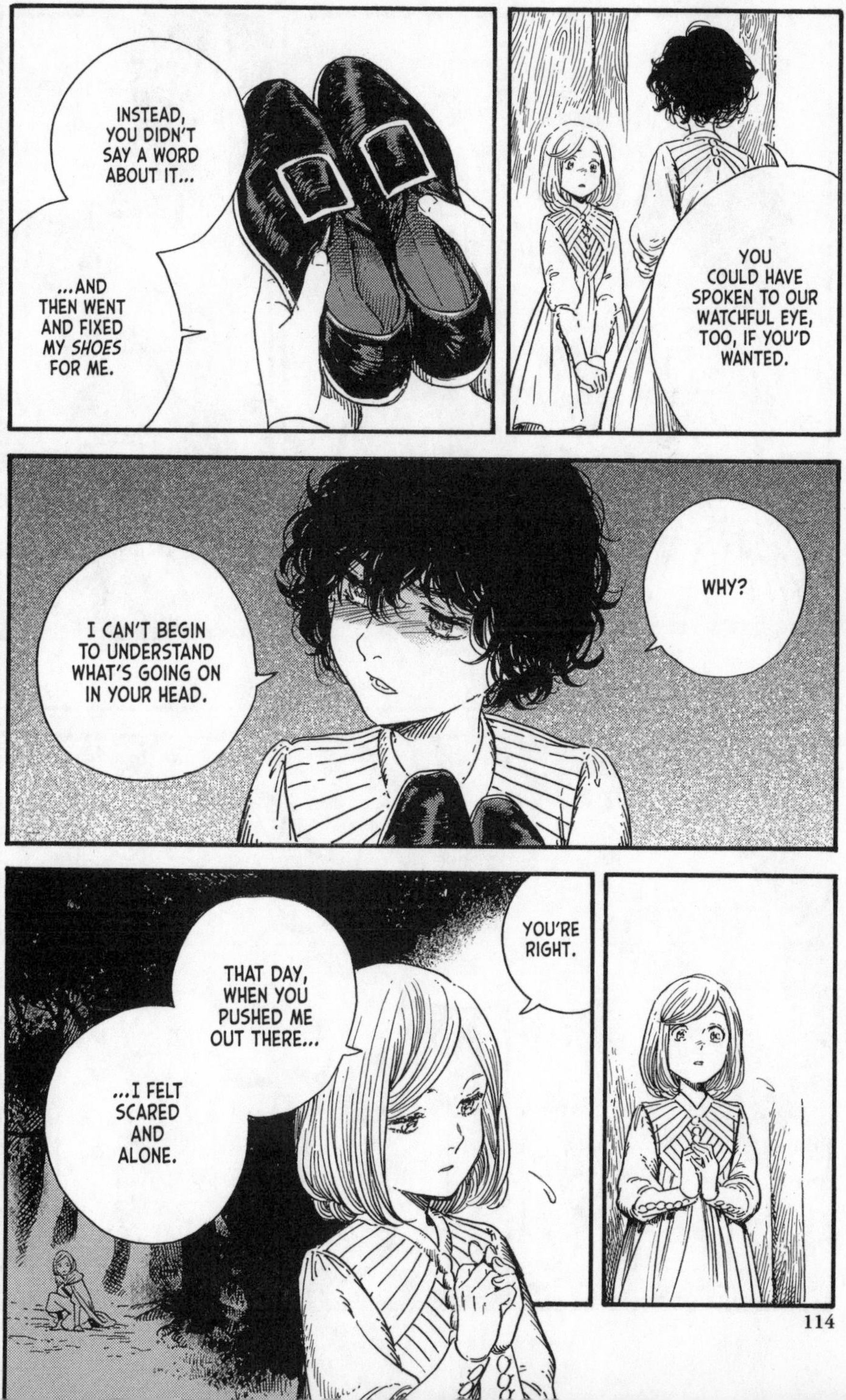
YOU COULD HAVE SPOKEN TO OUR WATCHFUL EYE, TOO, IF YOU'D WANTED.
INSTEAD, YOU DIDN'T SAY A WORD ABOUT IT...
...AND THEN WENT AND FIXED MY *SHOES* FOR ME.
WHY?
I CAN'T BEGIN TO UNDERSTAND WHAT'S GOING ON IN YOUR HEAD.
YOU'RE RIGHT.
THAT DAY, WHEN YOU PUSHED ME OUT THERE...
...I FELT SCARED AND ALONE.

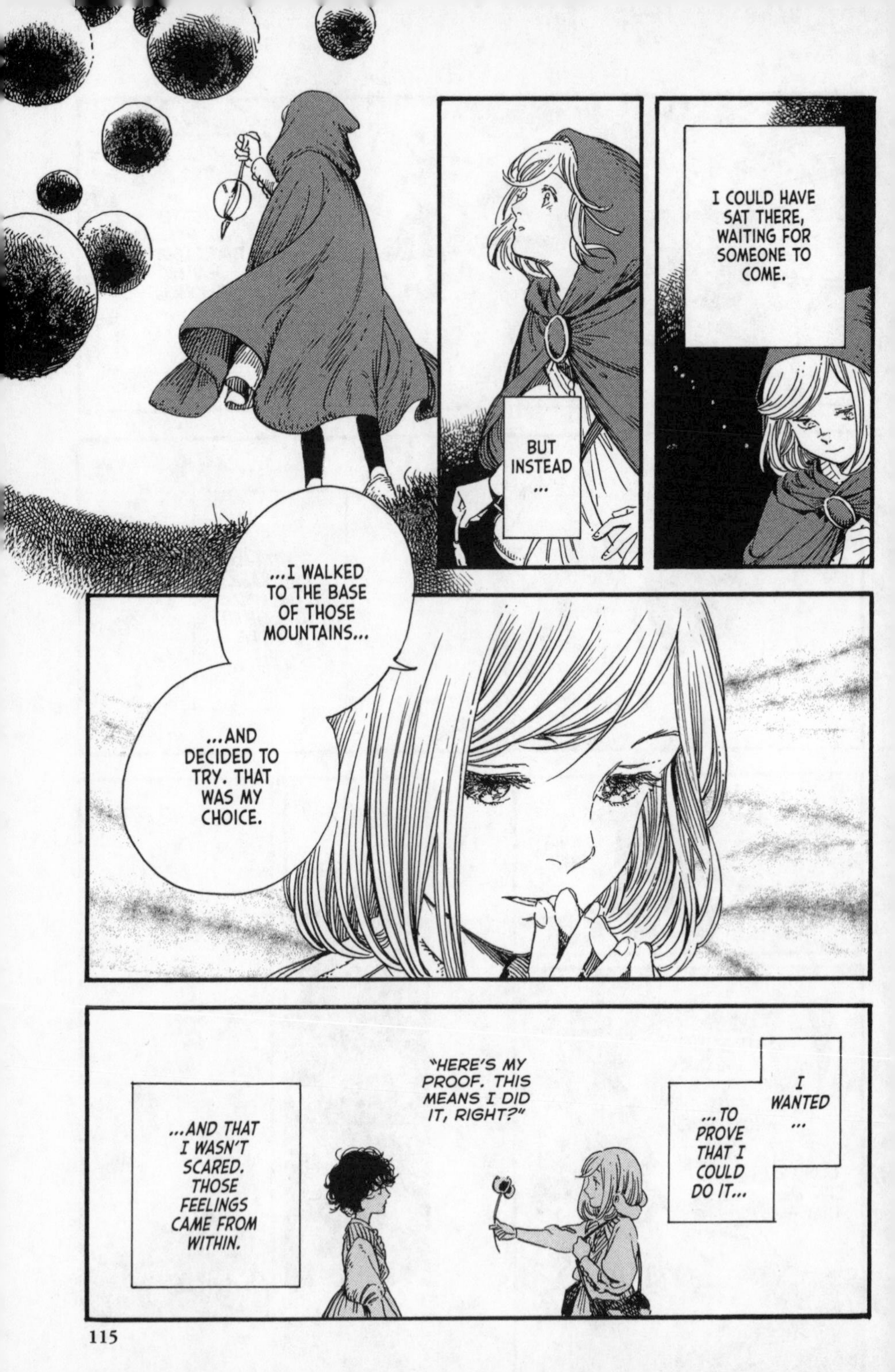
I COULD HAVE SAT THERE, WAITING FOR SOMEONE TO COME.
BUT INSTEAD ...
...I WALKED TO THE BASE OF THOSE MOUNTAINS...
...AND DECIDED TO TRY. THAT WAS MY CHOICE.
I WANTED ...
...TO PROVE THAT I COULD DO IT...
"HERE'S MY PROOF. THIS MEANS I DID IT, RIGHT?"
...AND THAT I WASN'T SCARED. THOSE FEELINGS CAME FROM WITHIN.

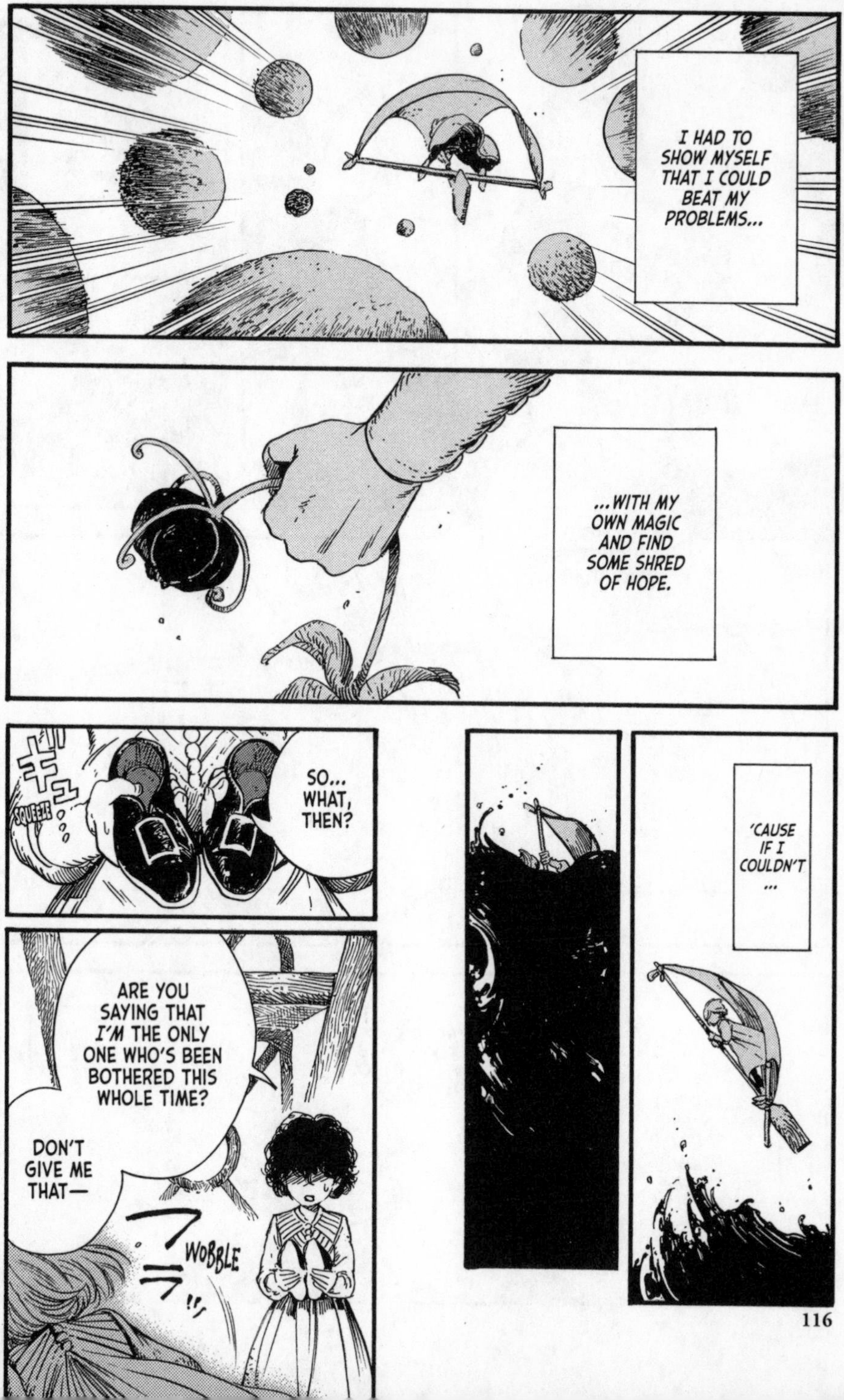
I HAD TO SHOW MYSELF THAT I COULD BEAT MY PROBLEMS...
...WITH MY OWN MAGIC AND FIND SOME SHRED OF HOPE.
'CAUSE IF I COULDN'T ...
SQUEEZE
SO... WHAT, THEN?
ARE YOU SAYING THAT *I'M* THE ONLY ONE WHO'S BEEN BOTHERED THIS WHOLE TIME?
DON'T GIVE ME THAT—
WOBBLE

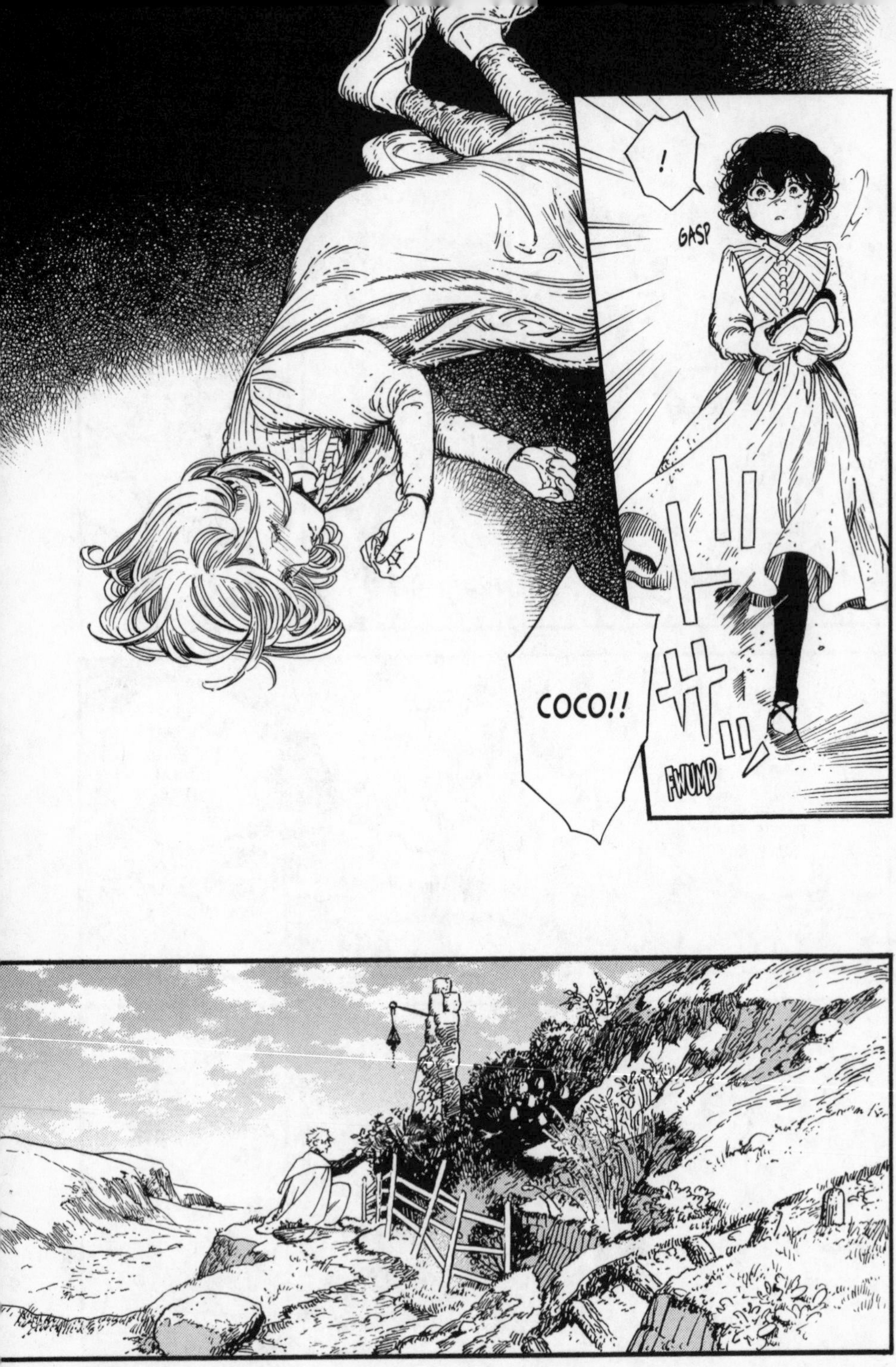
!
GASP
FWUMP
COCO!!

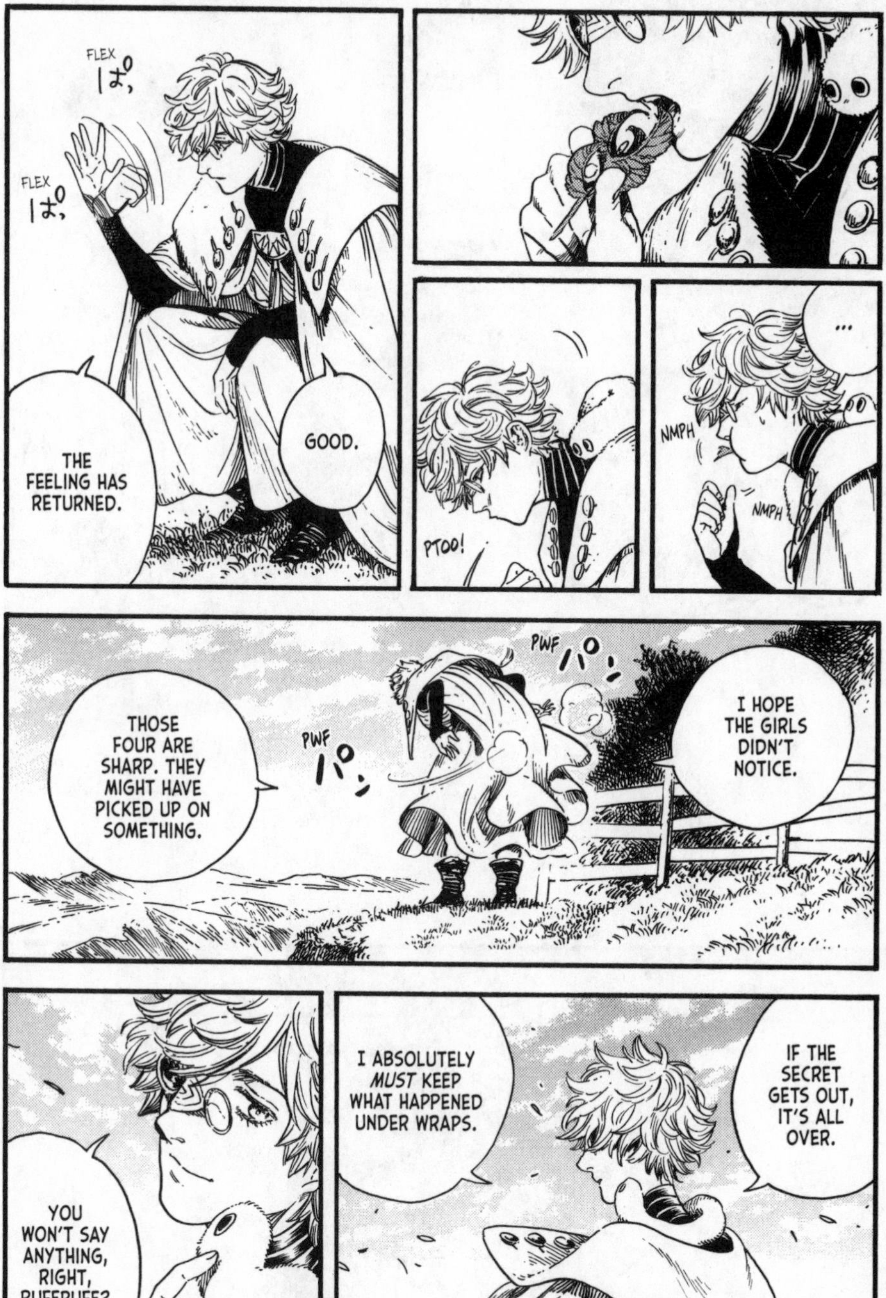
...
NMPH
NMPH
PTOO!
FLEX
ぱっ
FLEX
ぱっ
GOOD.
THE FEELING HAS RETURNED.
I HOPE THE GIRLS DIDN'T NOTICE.
PWF
パン
PWF
パン
THOSE FOUR ARE SHARP. THEY MIGHT HAVE PICKED UP ON SOMETHING.
IF THE SECRET GETS OUT, IT'S ALL OVER.
I ABSOLUTELY *MUST* KEEP WHAT HAPPENED UNDER WRAPS.
YOU WON'T SAY ANYTHING, RIGHT, PUFFPUFF?

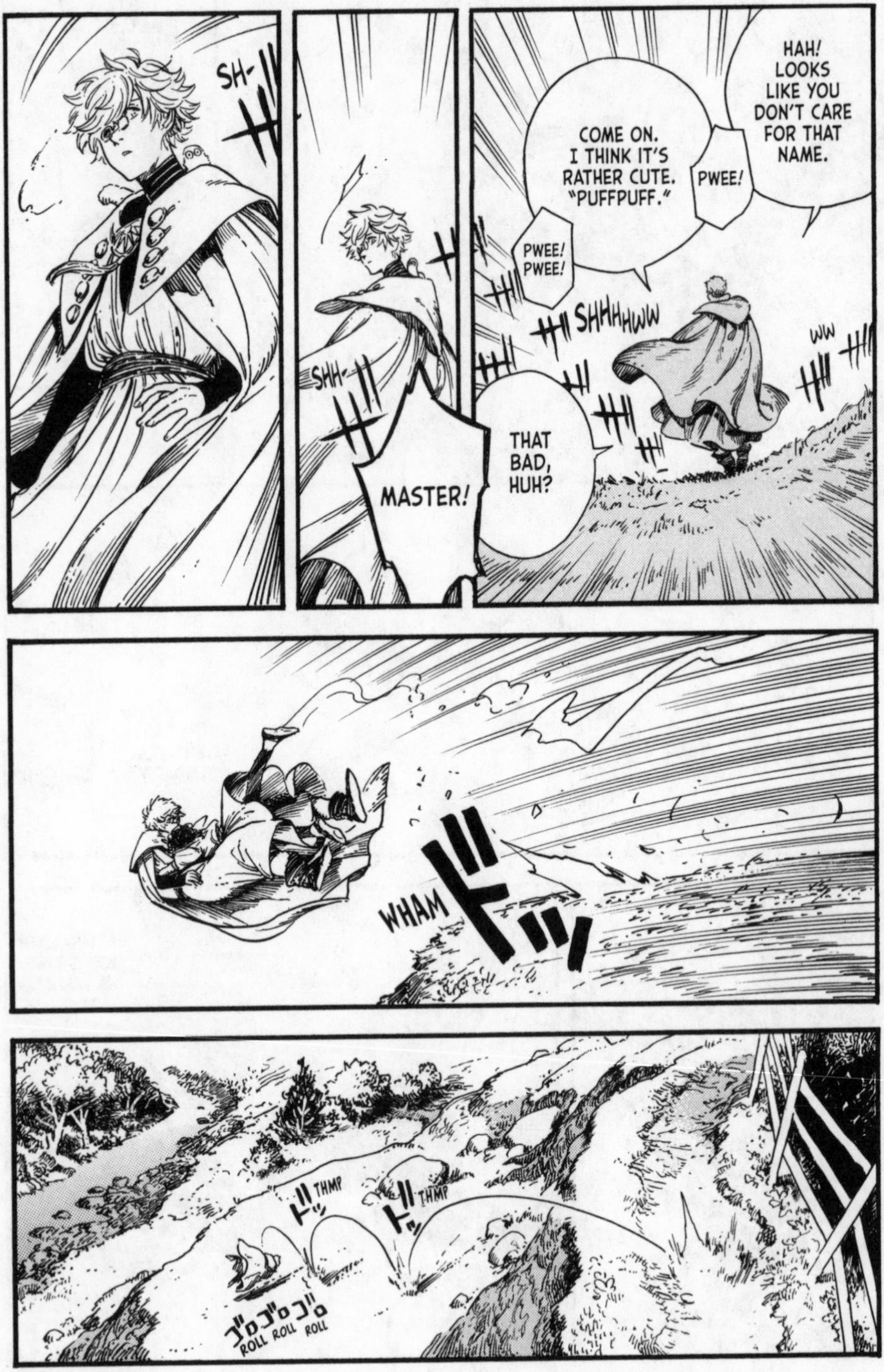
HAH! LOOKS LIKE YOU DON'T CARE FOR THAT NAME.
PWEE!
COME ON. I THINK IT'S RATHER CUTE. "PUFFPUFF."
PWEE! PWEE!
SHHHHWW
WW
THAT BAD, HUH?
SHH-
MASTER!
SH-
ドッ
WHAM
ドッ
THMP
ドッ
THMP
ゴロゴロゴロ
ROLL ROLL ROLL

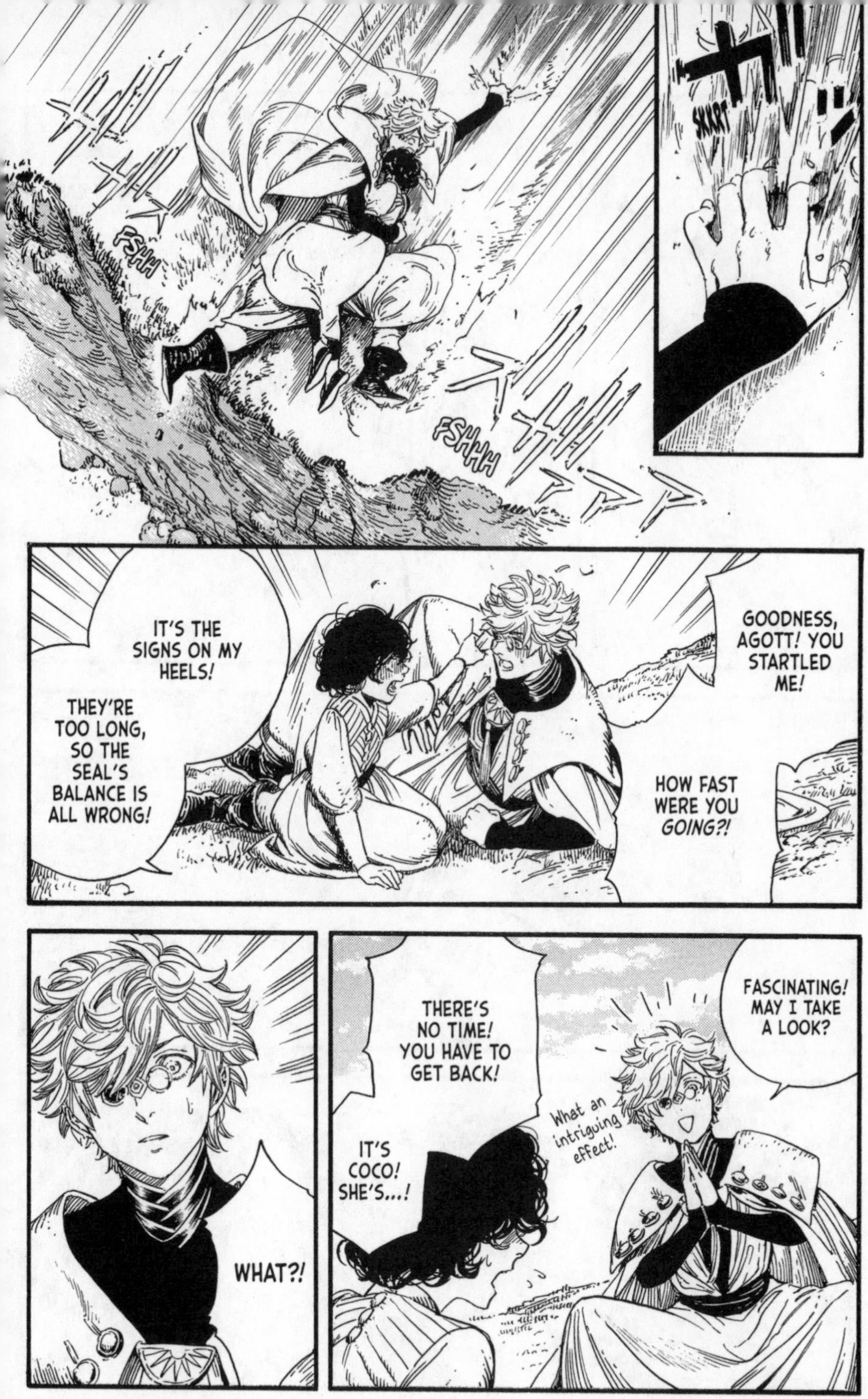
SKKRT
FSHH
FSHHH
GOODNESS, AGOTT! YOU STARTLED ME!
HOW FAST WERE YOU GOING?!
IT'S THE SIGNS ON MY HEELS!
THEY'RE TOO LONG, SO THE SEAL'S BALANCE IS ALL WRONG!
FASCINATING! MAY I TAKE A LOOK?
What an intriguing effect!
THERE'S NO TIME! YOU HAVE TO GET BACK!
IT'S COCO! SHE'S...!
WHAT?!

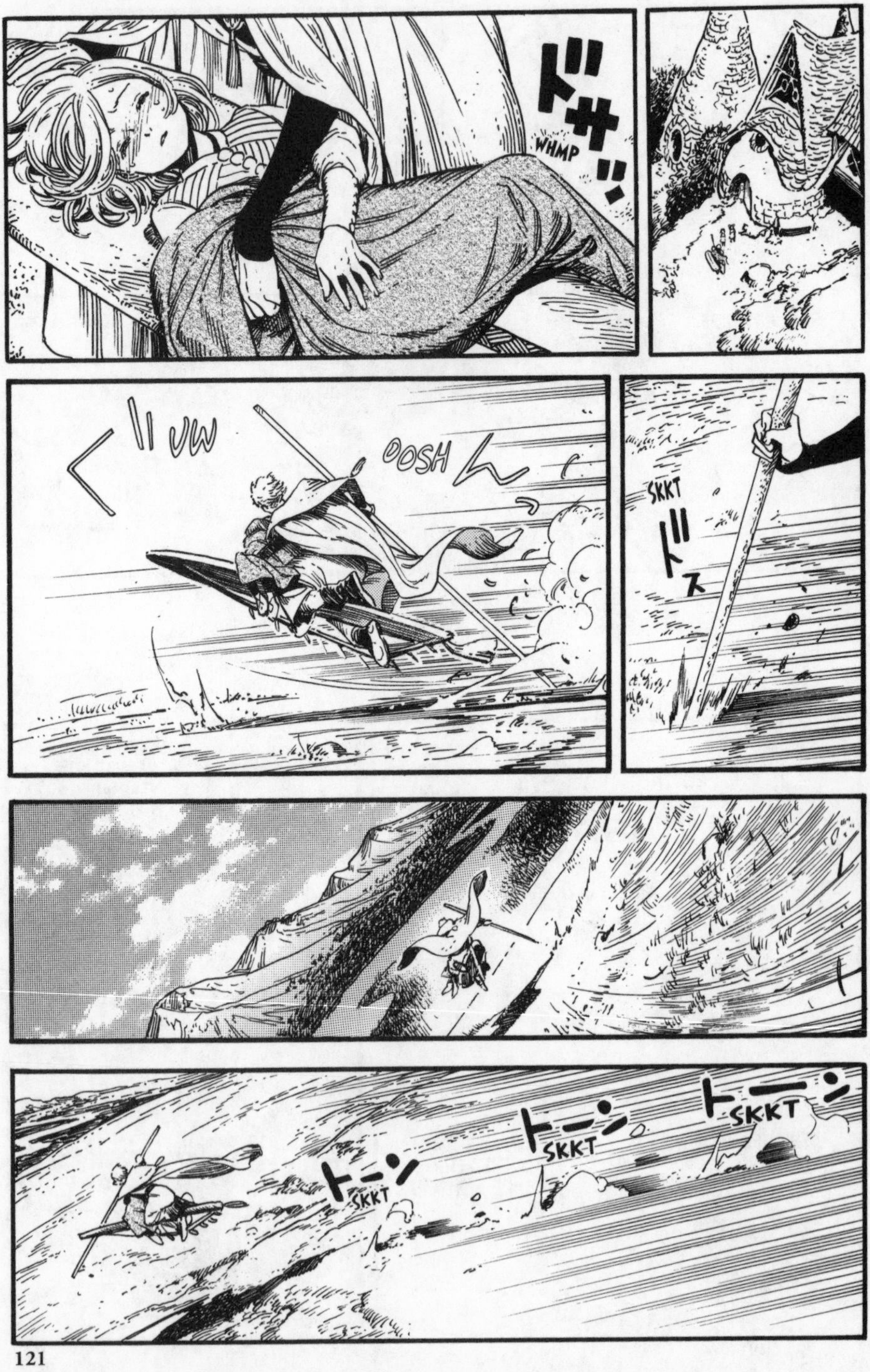
ドサッ
WHMP
ドス
SKKT
OOSH
トーーン
SKKT
トーン
SKKT
トーン
SKKT

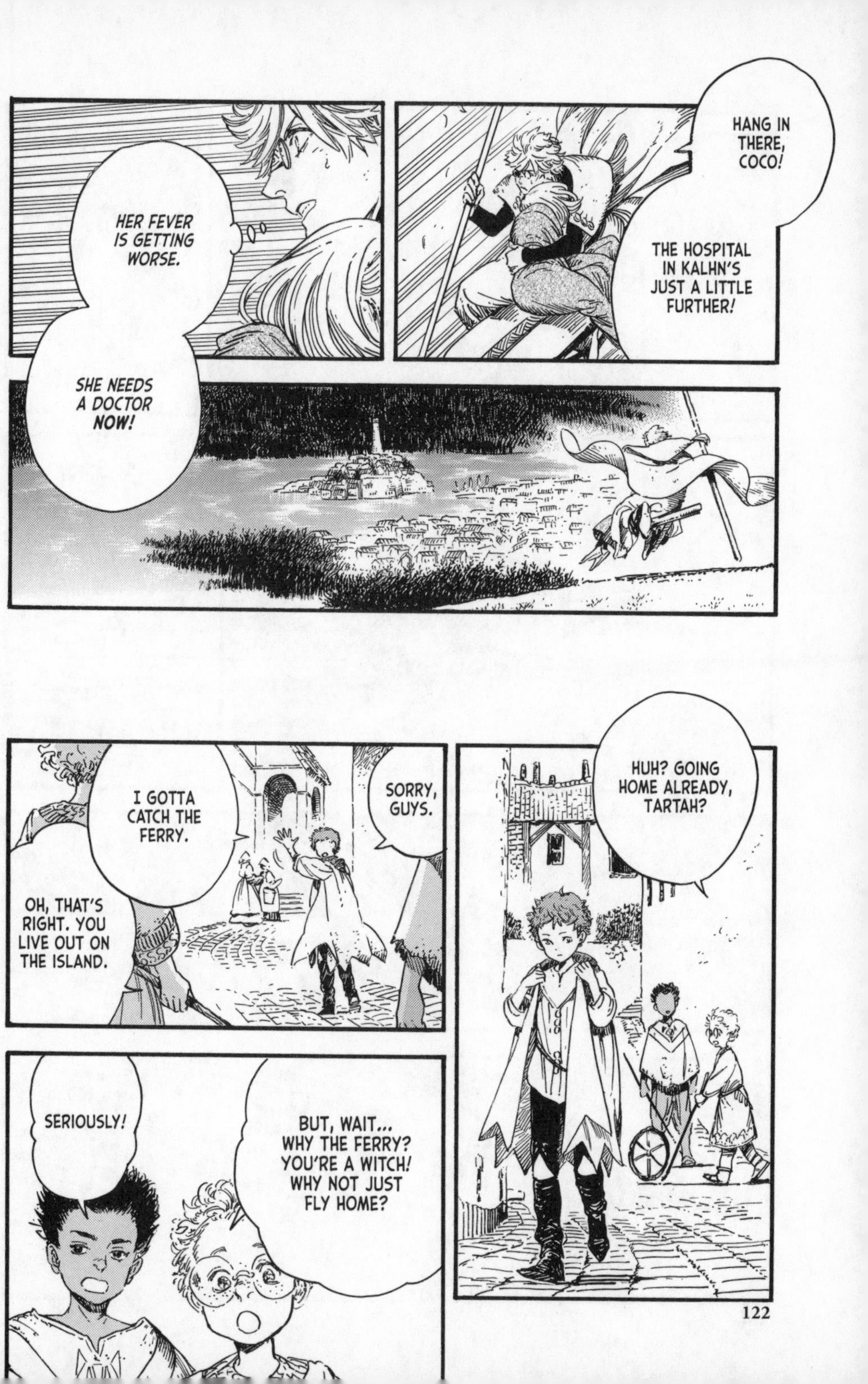
HANG IN THERE, COCO!
THE HOSPITAL IN KALHN'S JUST A LITTLE FURTHER!
HER FEVER IS GETTING WORSE.
SHE NEEDS A DOCTOR NOW!
HUH? GOING HOME ALREADY, TARTAH?
SORRY, GUYS.
I GOTTA CATCH THE FERRY.
OH, THAT'S RIGHT. YOU LIVE OUT ON THE ISLAND.
BUT, WAIT... WHY THE FERRY? YOU'RE A WITCH! WHY NOT JUST FLY HOME?
SERIOUSLY!

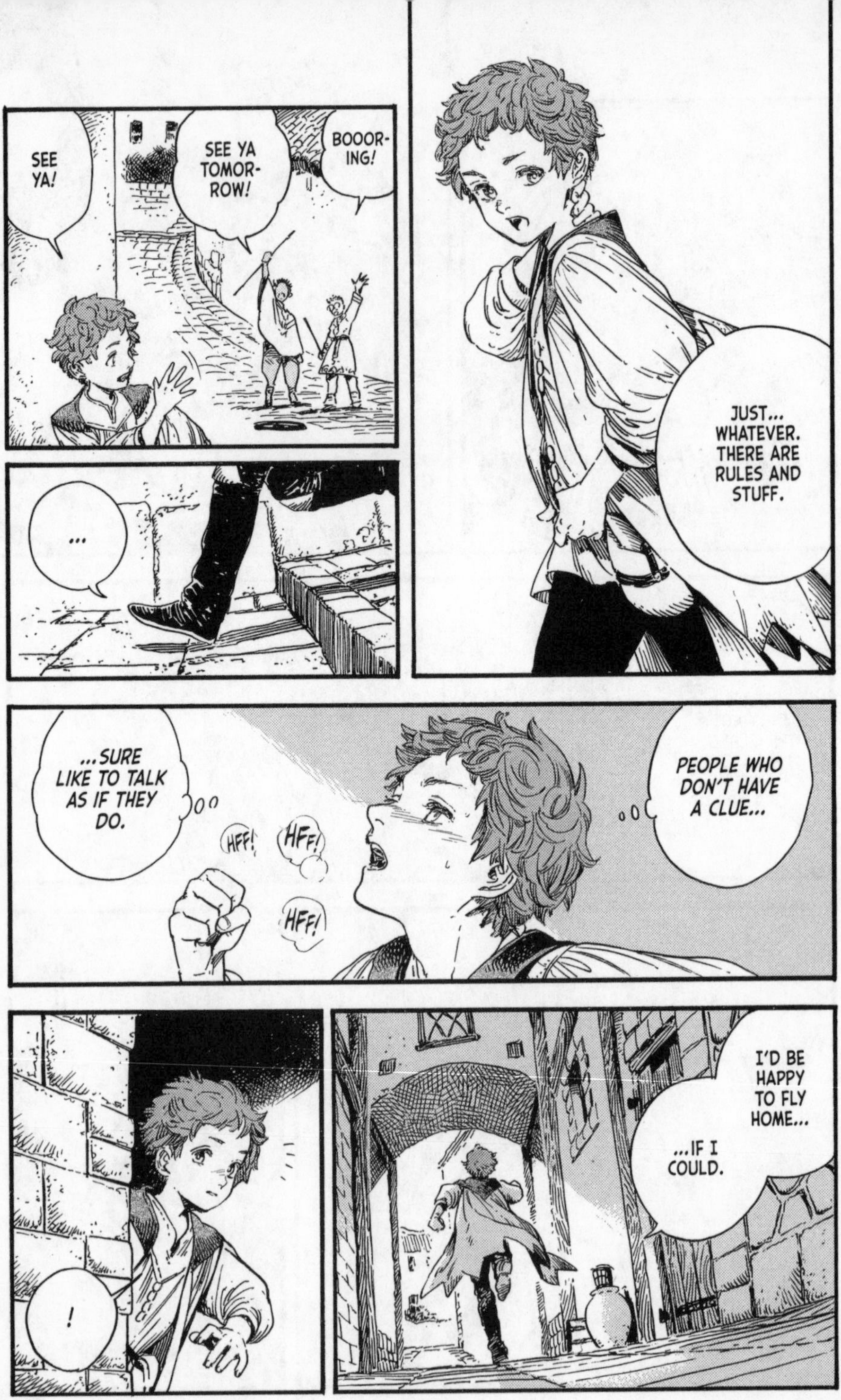
JUST... WHATEVER. THERE ARE RULES AND STUFF.
BOOORING!
SEE YA TOMORROW!
SEE YA!
...
PEOPLE WHO DON'T HAVE A CLUE...
HFF!
HFF!
HFF!
...SURE LIKE TO TALK AS IF THEY DO.
I'D BE HAPPY TO FLY HOME...
...IF I COULD.
!

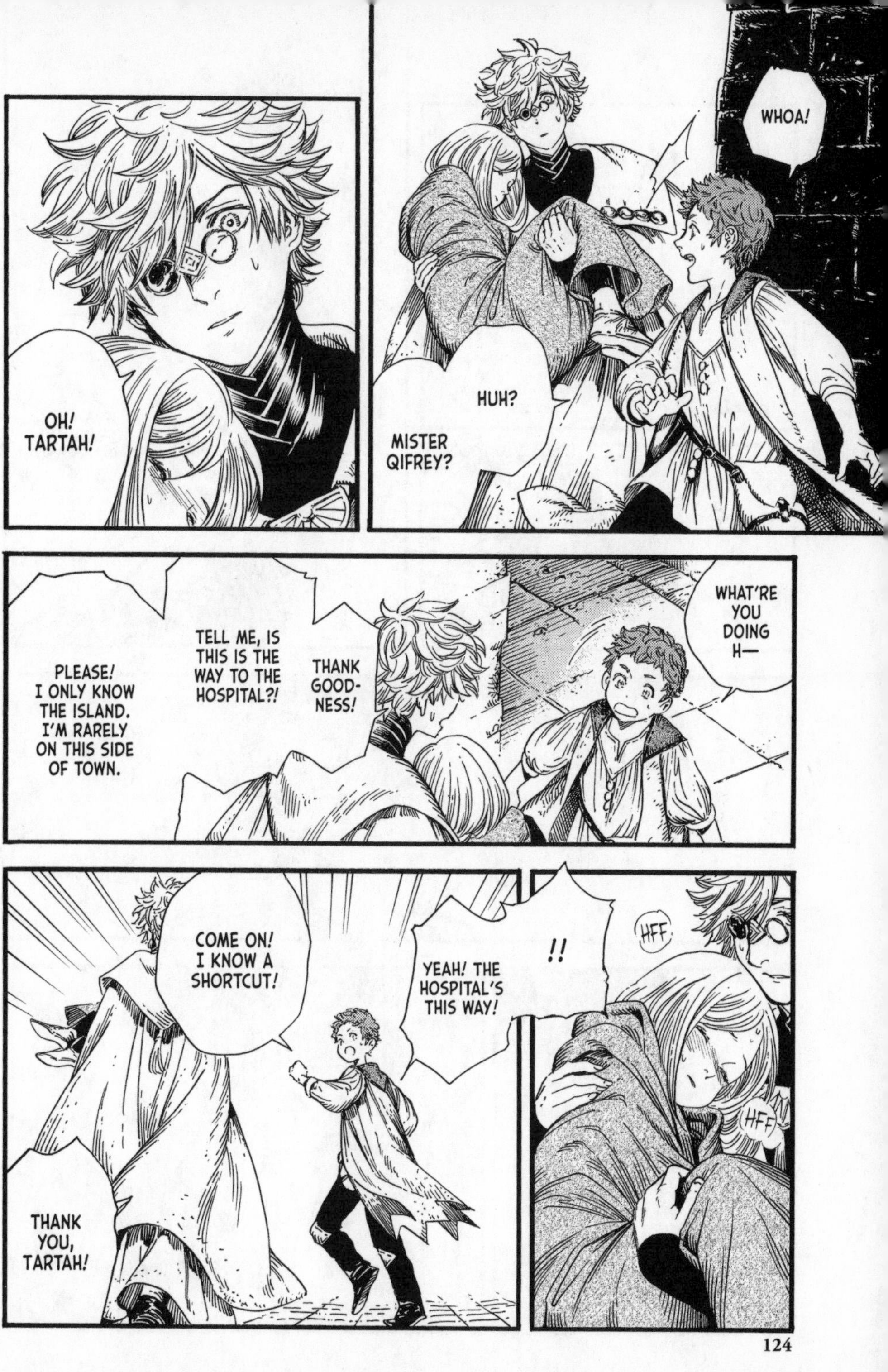
WHOA!
HUH?
MISTER QIFREY?
OH! TARTAH!
WHAT'RE YOU DOING H—
THANK GOOD-NESS!
TELL ME, IS THIS IS THE WAY TO THE HOSPITAL?!
PLEASE! I ONLY KNOW THE ISLAND. I'M RARELY ON THIS SIDE OF TOWN.
HFF
!!
HFF
YEAH! THE HOSPITAL'S THIS WAY!
COME ON! I KNOW A SHORTCUT!
THANK YOU, TARTAH!

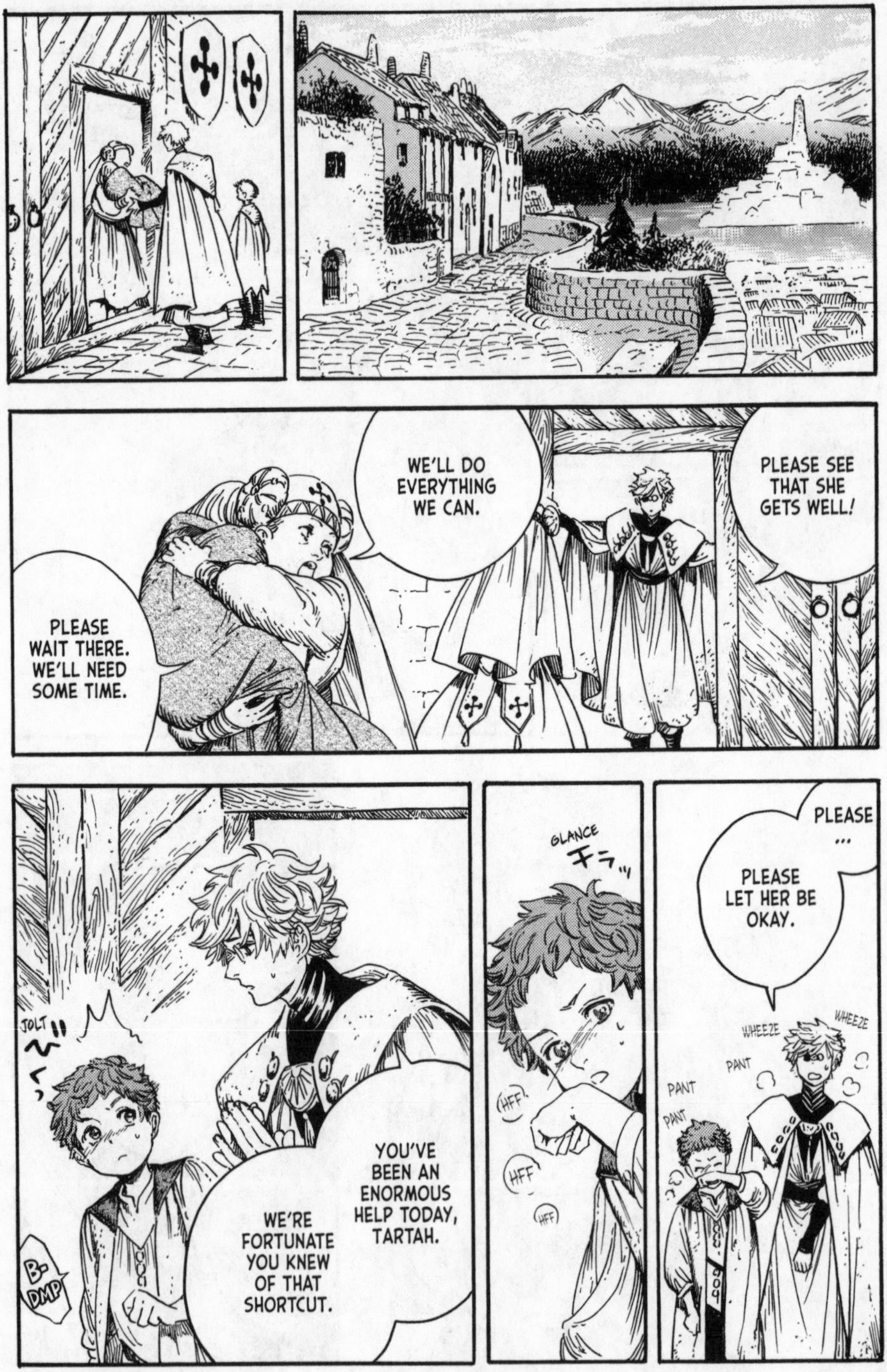
PLEASE SEE THAT SHE GETS WELL!
WE'LL DO EVERYTHING WE CAN.
PLEASE WAIT THERE. WE'LL NEED SOME TIME.
PLEASE ...
PLEASE LET HER BE OKAY.
WHEEZE
WHEEZE
PANT
PANT
PANT
GLANCE
HFF
HFF
HFF
JOLT
YOU'VE BEEN AN ENORMOUS HELP TODAY, TARTAH.
WE'RE FORTUNATE YOU KNEW OF THAT SHORTCUT.
B-DMP

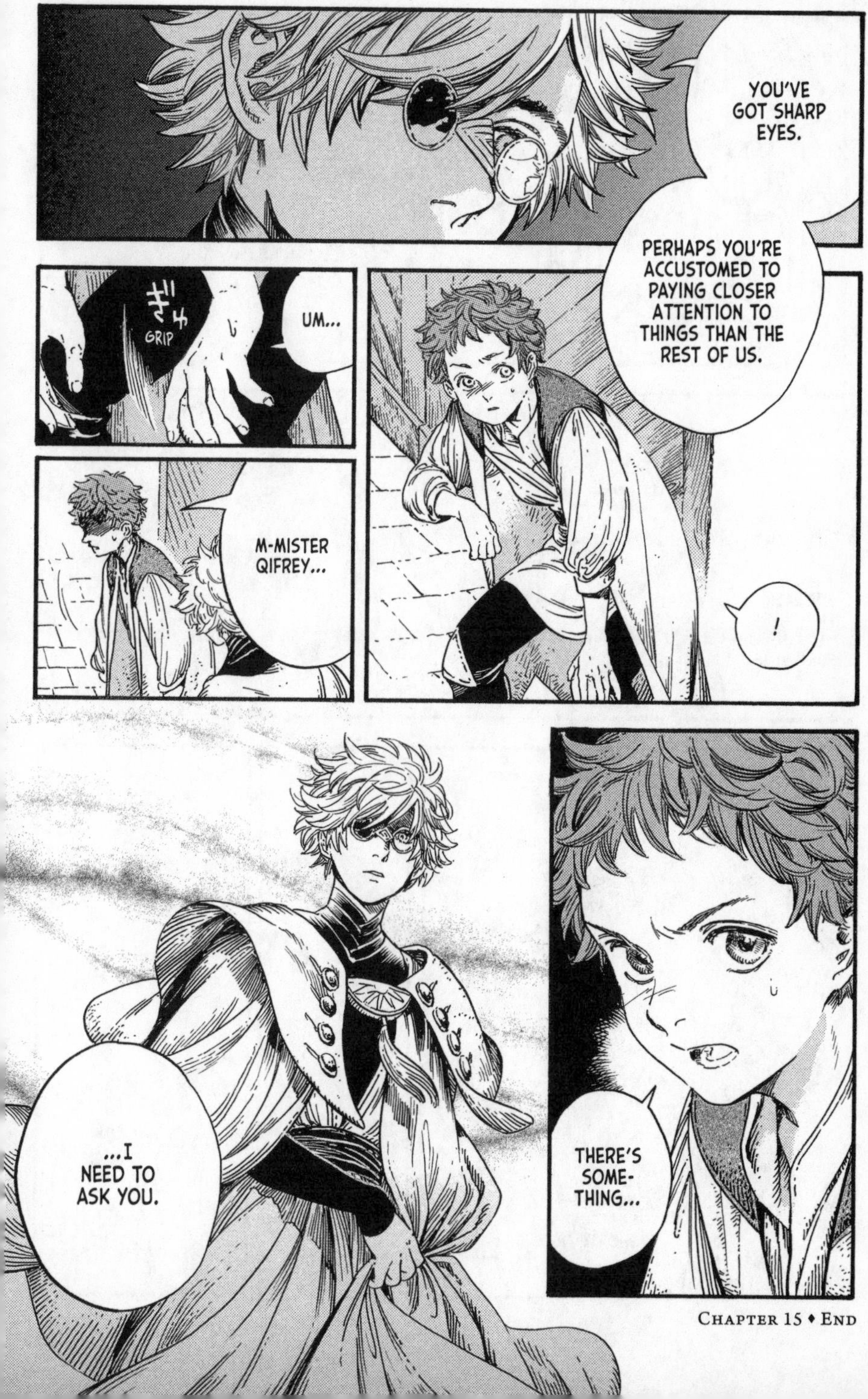
YOU'VE GOT SHARP EYES.
PERHAPS YOU'RE ACCUSTOMED TO PAYING CLOSER ATTENTION TO THINGS THAN THE REST OF US.
!
UM...
ぎゅ
GRIP
M-MISTER QIFREY...
THERE'S SOME-THING...
...I NEED TO ASK YOU.

Chapter 15 ♦ End

Witch Hat
Atelier

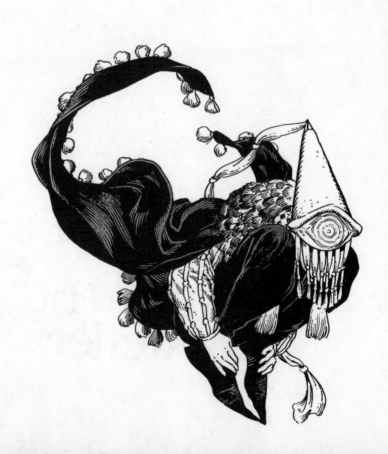

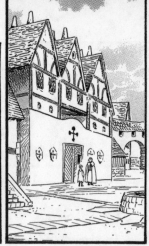

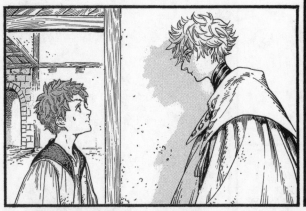

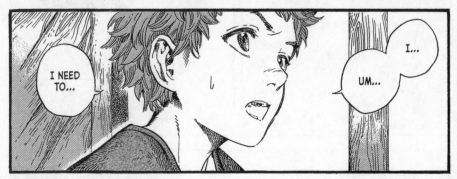

I NEED TO...

UM...

I...

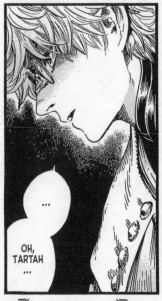

...

OH, TARTAH...

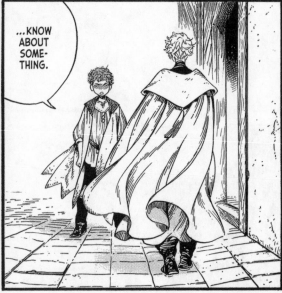

...KNOW ABOUT SOMETHING.

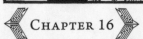

《 CHAPTER 16 》

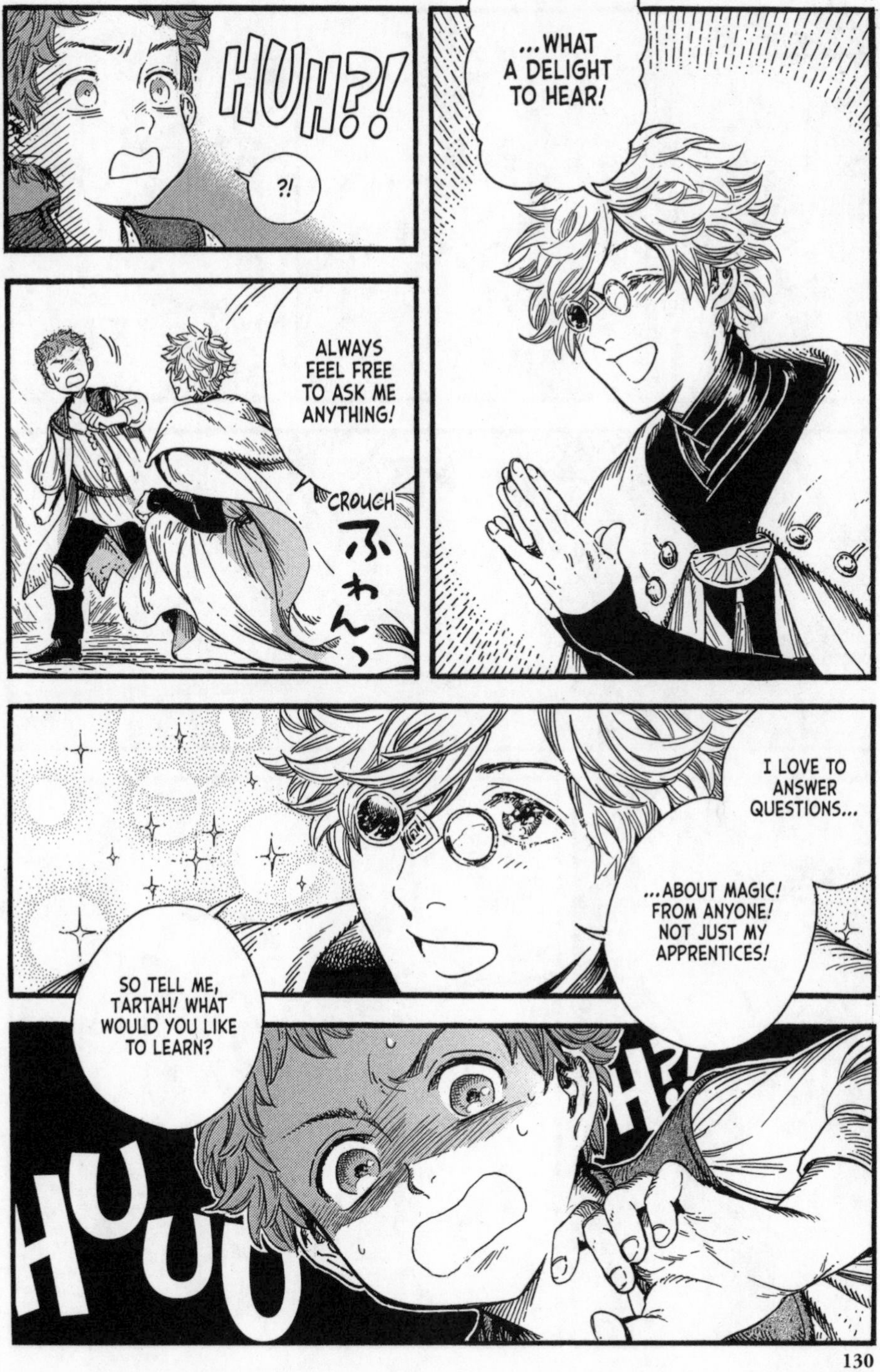
...WHAT A DELIGHT TO HEAR!
HUH?!
?!
ALWAYS FEEL FREE TO ASK ME ANYTHING!
CROUCH
ふわんっ
I LOVE TO ANSWER QUESTIONS...
...ABOUT MAGIC! FROM ANYONE! NOT JUST MY APPRENTICES!
SO TELL ME, TARTAH! WHAT WOULD YOU LIKE TO LEARN?
HUUU
H?!

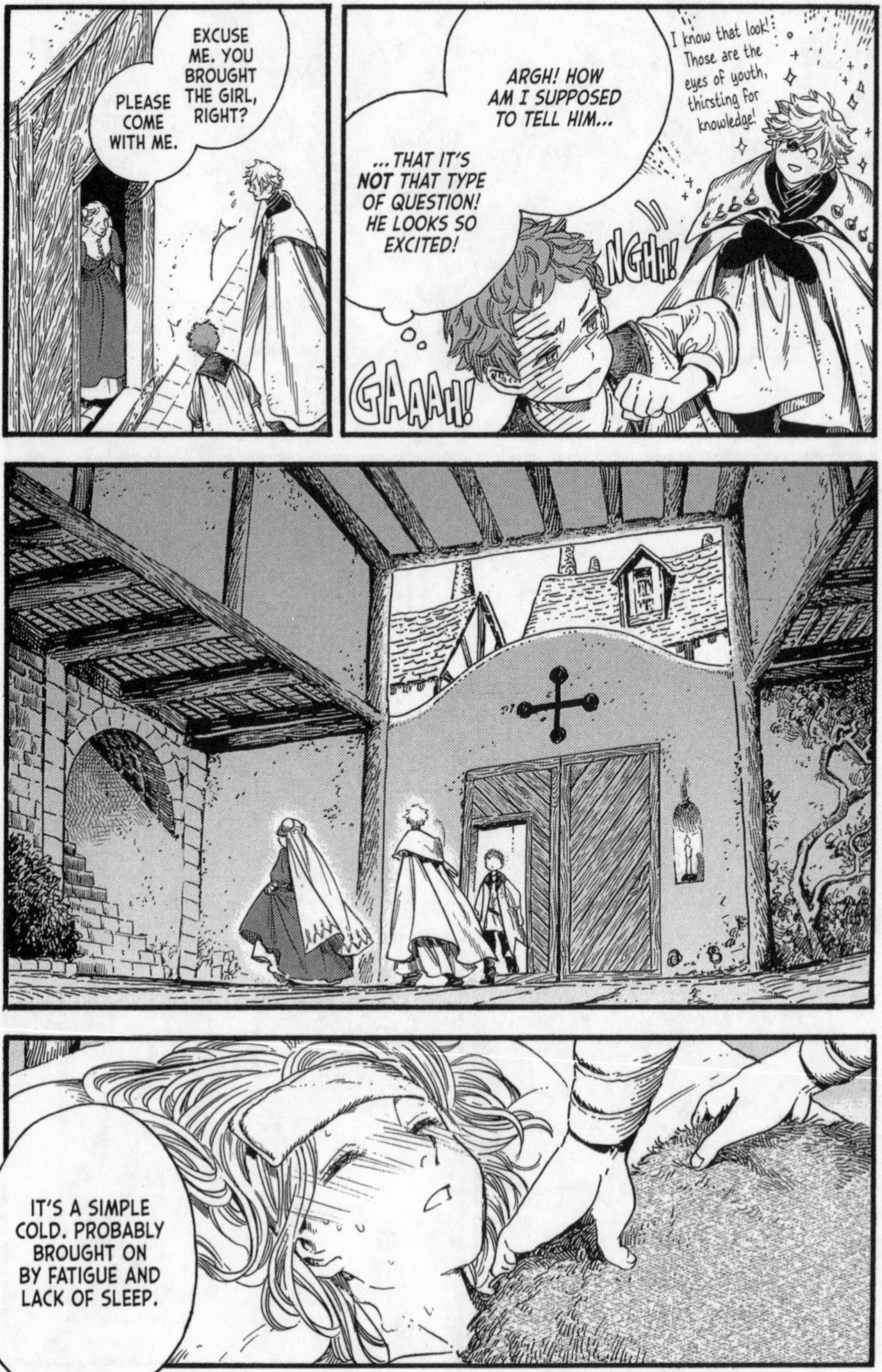
I know that look! Those are the eyes of youth, thirsting for knowledge!
ARGH! HOW AM I SUPPOSED TO TELL HIM...
...THAT IT'S **NOT** THAT TYPE OF QUESTION! HE LOOKS SO EXCITED!
NGHH!
GAAAH!
EXCUSE ME. YOU BROUGHT THE GIRL, RIGHT?
PLEASE COME WITH ME.
IT'S A SIMPLE COLD. PROBABLY BROUGHT ON BY FATIGUE AND LACK OF SLEEP.

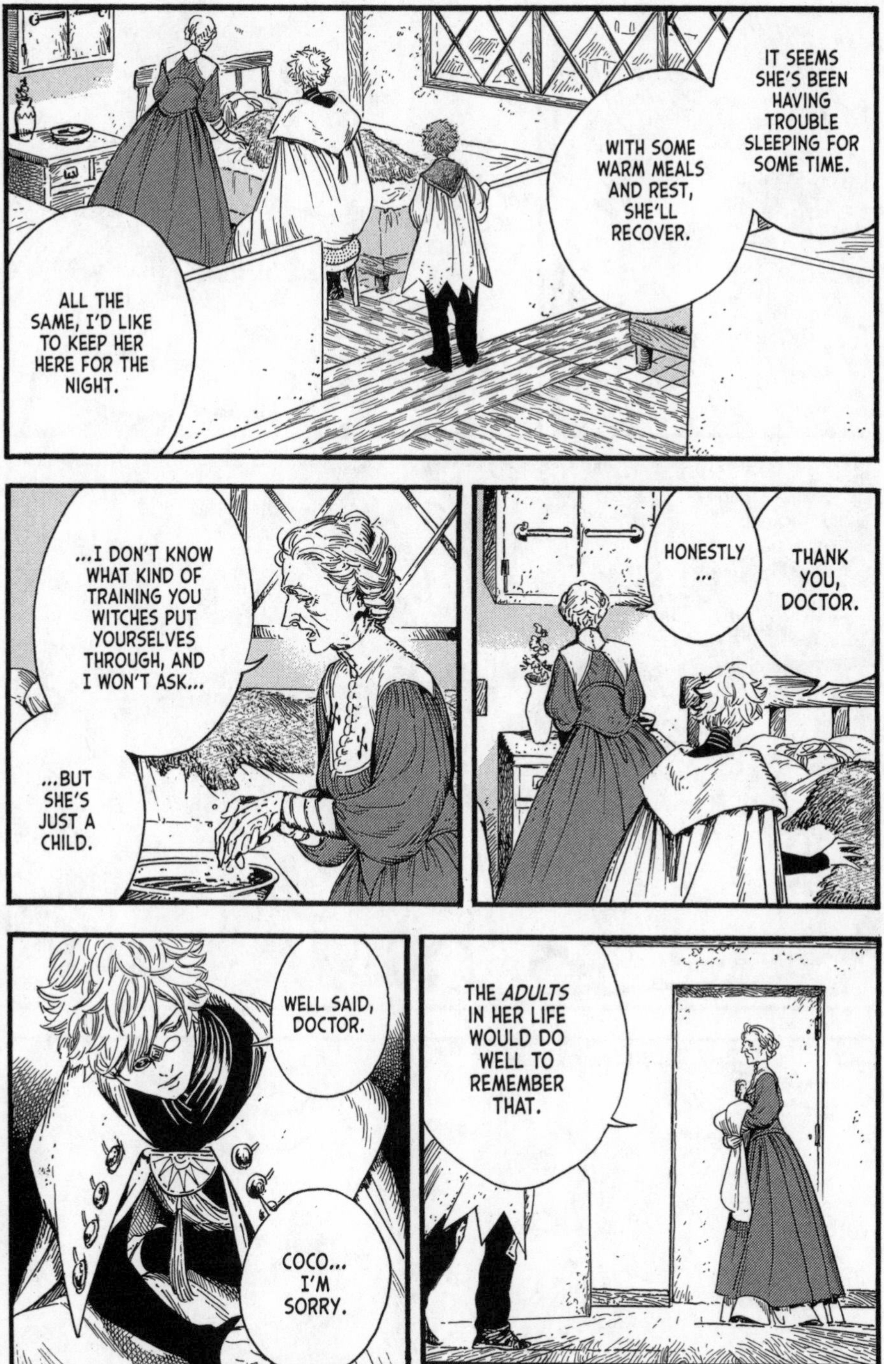
IT SEEMS SHE'S BEEN HAVING TROUBLE SLEEPING FOR SOME TIME.
WITH SOME WARM MEALS AND REST, SHE'LL RECOVER.
ALL THE SAME, I'D LIKE TO KEEP HER HERE FOR THE NIGHT.
THANK YOU, DOCTOR.
HONESTLY ...
...I DON'T KNOW WHAT KIND OF TRAINING YOU WITCHES PUT YOURSELVES THROUGH, AND I WON'T ASK...
...BUT SHE'S JUST A CHILD.
THE *ADULTS* IN HER LIFE WOULD DO WELL TO REMEMBER THAT.
WELL SAID, DOCTOR.
COCO... I'M SORRY.

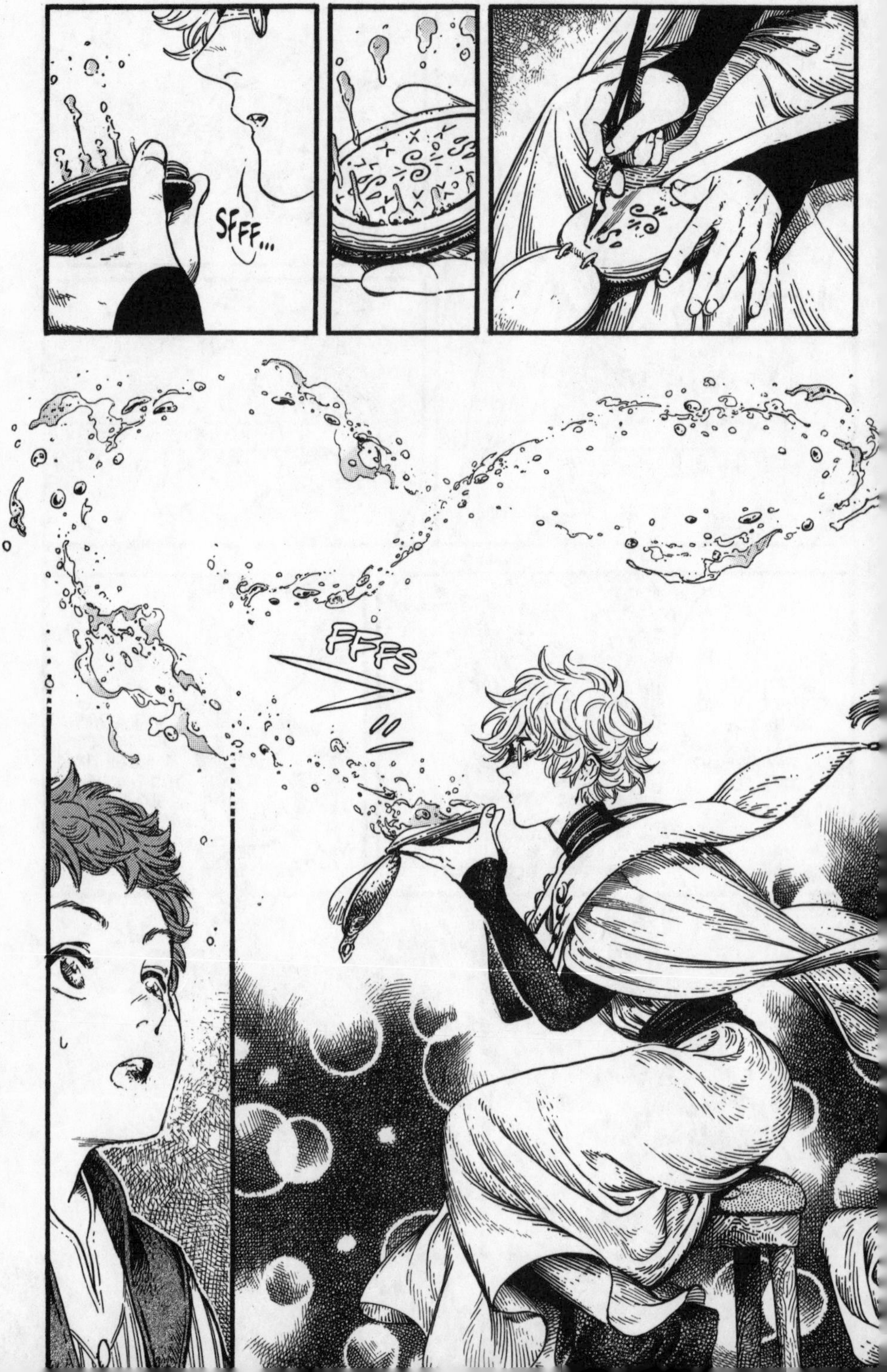
SFFF...
FFFS

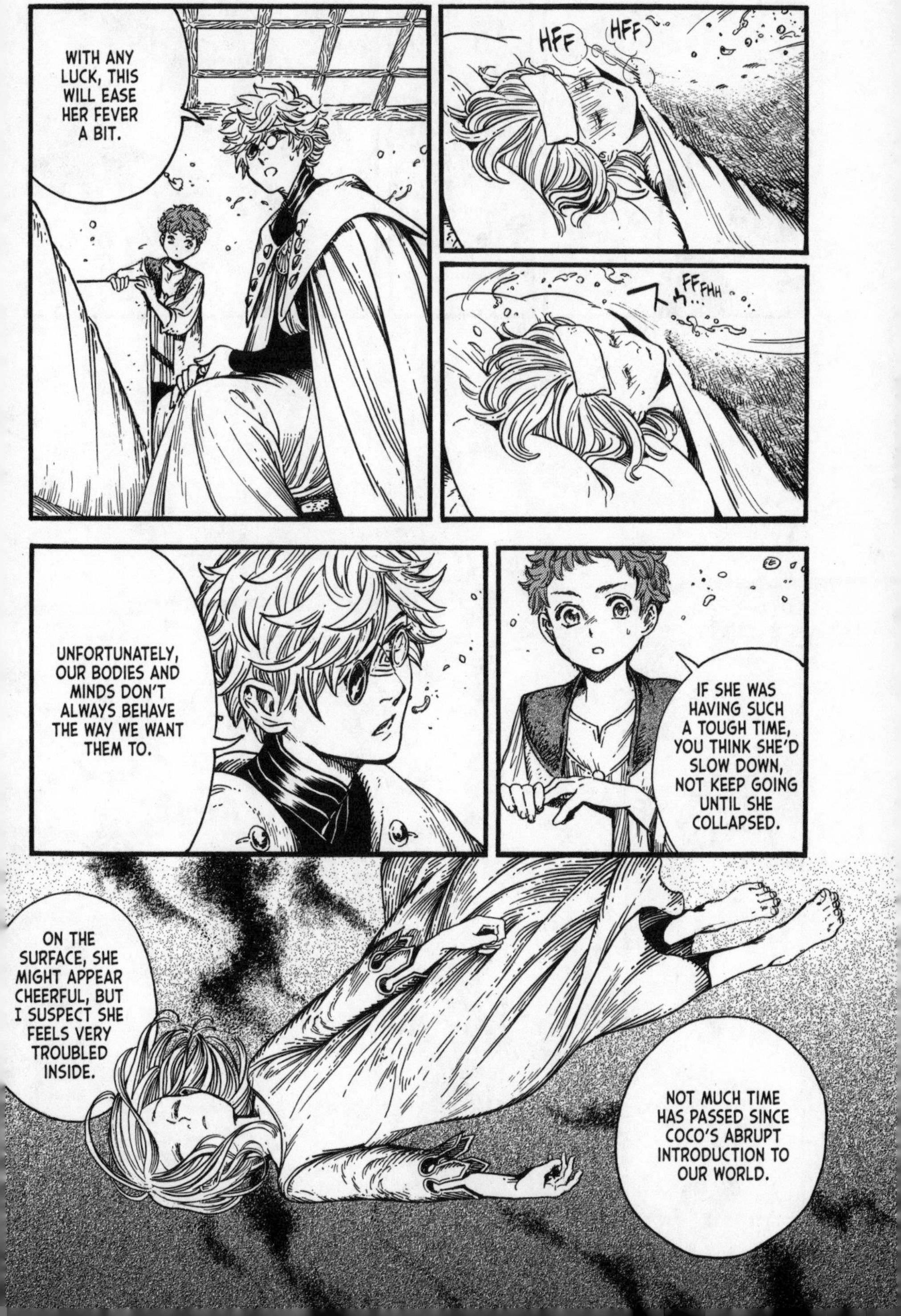
HFF
HFF
FFFHH...
WITH ANY LUCK, THIS WILL EASE HER FEVER A BIT.
IF SHE WAS HAVING SUCH A TOUGH TIME, YOU THINK SHE'D SLOW DOWN, NOT KEEP GOING UNTIL SHE COLLAPSED.
UNFORTUNATELY, OUR BODIES AND MINDS DON'T ALWAYS BEHAVE THE WAY WE WANT THEM TO.
NOT MUCH TIME HAS PASSED SINCE COCO'S ABRUPT INTRODUCTION TO OUR WORLD.
ON THE SURFACE, SHE MIGHT APPEAR CHEERFUL, BUT I SUSPECT SHE FEELS VERY TROUBLED INSIDE.

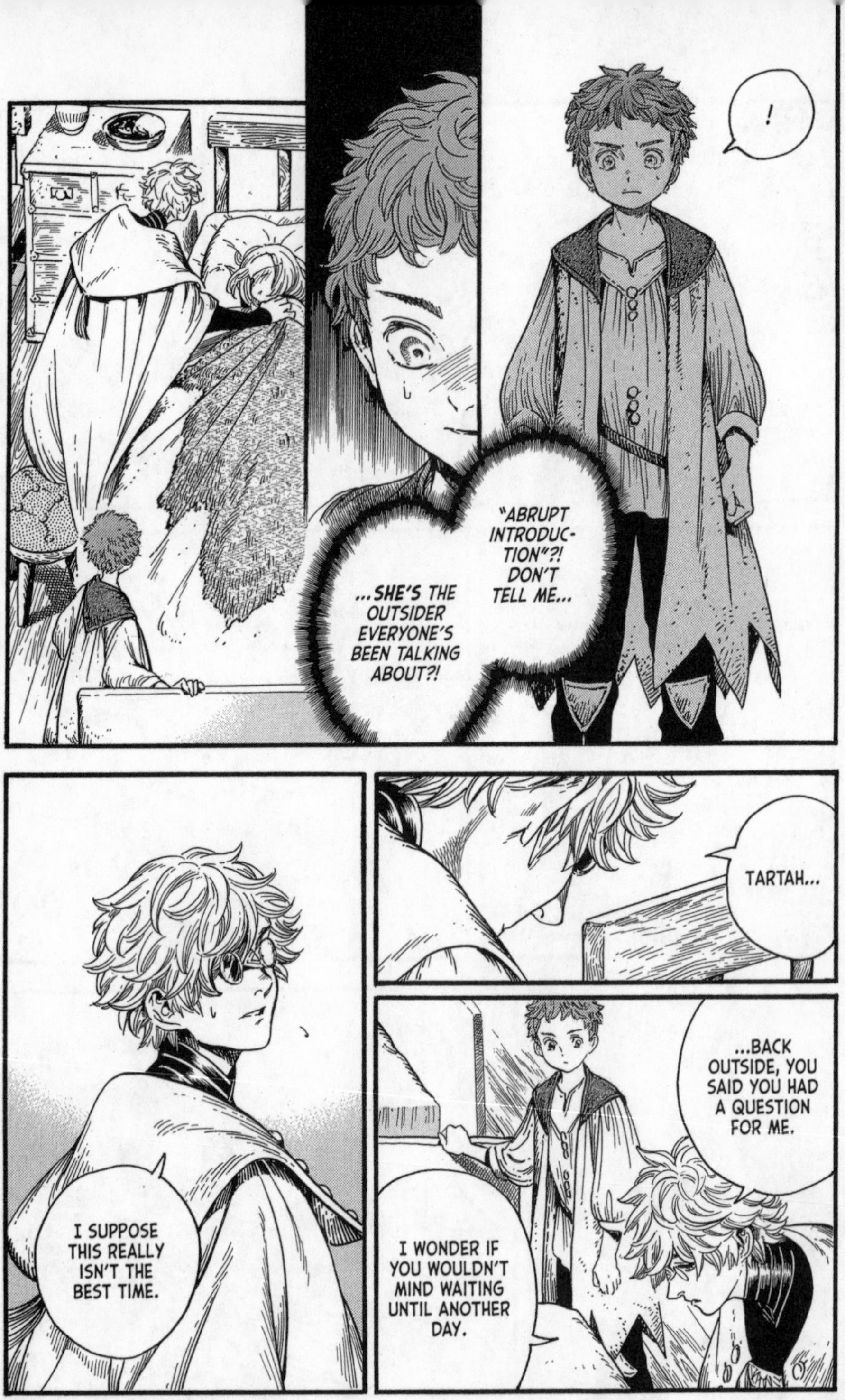
!
"ABRUPT INTRODUCTION"?! DON'T TELL ME...
...SHE'S THE OUTSIDER EVERYONE'S BEEN TALKING ABOUT?!
TARTAH...
...BACK OUTSIDE, YOU SAID YOU HAD A QUESTION FOR ME.
I WONDER IF YOU WOULDN'T MIND WAITING UNTIL ANOTHER DAY.
I SUPPOSE THIS REALLY ISN'T THE BEST TIME.

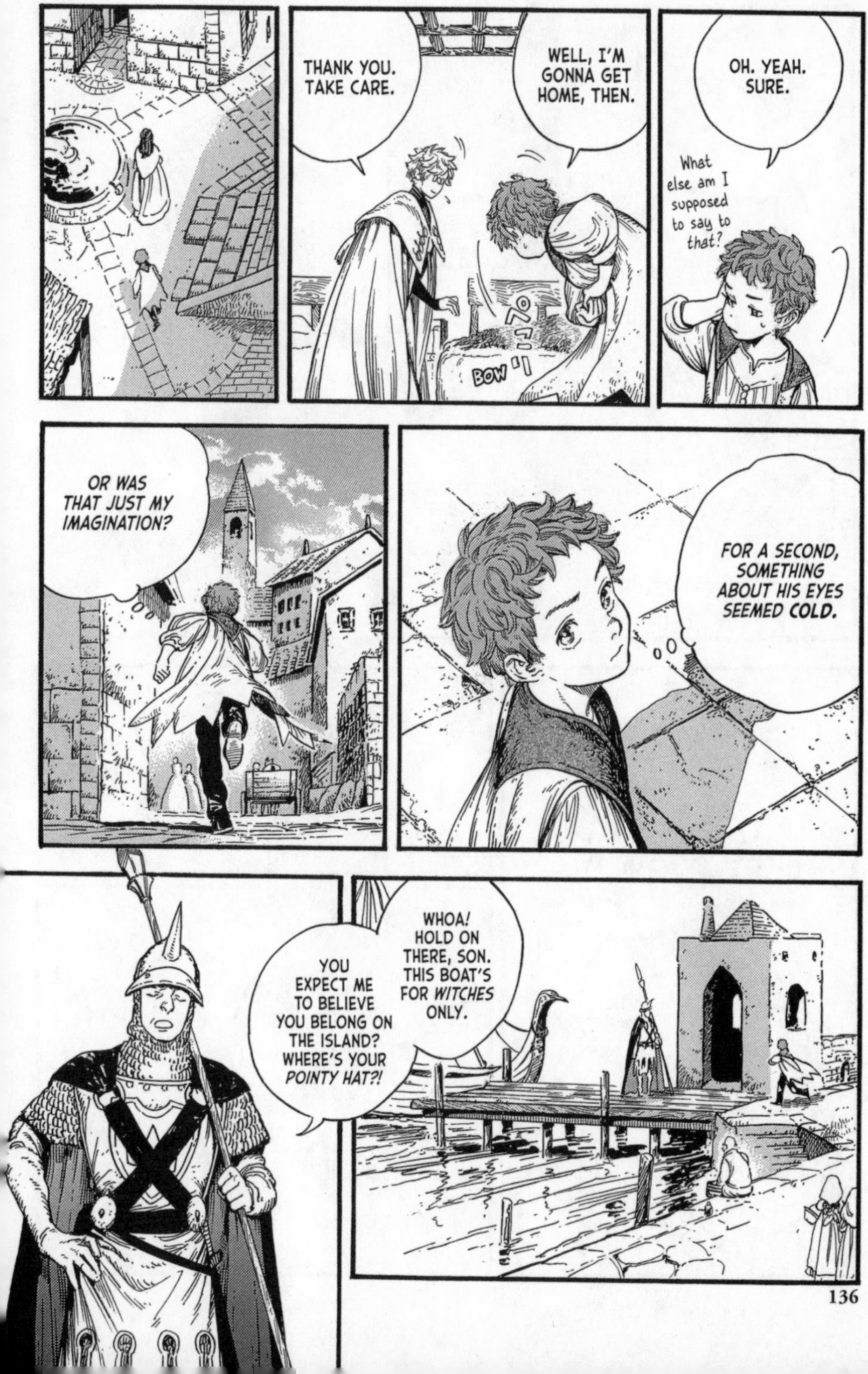
OH. YEAH. SURE.
What else am I supposed to say to that?
WELL, I'M GONNA GET HOME, THEN.
THANK YOU. TAKE CARE.
BOW
FOR A SECOND, SOMETHING ABOUT HIS EYES SEEMED COLD.
OR WAS THAT JUST MY IMAGINATION?
WHOA! HOLD ON THERE, SON. THIS BOAT'S FOR WITCHES ONLY.
YOU EXPECT ME TO BELIEVE YOU BELONG ON THE ISLAND? WHERE'S YOUR POINTY HAT?!

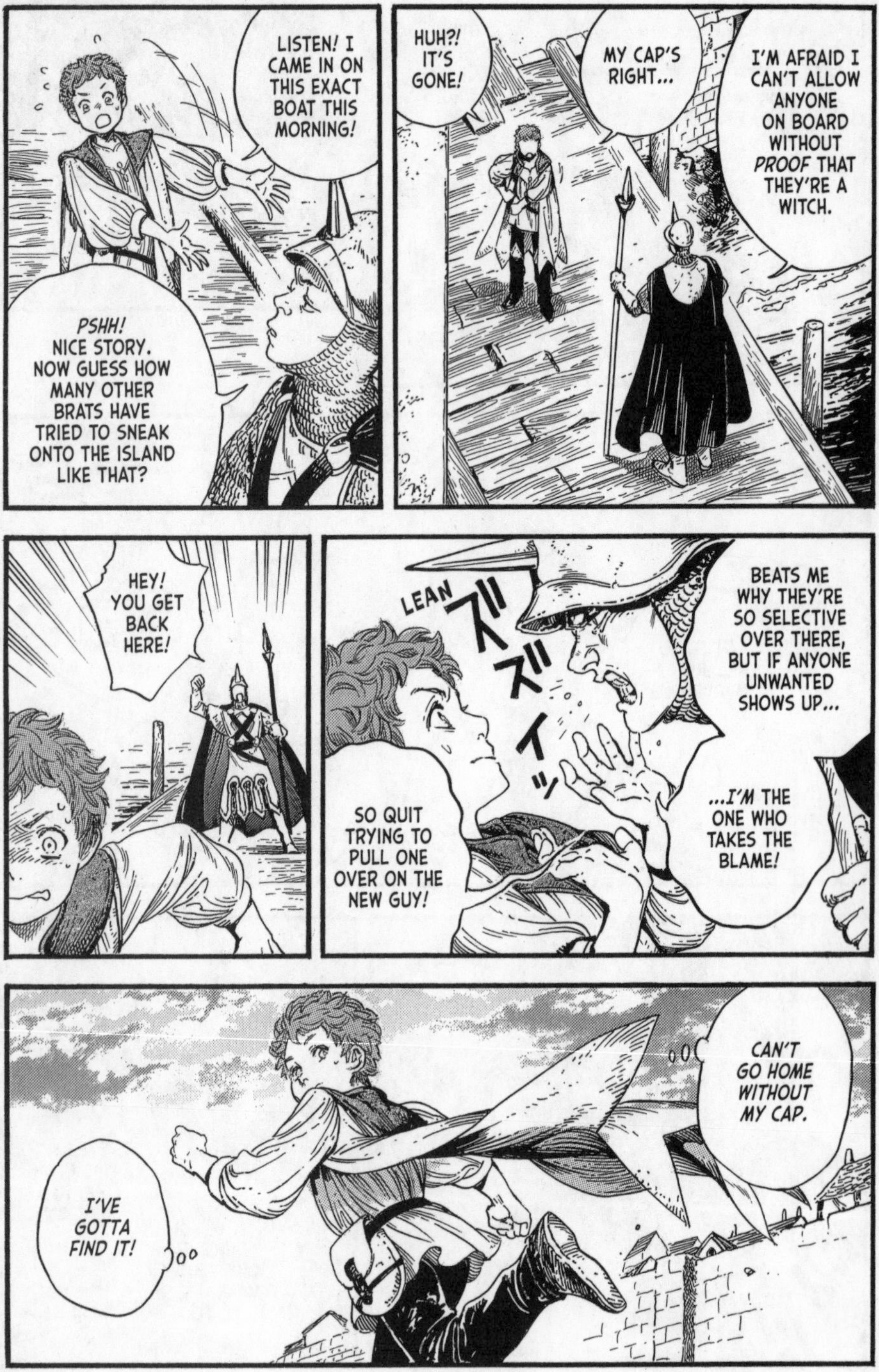
I'M AFRAID I CAN'T ALLOW ANYONE ON BOARD WITHOUT *PROOF* THAT THEY'RE A WITCH.
MY CAP'S RIGHT...
HUH?! IT'S GONE!
LISTEN! I CAME IN ON THIS EXACT BOAT THIS MORNING!
PSHH! NICE STORY. NOW GUESS HOW MANY OTHER BRATS HAVE TRIED TO SNEAK ONTO THE ISLAND LIKE THAT?
BEATS ME WHY THEY'RE SO SELECTIVE OVER THERE, BUT IF ANYONE UNWANTED SHOWS UP...
LEAN
ズズイッ
...*I'M* THE ONE WHO TAKES THE BLAME!
SO QUIT TRYING TO PULL ONE OVER ON THE NEW GUY!
HEY! YOU GET BACK HERE!
CAN'T GO HOME WITHOUT MY CAP.
I'VE GOTTA FIND IT!

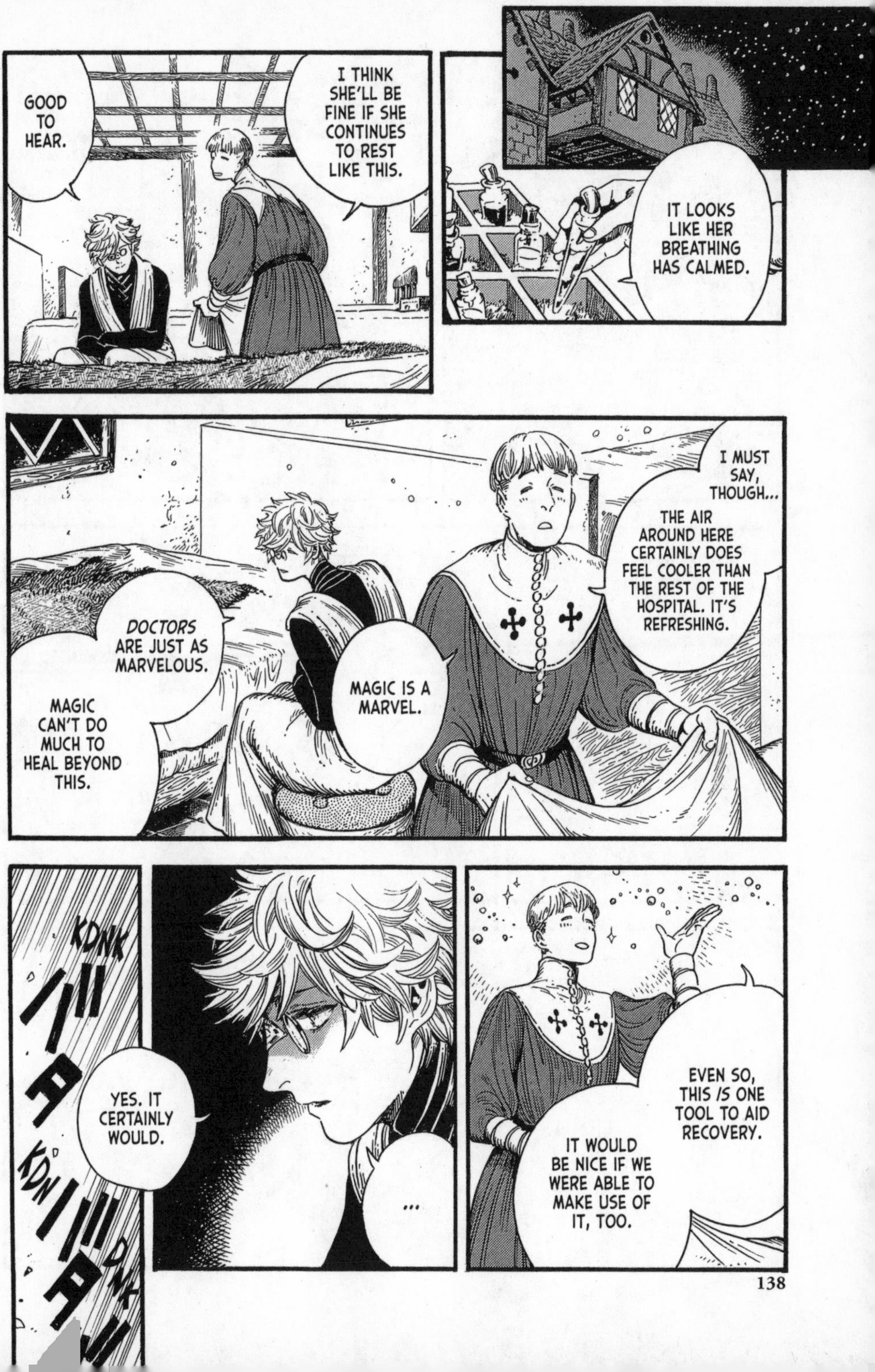
IT LOOKS LIKE HER BREATHING HAS CALMED.
I THINK SHE'LL BE FINE IF SHE CONTINUES TO REST LIKE THIS.
GOOD TO HEAR.
I MUST SAY, THOUGH...
THE AIR AROUND HERE CERTAINLY DOES FEEL COOLER THAN THE REST OF THE HOSPITAL. IT'S REFRESHING.
MAGIC IS A MARVEL.
DOCTORS ARE JUST AS MARVELOUS.
MAGIC CAN'T DO MUCH TO HEAL BEYOND THIS.
EVEN SO, THIS *IS* ONE TOOL TO AID RECOVERY.
IT WOULD BE NICE IF WE WERE ABLE TO MAKE USE OF IT, TOO.
YES. IT CERTAINLY WOULD.
...
KDNK
KDN
DNK

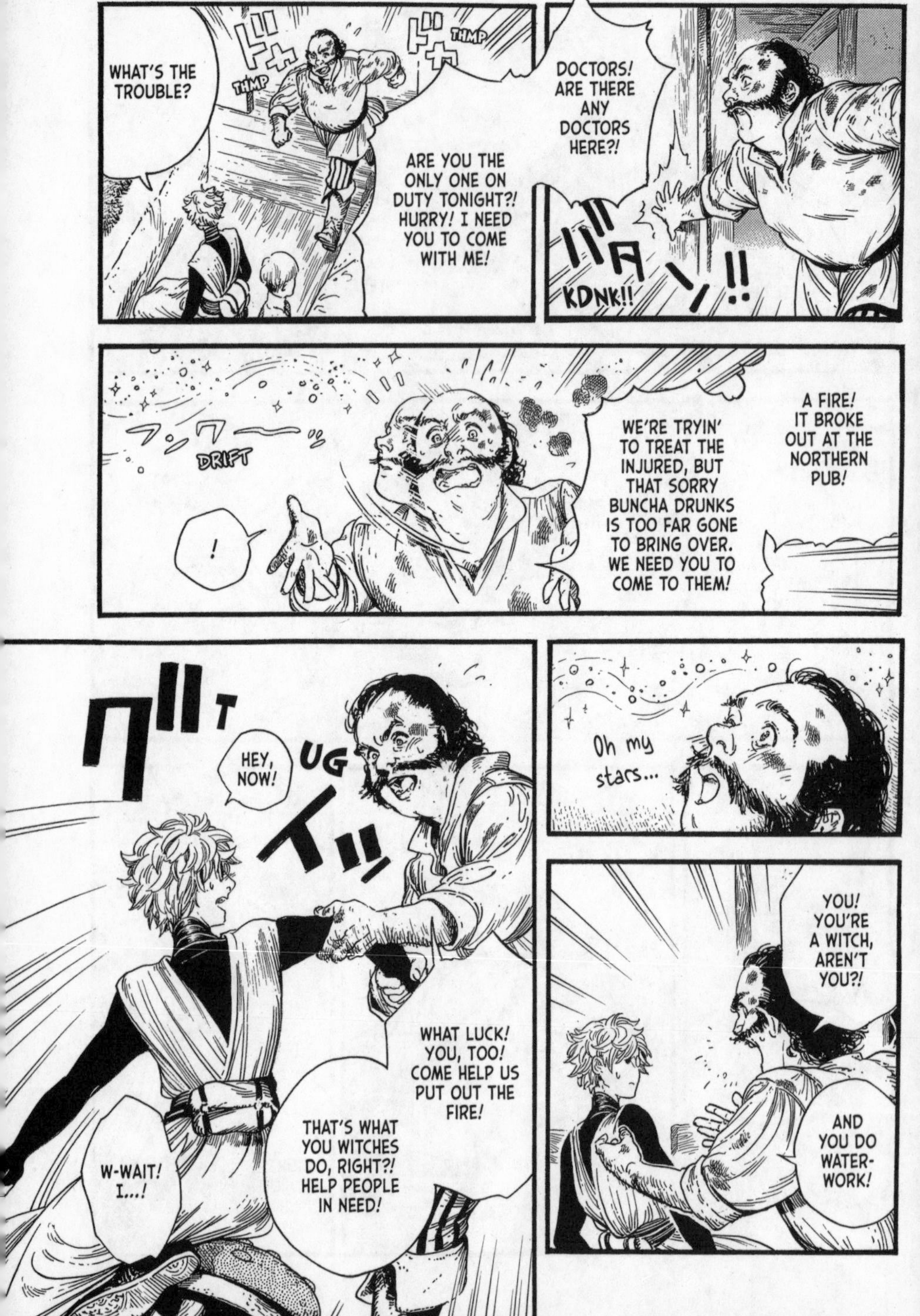
DOCTORS! ARE THERE ANY DOCTORS HERE?!
KDNK!!
THMP
WHAT'S THE TROUBLE?
ARE YOU THE ONLY ONE ON DUTY TONIGHT?! HURRY! I NEED YOU TO COME WITH ME!
THMP
A FIRE! IT BROKE OUT AT THE NORTHERN PUB!
WE'RE TRYIN' TO TREAT THE INJURED, BUT THAT SORRY BUNCHA DRUNKS IS TOO FAR GONE TO BRING OVER. WE NEED YOU TO COME TO THEM!
DRIFT
!
Oh my stars...
YOU! YOU'RE A WITCH, AREN'T YOU?!
AND YOU DO WATER-WORK!
TUG
HEY, NOW!
WHAT LUCK! YOU, TOO! COME HELP US PUT OUT THE FIRE!
THAT'S WHAT YOU WITCHES DO, RIGHT?! HELP PEOPLE IN NEED!
W-WAIT! I...!

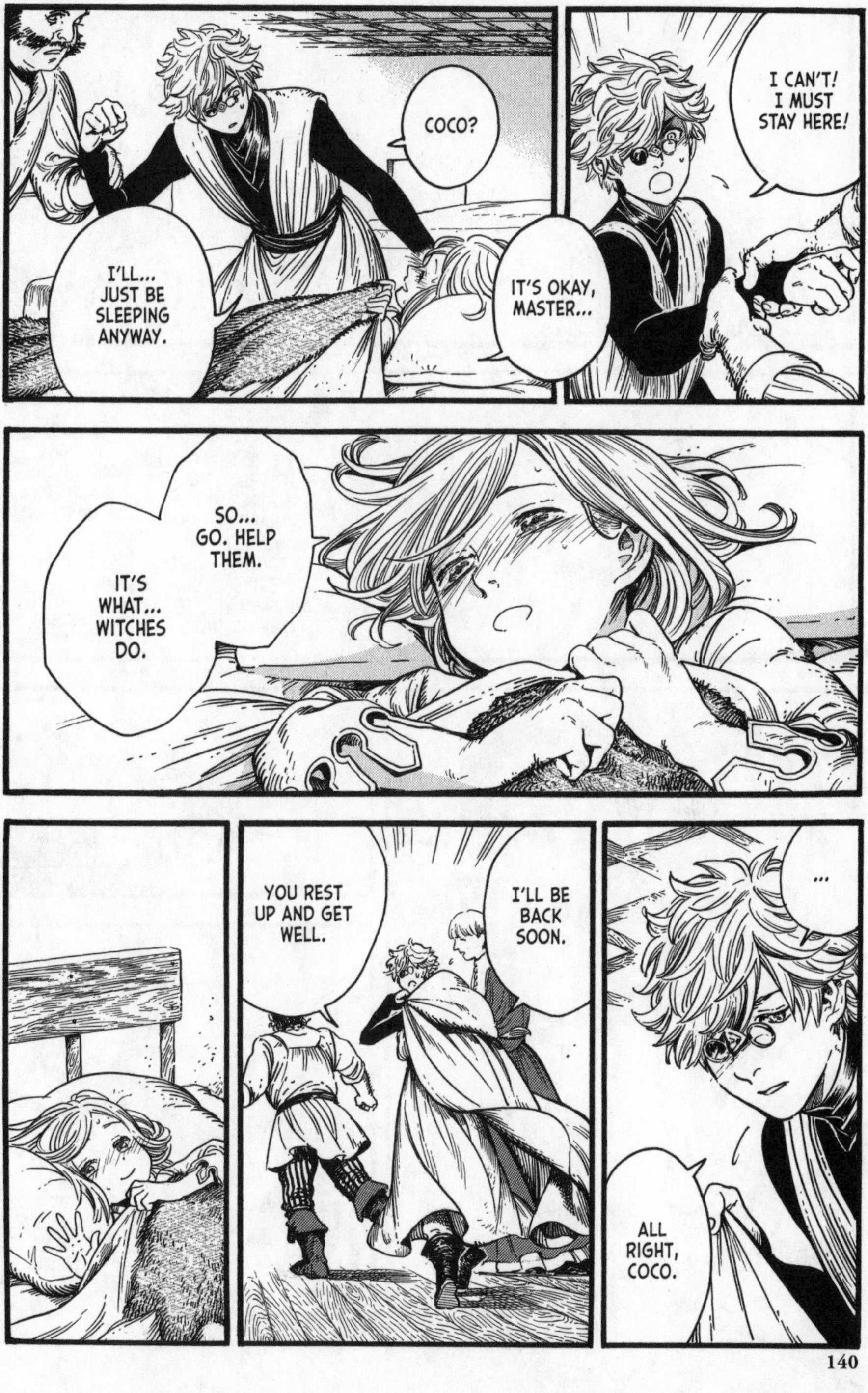
I CAN'T! I MUST STAY HERE!
IT'S OKAY, MASTER...
COCO?
I'LL... JUST BE SLEEPING ANYWAY.
SO... GO. HELP THEM.
IT'S WHAT... WITCHES DO.
...
ALL RIGHT, COCO.
I'LL BE BACK SOON.
YOU REST UP AND GET WELL.

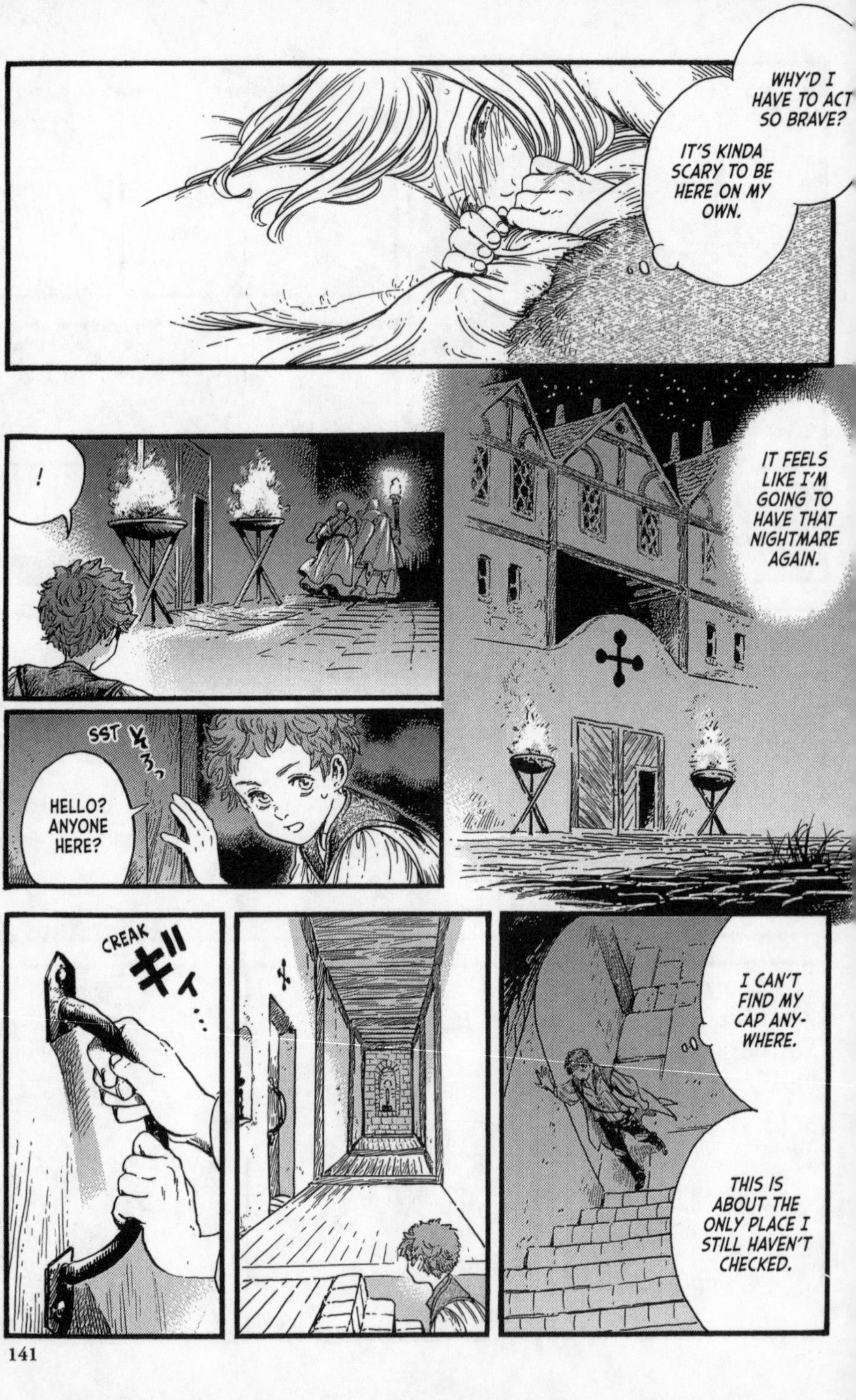
WHY'D I HAVE TO ACT SO BRAVE?
IT'S KINDA SCARY TO BE HERE ON MY OWN.
IT FEELS LIKE I'M GOING TO HAVE THAT NIGHTMARE AGAIN.
!
SST そろっ
HELLO? ANYONE HERE?
I CAN'T FIND MY CAP ANY-WHERE.
THIS IS ABOUT THE ONLY PLACE I STILL HAVEN'T CHECKED.
CREAK ギィ…

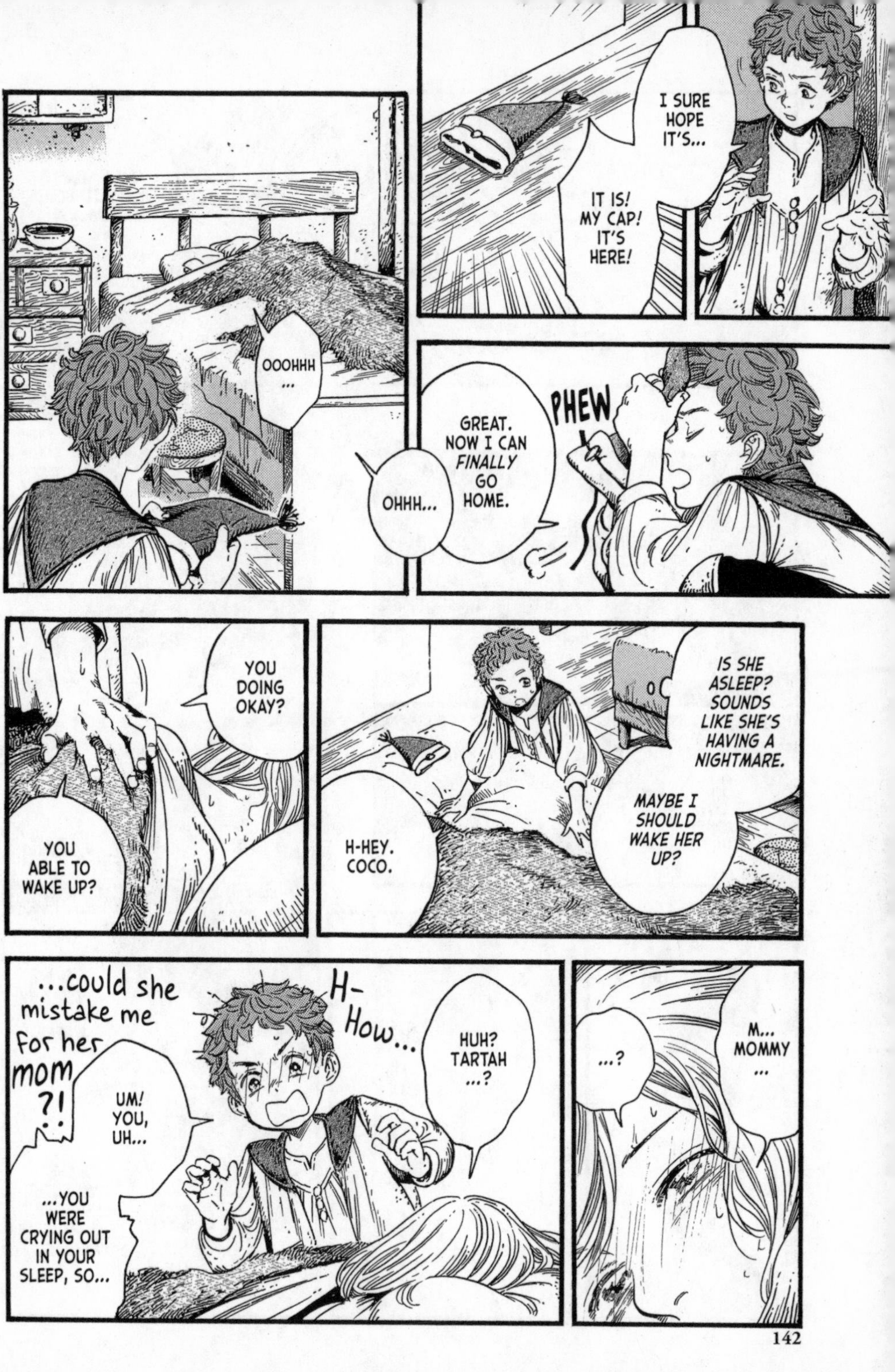

I SURE HOPE IT'S...
IT IS! MY CAP! IT'S HERE!
PHEW
GREAT. NOW I CAN FINALLY GO HOME.
OHHH...
OOOHHH...
IS SHE ASLEEP? SOUNDS LIKE SHE'S HAVING A NIGHTMARE.
MAYBE I SHOULD WAKE HER UP?
H-HEY. COCO.
YOU DOING OKAY?
YOU ABLE TO WAKE UP?
M... MOMMY...
...?
HUH? TARTAH...?
H-How...
...could she mistake me for her mom?!
UM! YOU, UH...
...YOU WERE CRYING OUT IN YOUR SLEEP, SO...

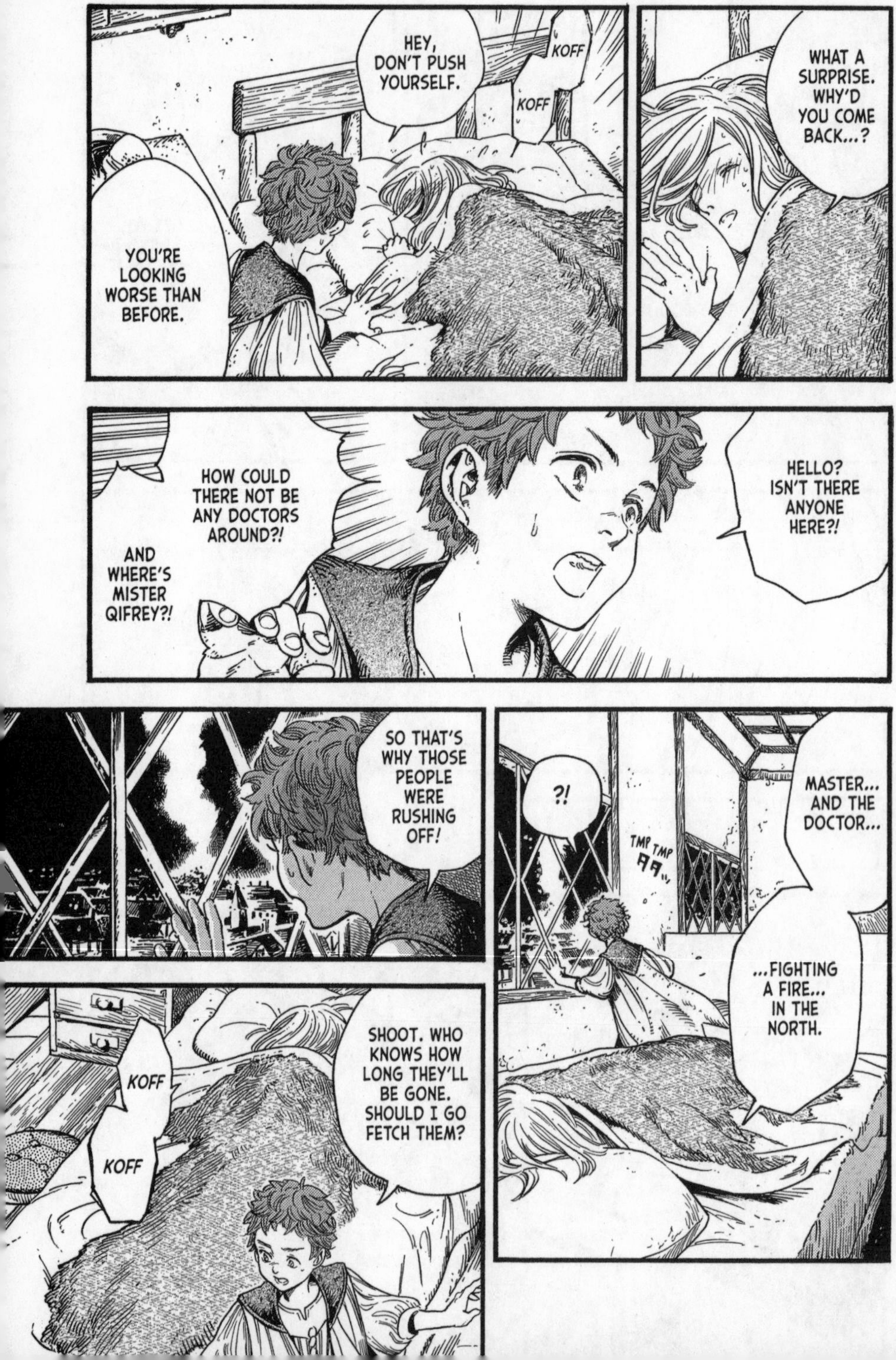
WHAT A SURPRISE. WHY'D YOU COME BACK...?
KOFF
KOFF
HEY, DON'T PUSH YOURSELF.
YOU'RE LOOKING WORSE THAN BEFORE.
HELLO? ISN'T THERE ANYONE HERE?!
HOW COULD THERE NOT BE ANY DOCTORS AROUND?!
AND WHERE'S MISTER QIFREY?!
MASTER... AND THE DOCTOR...
?!
TMP TMP
タタッ
...FIGHTING A FIRE... IN THE NORTH.
SO THAT'S WHY THOSE PEOPLE WERE RUSHING OFF!
SHOOT. WHO KNOWS HOW LONG THEY'LL BE GONE. SHOULD I GO FETCH THEM?
KOFF
KOFF

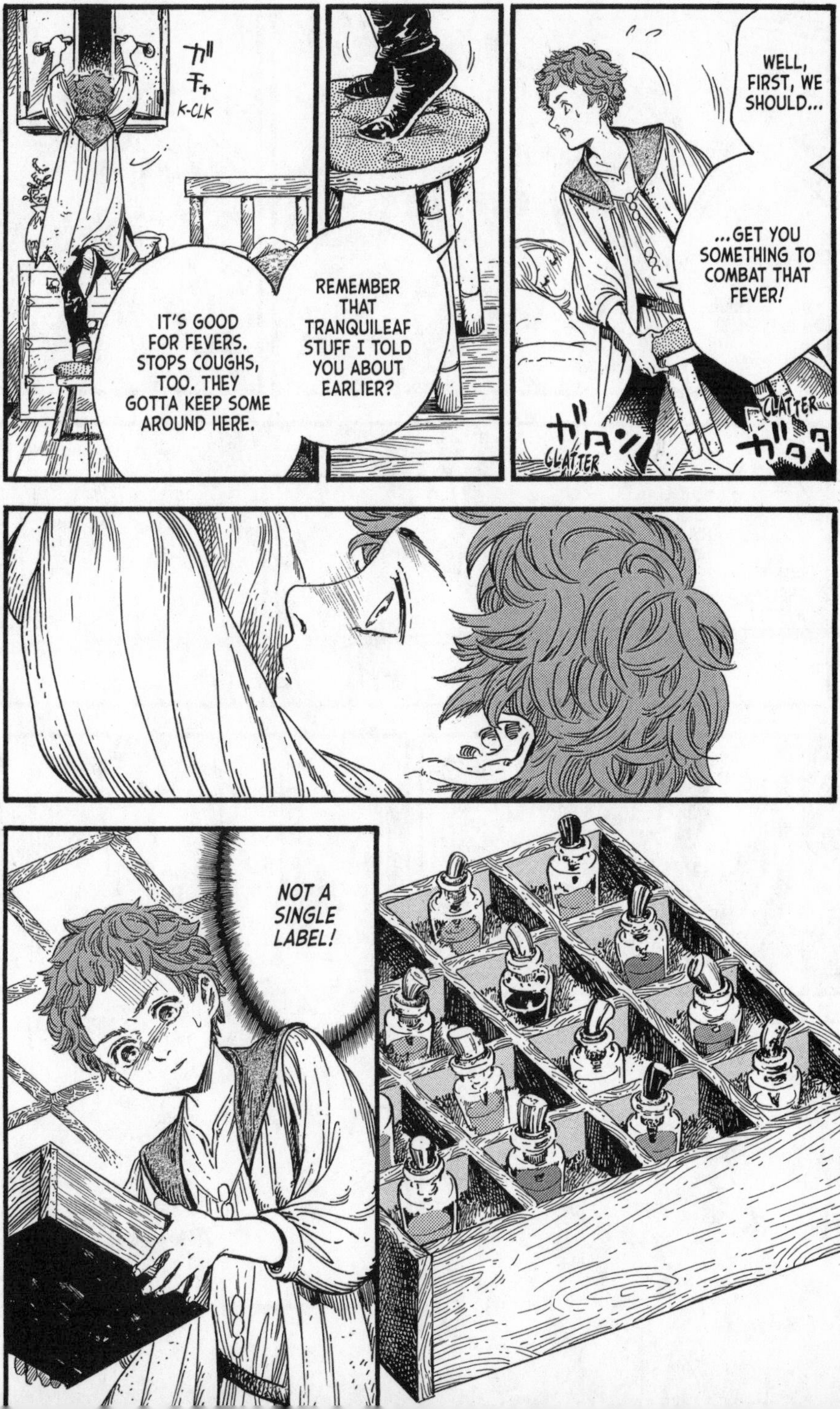
WELL, FIRST, WE SHOULD...
...GET YOU SOMETHING TO COMBAT THAT FEVER!
ガタタ
CLATTER
ガタン
CLATTER
REMEMBER THAT TRANQUILEAF STUFF I TOLD YOU ABOUT EARLIER?
ガチャ
K-CLK
IT'S GOOD FOR FEVERS. STOPS COUGHS, TOO. THEY GOTTA KEEP SOME AROUND HERE.
NOT A SINGLE LABEL!

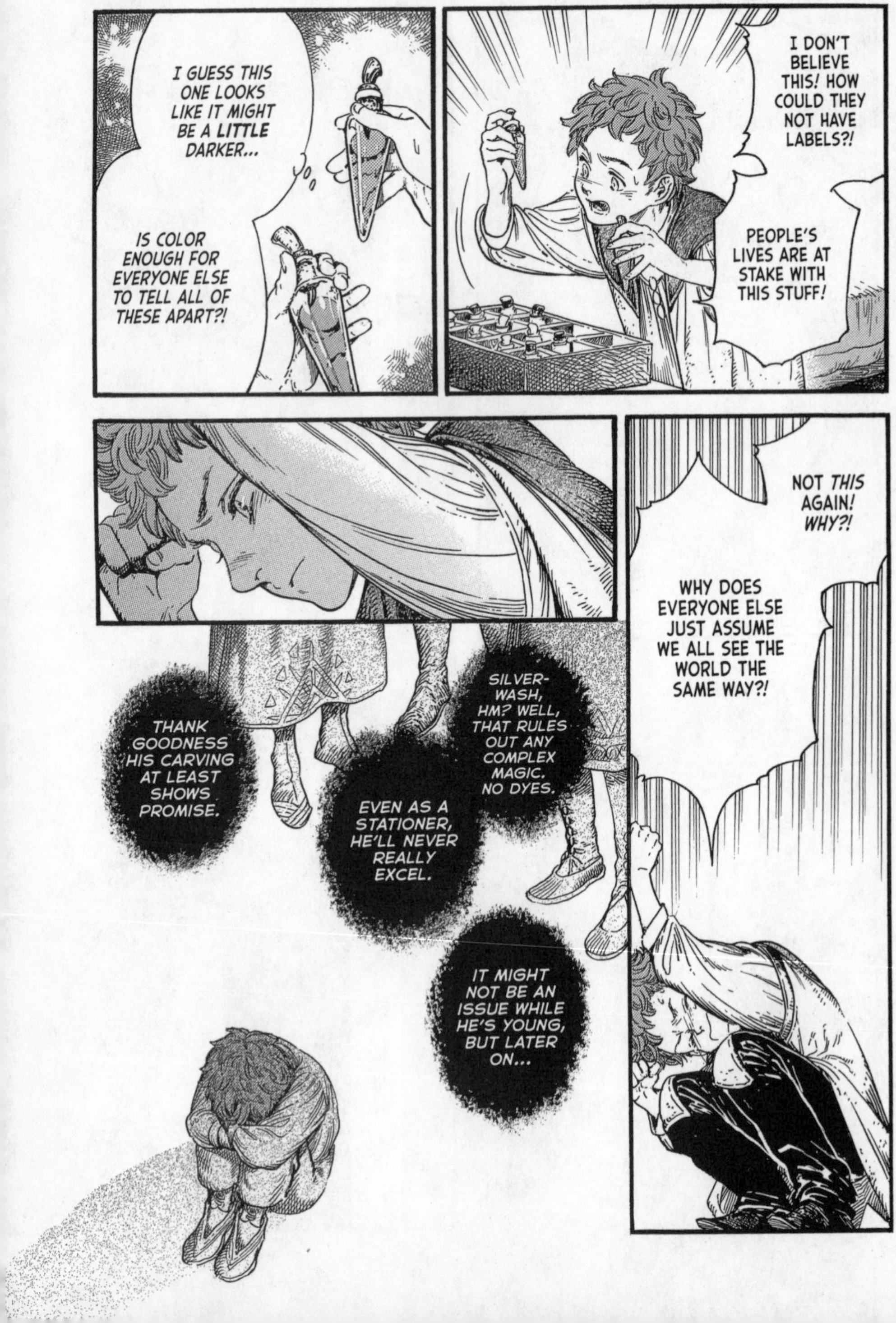
I DON'T BELIEVE THIS! HOW COULD THEY NOT HAVE LABELS?!
PEOPLE'S LIVES ARE AT STAKE WITH THIS STUFF!
I GUESS THIS ONE LOOKS LIKE IT MIGHT BE A LITTLE DARKER...
IS COLOR ENOUGH FOR EVERYONE ELSE TO TELL ALL OF THESE APART?!
NOT THIS AGAIN! WHY?!
WHY DOES EVERYONE ELSE JUST ASSUME WE ALL SEE THE WORLD THE SAME WAY?!
SILVER-WASH, HM? WELL, THAT RULES OUT ANY COMPLEX MAGIC. NO DYES.
THANK GOODNESS HIS CARVING AT LEAST SHOWS PROMISE.
EVEN AS A STATIONER, HE'LL NEVER REALLY EXCEL.
IT MIGHT NOT BE AN ISSUE WHILE HE'S YOUNG, BUT LATER ON...

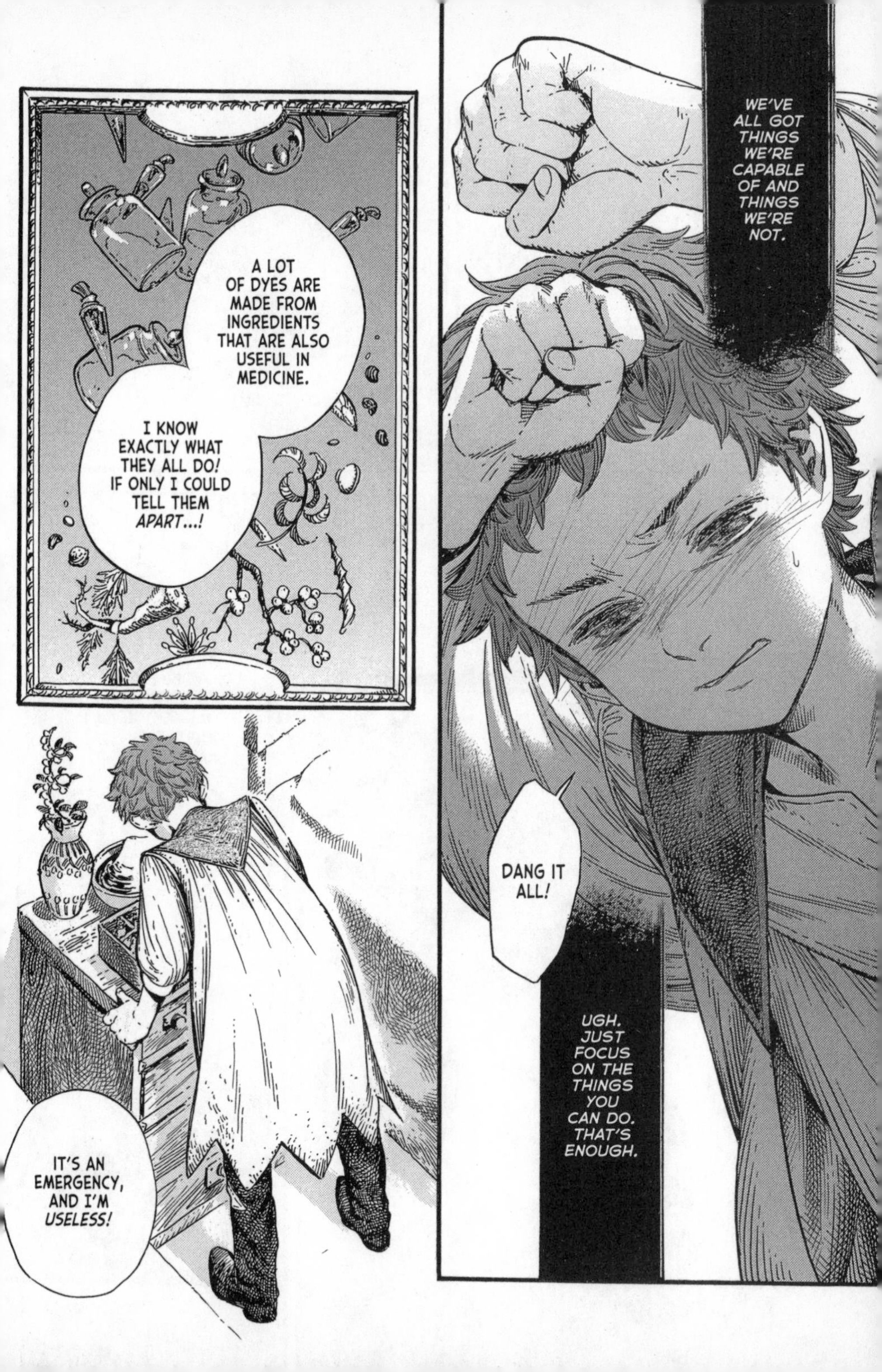
WE'VE ALL GOT THINGS WE'RE CAPABLE OF AND THINGS WE'RE NOT.
DANG IT ALL!
UGH. JUST FOCUS ON THE THINGS YOU CAN DO. THAT'S ENOUGH.
A LOT OF DYES ARE MADE FROM INGREDIENTS THAT ARE ALSO USEFUL IN MEDICINE.
I KNOW EXACTLY WHAT THEY ALL DO! IF ONLY I COULD TELL THEM *APART*...!
IT'S AN EMERGENCY, AND I'M *USELESS*!

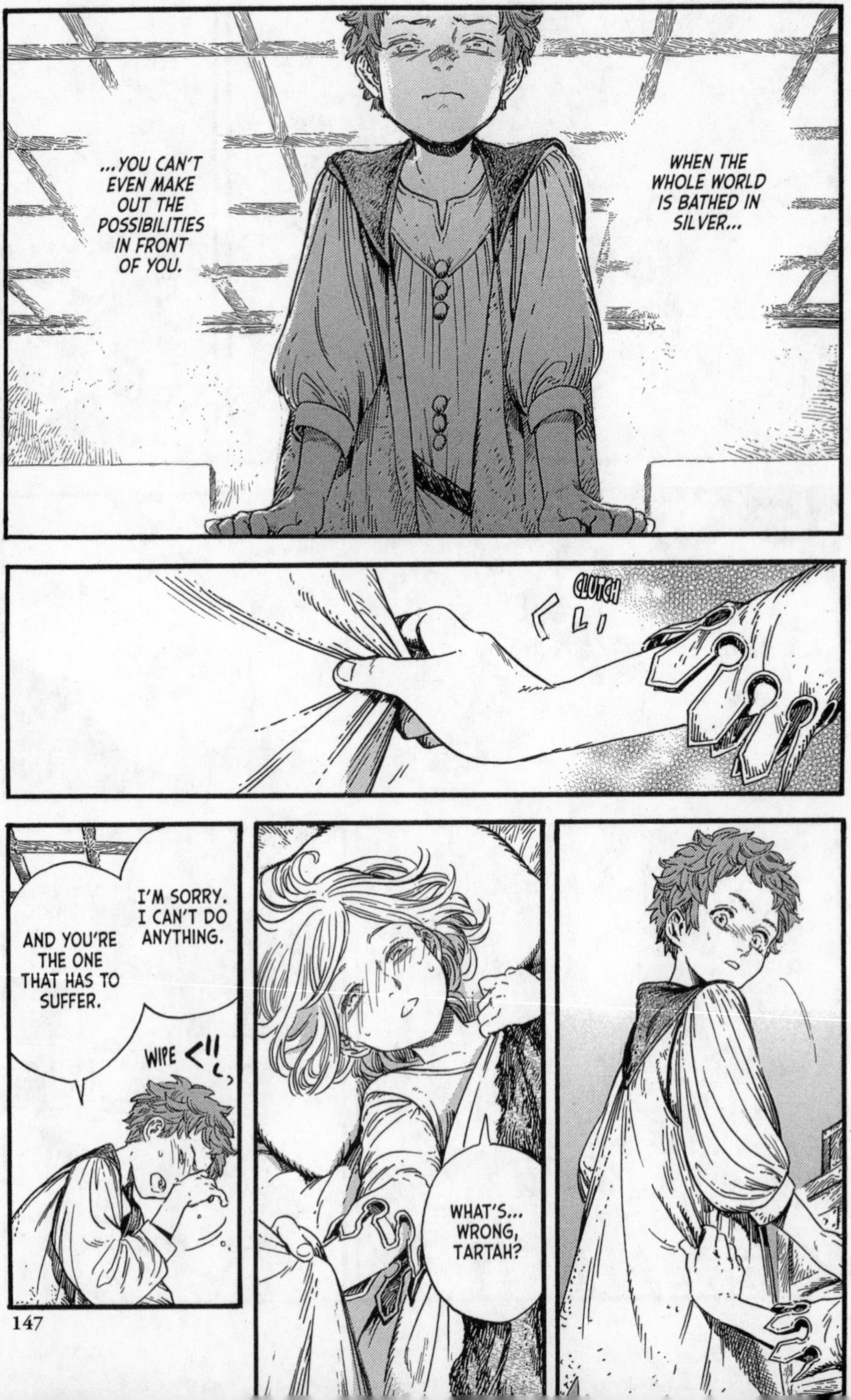
WHEN THE WHOLE WORLD IS BATHED IN SILVER...
...YOU CAN'T EVEN MAKE OUT THE POSSIBILITIES IN FRONT OF YOU.
CLUTCH
WHAT'S... WRONG, TARTAH?
I'M SORRY. I CAN'T DO ANYTHING.
AND YOU'RE THE ONE THAT HAS TO SUFFER.
WIPE

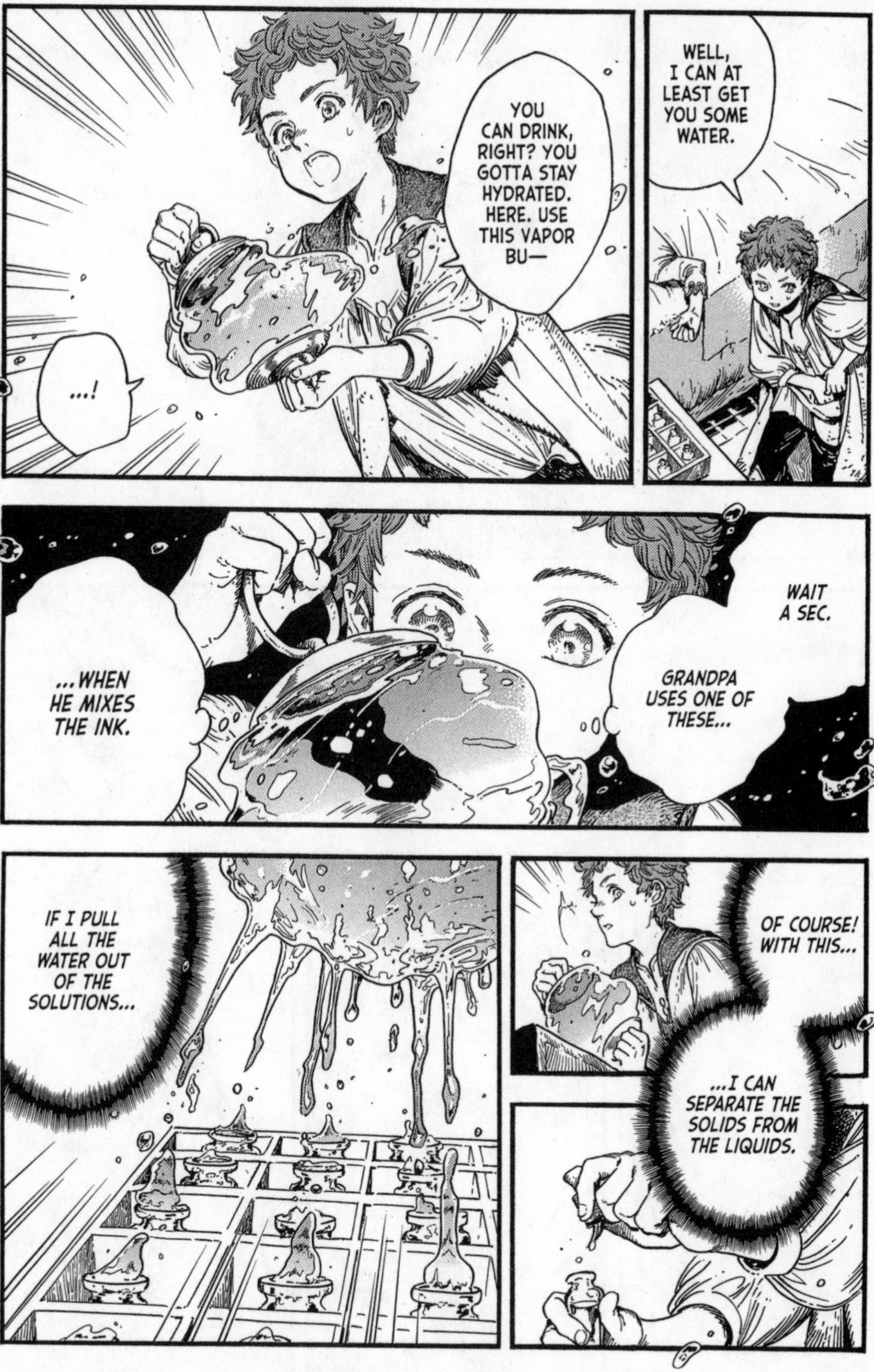
WELL, I CAN AT LEAST GET YOU SOME WATER.
YOU CAN DRINK, RIGHT? YOU GOTTA STAY HYDRATED. HERE. USE THIS VAPOR BU—
...!
WAIT A SEC.
GRANDPA USES ONE OF THESE...
...WHEN HE MIXES THE INK.
OF COURSE! WITH THIS...
...I CAN SEPARATE THE SOLIDS FROM THE LIQUIDS.
IF I PULL ALL THE WATER OUT OF THE SOLUTIONS...

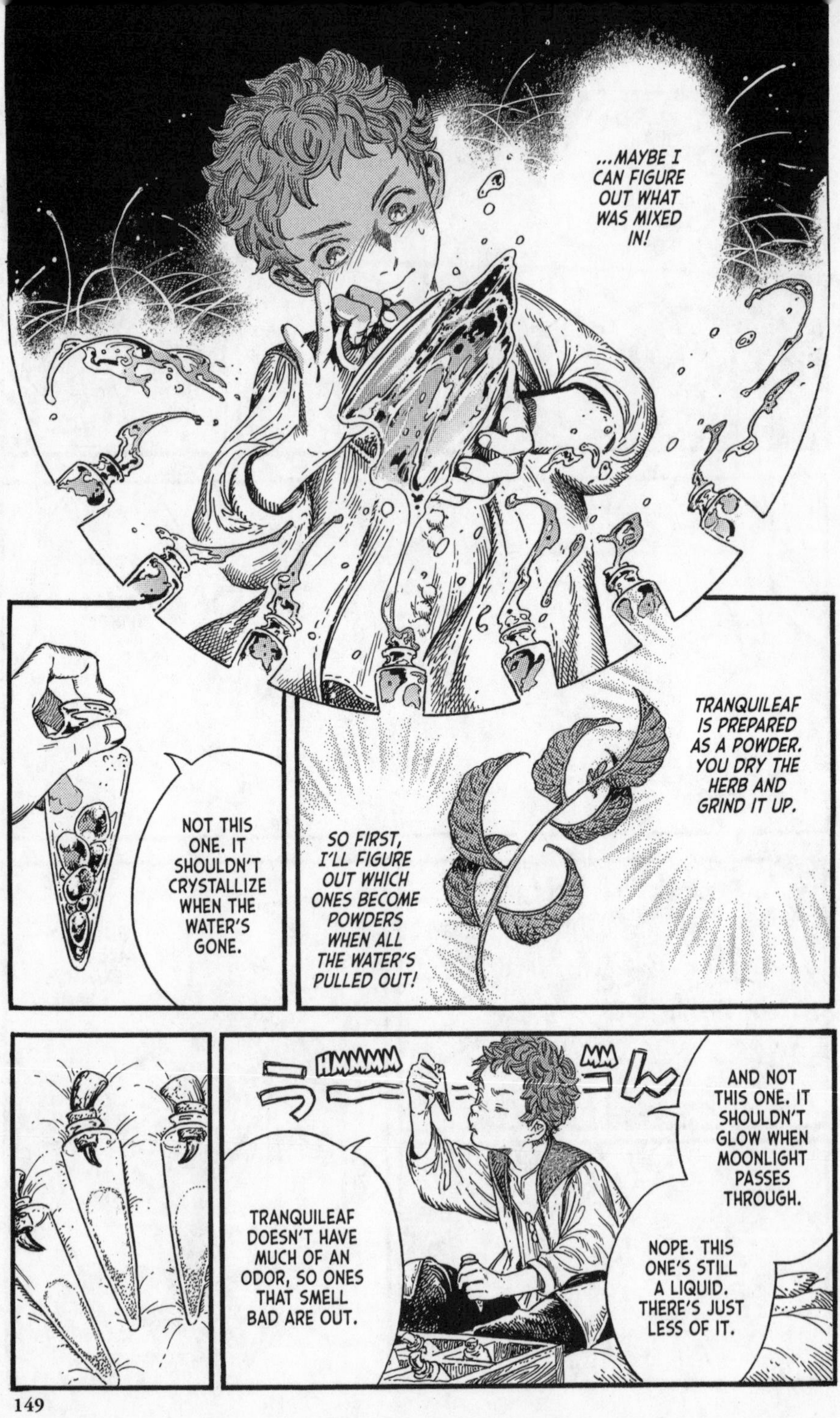
...MAYBE I CAN FIGURE OUT WHAT WAS MIXED IN!
TRANQUILEAF IS PREPARED AS A POWDER. YOU DRY THE HERB AND GRIND IT UP.
SO FIRST, I'LL FIGURE OUT WHICH ONES BECOME POWDERS WHEN ALL THE WATER'S PULLED OUT!
NOT THIS ONE. IT SHOULDN'T CRYSTALLIZE WHEN THE WATER'S GONE.
うーーーん
HMMMM MM
AND NOT THIS ONE. IT SHOULDN'T GLOW WHEN MOONLIGHT PASSES THROUGH.
NOPE. THIS ONE'S STILL A LIQUID. THERE'S JUST LESS OF IT.
TRANQUILEAF DOESN'T HAVE MUCH OF AN ODOR, SO ONES THAT SMELL BAD ARE OUT.

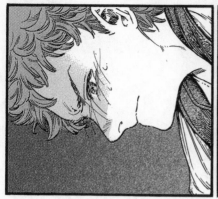

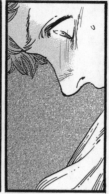

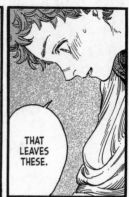

THAT LEAVES THESE.
IT'S DOWN TO JUST THESE THREE!
BUT THEY ALL LOOK EXACTLY THE SAME!
RUFFLE RUFFLE RUFFLE
わしゃ わしゃ わしゃ
ARGH! I'M SO CLOSE!
JUST A LITTLE FURTHER!
JUST A LITTLE—
NO... THIS IS AS FAR AS I CAN GO.

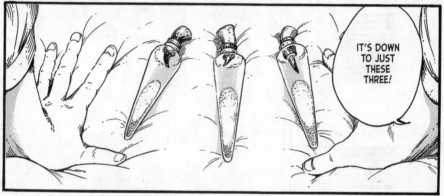

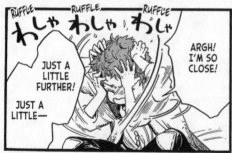

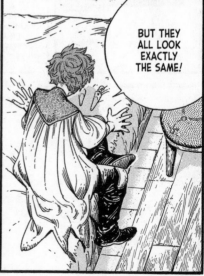

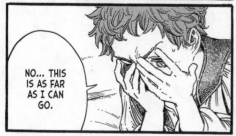

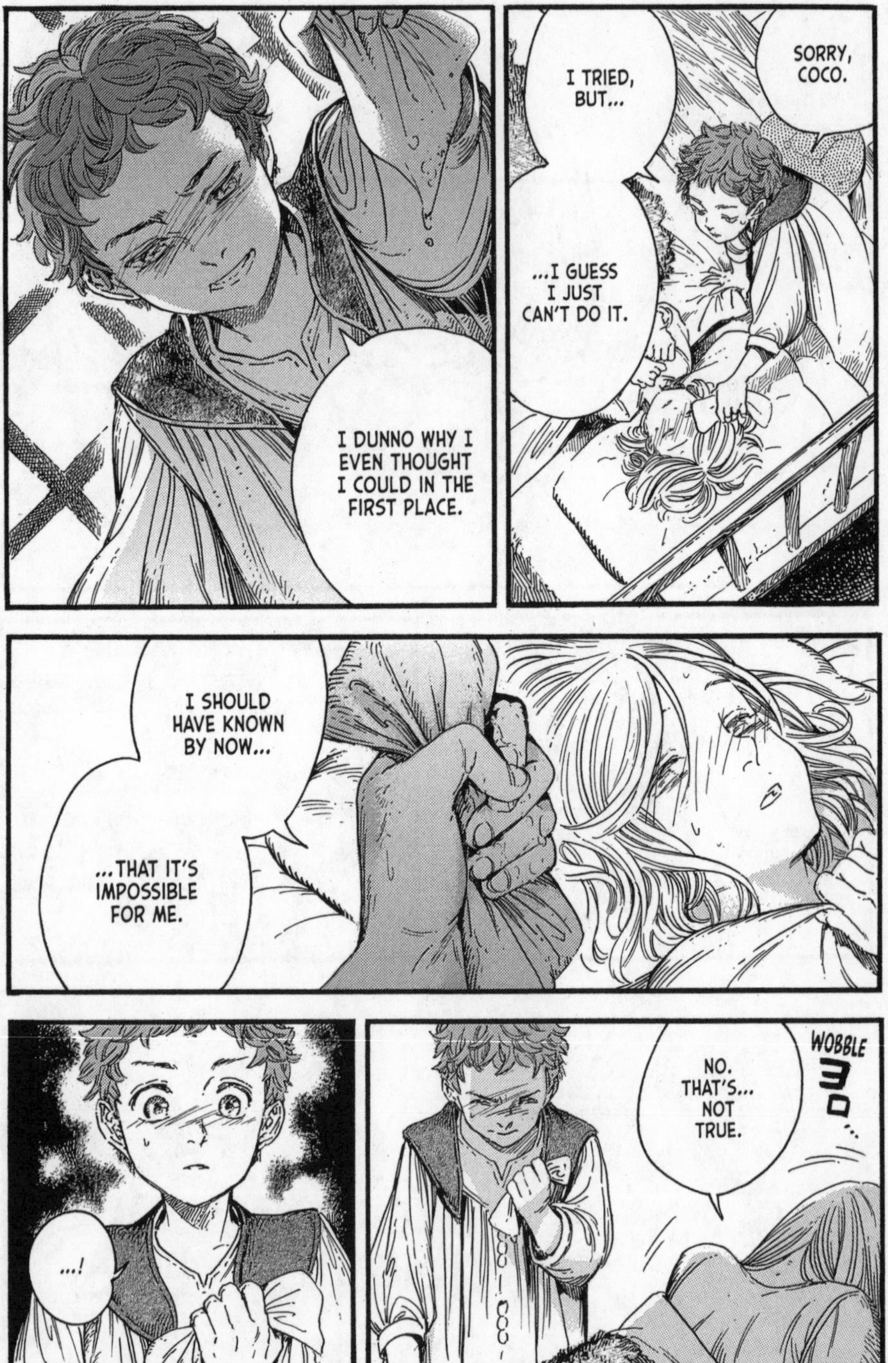
SORRY, COCO.
I TRIED, BUT...
...I GUESS I JUST CAN'T DO IT.
I DUNNO WHY I EVEN THOUGHT I COULD IN THE FIRST PLACE.
I SHOULD HAVE KNOWN BY NOW...
...THAT IT'S IMPOSSIBLE FOR ME.
WOBBLE
ヨロ...
NO. THAT'S... NOT TRUE.
...!

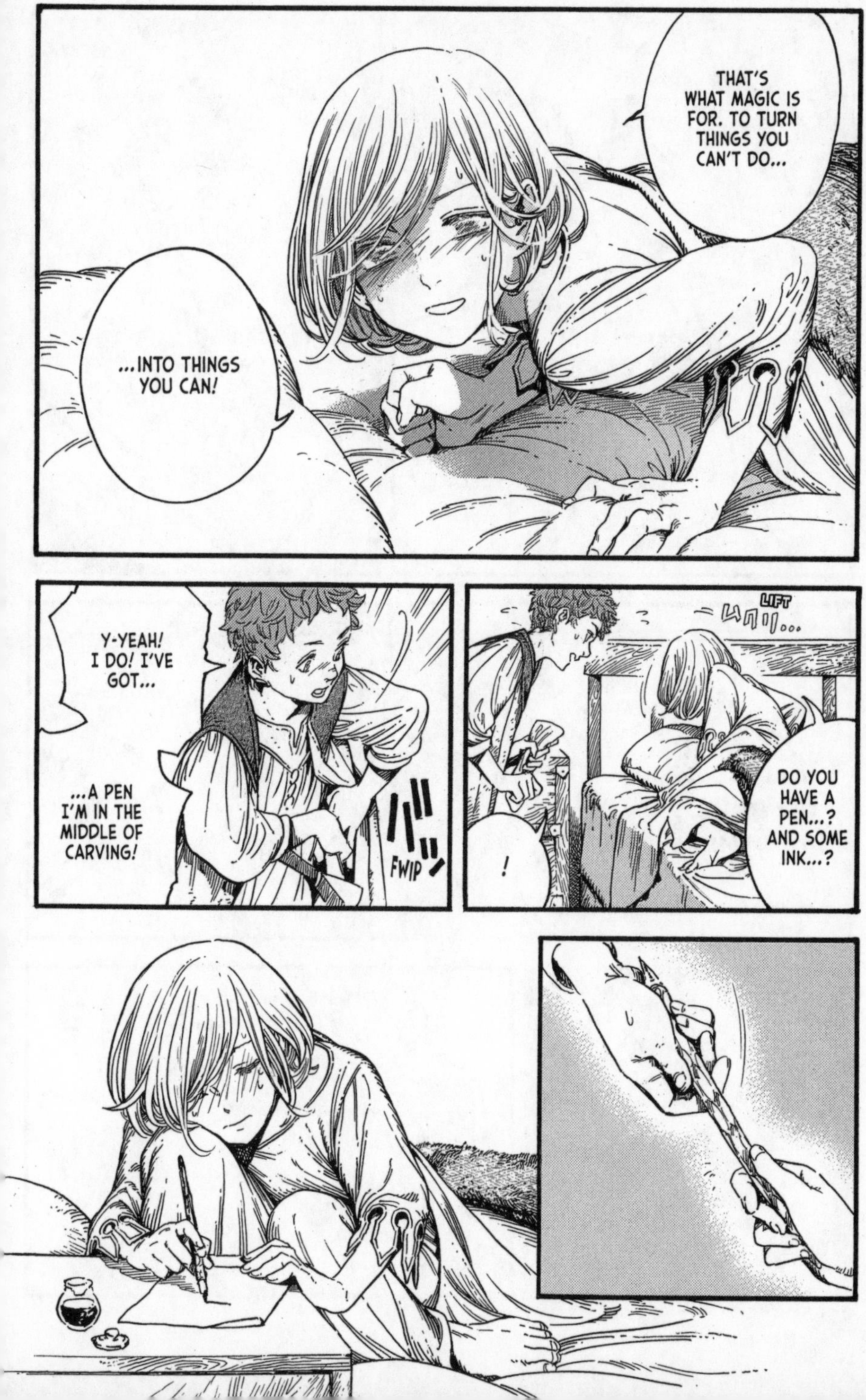
THAT'S WHAT MAGIC IS FOR. TO TURN THINGS YOU CAN'T DO...
...INTO THINGS YOU CAN!
LIFT
DO YOU HAVE A PEN...? AND SOME INK...?
!
Y-YEAH! I DO! I'VE GOT...
...A PEN I'M IN THE MIDDLE OF CARVING!
FWIP

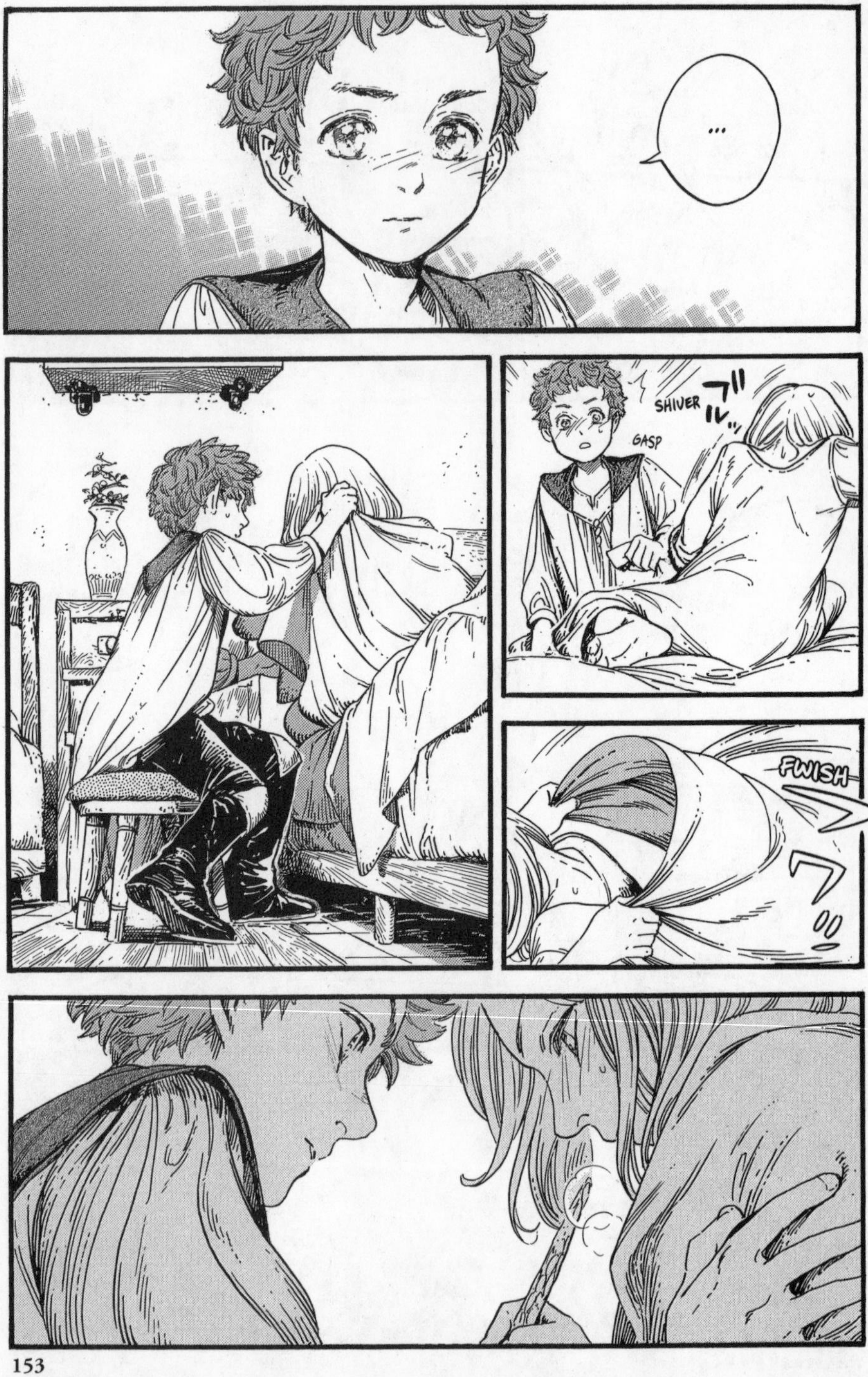
...
SHIVER
GASP
FWISH

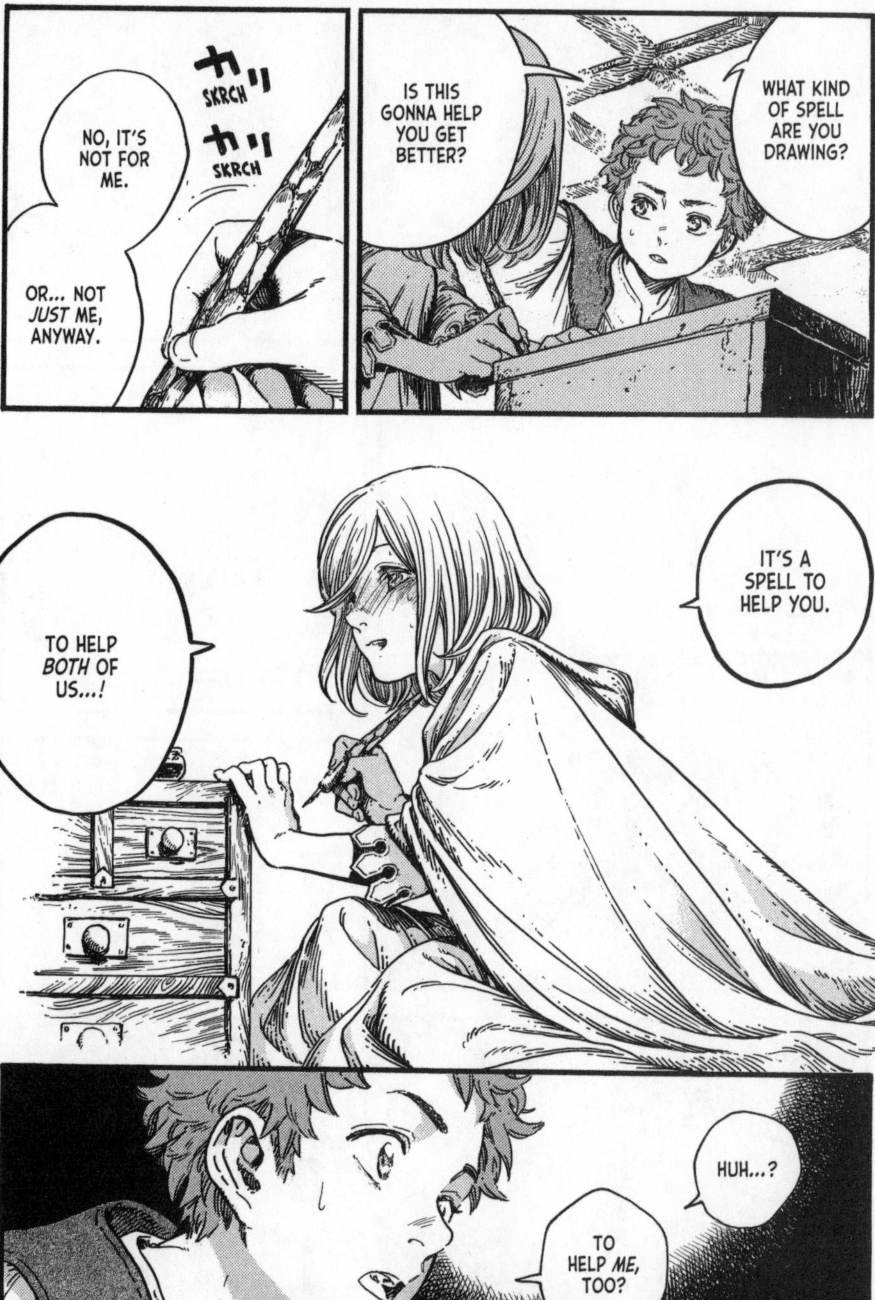
WHAT KIND OF SPELL ARE YOU DRAWING?
IS THIS GONNA HELP YOU GET BETTER?
カリ SKRCH
カリ SKRCH
NO, IT'S NOT FOR ME.
OR... NOT *JUST* ME, ANYWAY.
IT'S A SPELL TO HELP YOU.
TO HELP *BOTH* OF US...!
HUH...?
TO HELP *ME*, TOO?

Witch Hat Atelier

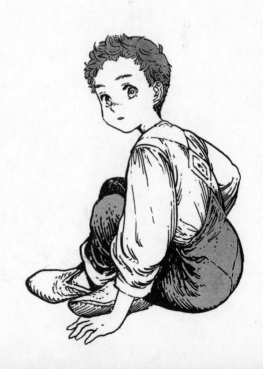

Chapter 17

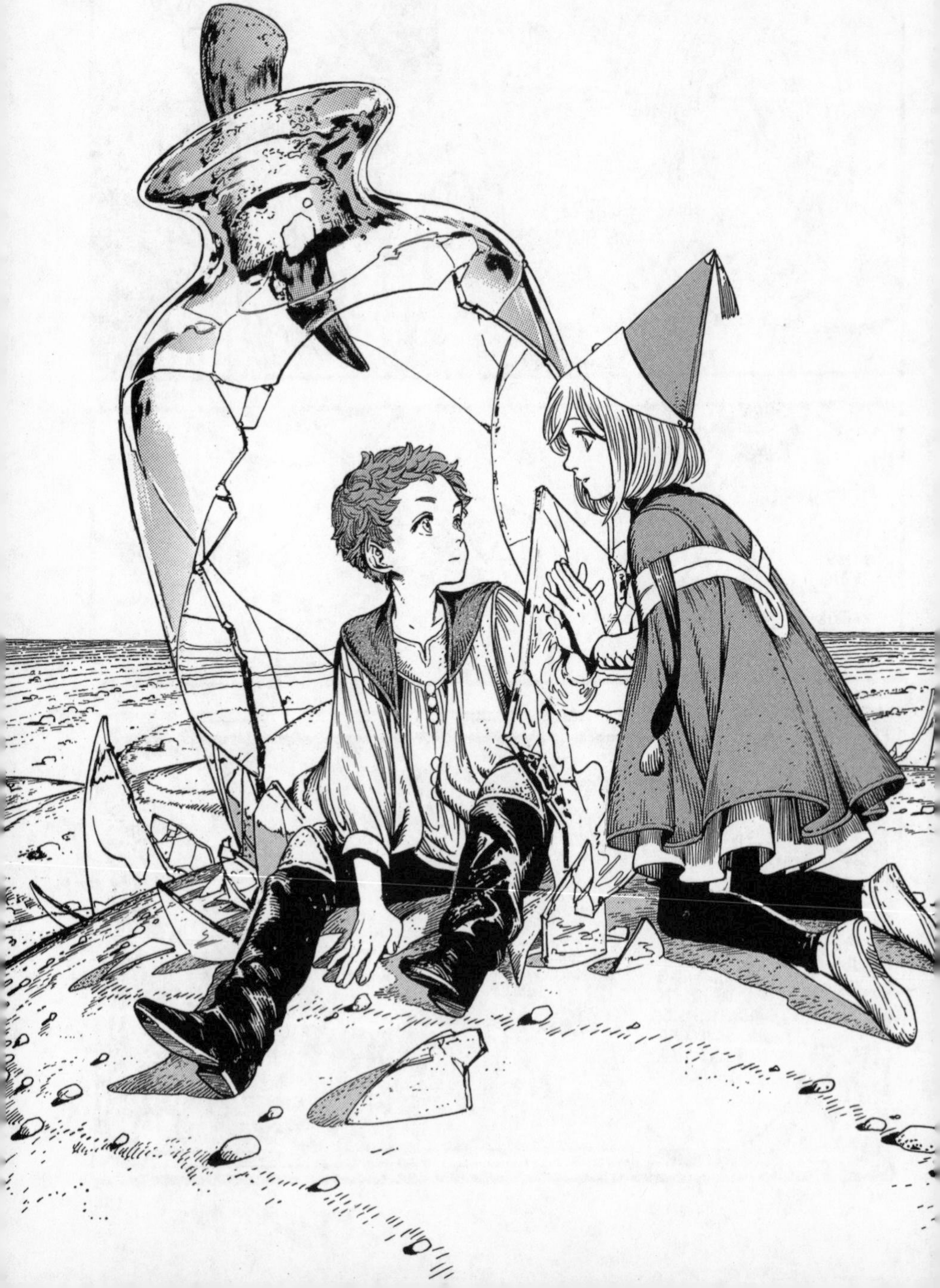

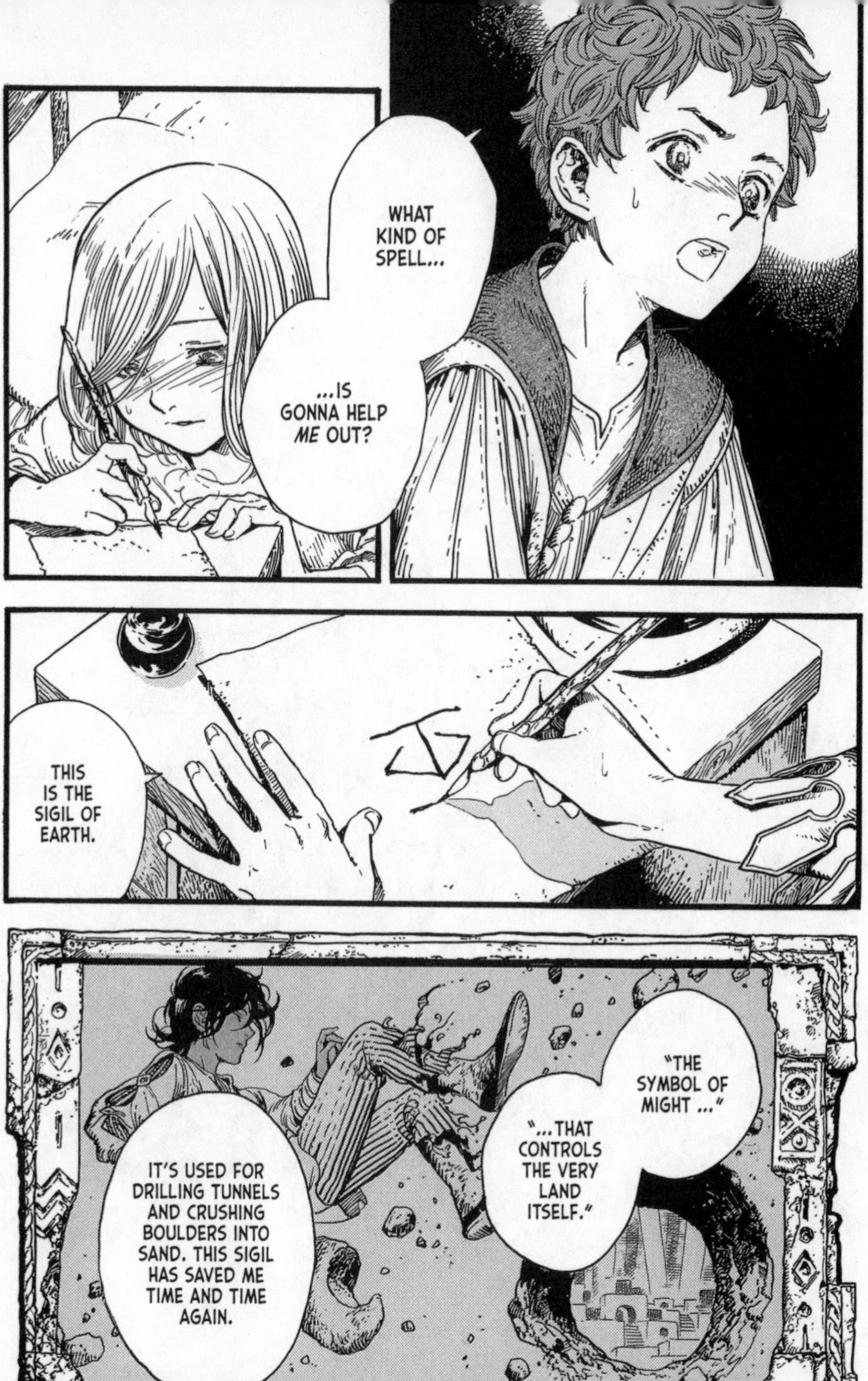
WHAT KIND OF SPELL...
...IS GONNA HELP *ME* OUT?
THIS IS THE SIGIL OF EARTH.
"THE SYMBOL OF MIGHT ..."
"...THAT CONTROLS THE VERY LAND ITSELF."
IT'S USED FOR DRILLING TUNNELS AND CRUSHING BOULDERS INTO SAND. THIS SIGIL HAS SAVED ME TIME AND TIME AGAIN.

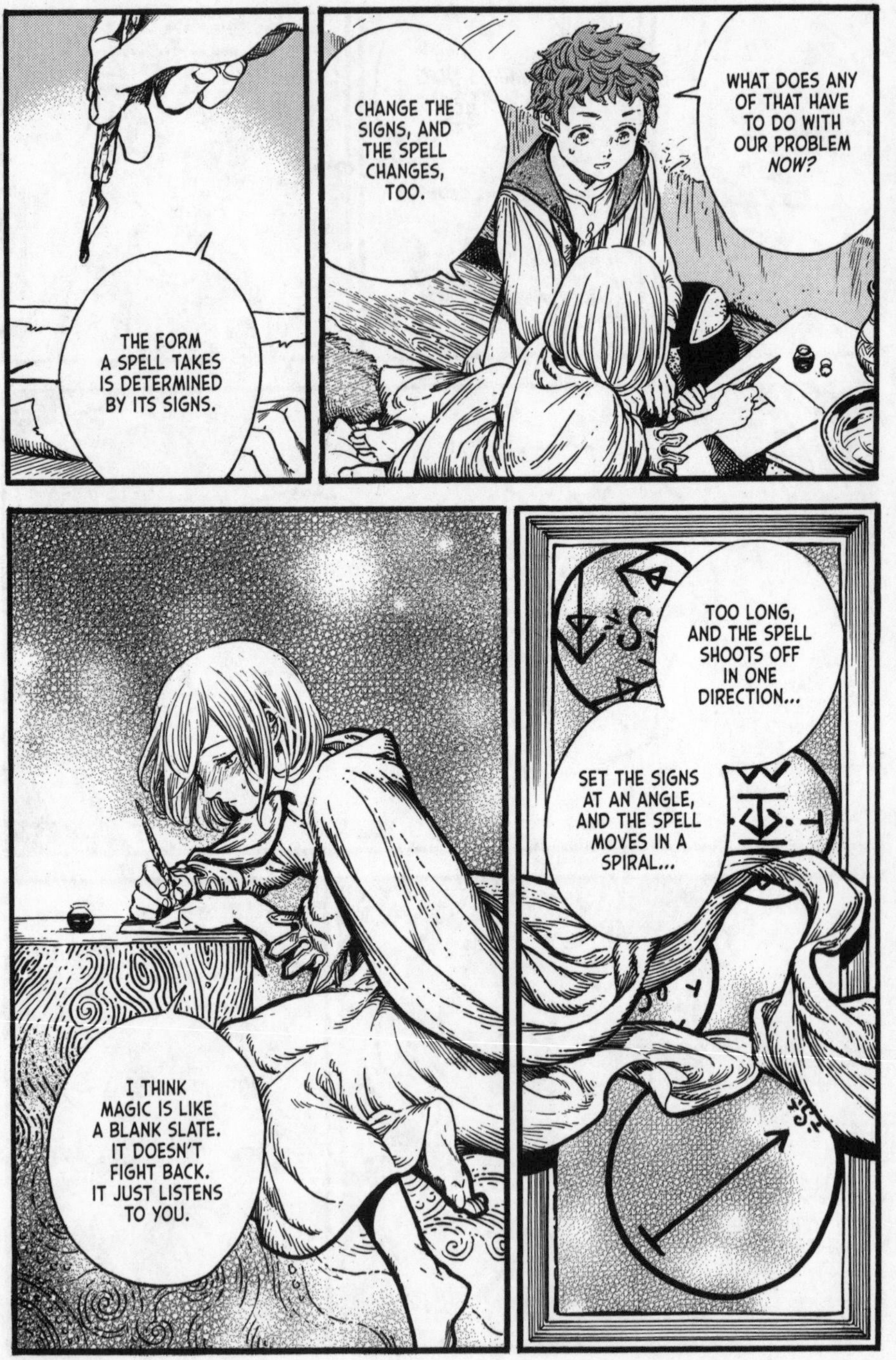
WHAT DOES ANY OF THAT HAVE TO DO WITH OUR PROBLEM *NOW?*
CHANGE THE SIGNS, AND THE SPELL CHANGES, TOO.
THE FORM A SPELL TAKES IS DETERMINED BY ITS SIGNS.
TOO LONG, AND THE SPELL SHOOTS OFF IN ONE DIRECTION...
SET THE SIGNS AT AN ANGLE, AND THE SPELL MOVES IN A SPIRAL...
I THINK MAGIC IS LIKE A BLANK SLATE. IT DOESN'T FIGHT BACK. IT JUST LISTENS TO YOU.

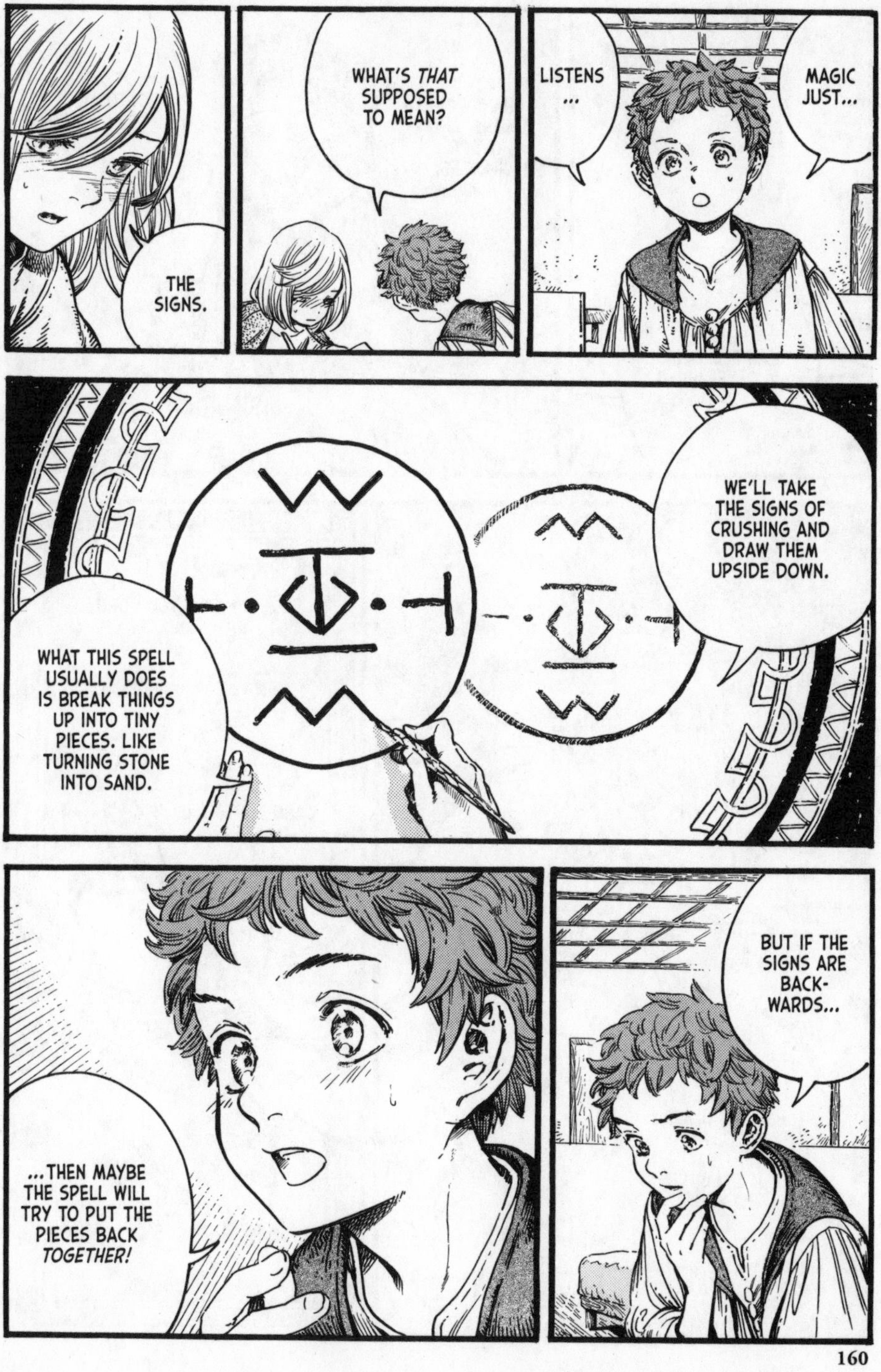
MAGIC JUST...
LISTENS ...
WHAT'S *THAT* SUPPOSED TO MEAN?
THE SIGNS.
WE'LL TAKE THE SIGNS OF CRUSHING AND DRAW THEM UPSIDE DOWN.
WHAT THIS SPELL USUALLY DOES IS BREAK THINGS UP INTO TINY PIECES. LIKE TURNING STONE INTO SAND.
BUT IF THE SIGNS ARE BACK-WARDS...
...THEN MAYBE THE SPELL WILL TRY TO PUT THE PIECES BACK *TOGETHER!*

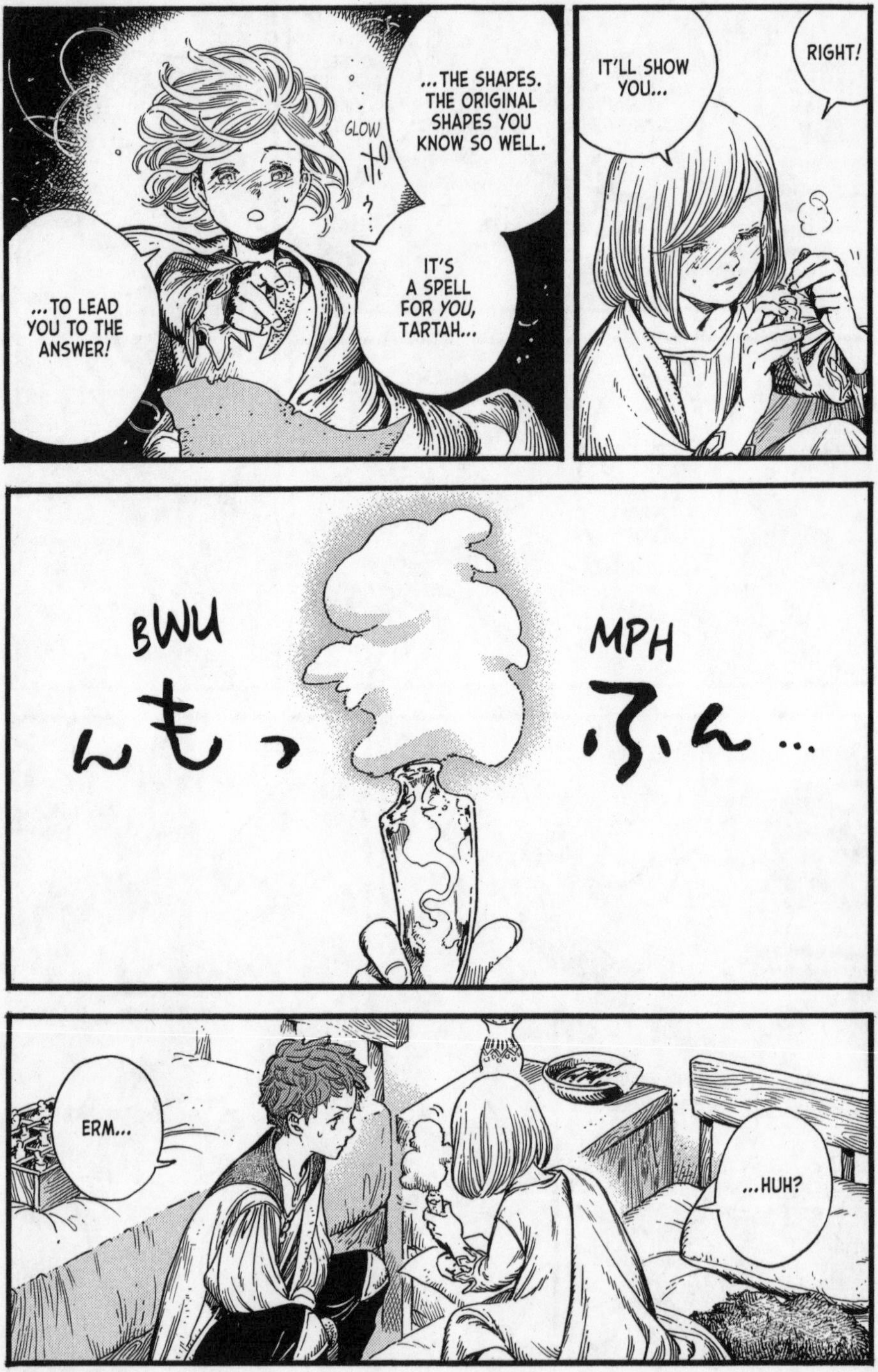
RIGHT!
IT'LL SHOW YOU...
...THE SHAPES. THE ORIGINAL SHAPES YOU KNOW SO WELL.
GLOW
IT'S A SPELL FOR *YOU*, TARTAH...
...TO LEAD YOU TO THE ANSWER!
BWU MPH
んもっ ふん…
...HUH?
ERM...

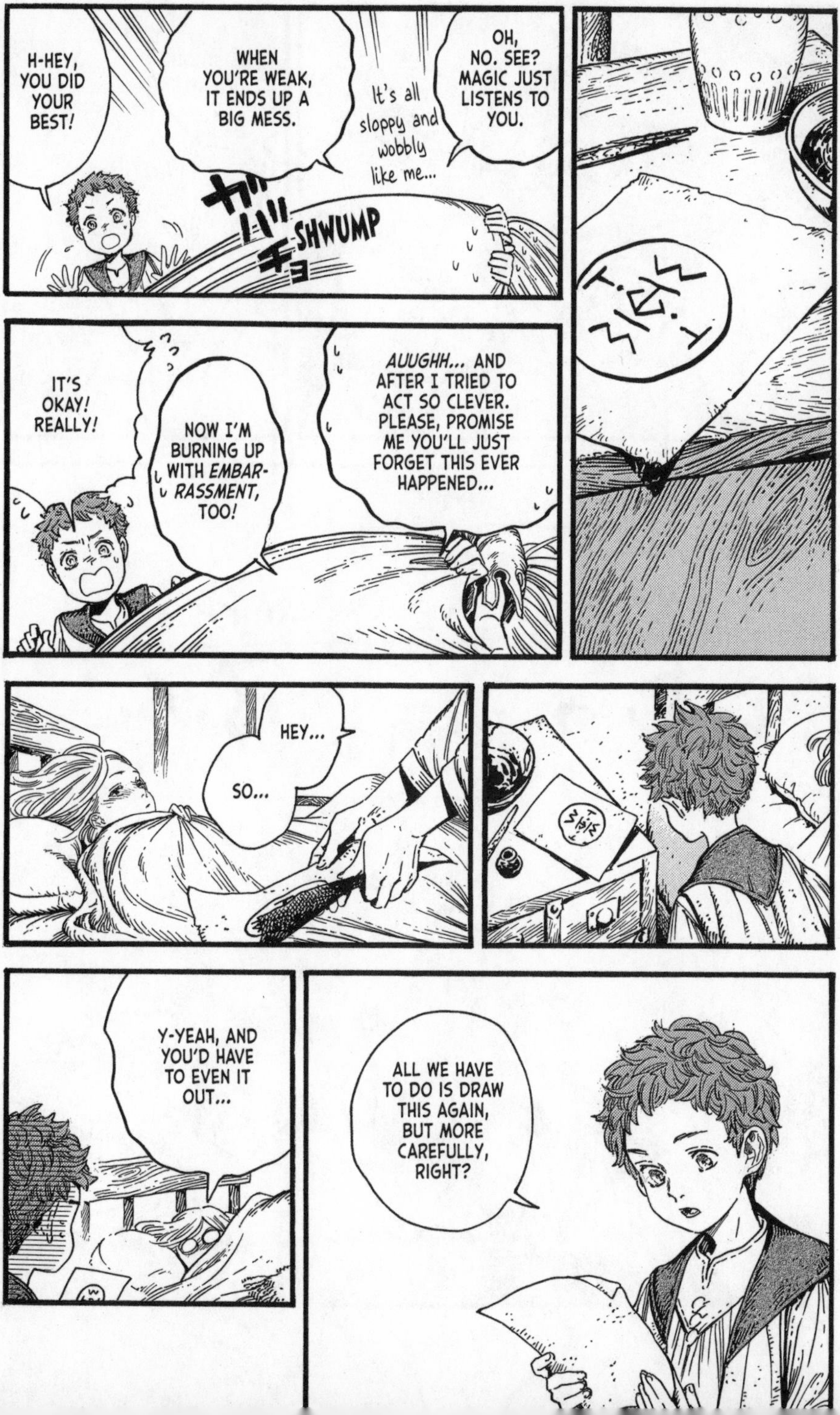
OH, NO. SEE? MAGIC JUST LISTENS TO YOU.
It's all sloppy and wobbly like me...
WHEN YOU'RE WEAK, IT ENDS UP A BIG MESS.
SHWUMP
H-HEY, YOU DID YOUR BEST!
AUUGHH... AND AFTER I TRIED TO ACT SO CLEVER. PLEASE, PROMISE ME YOU'LL JUST FORGET THIS EVER HAPPENED...
NOW I'M BURNING UP WITH *EMBARRASSMENT*, TOO!
IT'S OKAY! *REALLY!*
HEY...
SO...
ALL WE HAVE TO DO IS DRAW THIS AGAIN, BUT MORE CAREFULLY, RIGHT?
Y-YEAH, AND YOU'D HAVE TO EVEN IT OUT...

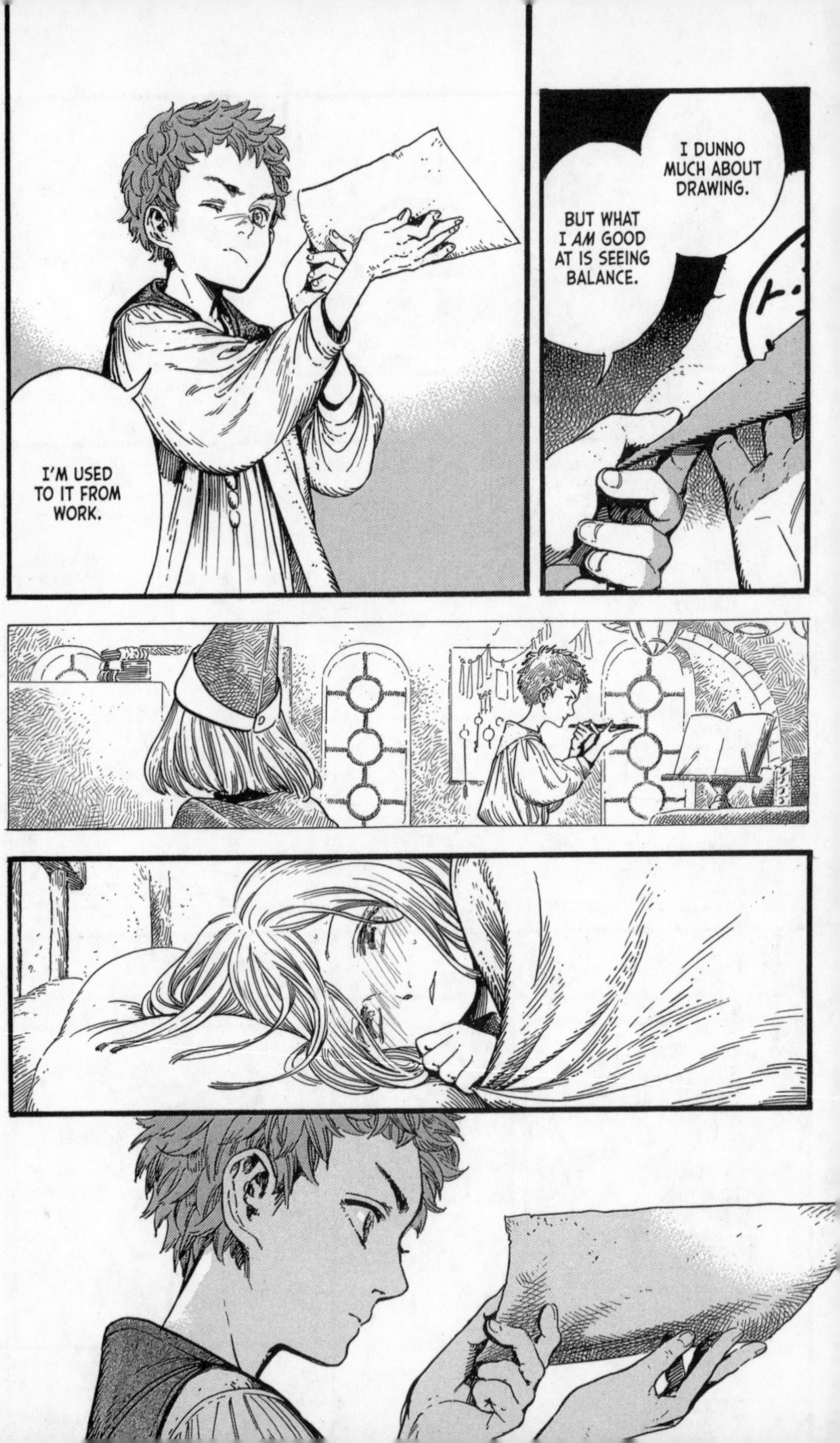
I DUNNO MUCH ABOUT DRAWING.
BUT WHAT I *AM* GOOD AT IS SEEING BALANCE.
I'M USED TO IT FROM WORK.

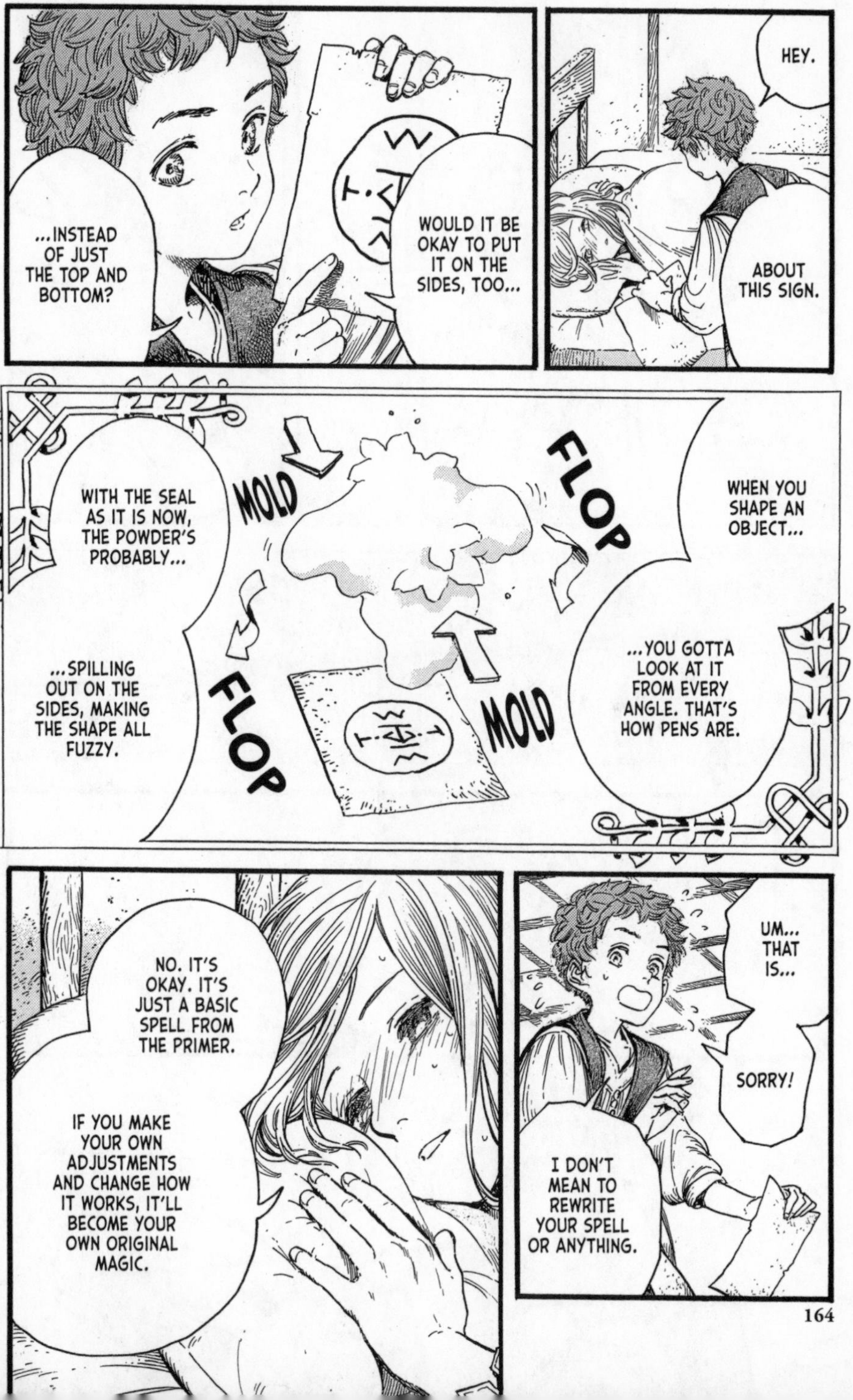
HEY.
ABOUT THIS SIGN.
WOULD IT BE OKAY TO PUT IT ON THE SIDES, TOO...
...INSTEAD OF JUST THE TOP AND BOTTOM?
WHEN YOU SHAPE AN OBJECT...
...YOU GOTTA LOOK AT IT FROM EVERY ANGLE. THAT'S HOW PENS ARE.
FLOP
MOLD
MOLD
FLOP
WITH THE SEAL AS IT IS NOW, THE POWDER'S PROBABLY...
...SPILLING OUT ON THE SIDES, MAKING THE SHAPE ALL FUZZY.
UM... THAT IS...
SORRY!
I DON'T MEAN TO REWRITE YOUR SPELL OR ANYTHING.
NO. IT'S OKAY. IT'S JUST A BASIC SPELL FROM THE PRIMER.
IF YOU MAKE YOUR OWN ADJUSTMENTS AND CHANGE HOW IT WORKS, IT'LL BECOME YOUR OWN ORIGINAL MAGIC.

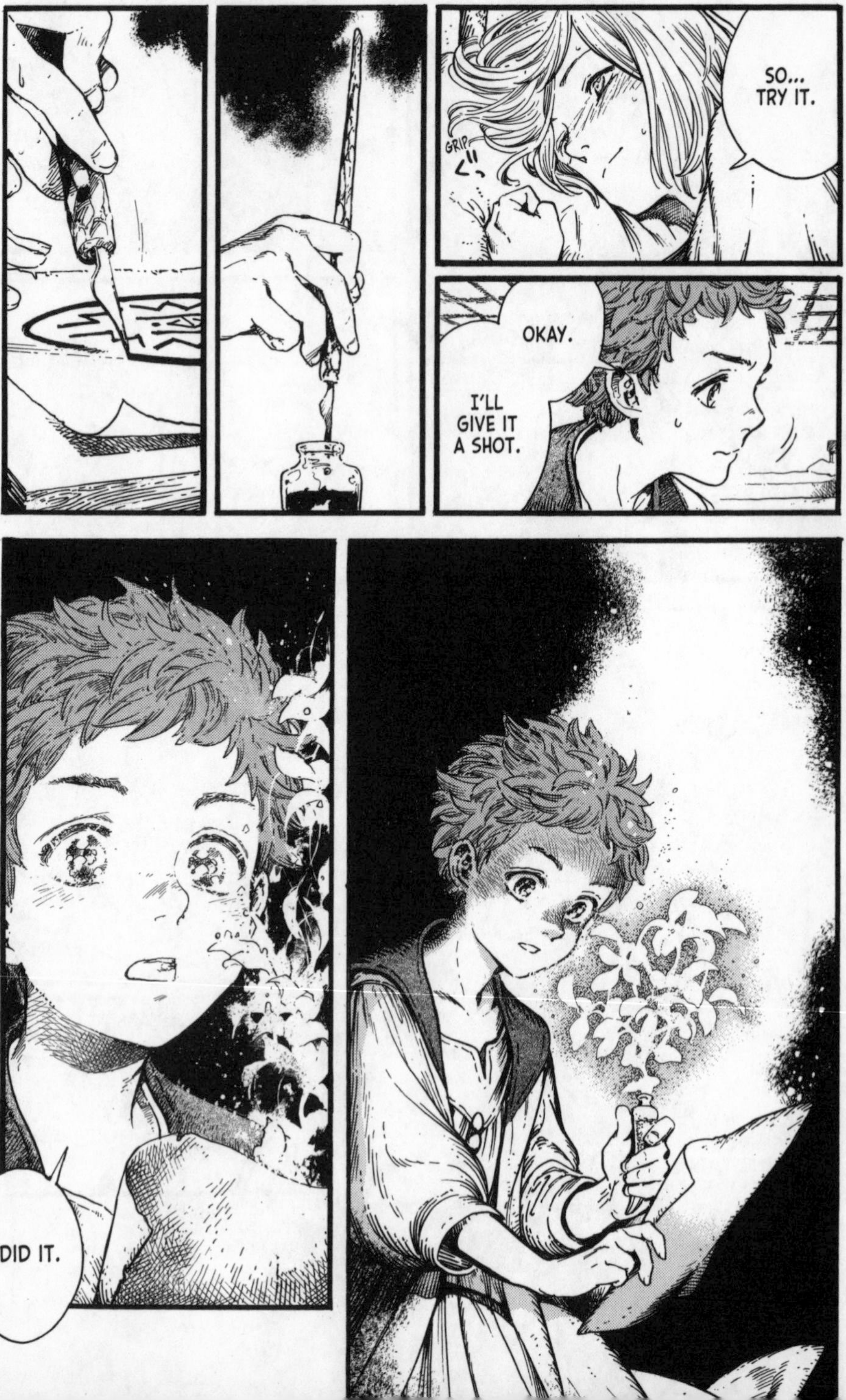
SO... TRY IT.
GRIP
OKAY.
I'LL GIVE IT A SHOT.
I DID IT.

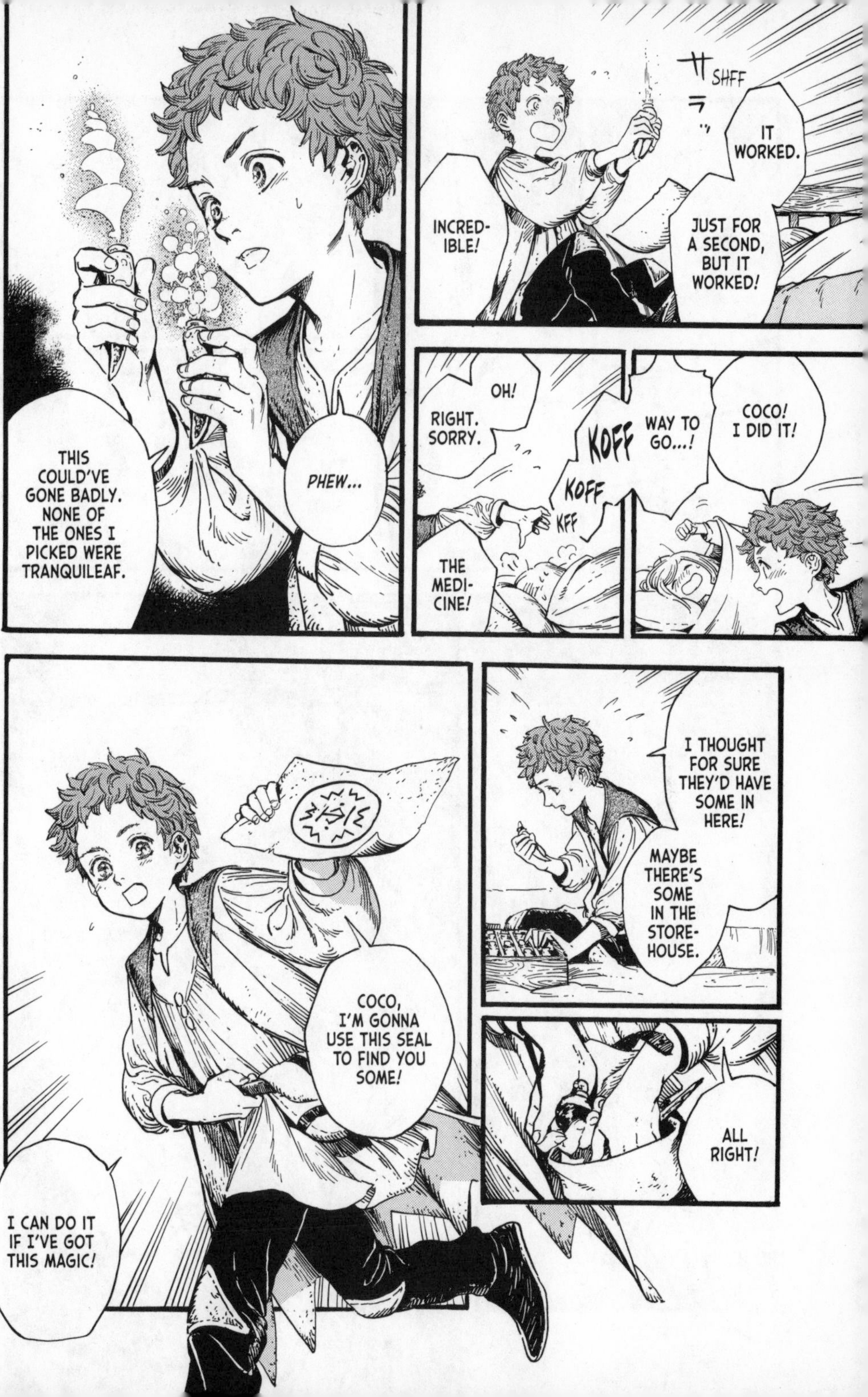
SHFF
IT WORKED.
JUST FOR A SECOND, BUT IT WORKED!
INCREDIBLE!
COCO! I DID IT!
WAY TO GO...!
KOFF
KOFF
KFF
OH!
RIGHT. SORRY.
THE MEDICINE!
PHEW...
THIS COULD'VE GONE BADLY. NONE OF THE ONES I PICKED WERE TRANQUILEAF.
I THOUGHT FOR SURE THEY'D HAVE SOME IN HERE!
MAYBE THERE'S SOME IN THE STORE-HOUSE.
ALL RIGHT!
COCO, I'M GONNA USE THIS SEAL TO FIND YOU SOME!
I CAN DO IT IF I'VE GOT THIS MAGIC!

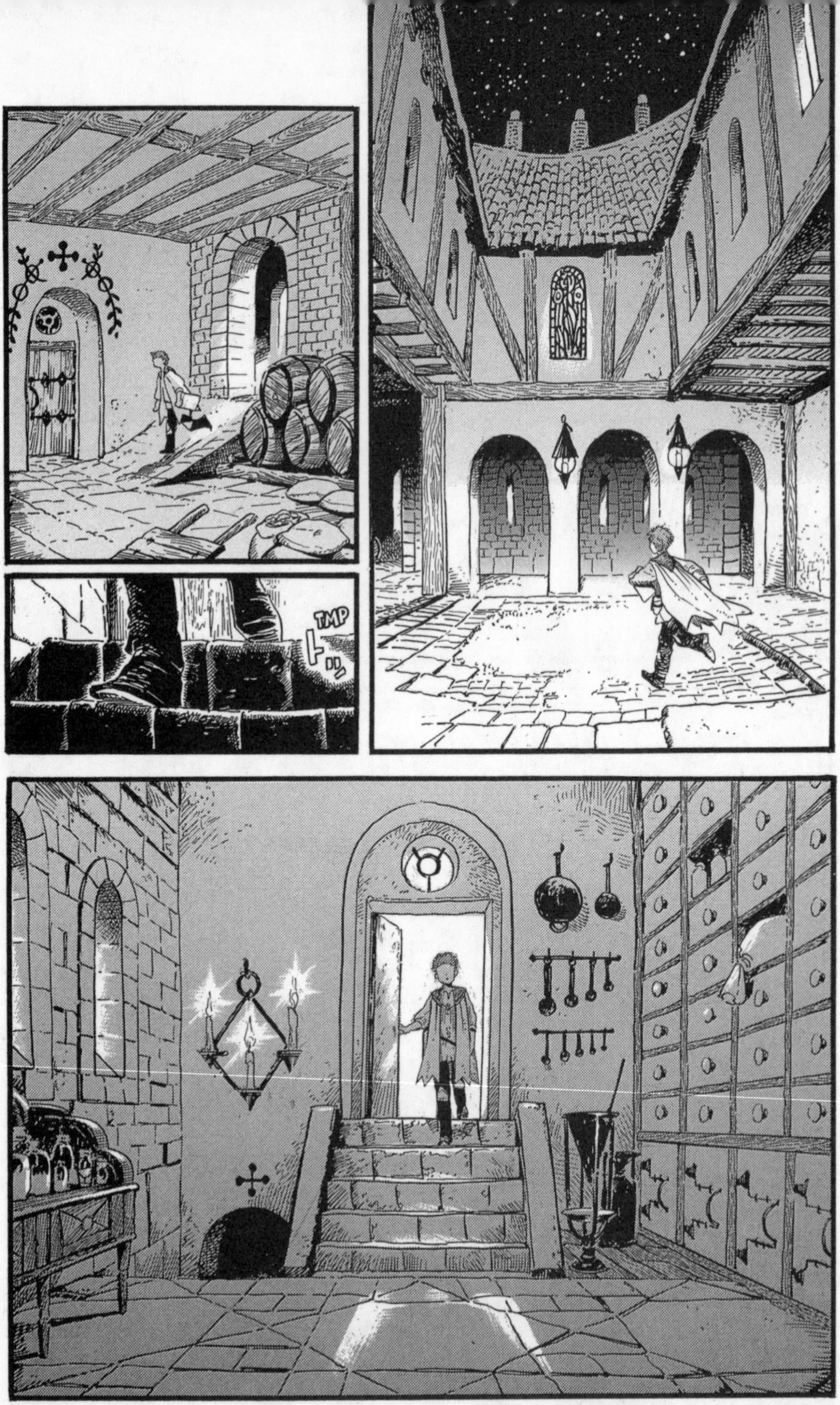
TMP
トッ

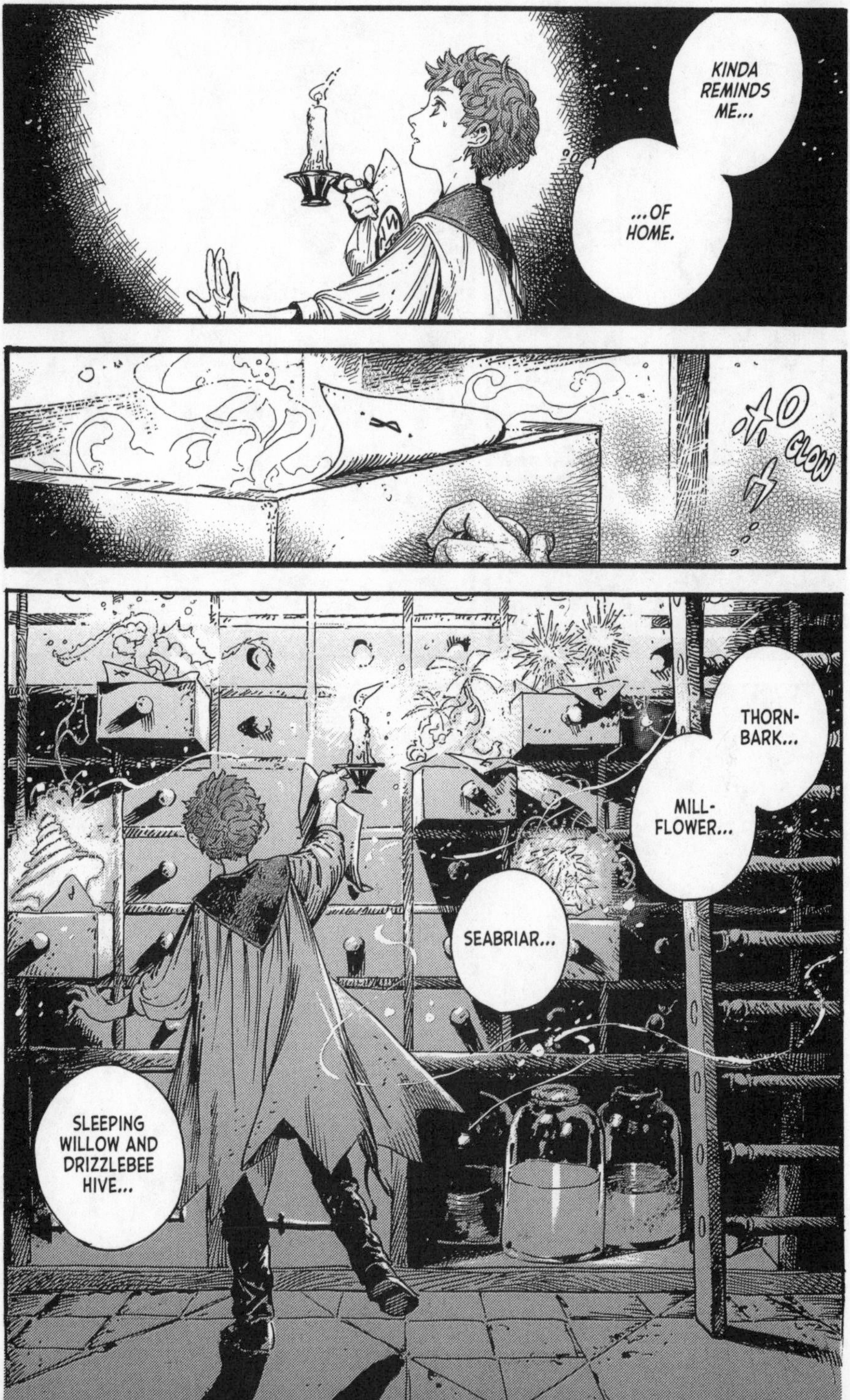
KINDA REMINDS ME...
...OF HOME.
GLOW
THORN-BARK...
MILL-FLOWER...
SEABRIAR...
SLEEPING WILLOW AND DRIZZLEBEE HIVE...

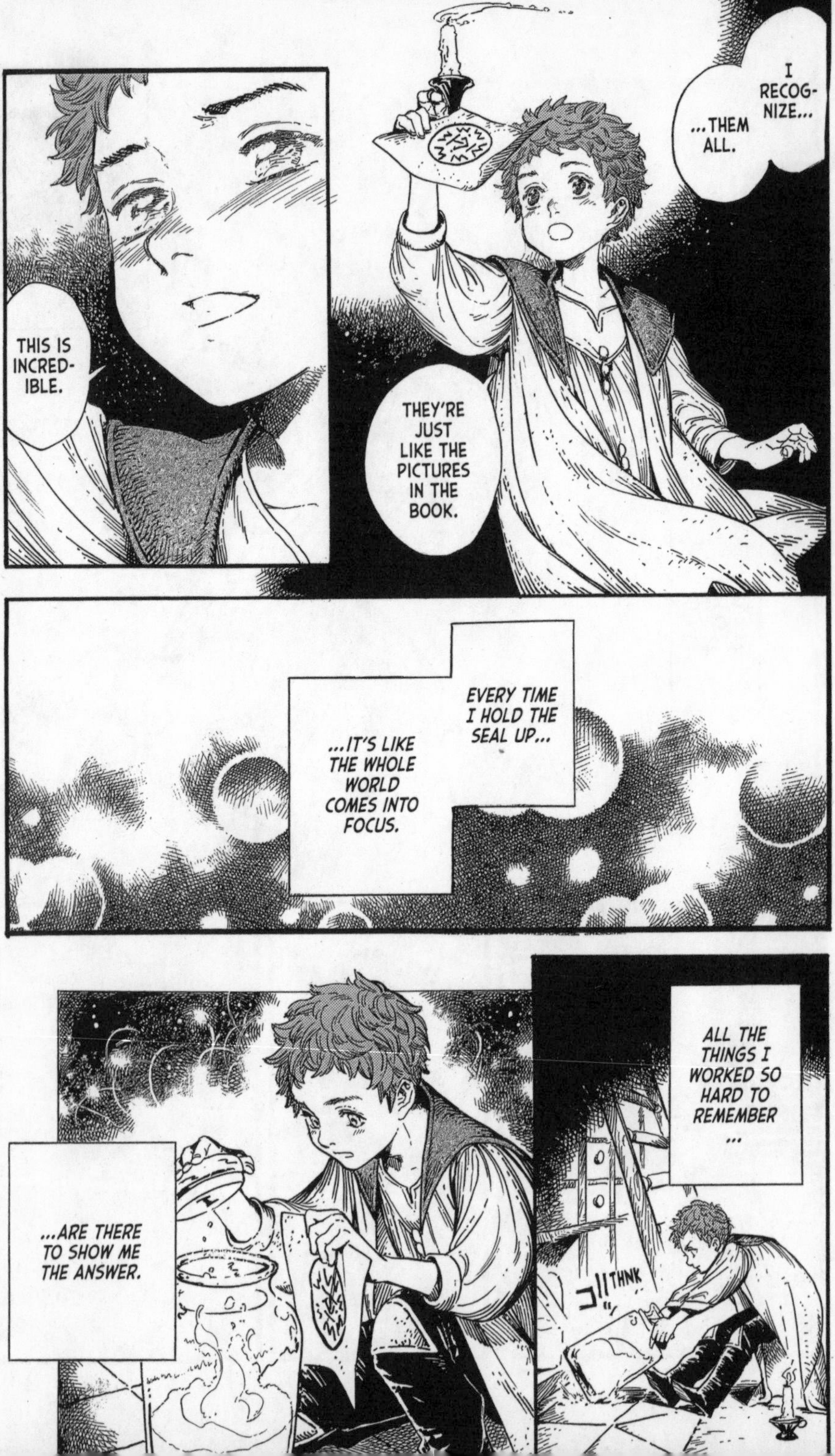
I RECOGNIZE...
...THEM ALL.
THEY'RE JUST LIKE THE PICTURES IN THE BOOK.
THIS IS INCREDIBLE.
EVERY TIME I HOLD THE SEAL UP...
...IT'S LIKE THE WHOLE WORLD COMES INTO FOCUS.
ALL THE THINGS I WORKED SO HARD TO REMEMBER ...
THNK
...ARE THERE TO SHOW ME THE ANSWER.

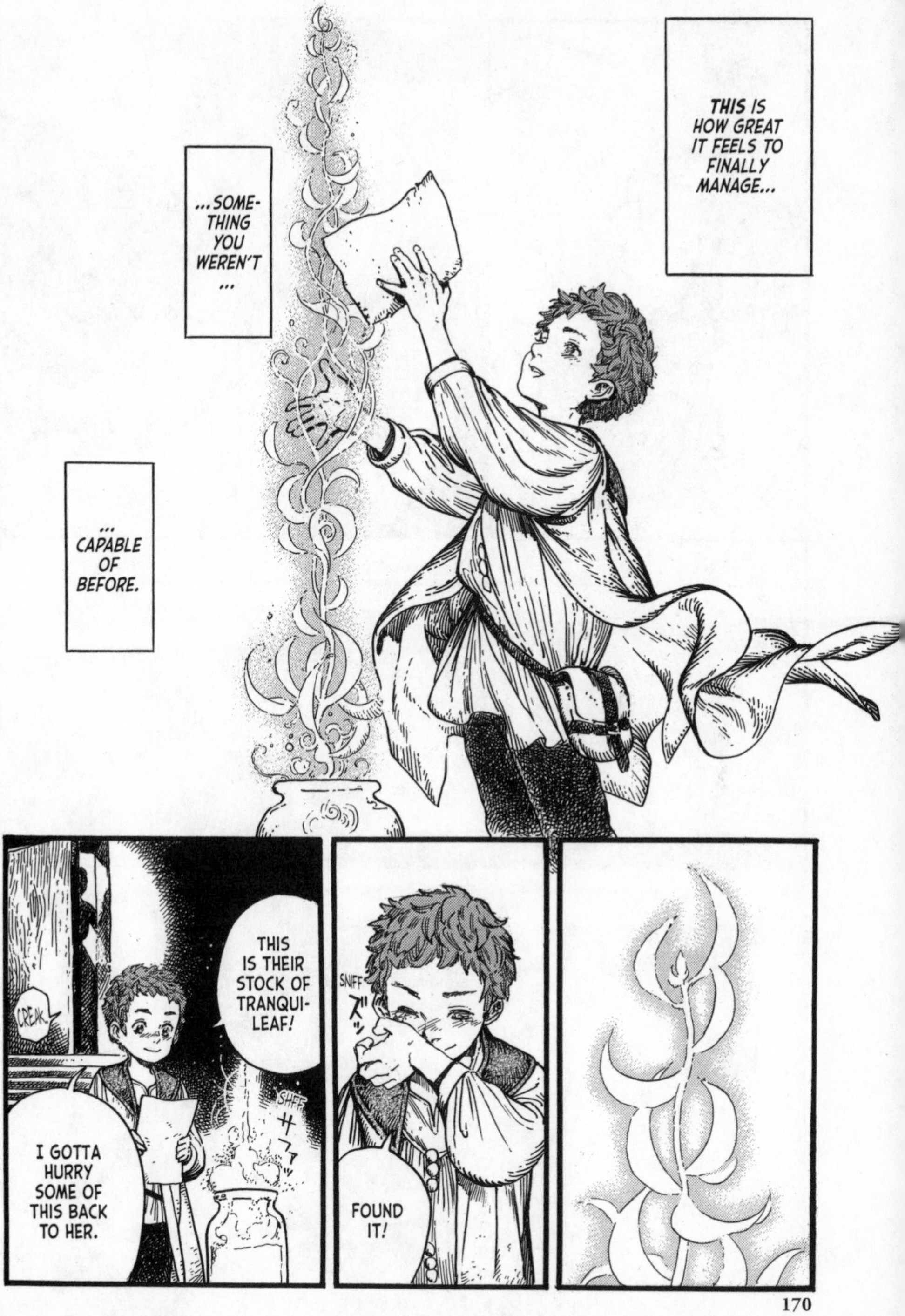
THIS IS HOW GREAT IT FEELS TO FINALLY MANAGE...
...SOME-THING YOU WEREN'T ...
... CAPABLE OF BEFORE.
SNIFF
ズッ
FOUND IT!
THIS IS THEIR STOCK OF TRANQUI-LEAF!
SHFF
サファッ
CREAK
I GOTTA HURRY SOME OF THIS BACK TO HER.

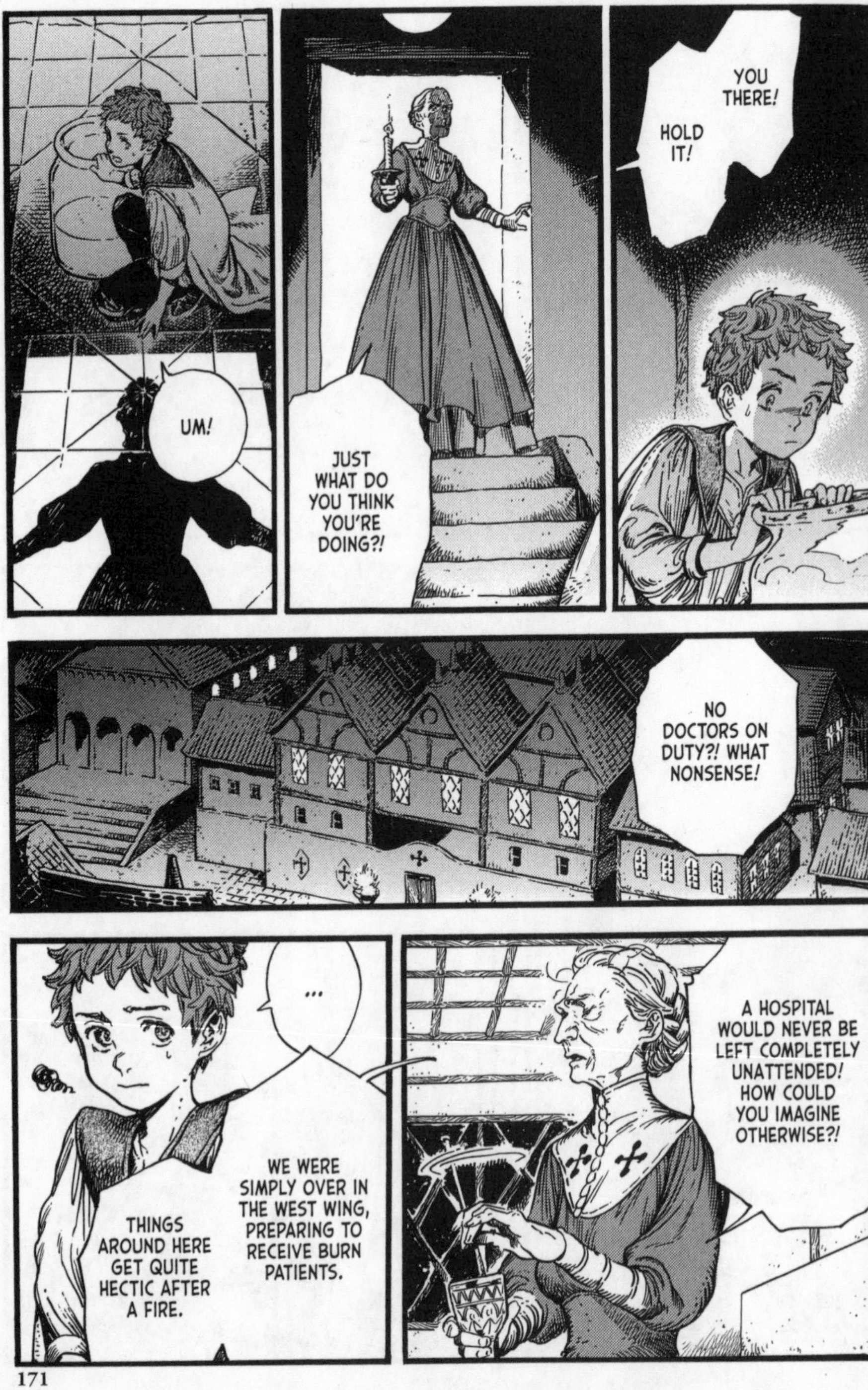
YOU THERE!
HOLD IT!
JUST WHAT DO YOU THINK YOU'RE DOING?!
UM!
NO DOCTORS ON DUTY?! WHAT NONSENSE!
A HOSPITAL WOULD NEVER BE LEFT COMPLETELY UNATTENDED! HOW COULD YOU IMAGINE OTHERWISE?!
...
WE WERE SIMPLY OVER IN THE WEST WING, PREPARING TO RECEIVE BURN PATIENTS.
THINGS AROUND HERE GET QUITE HECTIC AFTER A FIRE.

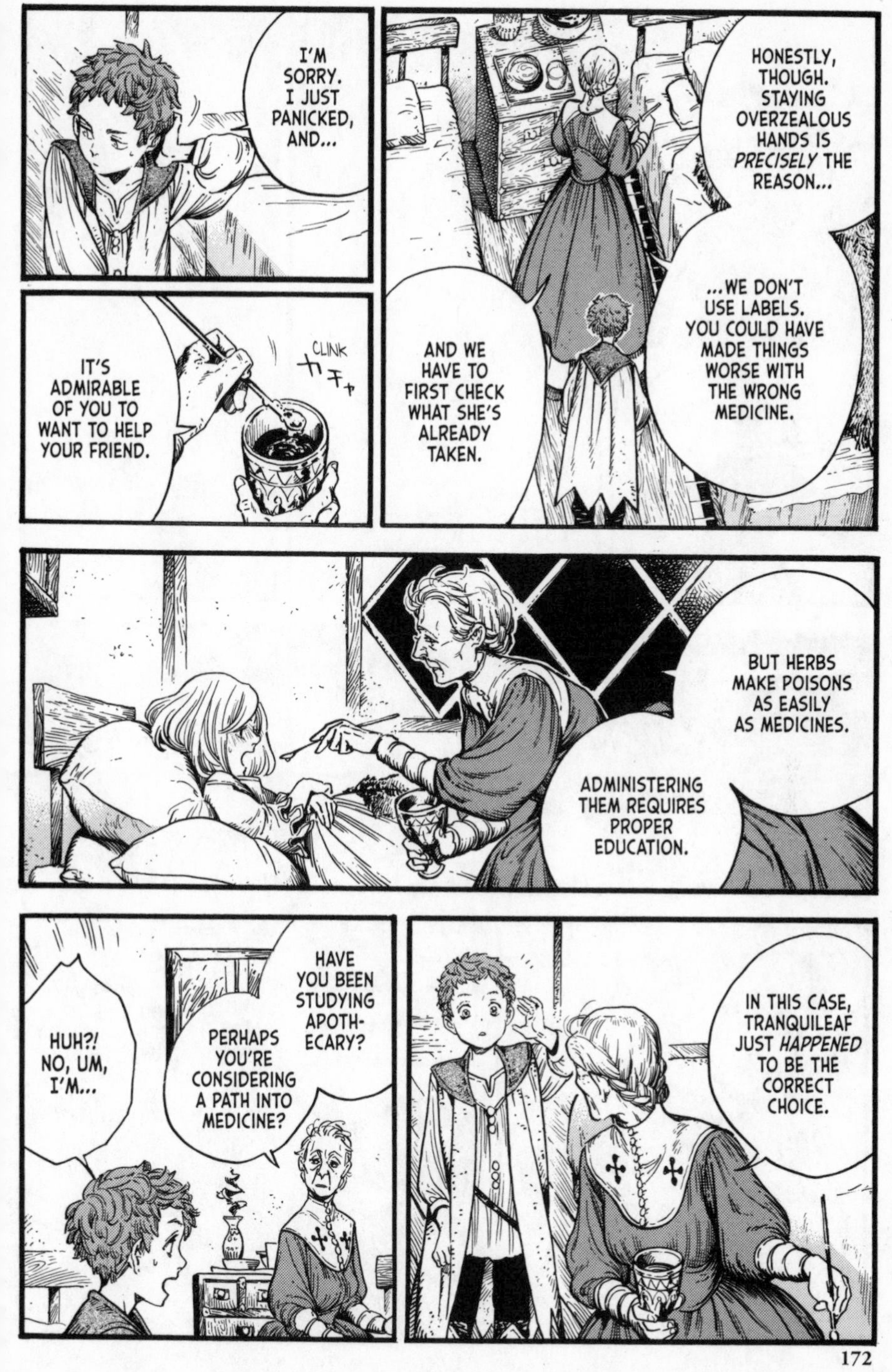
HONESTLY, THOUGH. STAYING OVERZEALOUS HANDS IS *PRECISELY* THE REASON...
...WE DON'T USE LABELS. YOU COULD HAVE MADE THINGS WORSE WITH THE WRONG MEDICINE.
AND WE HAVE TO FIRST CHECK WHAT SHE'S ALREADY TAKEN.
I'M SORRY. I JUST PANICKED, AND...
CLINK
カチャ
IT'S ADMIRABLE OF YOU TO WANT TO HELP YOUR FRIEND.
BUT HERBS MAKE POISONS AS EASILY AS MEDICINES.
ADMINISTERING THEM REQUIRES PROPER EDUCATION.
IN THIS CASE, TRANQUILEAF JUST *HAPPENED* TO BE THE CORRECT CHOICE.
HAVE YOU BEEN STUDYING APOTHECARY?
PERHAPS YOU'RE CONSIDERING A PATH INTO MEDICINE?
HUH?! NO, UM, I'M...

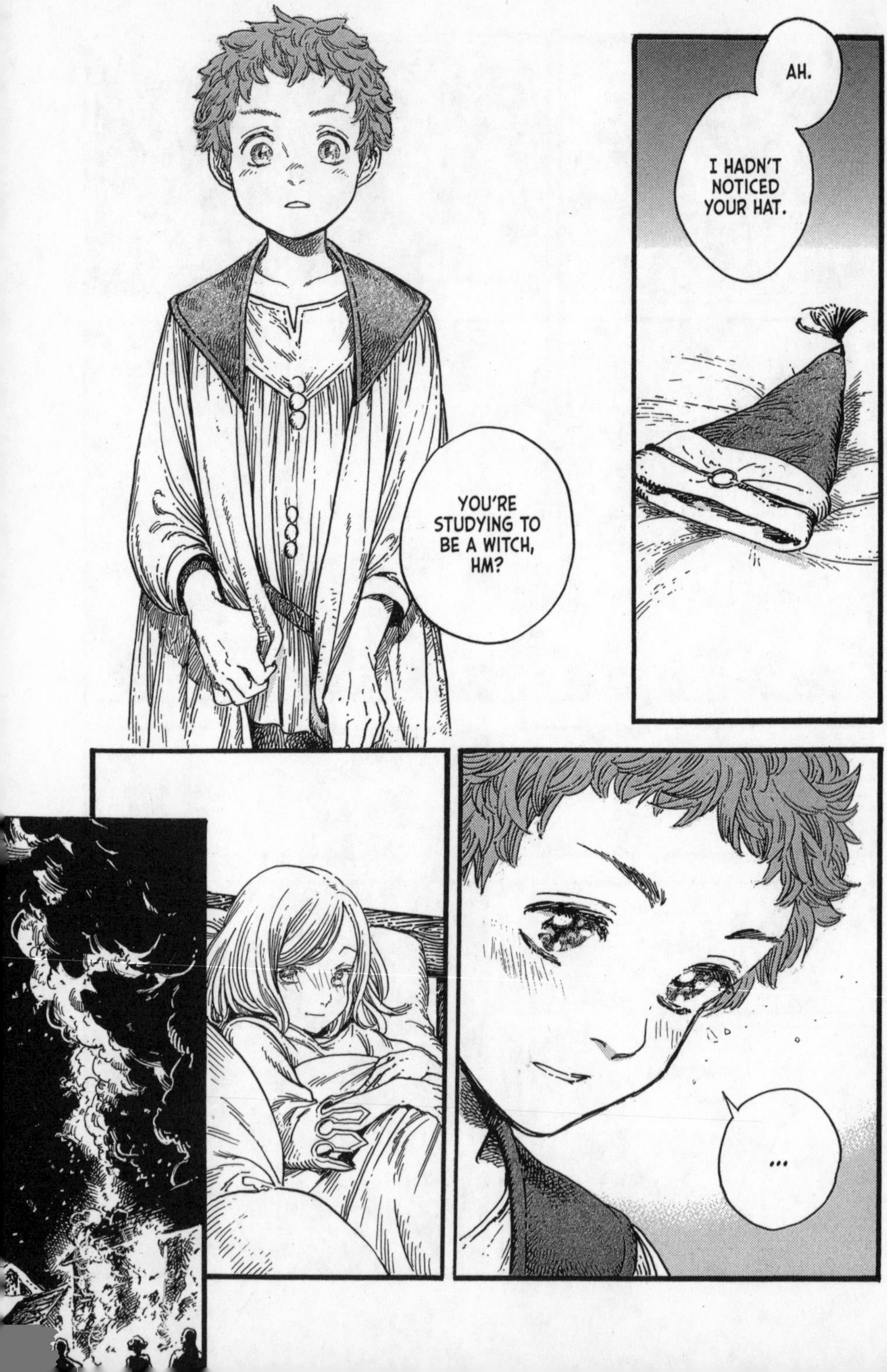
AH.
I HADN'T NOTICED YOUR HAT.
YOU'RE STUDYING TO BE A WITCH, HM?
...

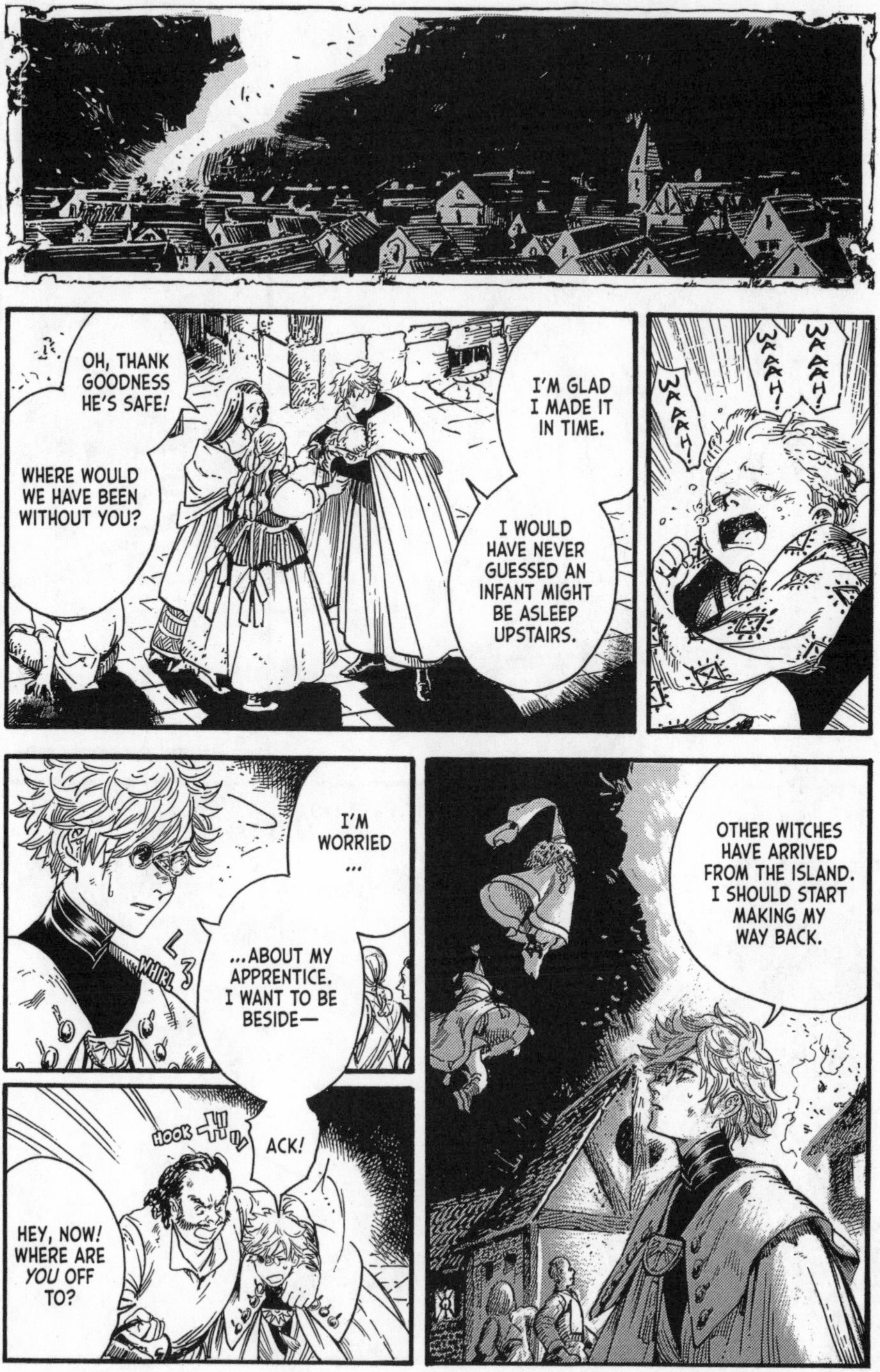
WAAAH!
WAAAH!
WAAAH!
I'M GLAD I MADE IT IN TIME.
I WOULD HAVE NEVER GUESSED AN INFANT MIGHT BE ASLEEP UPSTAIRS.
OH, THANK GOODNESS HE'S SAFE!
WHERE WOULD WE HAVE BEEN WITHOUT YOU?
OTHER WITCHES HAVE ARRIVED FROM THE ISLAND. I SHOULD START MAKING MY WAY BACK.
I'M WORRIED ...
...ABOUT MY APPRENTICE. I WANT TO BE BESIDE—
WHIRL
HOOK
ACK!
HEY, NOW! WHERE ARE *YOU* OFF TO?

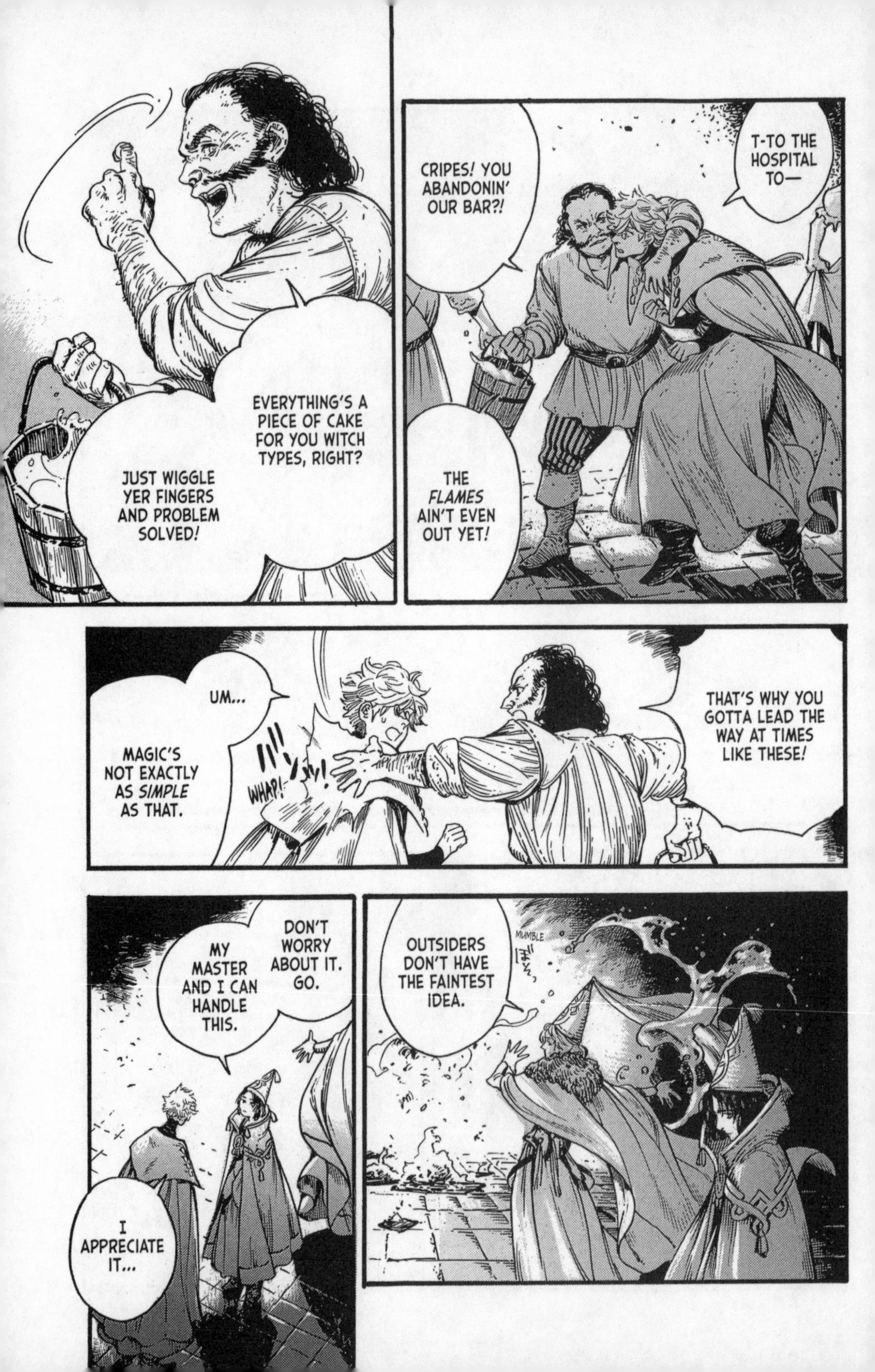
T-TO THE HOSPITAL TO—
CRIPES! YOU ABANDONIN' OUR BAR?!
THE *FLAMES* AIN'T EVEN OUT YET!
EVERYTHING'S A PIECE OF CAKE FOR YOU WITCH TYPES, RIGHT?
JUST WIGGLE YER FINGERS AND PROBLEM SOLVED*!*
THAT'S WHY YOU GOTTA LEAD THE WAY AT TIMES LIKE THESE*!*
WHAP!
UM...
MAGIC'S NOT EXACTLY AS *SIMPLE* AS THAT.
MUMBLE
OUTSIDERS DON'T HAVE THE FAINTEST IDEA.
DON'T WORRY ABOUT IT. GO.
MY MASTER AND I CAN HANDLE THIS.
I APPRECIATE IT...

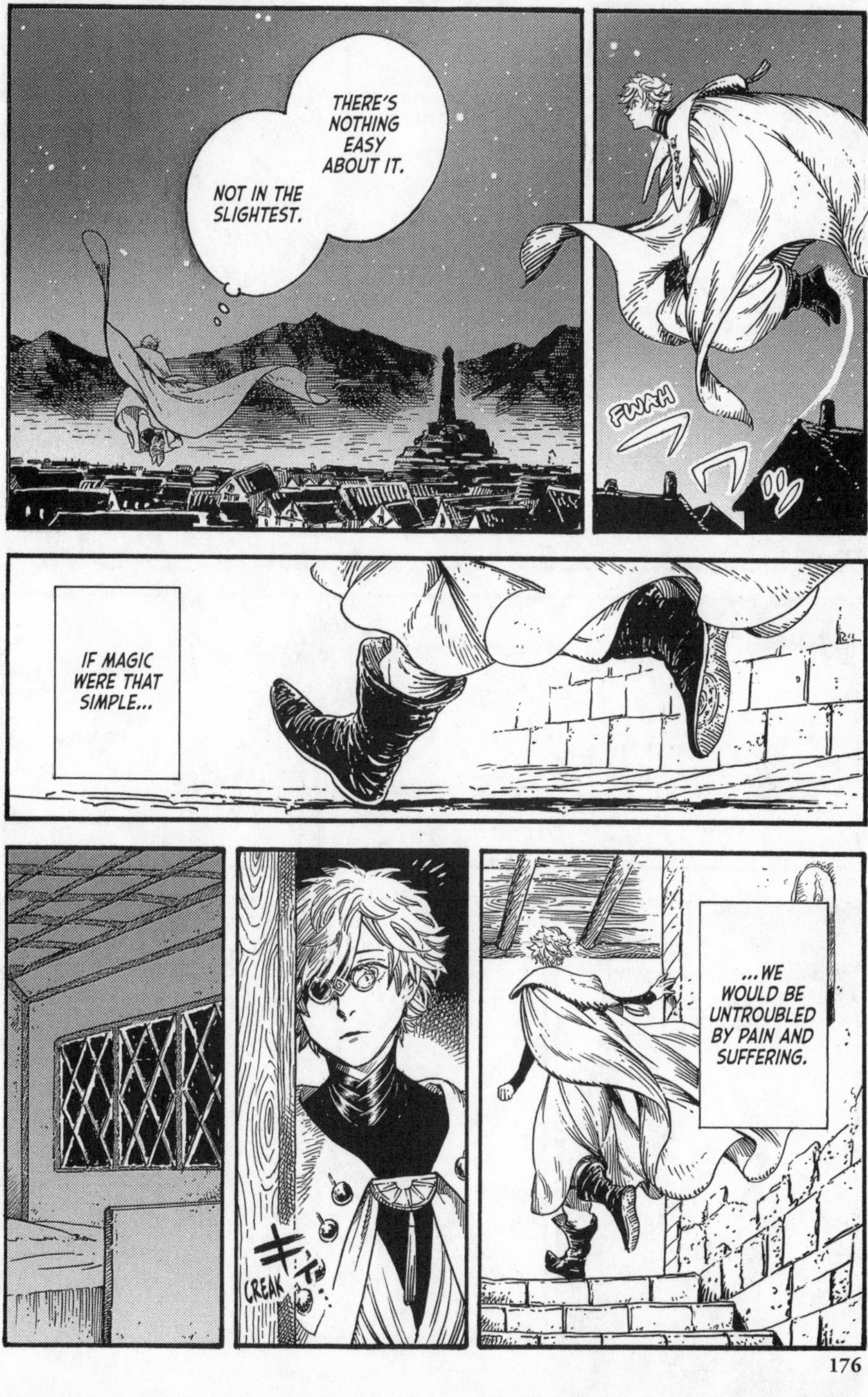
FWAH
THERE'S NOTHING EASY ABOUT IT.
NOT IN THE SLIGHTEST.
IF MAGIC WERE THAT SIMPLE...
...WE WOULD BE UNTROUBLED BY PAIN AND SUFFERING.
CREAK

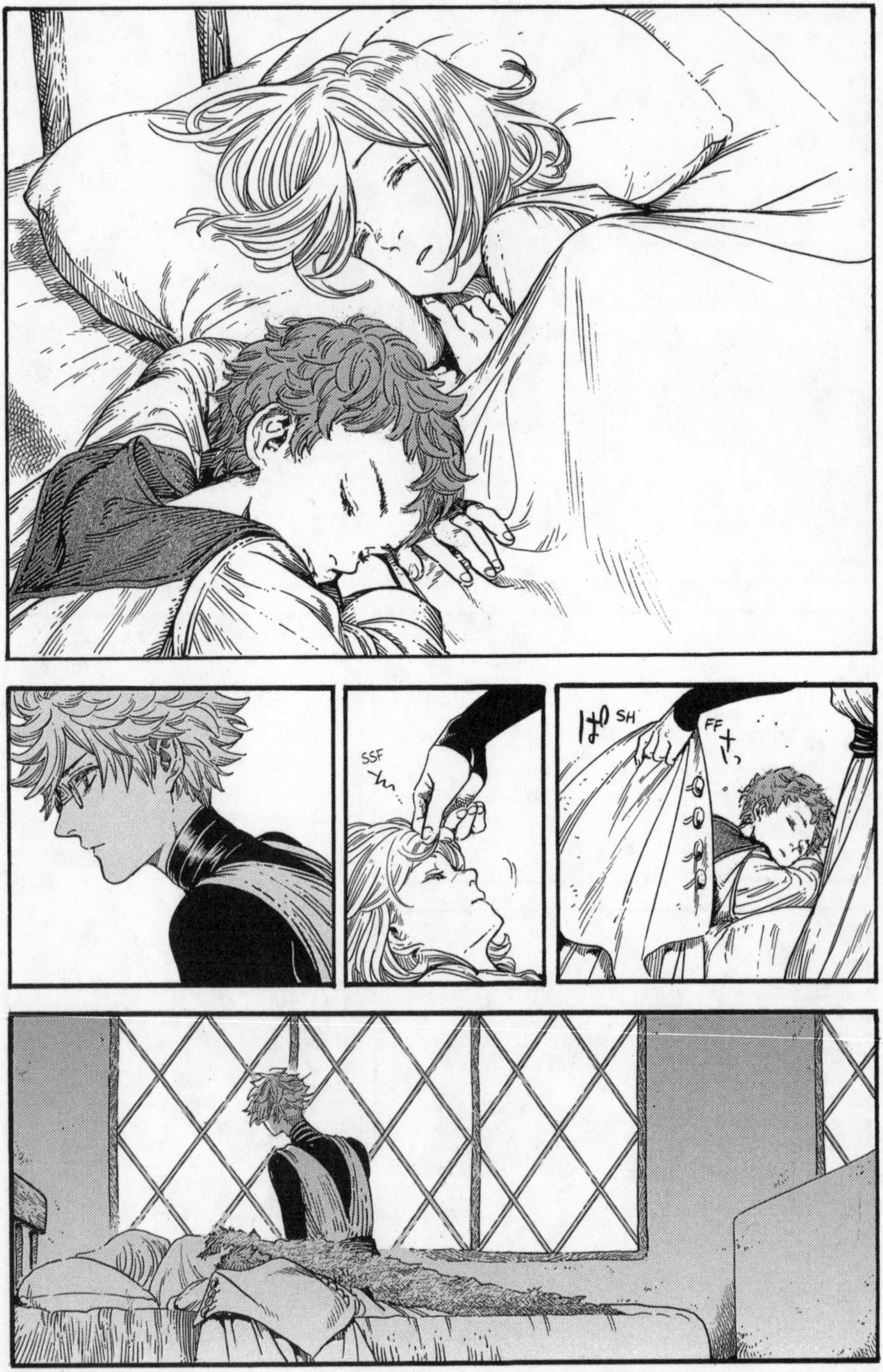
FF
SH
SSF

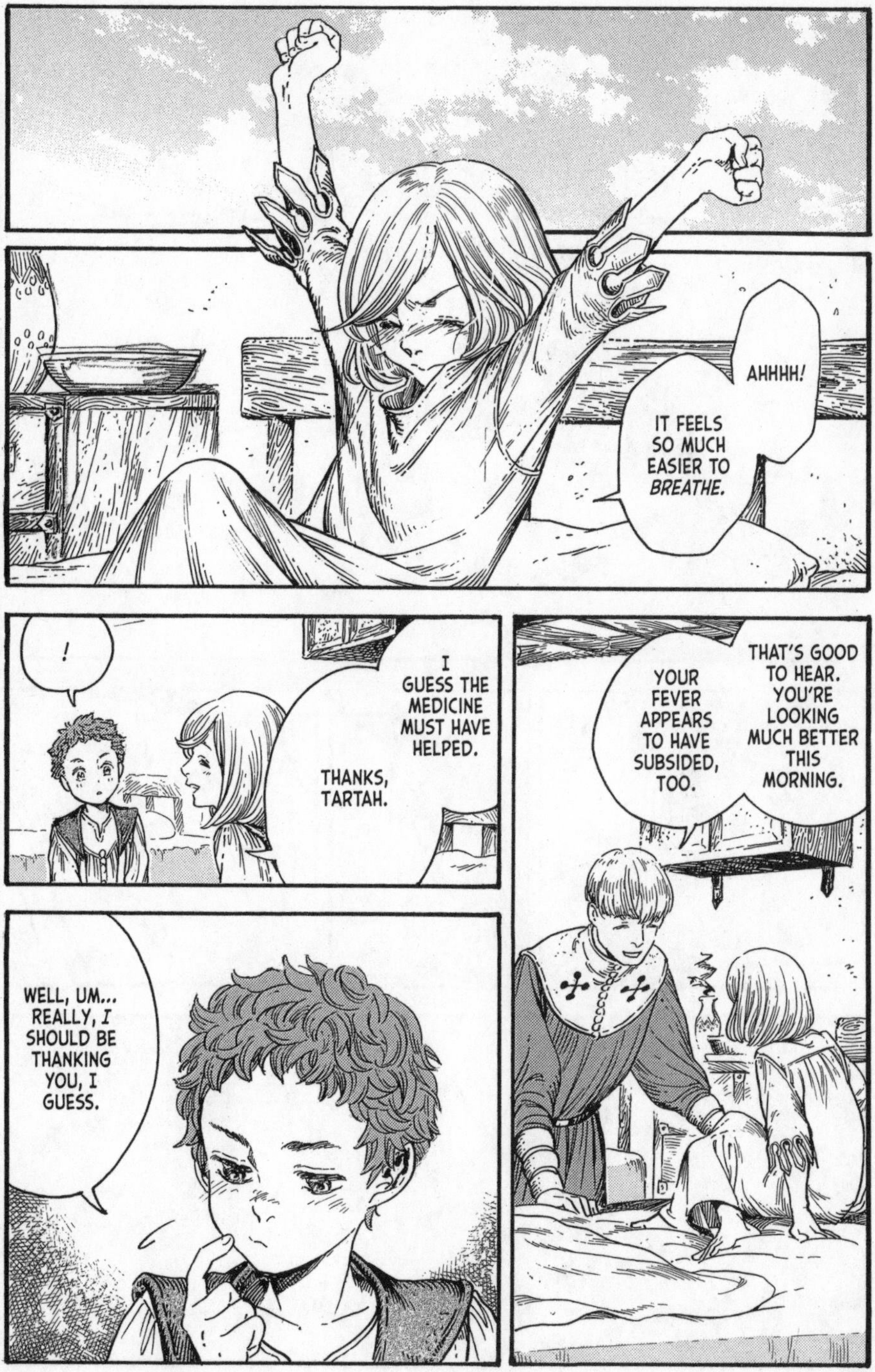
AHHHH!
IT FEELS SO MUCH EASIER TO *BREATHE.*
THAT'S GOOD TO HEAR. YOU'RE LOOKING MUCH BETTER THIS MORNING.
YOUR FEVER APPEARS TO HAVE SUBSIDED, TOO.
I GUESS THE MEDICINE MUST HAVE HELPED.
THANKS, TARTAH.
!
WELL, UM... REALLY, *I* SHOULD BE THANKING YOU, I GUESS.

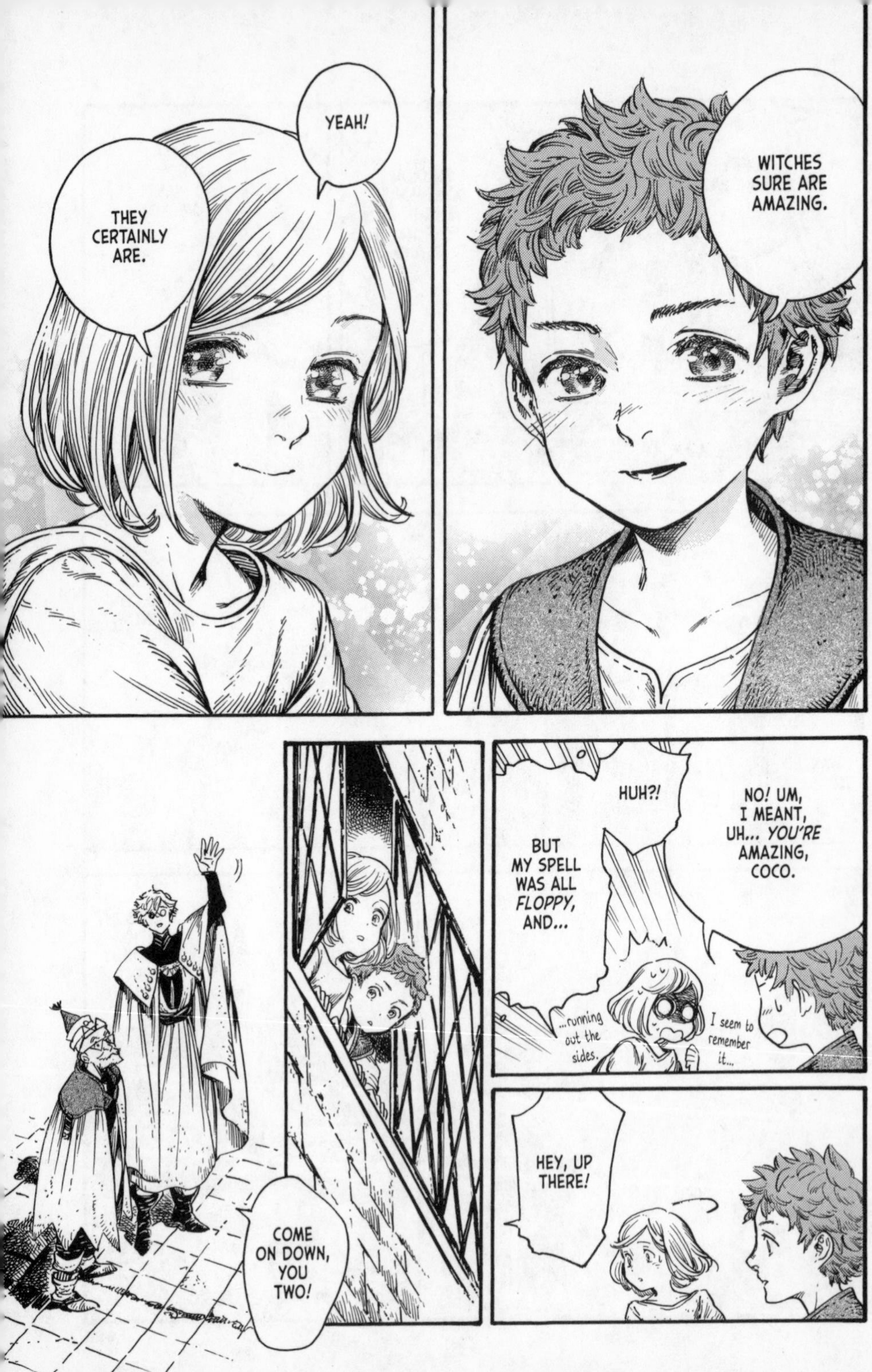
WITCHES SURE ARE AMAZING.
YEAH!
THEY CERTAINLY ARE.
NO! UM, I MEANT, UH... *YOU'RE* AMAZING, COCO.
HUH?!
BUT MY SPELL WAS ALL *FLOPPY*, AND...
I seem to remember it...
...running out the sides.
HEY, UP THERE!
COME ON DOWN, YOU TWO!

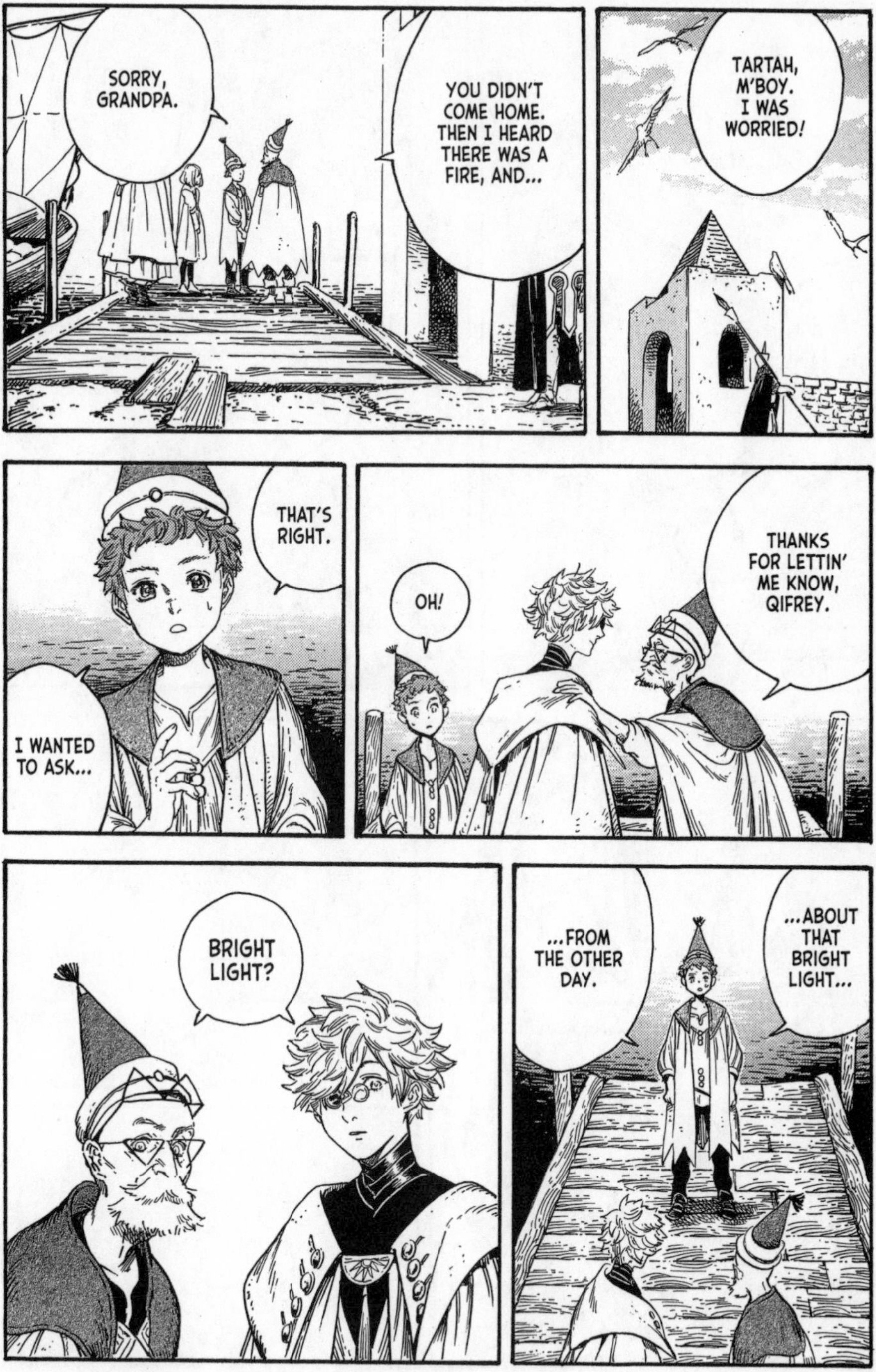
TARTAH, M'BOY. I WAS WORRIED!
YOU DIDN'T COME HOME. THEN I HEARD THERE WAS A FIRE, AND...
SORRY, GRANDPA.
THANKS FOR LETTIN' ME KNOW, QIFREY.
OH!
THAT'S RIGHT.
I WANTED TO ASK...
...ABOUT THAT BRIGHT LIGHT...
...FROM THE OTHER DAY.
BRIGHT LIGHT?

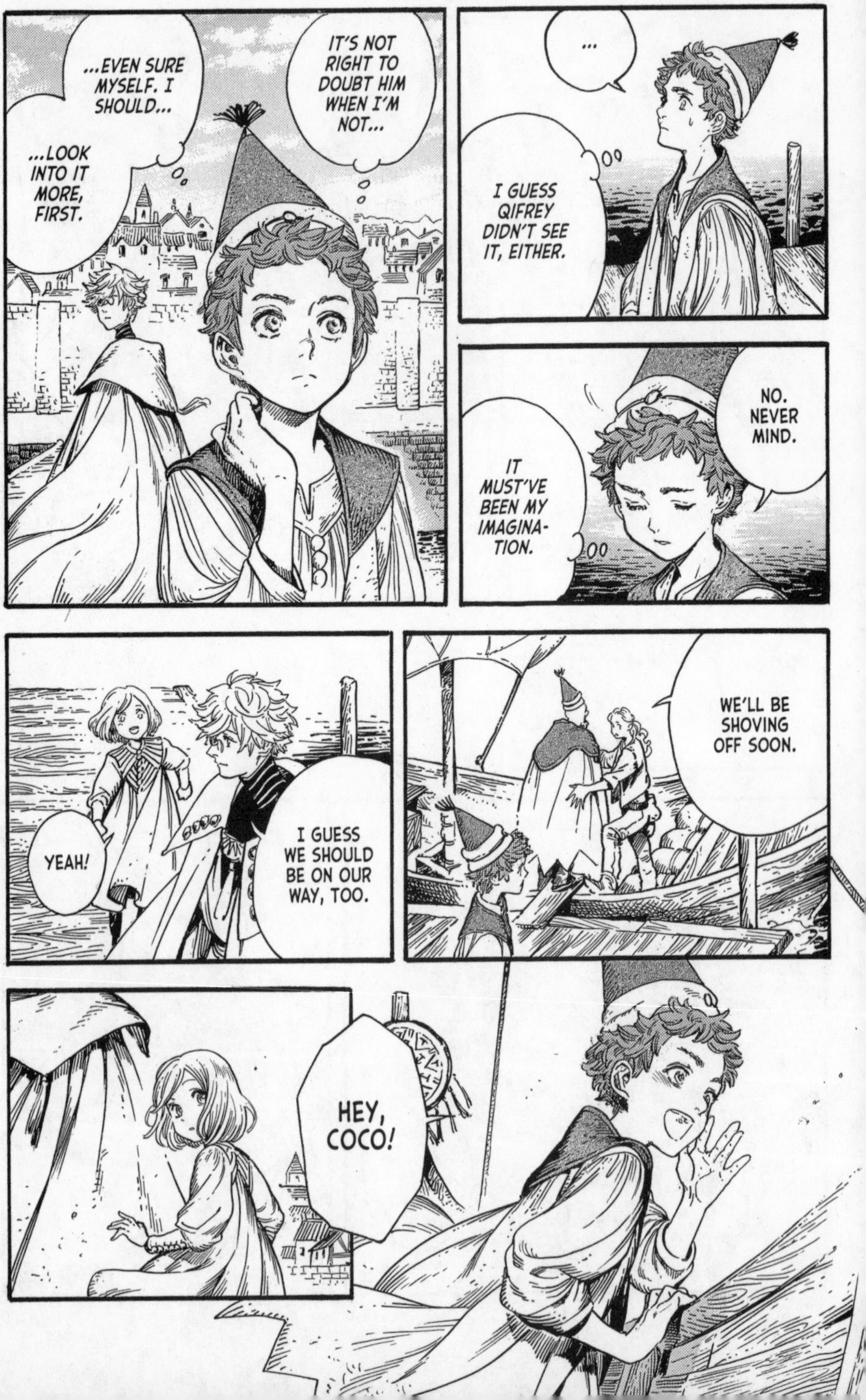
...
I GUESS QIFREY DIDN'T SEE IT, EITHER.
NO. NEVER MIND.
IT MUST'VE BEEN MY IMAGINATION.
IT'S NOT RIGHT TO DOUBT HIM WHEN I'M NOT...
...EVEN SURE MYSELF. I SHOULD...
...LOOK INTO IT MORE, FIRST.
WE'LL BE SHOVING OFF SOON.
I GUESS WE SHOULD BE ON OUR WAY, TOO.
YEAH!
HEY, COCO!

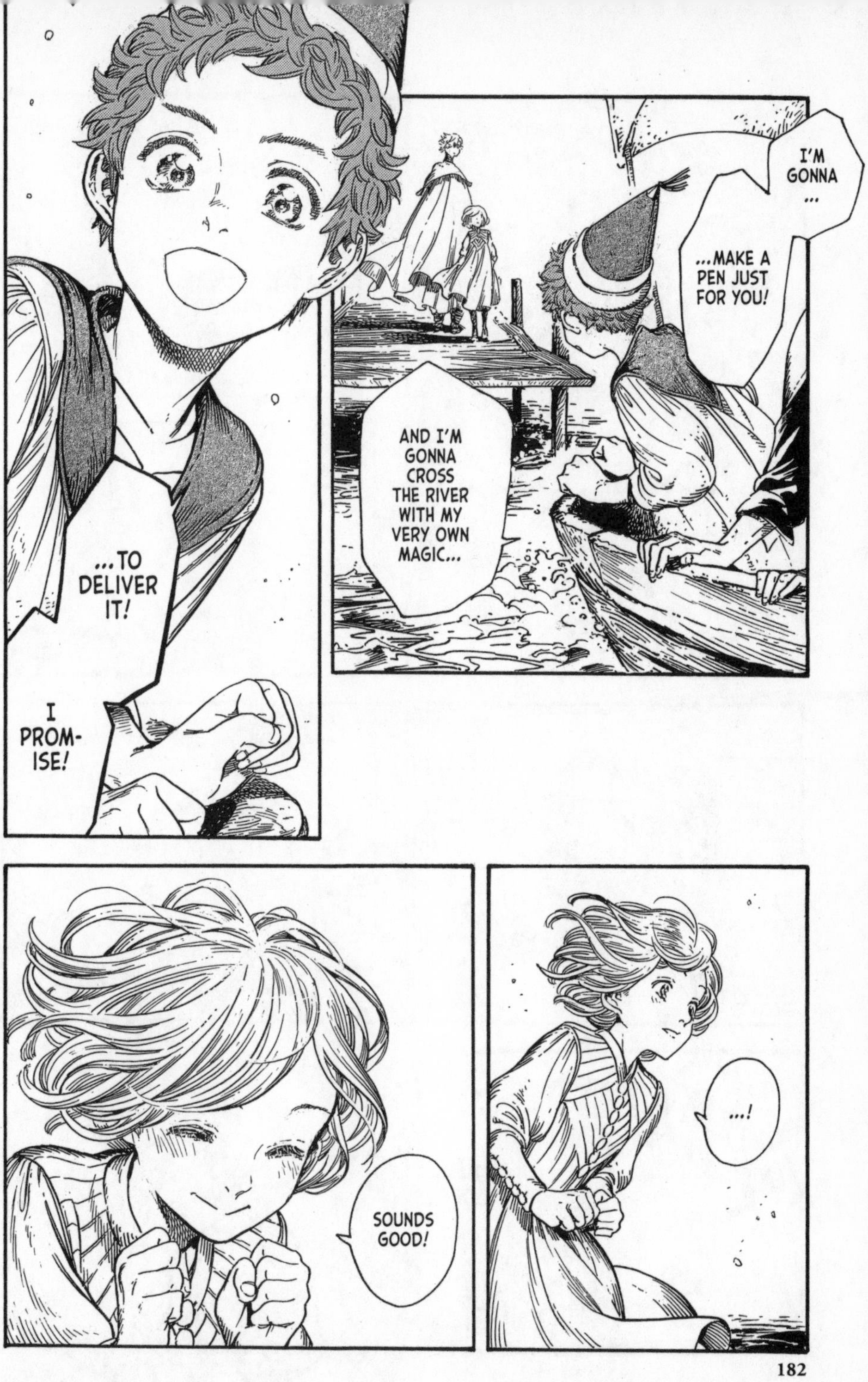
I'M GONNA ...
...MAKE A PEN JUST FOR YOU!
AND I'M GONNA CROSS THE RIVER WITH MY VERY OWN MAGIC...
...TO DELIVER IT!
I PROMISE!
...!
SOUNDS GOOD!

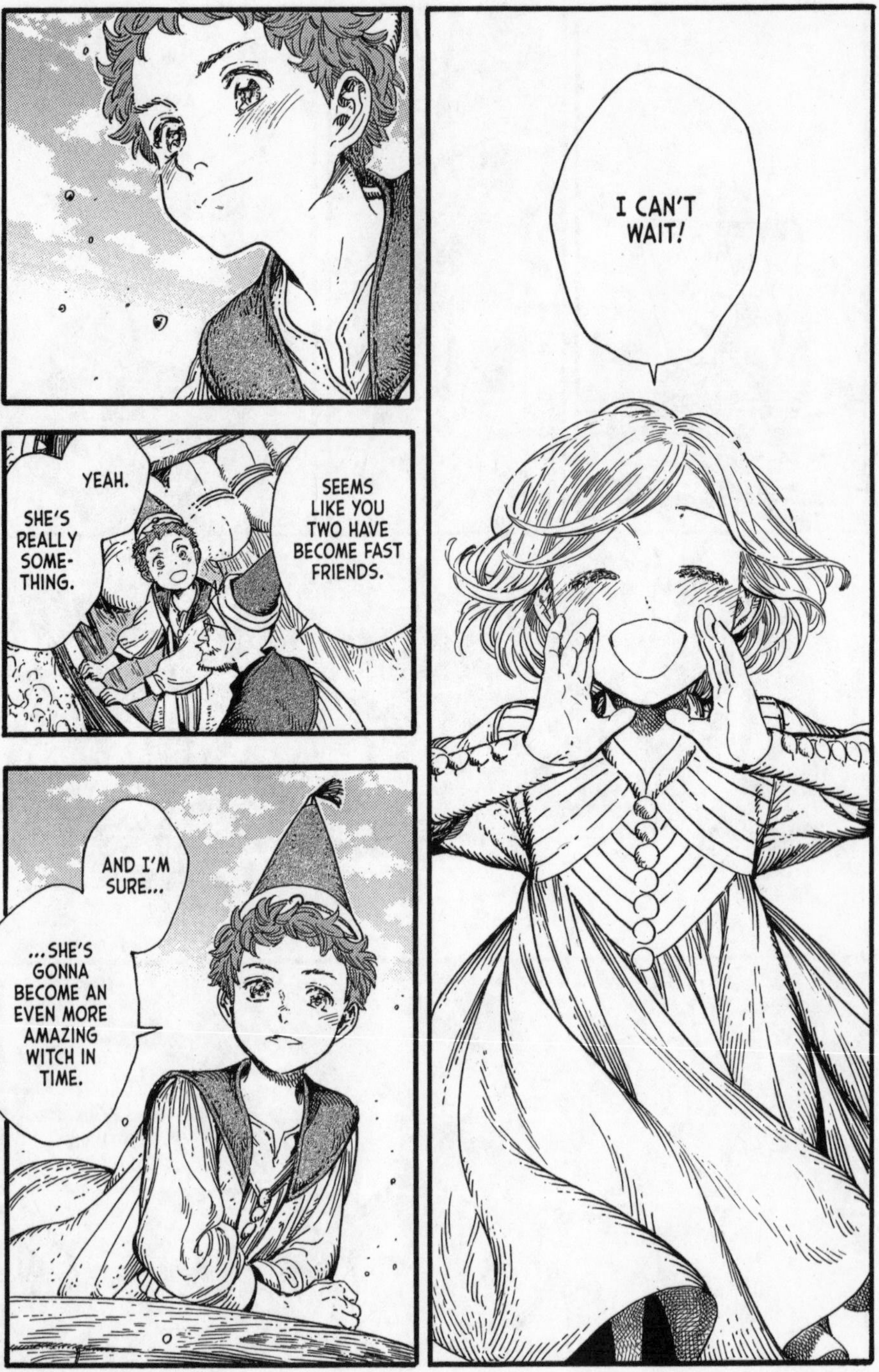
I CAN'T WAIT!
SEEMS LIKE YOU TWO HAVE BECOME FAST FRIENDS.
YEAH.
SHE'S REALLY SOME-THING.
AND I'M SURE...
...SHE'S GONNA BECOME AN EVEN MORE AMAZING WITCH IN TIME.

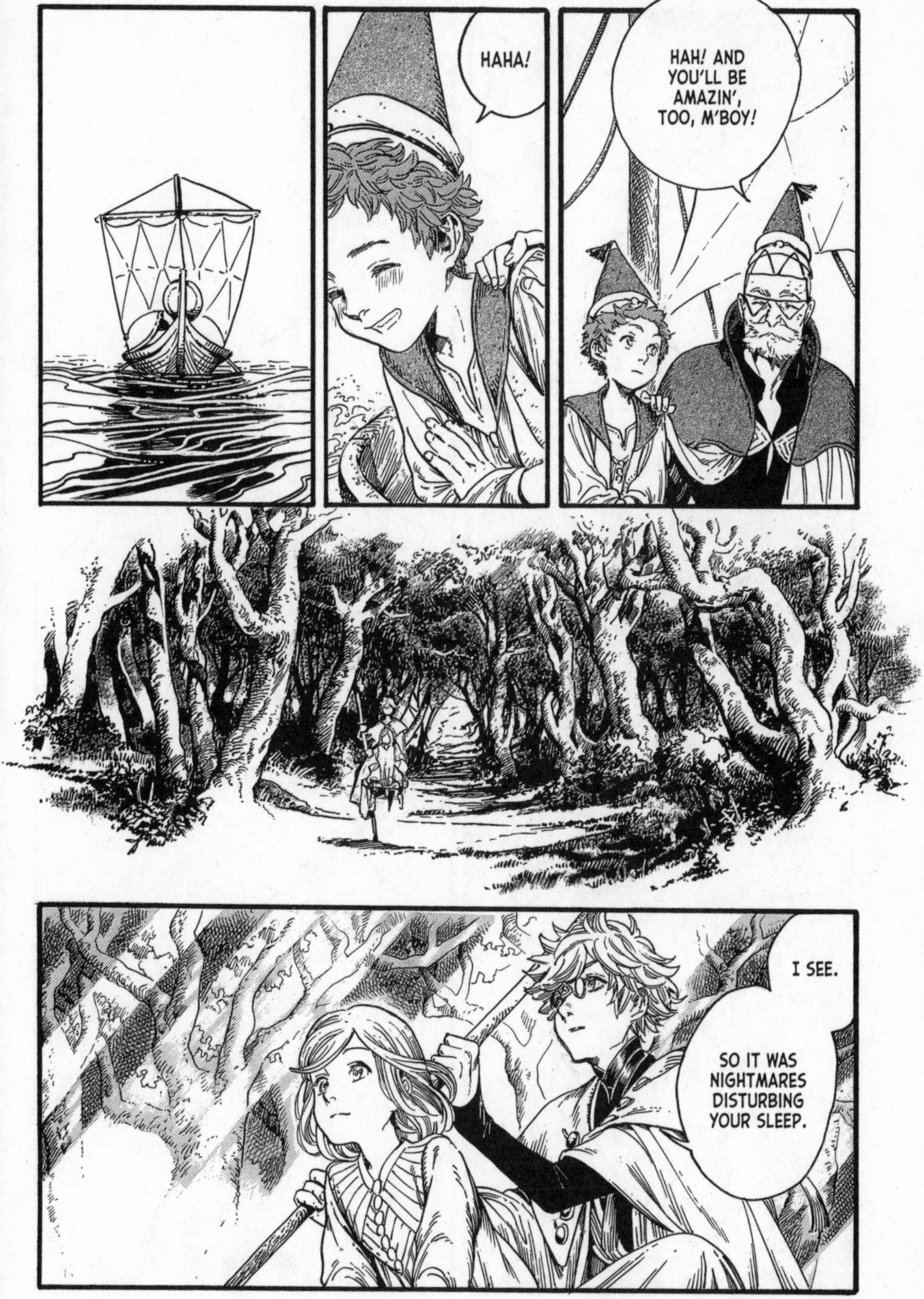
HAH! AND YOU'LL BE AMAZIN', TOO, M'BOY!
HAHA!
I SEE.
SO IT WAS NIGHTMARES DISTURBING YOUR SLEEP.

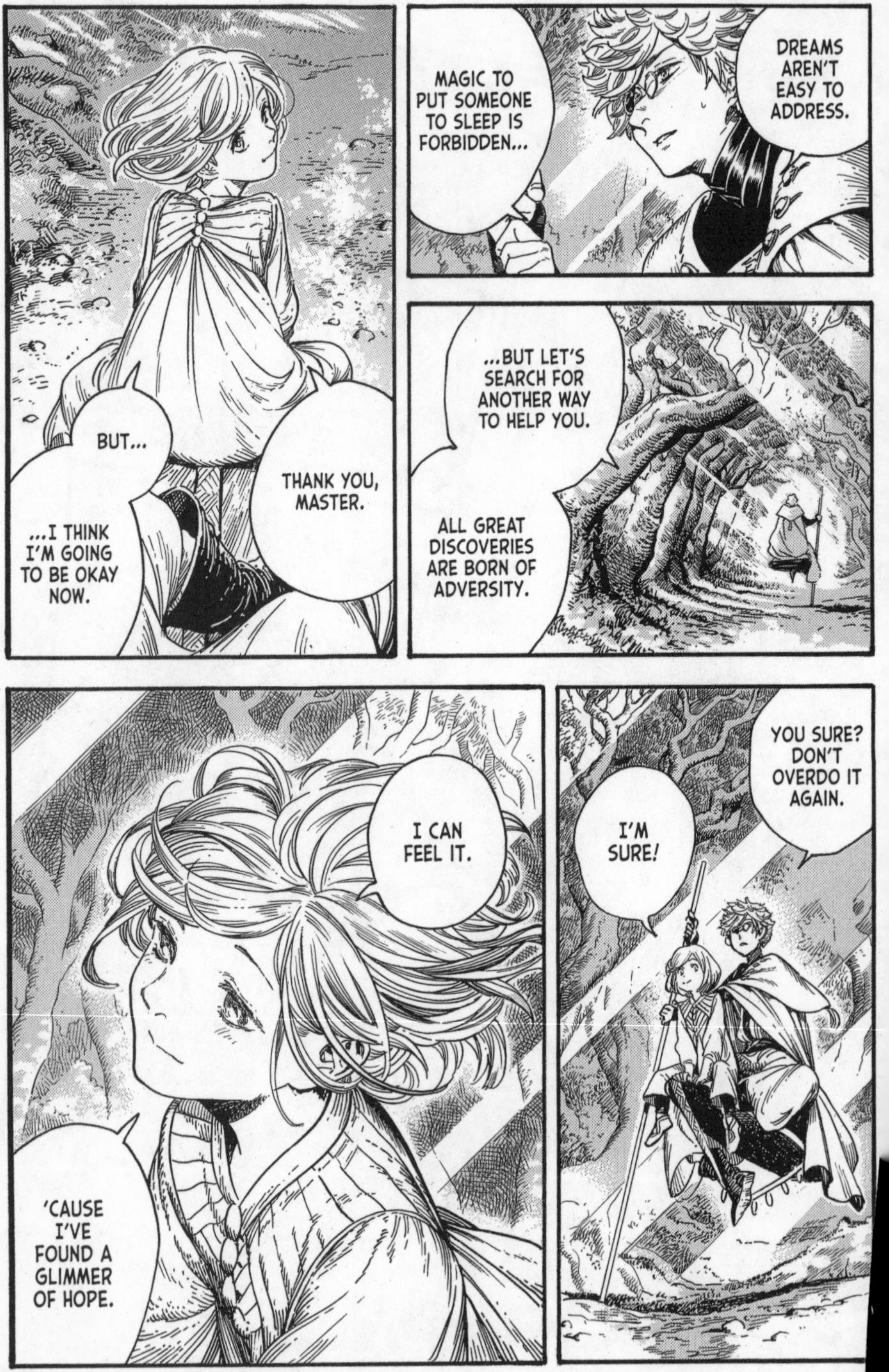
DREAMS AREN'T EASY TO ADDRESS.
MAGIC TO PUT SOMEONE TO SLEEP IS FORBIDDEN...
...BUT LET'S SEARCH FOR ANOTHER WAY TO HELP YOU.
ALL GREAT DISCOVERIES ARE BORN OF ADVERSITY.
THANK YOU, MASTER.
BUT...
...I THINK I'M GOING TO BE OKAY NOW.
YOU SURE? DON'T OVERDO IT AGAIN.
I'M SURE!
I CAN FEEL IT.
'CAUSE I'VE FOUND A GLIMMER OF HOPE.

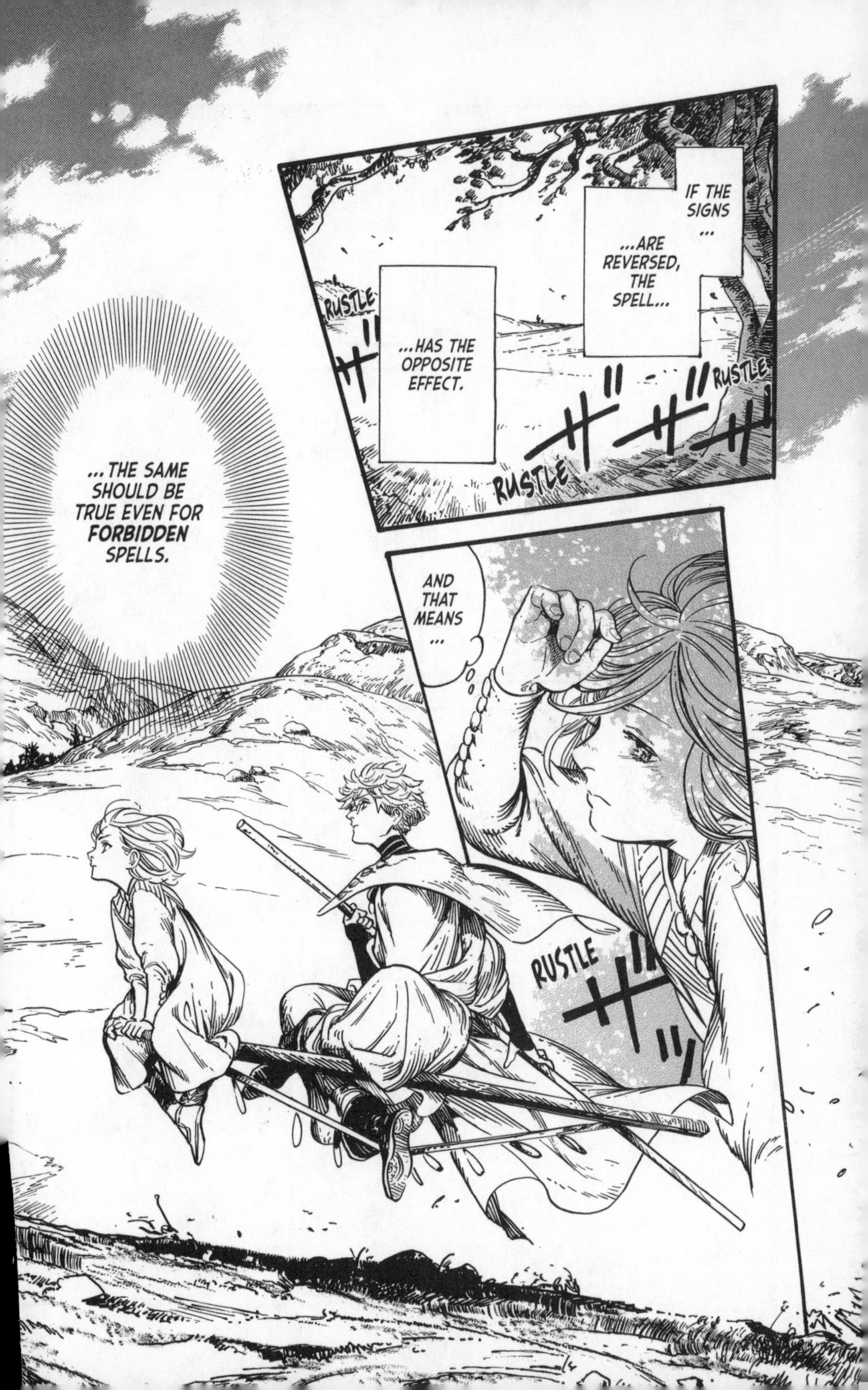
IF THE SIGNS...
...ARE REVERSED, THE SPELL...
...HAS THE OPPOSITE EFFECT.
RUSTLE
RUSTLE
RUSTLE
...THE SAME SHOULD BE TRUE EVEN FOR FORBIDDEN SPELLS.
AND THAT MEANS...
RUSTLE

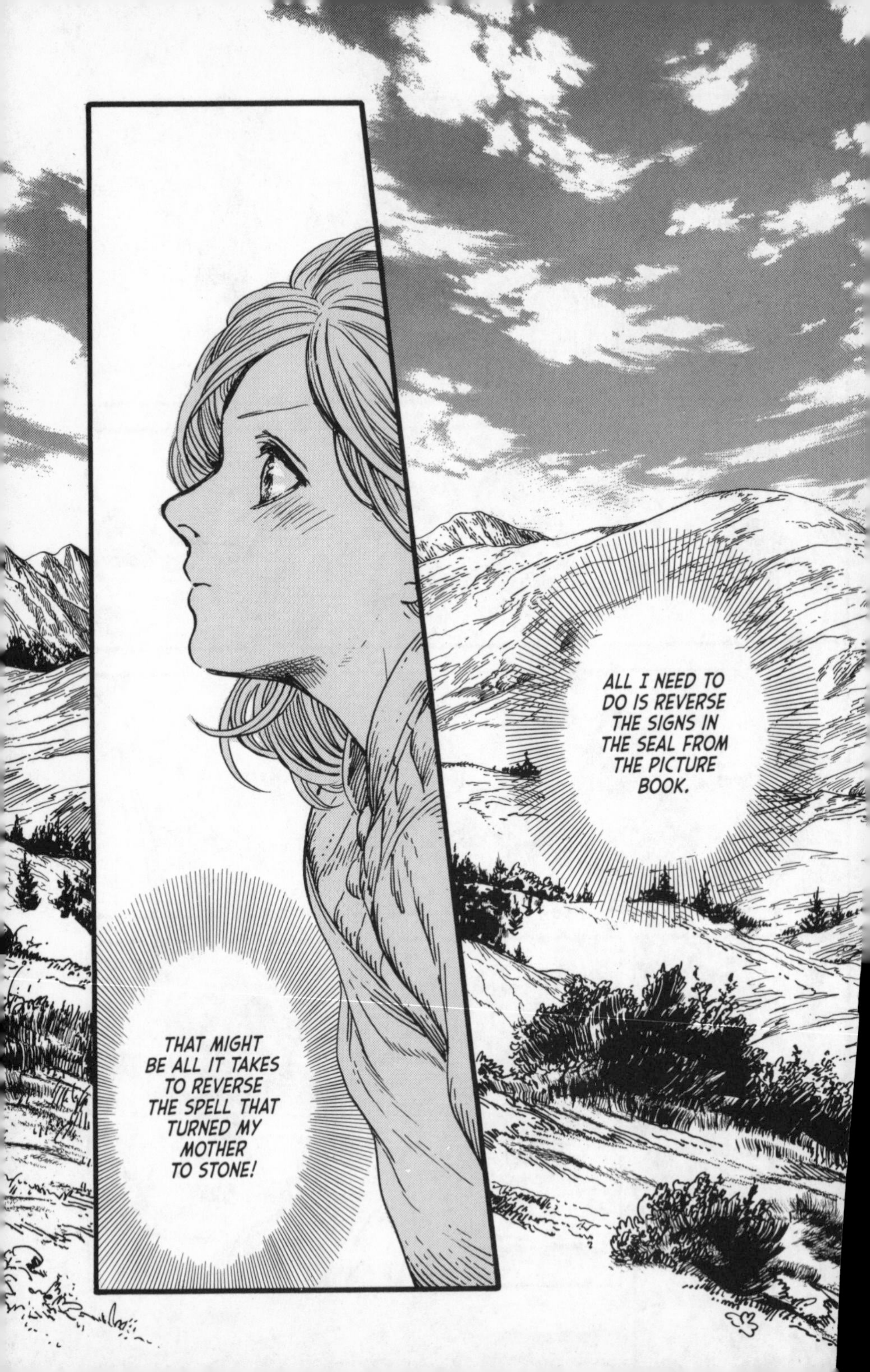
ALL I NEED TO DO IS REVERSE THE SIGNS IN THE SEAL FROM THE PICTURE BOOK.
THAT MIGHT BE ALL IT TAKES TO REVERSE THE SPELL THAT TURNED MY MOTHER TO STONE!

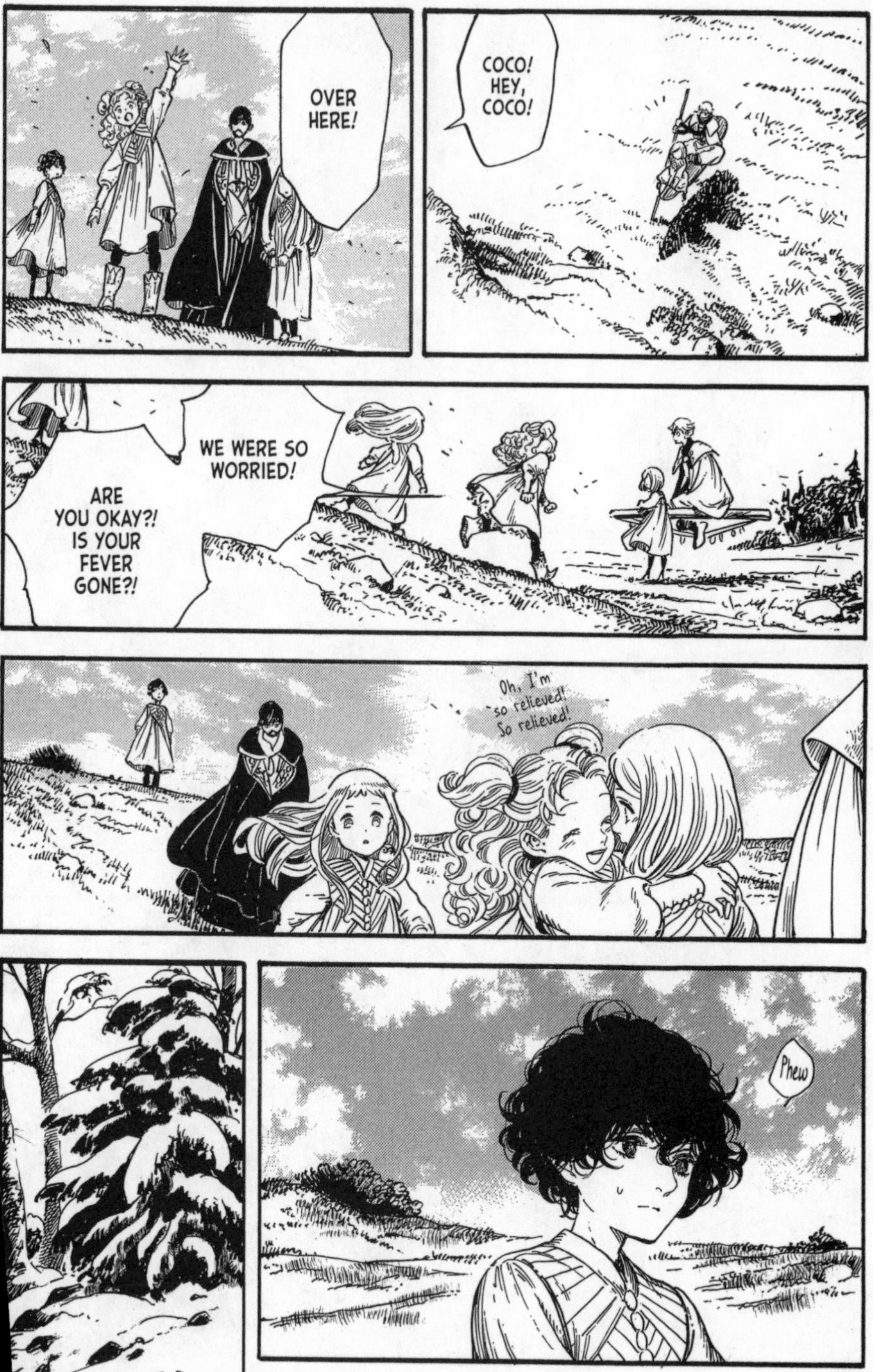
COCO! HEY, COCO!
OVER HERE!
WE WERE SO WORRIED!
ARE YOU OKAY?! IS YOUR FEVER GONE?!
Oh, I'm so relieved! So relieved!
Phew

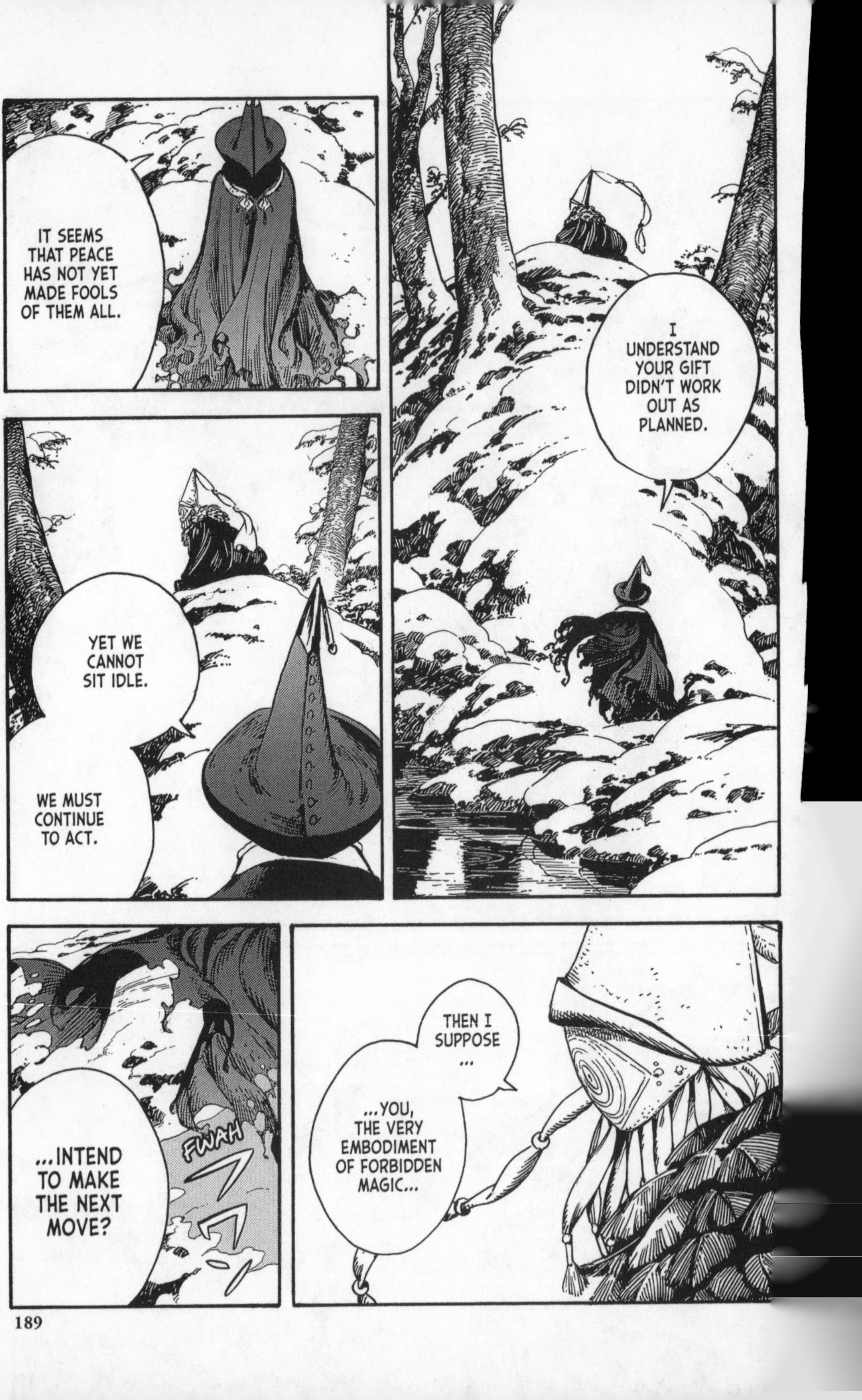
I UNDERSTAND YOUR GIFT DIDN'T WORK OUT AS PLANNED.
IT SEEMS THAT PEACE HAS NOT YET MADE FOOLS OF THEM ALL.
YET WE CANNOT SIT IDLE.
WE MUST CONTINUE TO ACT.
THEN I SUPPOSE ...
...YOU, THE VERY EMBODIMENT OF FORBIDDEN MAGIC...
FWAH
...INTEND TO MAKE THE NEXT MOVE?

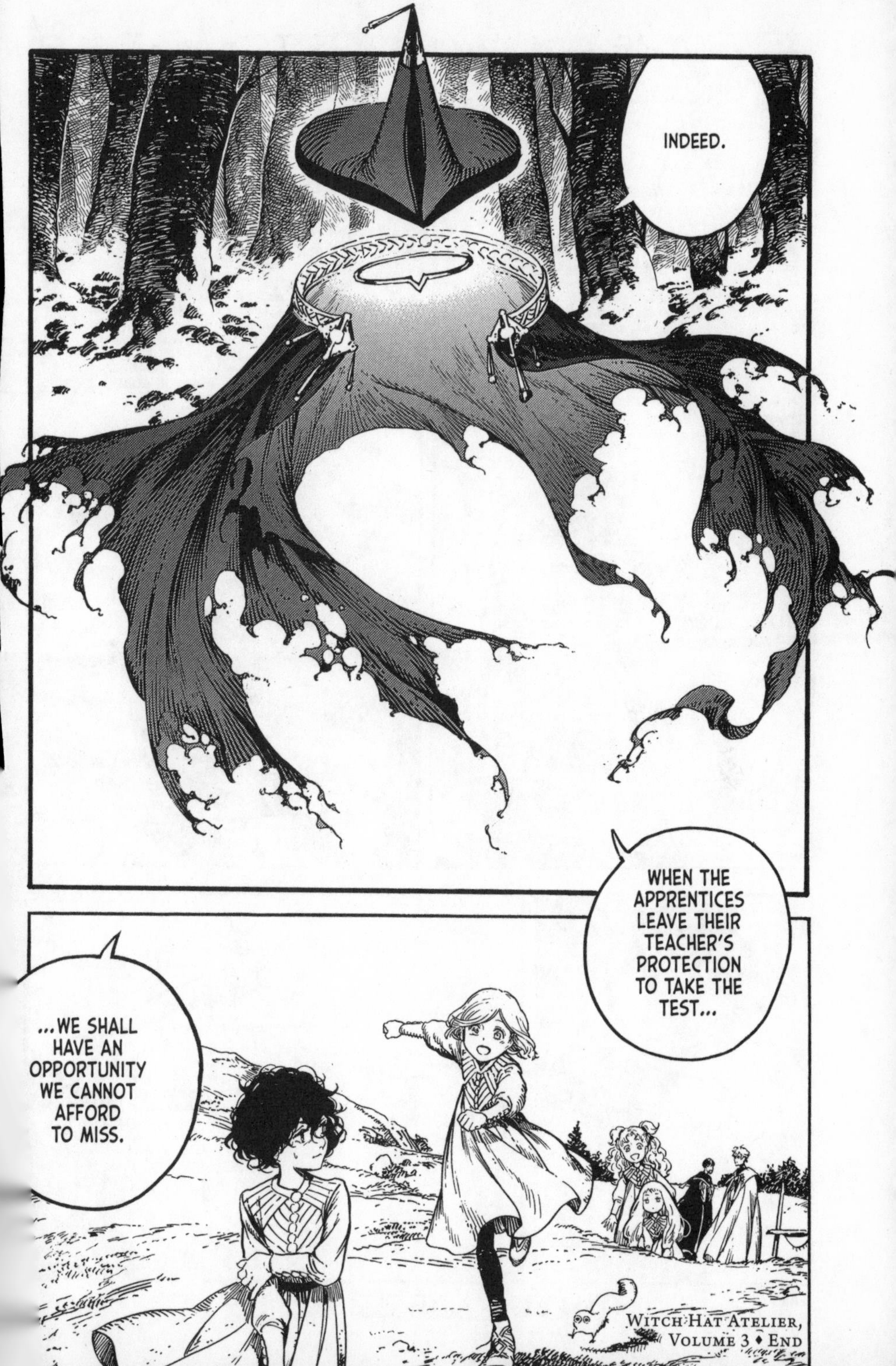
INDEED.
WHEN THE APPRENTICES LEAVE THEIR TEACHER'S PROTECTION TO TAKE THE TEST...
...WE SHALL HAVE AN OPPORTUNITY WE CANNOT AFFORD TO MISS.
WITCH HAT ATELIER, VOLUME 3 ♦ END

THE ANIMALS OF WITCH HAT

PEGASUS
FIRST APPEARS IN CHAPTER 1

WINGED STEEDS USED TO DRAW FLYING CARRIAGES. EVEN WITHIN THE CITIES, PASSAGE ON SUCH A CARRIAGE IMPLIES A CERTAIN DEGREE OF WEALTH. THE ANIMALS HAVE TWO PAIRS OF WINGS—ONE PAIR EACH SPROUTING FROM WHERE ONE WOULD EXPECT TO FIND THE EARS AND TAIL OF A NORMAL HORSE. THESE EXTRA APPENDAGES ARE CAUSE FOR SOME SCIENTIFIC DEBATE ABOUT WHETHER THE ANIMAL SHOULD BE CLASSIFIED AS HAVING FOUR OR EIGHT LIMBS. IN THE INTEREST OF AVOIDING LEG INJURIES, TAKEOFF FROM AND LANDING ON STONE SURFACES IS GENERALLY PROHIBITED. SLIGHTLY SLOWER THAN A NORMAL HORSE WHEN RUNNING ON THE GROUND.

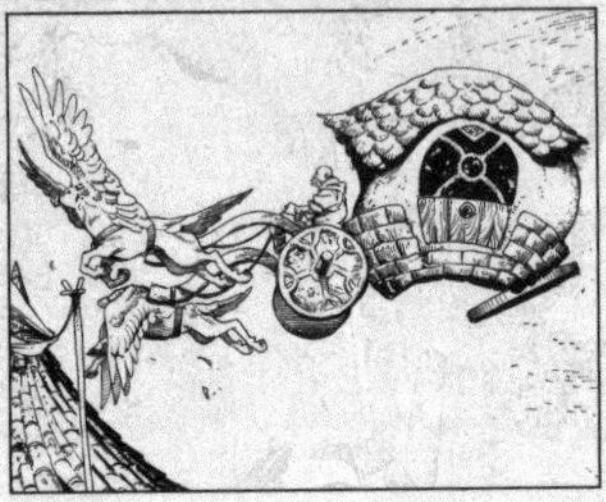

BRUSHBUDDY
FIRST APPEARS IN CHAPTER 4

SMALL CREATURES COVERED IN FUR LIKE THE SOFT BRISTLES OF A WRITING BRUSH. FOND OF THE SCENT OF CONJURING INK. WHEN GIVEN THE CHANCE, KNOWN TO COVER THEIR OWN BODIES IN INK AND FROLIC AROUND; AN INKPOT LEFT UNCOVERED AND UNATTENDED MAY RESULT I QUITE A MESSY ROOM IF ANY BRUSHBUDDIES ARE AROUND IN ADDITION TO THE WHITE-FURRED VARIETY, NUMEROUS OTHER COLORINGS EXIST—EVEN ONES WITH PATTERNED APPEARANCES. PREFERRED DIET INCLUDES NUTS AND FRUITS. EXHIBITS A MUCH SHORTER, ALMOST ROUND APPEARANCE AT BIRTH.

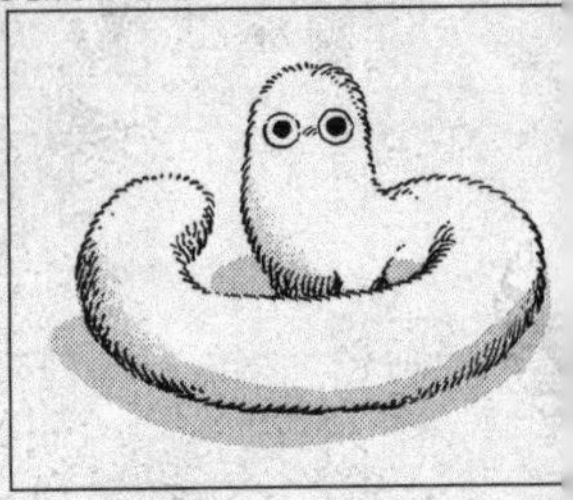

DRAGON
FIRST APPEARS IN CHAPTER 5

RARELY IF EVER SEEN NEAR CENTERS OF HUMAN POPULATION. DIET IS VARIED AND INCLUDES BOTH MEAT AND VEGETATION. EXTREMELY TERRITORIAL; KNOWN TO STRIKE AT INTRUDERS WITH ITS LONG, WHIPLIKE TAIL. CAPABLE OF GLIDING THROUGH THE AIR AND LARGELY UNAFFECTED BY FLAMES. THESE CREATURES' SCALES AND EGGSHELLS ARE SOURCES OF HIGHLY PRIZED CONJURING INK DYES.

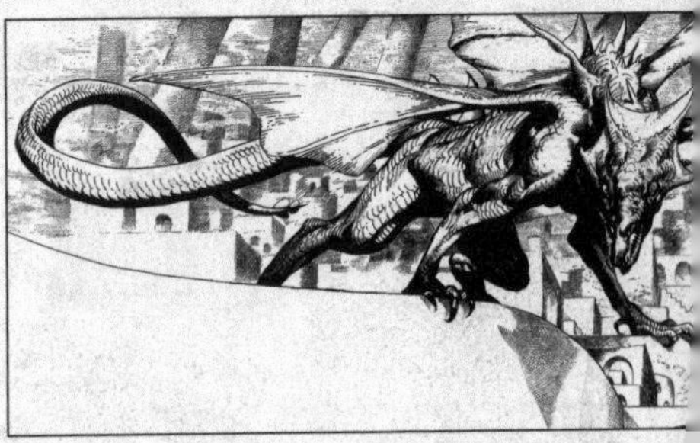

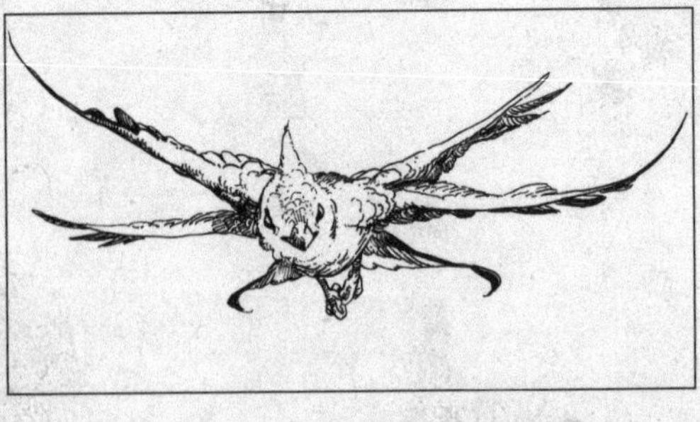

QUADRYPHON
FIRST APPEARS IN CHAPTER 8

RESEMBLES A DRAGONFLY WHEN IN FLIGHT, WITH EACH OF ITS FOUR WINGS BEATING INDEPENDENT THE OTHERS. ITS METHOD OF FLIGHT IS THEREFO QUITE UNLIKE THAT OF OTHER BIRDS, AND IT ENAB THE CREATURE TO QUICKLY CHANGE DIRECTIONS MIDAIR. BODY LENGTH TYPICALLY MEASURES 60 C AND WINGSPAN 150 CM. A RELATED SPECIES IS T "GRYPHON," WHICH EXHIBITS TWO ADDITIONAL LE INSTEAD OF THE EXTRA PAIR OF WINGS.

Witch Hat Atelier volume 3 is a work of fiction. Names, characters, places, and incidents are the products of the author's imagination or are used fictitiously. Any resemblance to actual events, locales, or persons, living or dead, is entirely coincidental.

A Kodansha Comics Trade Paperback Original.

Published in the United States by Kodansha Comics,
an imprint of Kodansha USA Publishing, LLC, New York.

Publication rights for this English edition arranged through Kodansha Ltd., Tokyo.

First published in Japan in 2018 by Kodansha Ltd., Tokyo, as *Tongari Bōshi no Atorie* volume 3.

ISBN 978-1-63236-805-8

Printed in the United States of America.

www.kodansha.us

9 8 7 6 5 4

Translation: Stephen Kohler
Lettering: Lys Blakeslee
Editing: Ajani Oloye
Kodansha Comics edition cover design: Phil Balsman